Jack London

John Griffith London (born John Griffith Chaney; January 12, 1876 – November 22, 1916) was an American novelist, journalist, and social activist. A pioneer in the world of commercial magazine fiction, he was one of the first writers to become a worldwide celebrity and earn a large fortune from writing. He was also an innovator in the genre that would later become known as science fiction. His most famous works include The Call of the Wild and White Fang, both set in the Klondike Gold Rush, as well as the short stories "To Build a Fire", "An Odyssey of the North", and "Love of Life". He also wrote about the South Pacific in stories such as "The Pearls of Parlay" and "The Heathen". London was part of the radical literary group "The Crowd" in San Francisco and a passionate advocate of unionization, socialism, and the rights of workers. He wrote several powerful works dealing with these topics, such as his dystopian novel The Iron Heel, his non-fiction exposé The People of the Abyss, and The War of the Classes. (Source: Wikipedia)

Literary works:

The Cruise of the Dazzler (1902)
A Daughter of the Snows (1902)
The Call of the Wild (1903)
The Kempton-Wace Letters (1903)
The Sea-Wolf (1904)
The Game (1905)
White Fang (1906)
Before Adam (1907)
The Iron Heel (1908)
Martin Eden (1909)
Burning Daylight (1910)
Adventure (1911)
The Scarlet Plague (1912)
A Son of the Sun (1912)
The Abysmal Brute (1913)
The Valley of the Moon (1913)

THE COLLECTED WORKS
OF
JACK LONDON
VOL. 23 (OF 25)

THE KEMPTON-WACE LETTERS
THE MUTINY OF THE ELSINORE

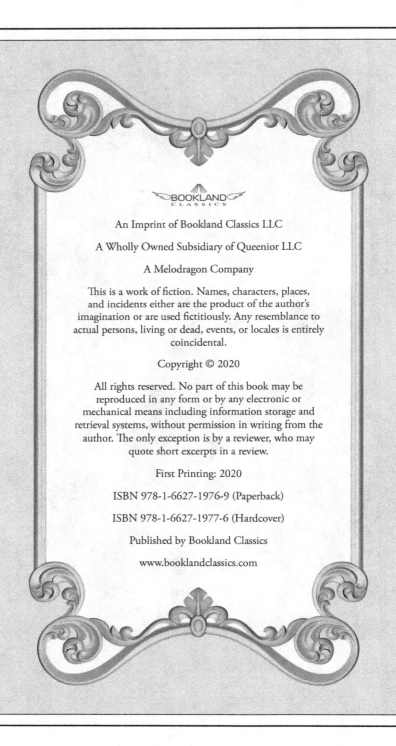

An Imprint of Bookland Classics LLC

A Wholly Owned Subsidiary of Queenior LLC

A Melodragon Company

First Printing: 2020

ISBN 978-1-6627-1976-9 (Paperback)

ISBN 978-1-6627-1977-6 (Hardcover)

Published by Bookland Classics

www.booklandclassics.com

Contents

THE COLLECTED WORKS

OF

JACK LONDON

VOL. 23 (OF 25)

THE KEMPTON-WACE
LETTERS

I. FROM DANE KEMPTON TO HERBERT WACE

London,

3 a Queen's Road, Chelsea, S.W.

August 14, 19—.

Yesterday I wrote formally, rising to the occasion like the conventional happy father rather than the man who believes in the miracle and lives for it. Yesterday I stinted myself. I took you in my arms, glad of what is and stately with respect for the fulness of your manhood. It is to-day that I let myself leap into yours in a passion of joy. I dwell on what has come to pass and inflate myself with pride in your fulfilment, more as a mother would, I think, and she your mother.

But why did you not write before? After all, the great event was not when you found your offer of marriage accepted, but when you found you had fallen in love. Then was your hour. Then was the time for congratulation, when the call was first sounded and the reveille of Time and About fell upon your soul and the march to another's destiny was begun. It is always more important to love than to be loved. I wish it had been vouchsafed me to be by when your spirit of a sudden grew willing to bestow itself without question or let or hope of return, when the self broke up and you grew fain to beat out your strength in praise and service for the woman who was soaring high in the blue wastes. You have known her long, and you must have been hers long, yet no word of her and of your love reached me. It was not kind to be silent.

Barbara spoke yesterday of your fastidiousness, and we told each other that you had gained a triumph of happiness in your love, for you are not of those who cheat themselves. You choose rigorously, straining for the heart of the end as do all rigorists who are also hedonists. Because we are in possession of this bit of data as to your temperamental cosmos we can congratulate you with the more abandon. Oh, Herbert, do you know that this is a rampant spring, and that on leaving Barbara I tramped out of the confines into the green, happier, it almost seems, than I have ever been? Do you know that because you love a woman and she loves you, and that because you are swept along by certain forces, that I am happy and feel myself in sight of my portion of immortality on earth, far more than because of my books, dear lad, far more?

I wish I could fly England and get to you. Should I have a shade less of you than formerly, if we were together now? From your too much green of wealth, a barrenness of friendship? It does not matter; what is her gain cannot be my loss. One power is mine,—without hindrance, in freedom and in right, to say to Ellen's son, "Godspeed!" to place Hester Stebbins's hand in his, and bid them forth to the sunrise, into the glory of day!

Ever your devoted father,

Dane Kempton.

II. FROM HERBERT WACE TO DANE KEMPTON

The Ridge,

Berkeley, California.

September 3, 19—.

Here I am, back in the old quarters once more, with the old afternoon climb across the campus and up into the sky, up to the old rooms, the old books, and the old view. You poor fog-begirt Dane Kempton, could you but have lounged with me on the window couch, an hour past, and watched the light pass out of the day through the Golden Gate and the night creep over the Berkeley Hills and down out of the east! Why should you linger on there in London town! We grow away from each other, it seems—you with your wonder-singing, I with my joyful science.

Poesy and economics! Alack! alack! How did I escape you, Dane, when mind and mood you mastered me? The auguries were fair. I, too, should have been a singer, and lo, I strive for science. All my boyhood was singing, what of you; and my father was a singer, too, in his own fine way. Dear to me is your likening of him to Waring.—"What's become of Waring?" He *was* Waring. I can think of him only as one who went away, "chose land travel or seafaring."

Gwynne says I am sometimes almost a poet—Gwynne, you know, Arthur Gwynne, who has come to live with me at The Ridge. "If it were not for your dismal science," he is sure to add; and to fire him I lay it to the defects of early training. I know he thinks that I never half appreciated you, and that I do not appreciate you now. If you will recollect, you praised his verses once. He cherishes that praise amongst his sweetest treasures. Poor dear good old Gwynne, tender, sensitive, shrinking, with the face of a seraph and the heart of a maid. Never were two men more incongruously companioned. I love him for himself. He tolerates me, I do secretly believe, because of you. He longs to meet you,—he knew you well through my father,—and we often talk you over. Be sure at every opportunity I tear off your halo and trundle it about. Trust me, you receive scant courtesy.

How I wander on. My pen is unruly after the long vacation; my thought yet wayward, what of the fever of successful wooing. And besides, ... how shall I say?... such was the gracious warmth of your letter, of both your letters, that I am at a loss. I feel weak, inadequate. It almost seems as though you had made a demand upon something that is not in me. Ah, you poets! It would seem your delight in my marriage were greater than mine. In my present mood, it is you who are young, you who love; I who have lived and am old.

Yes, I am going to be married. At this present moment, I doubt not, a million men and women are saying the same thing. Hewers of wood and drawers of water, princes and potentates, shy-shrinking maidens and brazen-faced hussies, all saying, "I am going to be married." And all looking forward to it as a crisis in their lives? No. After all, marriage is the way of the world. Considered biologically, it is an institution necessary for the perpetuation of the species. Why should it be a crisis? These million men and women will marry, and the work of the world go on just as it did before. Shuffle them about, and the work of the world would yet go on.

True, a month ago it did seem a crisis. I wrote you as much. It did seem a disturbing element in my life-work. One cannot view with equanimity that which appears to be totally disruptive of one's dear little system of living. But it only appeared so; I lacked perspective, that was all. As I look upon it now, everything fits well and all will run smoothly I am sure.

You know I had two years yet to work for my Doctorate. I still have them. As you see, I am back to the old quarters, settled down in the old groove, hammering away at the old grind. Nothing is changed. And besides my own studies, I have taken up an assistant instructorship in the Department of Economics. It is an ambitious course, and an important one. I don't know how they ever came to confide it to me, or how I found the temerity to attempt it,—which is neither here nor there. It is all agreed. Hester is a sensible girl.

The engagement is to be long. I shall continue my career as charted. Two years from now, when I shall have become a Doctor of Social Sciences (and candidate for numerous other things), I shall also become a benedict. My marriage and the presumably necessary honeymoon chime in with the summer vacation. There is no disturbing element even there. Oh, we are very practical, Hester and I. And we are both strong enough to lead each our own lives.

Which reminds me that you have not asked about her. First, let me shock you—she, too, is a scientist. It was in my undergraduate days that we met, and ere the half-hour struck we were quarrelling felicitously over Weismann and the neo-Darwinians. I was at Berkeley at the time, a cocksure junior; and she, far maturer as a freshman, was at Stanford, carrying more culture with her into her university than is given the average student to carry out.

Next, and here your arms open to her, she is a poet. Pre-eminently she is a poet—this must be always understood. She is the greater poet, I take it, in this dawning twentieth century, because she is a scientist; not in spite of being a scientist as some would hold. How shall I describe her? Perhaps as a George Eliot, fused with an Elizabeth Barrett, with a hint of Huxley and a trace of Keats. I may say she is something like all this, but I must say she is something other and different. There is about her a certain lightsomeness, a glow or flash almost Latin or oriental, or perhaps Celtic. Yes, that must be it—Celtic. But the high-stomached Norman is there and the stubborn Saxon. Her quickness and fine audacity are checked and poised, as it were, by that certain conservatism which gives stability to purpose and power to achievement. She is unafraid, and wide-looking and far-looking, but she is not over-looking. The Saxon grapples with the Celt, and the Norman forces the twain to do what the one would not dream of doing and what the other would dream beyond and never do. Do you catch me? Her most salient charm, is I think, her perfect poise, her exquisite adjustment.

Altogether she is a most wonderful woman, take my word for it. And after all she is described vicariously. Though she has published nothing and is exceeding shy, I shall send you some of her work. There will you find and know her. She is waiting for stronger voice and sings softly as yet. But hers will be no minor note, no middle flight. She is—well, she is Hester. In two years we shall be married. Two years, Dane. Surely you will be with us.

One thing more; in your letter a certain undertone which I could not fail to detect. *A shade less* of me than formerly?—I turn and look into your face—Waring's handiwork you remember—his painter's fancy of you in those golden days when I stood on the brink of the world, and you showed me the delights of the world and the way of my feet therein. So I turn and look, and look and wonder. A shade less of me, of you? Poesy and economics! Where lies the blame?

Herbert.

III. FROM DANE KEMPTON TO HERBERT WACE

London,

September 30, 19—.

It is because you know not what you do that I cannot forgive you. Could you know that your letter with its catalogue of advantages and arrangements must offend me as much as it belies (let us hope) you and the woman of your love, I would pardon the affront of it upon us all, and ascribe the unseemly want of warmth to reserve or to the sadness which grips the heart when joy is too palpitant. But something warns me that you are unaware of the chill your words breathe, and that is a lapse which it is impossible to meet with indulgence.

"He does not love her," was Barbara's quick decision, and she laid the open letter down with a definiteness which said that you, too, are laid out and laid low. Your sister's very wrists can be articulate. However, I laughed at her and she soon joined me. We do not mean to be extravagant with our fears. Who shall prescribe the letters of lovers to their sisters and foster-fathers? Yet there are some things their letters should be incapable of saying, and amongst them that love is not a crisis and a rebirth, but that it is common as the commonplace, a hit or miss affair which "shuffling" could not affect.

Barbara showed me your note to her. "Had I written like this of myself and Earl—"

"You could not," I objected.

"Then Herbert should have been as little able to do it," she deduced with emphasis. Here I might have told her that men and women are races apart, but no one talks cant to Barbara. So I did not console her, and it stands against you in our minds that on this critical occasion you have baffled us with coldness.

An absence of six years, broken into twice by a brief few months, must work changes. When Barbara called your letter unnatural, she forgot how little she knows what is natural to you. She and I have been wont to predetermine you, your character, foothold, and outlook, by—say by the fact that you knew your Wordsworth and that you knew him without being able to take for yourself his austere peace. Youth which lives by hope is riven by unrest.

> "I made no vows; vows were made for me,
>
> Bond unknown to me was given
>
> That I should be, else sinning gently,
>
> A dedicated spirit."

That pale sunrise seen from Mt. Tamalpais and your voice vibrant to fierceness on the "else sinning gently"—to me the splendour of rose on piled-up ridges of mist spoke all for you, so dear have you always been. It rested on the possible wonder of your life. It threw you into the scintillant Dawn with an abandon meet to a son of Waring.

Tell me, do you still read your Wordsworth on your knees? I am bent with regret for the time when your mind had no surprises for me, when the days were flushed halcyon with my hope in you. I resent your development if it is because of it that you speak prosaically of a prosaic marriage and of a honeymoon simultaneous with the Degree. I think you are too well pleased with the simultaneousness.

Yet the fact of the letter is fair. It cannot be that the soul of it is not. Hester Stebbins is a poet. I lean forward and think it out as I did some days ago when the news came. I conjure up the look of love. If the woman is content (how much more than content the feeling she bounds with in knowing you hers as she is yours), what better test that all is well? I conjure up the look of love. It is thus at meeting and thus at parting. Even here, to-night, when all is chill and hard to understand, I catch the flash and the warmth, and what I see restores you to me, but how deep the plummet of my mind needed to sound before it reached you. It is because you permitted yourself to speak when silence had expressed you better.

Show me the ideally real Hester Stebbins, the spark of fire which is she. The storms have not broken over her head. She will laugh and make poetry of her laughter. If before she met you she wept, that, too, will help the smiling. There is laughter which is the echo of a Miserere sobbed by the ages. Men chuckle in the irony of pain, and they smile cold, lessoned smiles in resignation; they laugh in forgetfulness and they laugh lest they die of sadness. A shrug of the shoulders, a widening of the lips, a heaving forth of sound, and the life is saved. The remedy is as drastic as are the drugs used for epilepsy, which in quelling the spasm bring idiocy to the patient. If we are made idiots by our laughter, we are paying dearly for the privilege of continuing in life.

Hester shall laugh because she is glad and must tell her joy, and she will not lose it in the telling. Greet her for me and hasten to prove yourself, for

"The Poet, gentle creature that he is,

Hath like the Lover, his unruly times;

His fits when he is neither sick nor well,

Though no distress be near him but his own

Unmanageable thoughts."

You will judge by this letter that I am neither sick nor well, and that I reach for a distress which is not near. If I were Merchant rather than Poet, it would be otherwise with me.

Dane.

23

IV. FROM HERBERT WACE TO DANE KEMPTON

The Ridge,

Berkeley, California.

October 27, 19—.

Do I still read my Wordsworth on my knees? Well, we may as well have it out. I have foreseen this day so long and shunned it that now I meet it almost with extended hands. No, I do not read my Wordsworth on my knees. My mind is filled with other things. I have not the time. I am not the Herbert Wace of six years gone. It is fair that you should know this; fair, also, that you should know the Herbert Wace of six years gone was not quite the lad you deemed him.

There is no more pathetic and terrible thing than the prejudice of love. Both you and I have suffered from it. Six years ago, ay, and before that, I felt and resented the growing difference between us. When under your spell, it seemed that I was born to lisp in numbers and devote myself to singing, that the world was good and all of it fit for singing. But away from you, even then, doubts faced me, and I knew in vague fashion that we lived in different worlds. At first in vague fashion, I say; and when with you again, your spell dominated me and I could not question. You were true, you were good, I argued, all that was wonderful and glorious; therefore, you were also right. You mastered me with your charm, as you were wont to master those who loved you.

But there came times when your sympathy failed me and I stood alone on outlooks I had achieved alone. There was no response from you. I could not hear your voice. I looked down upon a real world; you were caught up in a beautiful cloudland and shut away from me. Possibly it was because life of itself appealed to you, while to me appealed the mechanics of life. But be it as it may, yours was a world of ideas and fancies, mine a world of things and facts.

Enters here the prejudice of love. It was the lad that discovered our difference and concealed; it was the man who was blind and could not discover. There we erred, man and boy; and here, both men now, we make all well again.

Let me be explicit. Do you remember the passion with which I read the "Intellectual Development of Europe?" I understood not the tithe of it, but I was thrilled. My common sense was thrilled, I suppose; but it was all very joyous, gripping hold of the tangible world for the first time. And when I came to you, warm with the glow of adventure, you looked blankly, then smiled indulgently and did not answer. You regarded my ardour complacently. A passing humour of adolescence, you thought; and I thought: "Dane does not read his Draper on his knees." Wordsworth was great to me; Draper was great also. You had no patience with him, and I know now, as I felt then, your consistent revolt against his materialistic philosophy.

Only the other day you complained of a letter of mine, calling it cold and analytical. That I should be cold and analytical despite all the prodding and pressing and moulding I have received at your hands, and the hands of Waring, marks only more clearly our temperamental difference; but it does not mark that one or the other of us is less a dedicated spirit. If I have wandered away from the warmth of poesy and become practical, have you not remained and become confirmed in all that is beautifully impractical? If I have adventured in a new world of common things, have you not lingered in the old world of great and impossible things? If I have shivered in the gray dawn of a new day, have you not crouched over the dying embers of the fire of yesterday? Ah, Dane, you cannot rekindle that fire. The whirl of the world scatters its ashes wide and far, like volcanic dust, to make beautiful crimson sunsets for a time and then to vanish.

None the less are you a dedicated spirit, priest that you are of a dying faith. Your prayers are futile, your altars crumbling, and the light flickers and drops down into night. Poetry is empty these days, empty and worthless and dead. All the old-world epic and lyric-singing will not put this very miserable earth of ours to rights. So long as the singers sing of the things of yesterday, glorifying the things of yesterday and lamenting their departure, so long will poetry be a vain thing and without avail. The old world is dead, dead and buried along with its heroes and Helens and knights and ladies and tournaments and pageants. You cannot sing of the truth and wonder of to-day in terms of yesterday. And no one will listen to your singing till you sing of to-day in terms of to-day.

This is the day of the common man. Do you glorify the common man? This is the day of the machine. When have you sung of the machine? The crusades are here again, not the Crusades of Christ but the Crusades of the Machine—have you found motive in them for your song? We are crusading to-day, not for the remission of sins, but for the abolition of sinning, of economic and industrial sinning. The crusade to Christ's sepulchre was paltry compared with the splendour and might of our crusade to-day toward manhood. There are millions of us afoot. In the stillness of the night have you never listened to the trampling of our feet and been caught up by the glory and the romance of it? Oh, Dane! Dane! Our captains sit in council, our heroes take the field, our fighting men are buckling on their harness, our martyrs have already died, and you are blind to it, blind to it all!

We have no poets these days, and perforce we are singing with our hands. The walking delegate is a greater singer and a finer singer than you, Dane Kempton. The cold, analytical economist, delving in the dynamics of society, is more the prophet than you. The carpenter at his bench, the blacksmith by his forge, the boiler-maker clanging and clattering, are all warbling more sweetly than you. The sledge-wielder pours out more strength and certitude and joy in every blow than do you in your whole sheaf of songs. Why, the very socialist agitator, hustled by the police on a street corner amid the jeers of the mob, has caught the romance of to-day as you have not caught it and where you have missed it. He knows life and is living. Are you living, Dane Kempton?

Forgive me. I had begun to explain and reconcile our difference. I find I am lecturing and censuring you. In defending myself, I offend. But this I wish to say: We are so made, you and I, that your function in life is to dream, mine to work. That you failed to make a dreamer of me is no cause for heartache and chagrin. What of my practical nature and analytical mind, I have generalised in my own way upon the data of life and achieved a different code from yours. Yet I seek truth as passionately as you. I still believe myself to be a dedicated spirit.

And what boots it, all of it? When the last word is said, we are two men, by a thousand ties very dear to each other. There is room in our hearts for each other as there is room in the world for both of us. Though we have many things not in common, yet you are my dearest friend on earth, you who have been a second father to me as well.

You have long merited this explanation, and it was cowardly of me not to have made it before. My hope is that I have been sufficiently clear for you to understand.

Herbert.

V. FROM DANE KEMPTON TO HERBERT WACE

London,

3 a Queen's Road, Chelsea, S.W.

November 16, 19—.

You sigh "Poesy and Economics," supplying the cause and thereby admitting the fact. I wish you had shown some reluctance to see my meaning, that you had preferred to waive the matter on the ground of insufficient data, that you had been less eager to ferret out the science of the thing. Do you remember how your boy's respect rose for little Barbara whenever she cried when too readily forgiven? "She dreads a double standard," you explained to me with generous heat. You sympathised with her fear lest I demand less of her than of you, honouring her insistence on an equality of duty as well as of privilege. Is the man Herbert less proud than the child Barbara, that you speak of a temperamental difference and ask for a special dispensation?

You are not in love (this you say in not gainsaying my attack on you, and so far I understand), because you are a student of Economics. At the last I stop. What is this about economics and poesy? About your emancipation from my riotously lyric sway? The hand of the forces by which you have been moulded cannot detain you from going out upon the love-quest. The fact of your preference for Draper cannot forestall your spirit's need of love. There are many codes, but there is one law, binding alike on the economist and poet. It springs out of the common and unappeasable hunger, commanding that love seek love through night to day and through day to night.

Yet it is possible to put oneself outside the pale of the law, to refuse the gift of life and snap the tie between time and space and creature. It is possible to be too emaciated for interest or feeling. The men and women of the People know neither love nor art because they are too weary. They lie in sleep prostrate from great fatigue. Their bodies are too much tried with the hungers of the body and their spirits too dimly illumined with the hope of fair chances. It is also possible to fill oneself so full with an interest that all else is crowded out. You have done this. Like the cobbler who is a cobbler typically, the teacher who is a pedagogue, the physician and the lawyer who are pathologists merely, you are a fanatic of a text. You are in the toils of an idea, the idea of selection, as I well know, and you exploit it like a drudge. When a man finds that he cannot deal in petroleum without smelling of it, it is time that he turn to something else. Every man is engaged in the cause of keeping himself whole, in watching himself lest his man turn machine, in watching lest the outside world assail the inner. Nature spares the type, but the individual must spare himself. He is strong who is sensitive and who responds subtly to everything in his environment, but his response must be characteristic; he must sustain his personality and become more himself through the years. He alone is vital in the social scheme who lets nothing in him atrophy and who persists in being varied from all others in the scale of character to the degree of variability that was his at the beginning.

I read in your letter nothing but a decision to stop short and give over, as if you had strength for no more than your book and your theory! You have become slave to a small point of inquiry, and you call it the advance to a new time. "The crusade is on," you say. Coronation rites for the commoners and destruction to superstition. I put my hand out to you in joy. The joy is in unholy worship of a fetish, the pain that there is no joy also deference to a fetish. Your creed thunders "Thou shalt not." Love is a thing of yesterday. No room for anything that intimately concerns the self. But what are the apostles of the young thought preaching if it is not the right of men to their own, and what would it avail them to come into their own if life be stripped of romance?

I am dissatisfied because you are willing to live as others must live. You should stay aristocrat. Ferdinand Lassalle dressed with elegance for his working-men audiences, with the hope, he said, of reminding them that there was something better than their shabbiness. You are of the favoured, Herbert. It devolves upon you to endear your life to yourself. You do not agree with me. You do not believe that love is the law which controls freedom and life. Slave to your theory and rebel to the law, you lose your soul and imperil another's.

"Gently! Gently!" I say to myself. Old sorrows and wrongs oppress me and I grow harsh. My heat only helps to convince you that my position is not based on the *rational rightness* you hold so essential and that therefore it is unlivable. I will state calmly, then, that it is wrong to marry without love. "For the perpetuation of the species"—that is noble of you! So you strip yourself of the thousand years of civilisation that have fostered you, you abandon your prerogative as a creature high in the scale of existence to obey an instinct and fulfil a function? You say: "These men and women will marry, and the work of the world go on just as it did before. Shuffle them about and the work of the world would yet go on." And you are content. You feel no need of anything different from this condition.

Believe me, Herbert, these million men and women will not let you shuffle them about. There are forces stronger than force, shadows more real than reality. We know that the need of the unhungered for the one friend, one comrade, one mate, is good. We honour the love that persists in loving. More beautiful than starlight is the face of the lover when the Voice and the Vision enfold him. The race is consecrated to the worship of idea, and the lover who lays his all on the altar of romance (which is idea) is at one with the race. The arms of the unloved girl close about the formless air and more real than her loneliness and her sorrow is the imagined embrace, the awaited warm, close pressure of the hands, the fancied gaze. What does it mean? What secret was there for Leonardo in Mona Lisa's smile, what for him in the motion of waters? You cannot explain the bloom, the charm, the smile of life, that which rains sunshine into our hearts, which tells us we are wise to hope and to have faith, which buckles on us an armour of activity, which lights the fires of the spirit, which gives us Godhead and renders us indomitable. Comparative anatomy cannot reason it down. It is sensibility, romance, idea. It is a fact of life toward which all other facts make. For the flush of rose-light in the heavens, the touch of a hand, the colour and shape of fruit, the tears that come for unnamed sorrows, the regrets of old men, are more significant than all the building and inventing done since the first social compact.

Forgive my tediousness. I have flaunted these truisms before you in order to exorcise that modern slang of yours which is more false than the overstrained forms of a feudal France. To shut out glory is not to be practical. You are not adjusting your life artistically; there is too much strain, too little warmth, too much self-complacence. I see that you are really younger than I thought. The world never censures the crimes of the spirit. You are safe from the world's tongue lashings, and in that safety is the danger against which my friendship warns you.

I have been reading Hester's poems, and I know that she is like them, nervous, vibrant, throbbing, sensitive. I have been reading your letters, and I think her soul will escape yours. If you have not love like hers, you have nothing with which to keep her. This I have undertaken to say to you. It is a strange role, yet conventional. I am the father whose matrimonial whims are not met by the son. The stock measure is to disinherit. But the cause of our quarrel is somewhat unusual, and I can be neither so practical nor so vulgar as to set about making codicils. Love is of no value to financiers; there is no bank for it nor may it be made over in a will. Rather is it carried on in the blood, even as Barbara carried it on into the life of her girl-babe. Your sister keeps me strong with the faith of love. May God be good to her! It was five years ago that she came to me and whispered, "Earl." When she saw I could not turn to her in joy, she leaned her little head back against the roses of the porch and wept, more than was right, I fear, for a girl just betrothed. Earl was a cripple and poor and helpless, but Barbara knew better than we, for she knew how to give herself. Poor little one, whom nobody congratulated! She sends you and Hester her love, unfolding you both in her eager tenderness.

Dane.

VI. FROM THE SAME TO THE SAME

London.

November 19, 19—.

Metaphysics is contagious. I caught it from Barbara, and I cannot resist the impulse to pass it on, and to you of all others.

The mood leapt upon Barbara out of the pages of "Katia," a story by Tolstoy. To my mind, it is a painful tale of lovers who outlive their love, killing it with their own hands, but the author means it to be a happily ending novel. Tolstoy attempts to show that men and women can find happiness only when they grow content to give over seeking love from one another. They may keep the memory but must banish the hope. "Hereafter, think of me only as the father of your children," and the woman who had pined for that which had been theirs in the beginning of their union weeps softly, and agrees. Tolstoy calls this peace, but for Barbara and me this gain is loss, this end an end indeed, replete with all the tragedy of ending.

I found Barbara to-day on the last page of "Katia," and much disturbed. "Dear, I saw a spirit break," she said. I waited before asking whose, and when I did, she answered, "That of three-quarters of the world. The ghost of a Dream walked to-day—when after the spirit broke, I saw it—and myself and my Earl vanished in shadow. We and our love thinned away before the thought-shape."

"Your dreaming, Barbara, can scarce be better than your living."

We looked long at each other. She knew herself a happy woman, yet to-day the ghost had walked in the light, and her eyes were not held, and she saw. Even her life was not sufficient, even her plans were paltry, even her heart's love was cramped. Such times of seeing come to happy men and to happy women. Barbara was reading the opinions of the world and the acceptances of the world, and in disliking them she came to doubt herself. Perhaps she, too, should be less at peace, she too may be amongst Pharisees a Pharisee.

"In the midst of the breaking of spirit, how can I know?" she demanded. "Love is sure," I prompted, my hand on her forehead. "Earl and I are sure, dear," she laughed low, and a drift of sobbing swept through the music; "it is not that we are in doubt about ourselves, but sometimes, like to-day, you understand, one finds oneself bitten by the sharp tooth of the world, and a despair courses through the veins and blinds the eyes, and then, in the midst of the bitterest throe, comes a great visioning."

I heard her and understood, and my heart leapt as it had not done for long. Think of it, Herbert, fifty-three and still young! When was it that I last fluttered with joy? Ah, yes, that time the summer and the woods had a great deal to do with it, and a few words spoken by a boy. I think Barbara's majesty of attainment through vicarious breaking of spirit a greater cause for rejoicing.

And then, in the midst of the bitterest throe, came a great visioning. When pain is good and to be thanked for, how good life is! By this alone may you know the proportion and the value of the good of being. Three-quarters of the world are broken spirited, but from out the wreckage a thought-shape, and it is well. The Vision fastens upon us, and what was full seems shrunken, what whole and of all time a passing bit, an untraceable flash. And that is well, for the dream recalls the hope, and the heart grows hardy with hoping and dreaming.

So Barbara.

And you? You do not repine because of these things. Let the Grand Mujik mutter a thousand heresies, let three-quarters of the world accept and live them, you would not think the unaspiring three-quarters broken-spirited. You would hail them right practical. And if you held a thought as firmly as your sister holds the thought of love, and you found yourself alone in your esteem of it, you would part from it and go over to the others. You would not be the fanatic your sister is, to stay so much the closer by it that of necessity she must doubt her own allegiance, fearing in her devotion that, without knowing it, she, too, is cold and but half alive. You would not see visions that would put your best to shame. The thought-shape of the more you could be, were you and the whole world finer and greater, would not walk before you. You would rest content and assured, and—I regret your assurance.

Always yours,

Dane Kempton.

VII. FROM HERBERT WACE TO DANE KEMPTON

The Ridge,

Berkeley, California.

December 6, 19—.

No, I am not in love. I am very thankful that I am not. I pride myself on the fact. As you say, I may not be adjusting my life artistically to its environment (there is room for discussion there), but I do know that I am adjusting it scientifically. I am arranging my life so that I may get the most out of it, while the one thing to disorder it, worse than flood and fire and the public enemy, is love.

I have told you, from time to time, of my book. I have decided to call it "The Economic Man." I am going over the proofs now, and my brain is in perfect working order. On the other hand, there is Professor Bidwell, who is likewise correcting proofs. Poor devil, he is in despair. He can do nothing with them. "I positively cannot think," he complains to me, his hair rumpled and face flushed. He did not answer my knock the other day, and I came upon him with the neglected proofs under his elbows and his absent gaze directed through window and out of doors to some rosy cloudland beyond my ken. "It will be a failure, I know it will," he growled to me. "My brain is dull. It refuses to act. I cannot imagine what has come over me." But I could imagine very easily. He is in love (madly in love with what I take to be a very ordinary sort of girl), and expects shortly to be married. "Postpone the book for a time," I suggested. He looked at me for a moment, then brought his fist down on the general disarray with a thumping "I will!" And take my word for it, Dane, a year hence, when the very ordinary girl greets him with the matronly kiss and his fever and folly have left him, he will take up the book and make a success of it.

Of course I am not in love. I have just come back from Hester—I ran down Saturday to Stanford and stopped over Sunday. Time did not pass tediously on the train. I did not look at my watch every other minute. I read the morning papers with interest and without impatience. The scenery was charming and I was unaware of the slightest hurry to reach my destination. I remember noting, when I came up the gravel walk between the rose-bushes, that my heart was not in my mouth as it should have been according to convention. In fact, the sun was uncomfortable, and I mopped my brow and decided that the roses stood in need of trimming. And really, you know, I had seen brighter days, and fairer views, and the world in more beautiful moods.

And when Hester stood on the veranda and held out her hands, my heart did not leap as though it were going to part company with me. Nor was I dizzy with—rapture, I believe. Nor did all the world vanish, and everything blot out, and leave only Hester standing there, lips curved and arms outstretched in welcome. Oh, I saw the curved lips and outstretched arms, and all the splendid young womanhood swaying there, and I was pleased and all that; but I did not think it too wonderful and impossible and miraculous and the rest of the fond rubbish I am sure poor Bidwell thinks when his eyes are gladdened by his ordinary sort of girl when he calls upon her.

What a comely young woman, is what I thought as I pressed Hester's hands; and none of the ordinary sort either. She has health and strength and beauty and youth, and she will certainly make a most charming wife and excellent mother. Thus I thought, and then we chatted, had lunch, and passed a delightful afternoon together—an afternoon such as I might pass with you, or any good comrade, or with my wife.

All of which rational rightness is, I know, distasteful to you, Dane. And I confess I depict it with brutal frankness, failing to give credit to the gentler, tenderer side of me. Believe me, I am very fond of Hester. I respect and admire her. I am proud of her, too, and proud of myself that so fine a creature should find enough in me to be willing to mate with me. It will be a happy marriage. There is nothing cramped or narrow or incompatible about it. We know each other well—a wisdom that is acquired by lovers only after marriage, and even then with the likelihood of it being a painful wisdom. We, on the other hand, are not blinded by love madness, and we see clearly and sanely and are confident of our ability to live out the years together.

Herbert.

VIII. FROM THE SAME TO THE SAME

The Ridge,

Berkeley, California.

December 11, 19—.

I have been thinking about your romance and my rational rightness, and so this letter.

"One loves because he loves: this explanation is, as yet, the most serious and most decisive that has been found for the solution of this problem." I do not know who has said this, but it might well have been you. And you might well say with Mlle. de Scudéri: *"Love is—I know not what: which comes—I know not when: which is formed—I know not how: which enchants—I know not by what: and which ends—I know not when or why."*

You explain love by asserting that it is not to be explained. And therein lies our difference. You accept results; I search for causes. You stop at the gate of the mystery, worshipful and content. I go on and through, flinging the gate wide and formulating the law of the mystery which is a mystery no longer. It is our way. You worship the idea; I believe in the fact. If the stone fall, the wind blow, the grass and green things sprout; if the inorganic be vitalised, and take on sensibility, and perform functions, and die; if there be passions and pains, dreams and ambitions, flickerings of infinity and glimmerings of Godhead—it is for you to be smitten with the wonder of it and to memorialise it in pretty song, while for me remains to classify it as so much related phenomena, so much play and interplay of force and matter in obedience to ascertainable law.

There are two kinds of men: the wonderers and the doers; the feelers and the thinkers; the emotionals and the intellectuals. You take an emotional delight in living; I an intellectual delight. You feel a thing to be beautiful and joyful; I seek to know why it is beautiful and joyful. You are content that it is, no matter how it came to be; I, when I have learned why, strive that we may have more beautiful and joyful things. "The bloom, the charm, the smile of life" is all too wonderful for you to know; to me it is chiefly wonderful because I may know.

Oh, well, it is an ancient quarrel which neither you nor I shall outlive. I am rational, you are romantic,—that is all there is to it. You are more beautiful; I am more useful; and though you will not see it and will never be able to see it, you and your beauty rest on me. I came into the world before you, and I made the way for you. I was a hunter of beasts and a fighter of men. I discovered fire and covered my nakedness with the skins of animals. I built cunning traps, and wove branches and long grasses and rushes and reeds into the thatch and roof-tree. I fashioned arrows and spears of bone and flint. I drew iron from the earth, and broke the first ground, and planted the first seed. I gave law and order to the tribe and taught it to fight with craft and wisdom. I enabled the young men to grow strong and lusty, and the women to find favour with them; and I gave safety to the women when their progeny came forth, and safety to the progeny while it gathered strength and years.

I did many things. Out of my blood and sweat and toil I made it possible that all men need not all the time hunt and fish and fight. The muscle and brain of every man were no longer called to satisfy the belly need. And then, when of my blood and sweat and toil I had made room, you came, high priest of mystery and things unknowable, singer of songs and seer of visions.

And I did you honour, and gave you place by feast and fire. And of the meat I gave you the tenderest, and of the furs the softest. Need I say that of women you took the fairest? And you sang of the souls of dead men and of immortality, of the hidden things, and of the wonder; you sang of voices whispering down the wind, of the secrets of light and darkness, and the ripple of running fountains. You told of the powers that pulsed the tides, swept the sun across the firmaments, and held the stars in their courses. Ay, and you scaled the sky and created for me the hierarchy of heaven.

These things you did, Dane; but it was I who made you, and fed you, and protected you. While you dreamed and sang, I laboured sore. And when danger came, and there was a cry in the night, and women and children huddling in fear, and strong men broken, and blare of trumpets and cry of battle at the outer gate—you fled to your altars and called vainly on your phantoms of earth and sea and sky. And I? I girded my loins, and strapped my harness on, and smote in the fighting line; and died, perchance, that you and the women and children might live.

And in times of peace you throve and waxed fat. But only by our brain and blood did we men of the fighting line make possible those times of peace. And when you throve, you looked about you and saw the beauty of the world and fancied yet greater beauty. And because of me your fancy became fact, and marvels arose in stone and bronze and costly wood.

And while your brows were bright, and you visioned things of the spirit, and rose above time and space to probe eternity, I concerned myself with the work of head and hand. I employed myself with the mastery of matter. I studied the times and seasons and the crops, and made the earth fruitful. I built roads and bridges and moles, and won the secrets of metals and virtues of the elements. Bit by bit, and with great travail, I have conquered and enslaved the blind forces. I built ships and ventured the sea, and beyond the baths of sunset found new lands. I conquered peoples, and organised nations and knit empires, and gave periods of peace to vast territories.

And the arts of peace flourished, and you multiplied yourself in divers ways. You were priest and singer and dancer and musician. You expressed your fancies in colours and metals and marbles. You wrote epics and lyrics— ay, as you to-day write lyrics, Dane Kempton. And I multiplied myself. I kept hunger afar off, and fire and sword from your habitation, and the bondsmen in obedience under you. I solved methods of government and invented systems of jurisprudence. Out of my toil sprang forms and institutions. You sang of them and were the slave of them, but I was the maker of them and the changer of them.

You worshipped at the shrine of the idea. I sought the fact and the law behind the fact. I was the worker and maker and liberator. You were conventional. Tradition bound you. You were full bellied and content, and you sang of the things that were. You were mastered by dogma. Did the

Mediæval Church say the earth was flat, you sang of an earth that was flat, and danced and made your little shows on an earth that was flat. And you helped to bind me with chains and burn me with fire when my facts and the laws behind my facts shook your dogmas. Dante's highest audacity could not transcend a material inferno. Milton could not shake off Lucifer and hell.

You were more beautiful. But not only was I more useful, but I made the way for you that there might be greater beauty. You did not reck of that. To you the heart was the seat of the emotions. I formulated the circulation of the blood. You gave charms and indulgences to the world; I gave it medicine and surgery. To you, famine and pestilence were acts of providence and punishment of sin: I made the world a granary and drained its cities. To you the mass of the people were poor lost wretches who would be rewarded in paradise or baked in hell. You could offer them no earthly happiness of decency. Forsooth, beggars as well as kings were of divine right. But I shattered the royal prerogatives and overturned the thrones of the one and lifted the other somewhat out of the dirt.

Nor is my work done. With my inventions and discoveries and rational enterprise, I draw the world together and make it kin. The uplift is but begun. And in the great world I am making I shall be as of old to you, Dane. I, who have made you and freed you, shall give you space and greater freedom. And, as of old, we shall quarrel as when first you came to me and found me at my rude earth-work. You shall be the scorner of matter, and I the master of matter. You may laugh at me and my work, but you shall not be absent from the feast nor shall your voice be silent. For, when I have conquered the globe, and enthralled the elements, and harnessed the stars, you shall sing the epic of man, and as of old it shall be of the deeds I have done.

Herbert.

IX. FROM DANE KEMPTON TO HERBERT WACE

3a Queen's Road, Chelsea, S.W.

December 28, 19—.

The curtain is rung down on an illusion, but it rises again on another, this time, as before, with the look of the absolute Good and True upon it. It is because we are at once actor and spectator that we find no fault with blinking sight and slothful thought. We are finite branded and content, except during the shrill, undermining moments when the orchestra is tuning up. "Thus we half-men struggle."

I follow your letter and wonder whether your illusions have qualities of beauty which escape me. I give you the benefit of every doubt which it is possible for me to harbour with regard to my own system of illusions. You glorify the crowd practical. You attach yourself to the ranks that carried thought into action. You inspire yourself with rugged strength by dwelling on the achievements of ruggedness, forgetting that the progress of the world is not marshalled by those who work with line and rule. It was not his crew, but Columbus, who discovered America. The crew stood between the Old and the New, as indeed the crew always does. Between the idealist and his hope were hosts of practical enemies whom he had to subdue before he reached land. But I must not fall into your mistake of dividing men into categories. Men are not either intellectual or emotional; they are both. It is a rounded not an angular development which we follow. Feeling and thinking are not mutually exclusive, and the great personality feels deeply because he thinks highly, feels keenly because he sees widely. Common sense is not incompatible with uncommon sense, evil does not of necessity attend beauty, nor weakness the strength of genius.

I shall sing of the deeds you have done if your deeds are worthy of song. I shall sing a Song of the Sword, too, should the sword "thrust through the fatuous, thrust through the fungous brood." Whatever helps the races to better life sings itself into racial lore, and I alone shall not refuse the tribute.

When you come to see that the Iliad is as great a gift to the race as the doings of Achilles, that the Iliads are more significant than the doings they celebrate, you will cease to classify men into doers and singers. You will cease to dishonour yourself in the eyes of the singers with the hope that in so doing you gain somewhat elsewhere.

Professor Bidwell is in love and it interferes with his work. You have the advantage of him there, no doubt. However, you lose more than you gain. You have shattered the dream and have awakened. To what? What is this reality in which your universe is hung? Where shine the stars of your scientific heaven? By the beauty of your dreaming alone, Herbert, shall you be judged and known. You dream that you have learned the lesson, solved the problem, pierced the mystery, and become a prophet of matter. But matter does not include spirit, so the motif of your dream grows all confused. Your race epic omits the race. You sing the branch and the leaf rather than the sunlit and tenebral wood. Bidwell thinks his ordinary sort of girl a "lyric love, half angel and half bird, and all a wonder and a wild desire." Bidwell exaggerates, perhaps, but unless he feels this for his wife, he has no wife. Barbara obeyed the voice of her heart. That sounds sentimental, but it is none the less a courageous thing to do. I was inconsistent enough to be sorry because she loved a crippled man. Bidwell and Barbara are wiser and happier than you can be, Herbert, than you from whose hand the map of Parnassus Hill has been filched.

Is there one state of consciousness better than another? I think yes. Better to have long, youthful thoughts and to thrill to vibrant emotions than to grovel sluggishly; better to hope and dream and aspire and sway to great harmonies than to be blind and deaf and dumb—better for the type, better for the immortality of the world's soul. This to me is a vital thought, therefore life or death is in the issue. For the rest I know not. By the glimmer of light lent me, I can but guess greatness and descry vagueness. You go further and would touch the phantasmagorial veil. "Right!" I say, and I pray, "Godspeed." But there must be intensity. Are you thrilled? Do you stretch out your arms and dream the beauty? It is only when you gaze into a reality empty of the voices of life that I would wake you to bid you dream better.

Well, Herbert, I have quarrelled with you and shall to the end, I promise. I wish I could take you away, hide you from your Hester's sight, and pour my poetic spleen out on you. Oh, I shall torment you into reason and passion! Whatever you may choose to be, you are my son. I must take you and keep you as you are, of course, but I choose to tell the truth to you though I do love you and hold you mine. Disagreeable of me, but how else?

Dane.

X. FROM THE SAME TO THE SAME

London.

Sunday, January 1, 19—.

Behold, I have lived! I press your face to the breathing, stinging roses of my days, and bid you drink in the sweet and throb with the pain. What is my philosophy but a translation of the facts which have stamped me? Perhaps if I let you read these facts, you will the sooner come to share my consecration and my faith. I must teach you to know that you are the fact of my whole tangled web of facts, and that all that I have and am, and all that might have been I and mine, stretches itself out in the unmarked path which is before you.

I take you back with me to the road, white with dust, upon which like a Viking and like a feeble girl I have travelled. It is not long, but how many paths, what byways and what turns! What sudden glimpses of sea and sky, what inaccessibleness! Hark, from the wood on either side murmurings of hope and hard sobbing of despair, young laughter of joy and aged renunciations! See from amongst the pines the farewell gleam of a white hand. All of it dear—dearly bought and precious and miraculous, the heartache even as the gladness.

"Life is worth living

Through every grain of it,

From the foundations

To the last edge

Of the cornerstone, death."

Ay, through every grain of it. Even that morning in the wood, thirty years ago, when your mother put her hand in mine and looked a great pity into my eyes. Indeed, she loved me well, but romance shone on the brow of John Wace. For her his face was sunlit, and she needs must take it between her hands and hold it forever. He was her Siegfried, her master. Thus the gods decreed, and we three obeyed. What else was there to do? We must be honest before all, and Ellen did not love me any more, and I must know it, and wipe out a past of deepest mutuality, and strengthen and console and restore the woman whose hand held mine while her eyes were turned elsewhere.

Before that bright, black summer morning which saw me woman-pitied, I knew I should have to renounce her. Their souls rushed together in their first meeting. John had been away, knocking about museums and colleges, and carrying on tempestuous radical work. He was splendidly picturesque. I was a youth of twenty-three, almost ten years his junior, a boy full of half-defined aims and groping powers, reaching toward what he had firm in his grasp. Ellen talked of his coming, and she planned that she should meet this my one friend in the environment she loved best—in my rooms, whose atmosphere, she declared, belonged to an earlier time and place. (She found in me Nolly Goldsmith and all of Grub Street.) So they met at the tea-table in my study, and a great warmth stole over your father. He spoke without looking at either of us, while Ellen looked as if her destiny had just begun.

Without, it rained. I strode to the window and in a dazed way stared at the lamp-post which was sticking out its flaming little tongue to the night. Why was I mocked? There was no mocking and there should have been no bitterness. Of that there was none either, after a while.

Ellen put her hand on my hair, and a strong primal emotion rose in me. In that moment civilisation was as if it had not been. I reverted to the primitive. The blood of forgotten ancestors, cave-men and river-men, reasoned me my ethics. I turned to her, met her flushed cheeks and moved being and the glory of dawning in her eyes. I measured my strength with hers and your father's, Herbert. Easily, great strength was mine in my passion, easily I could carry her off!

You, too, have had moments of upheaval when you heard the growling of the tiger and the bear, when the brute crowded out the man. Then your soul writhed in derision, you scoffed at that which you had held to be the nobility of the soul, and you minced words satirically over the exquisiteness of the type which we have evolved. Then the experiment of life turned farce, the heavens fell about your ears and "Fool!" was upon your lips. Oh, the hurricane that sweeps over the soul when it is cheated of its joy! In the first instant of Ellen's indifference, when I felt myself pushed out of her life, I forgot everything but my desire. I could not renounce her. I was in the throes of the passion for ownership.

Gentle girl between whom and myself there had been naught but sweetness and fellowship! How often had we talked large (we were very young!) of our sublimities and potentialities, how often had we pictured tragedies of surrender and greatened in the speaking! Ah, it should come true. For her and for me there must be miracles, and there were. So was the strength of the spirit proven, so was it shown to be "pure waft of the Will." So was I confirmed in the creed which believes that to keep we must lose, and to live we must die. So was I assured that there may be but one way, and that, the way of service.

I did not grip her passionately in my arms. I withdrew; I did much to make her task of leaving me an easy one. Were it not for my efforts, it would have been harder for her to obey a mandate which made for my pain. She could not quite drown an old, Puritan voice, speaking with the authority of tradition, which bade her hold to her vows. Yes, I made it easy for her. Harrow my soul with theories of selection and survival if you dare!

In those days the spires of the temple were golden, the shrine white. The door was seen from every point in the fog-begirt world. We who worshipped knew not of doubt. Stirred by the rumbling organ tones of causes and ideas, we immolated our lives gladly. High priests of thought, we swung the censers and rose on the breast of the incense. Ellen and John and myself glorified God and enjoyed Him forever,—God, the Type, the Final Humanity, the giant Body Soul of man. In our hearts dwelt a religion which compelled us to serve the ideal. We strove to become what organically we felt the "Human with his drippings of warm tears" may become. We were the standard-bearers of the advancing margin of the world. We were the high-water mark toward which all the tides forever make. We were soldiers and priests.

And so when Ellen loved, and lacked courage for her love, I helped her. A past of kindness and ardour riveted her to my side. She knew that we were in feeling and fact divorced from each other by virtue of her stronger love for John, yet did she do battle with the rich young love. For two years we had been close; she had been so much my friend, she could not in maiden charity seal for me a so unwelcome fate. I had awakened her slumbering soul with my first look into the sphinx wonder of her eyes. For me she had become fire and dew, flame of the sun, and flower of the hill. Without me to help her do it she could not leave me.

To the master of matter this coping with spiritual abstractions must appear like juggling with intellectual phantasmagoria. Yet I protest that life is finally for intangible triumphs. Unnamed fragrances steal upon the senses and the soul revels and greatens. Unseen hands draw us to worlds afar, and we are gathered up in the dignity of the human spirit. Unknown ideas attract and hold us, and we take our place in the universe as intellectual factors. In giving up Ellen I helped her, and, sacredly better still, I sent on into a world of vague thinking and weak acting the impulse of devotion to revealed truth.

She had a sweet way of sitting low and resting her head on my knee. She sat through one whole day with me thus, and for hours I could have thought her asleep were it not for the waves of feeling which surged in her upturned face. Toward the end she raised her head, ecstasy in her eyes and on her cheek and lip. "Dane, I love you. Dane! Dane!" The whole of me was caught up in the accents of that tremulousness. She had know John three months; but her love for him was young, it had come unexpectedly, it was still unexpressed and ineffable. Her yearning for him led to softness toward me, and though she rose out of her mood as one does from a dream, the hours when we were like the angels, all love and all speech, were mine. So much was vouchsafed me.

Memories and echoes, gusts of sweet breath from the violets on your mother's grave—the prophet of matter will have none of them, and, I fear, will pity me that I am so much theirs. I am yours also, dear lad, and I wish to serve you.

Dane Kempton.

XI. FROM HERBERT WACE TO DANE KEMPTON

The Ridge,

Berkeley, California.

January 20, 19—.

I do not know whether to laugh or weep. I have just finished reading your letter, and I can hardly think. Words seem to have lost their meaning, and words, used as you use them, are without significance. You appear to speak a tongue strangely familiar, yet one I cannot understand. You are unintelligible, as, I dare say, I am to you.

And small wonder that we are unintelligible. Our difference presents itself quite clearly to the scientific mind, and somewhat in this fashion: Man acquires knowledge of the outer world through his sensations and perceptions. Sensation ends in sentiment, and perception ends in reason. These are the two sides of man's nature, and the individual is determined and ruled by whichever side in him happens to be temperamentally dominant. I have already classed you as a feeler, myself as a thinker. This is, I *think* true. You, I am confident, *feel* it to be true. I reason why it is true. You accept it on faith as true, lose sight of the argument forthwith, and proceed to express it in emotional terms—which is to say that you take it to heart and feel badly because it happens to be so.

You feign to know this modern scientific slang, and you are contemptuous of it because you do not know it. The terms I use freight no ideas to you. They are sounds, rhythmic and musical, but they are not definite symbols of thought. Their facts you do not grasp. For instance, the prehensile organs of insects, the great toothed mandibles of the black stag-beetle, the amorous din of the male cicada and the muteness of his mate—these are facts which you cannot relate, one with the other, nor can you generalise upon them. Let me add to these related characters, and you cannot discern the law which is alike to all. What to you the fluttering moth, decked in gold and crimson, brilliant, iridescent, splendid? The beauty of it bids you bend to deity, otherwise it has no worth; it is a stimulus to religion, and that is all. So with the glowing incandescence of the stickleback and its polished scales of silver. What make you of the hoarse voice of the gorilla? Is not the dewlap of the ox inscrutable? the mane of the lion? the tusks of the boar? the musk-sack of the deer? In the amethyst and sapphire of the peacock's wing you find no rationality; to you it is a manifestation of the wonder which is taboo. And so with the cock bird, displaying his feathered ruffs and furbelows, dancing strange antics and spilling out his heart in song.

I, on the other hand, dare to gather all these phenomena together, and find out the common truth, the common fact, the common law, which is generalisation, which is Science. I learn that there are two functions which all life must perform: Nutrition and Reproduction. And I learn that in all life, the performance, according to time and space and degree, is very like. The slug must take to itself food, else it will perish; and so I. The slug must procreate its kind, or its kind will perish; and so I. The need being the same, the only difference is in the expression. In all life come times and seasons when the individuals are aware of dim yearnings and blind compulsions and masterful desires. The senses are quickened and alert to the call of kind. And just as the fish and the reptile glimmeringly adumbrate man, so do these yearnings and desires adumbrate what man in himself calls "love," spelled all out in capitals. I repeat, the need is the same. From the amœba, up the ladder of life to you and me, comes this passion of perpetuation. And in yourself, refine and sublimate as you will, it is none the less blind, unreasoning, and compelling.

And now we come to the point. In the development of life from low to high, there came a dividing of the ways. Instinct, as a factor of development, had its limitations. It culminated in that remarkable mechanism, the bee-swarm. It could go no farther. In that direction life was thwarted. But life, splendid and invincible, not to be thwarted, changed the direction of its advance, and reason became the all-potent developmental factor. Reason dawned far down in the scale of life; but it culminates in man and the end is not yet.

The lever in his arm he duplicates in wood and steel; the lenses in his eyes in glass; the visual impressions of his brain on chemically sensitised wood-pulp. He is able, reasoning from events and knowing the law, to control the blind forces and direct their operation. Having ascertained the laws of development, he is able to take hold of life and mould and knead it into more beautiful and useful forms. Domestic selection it is called. Does he wish horses which are fast, he selects the fastest. He studies the physics of velocity in relation to equine locomotion, and with an eye to withers, loins, hocks, and haunches, he segregates his brood mares and his stallions. And behold, in the course of a few years, he has a thoroughbred stock, swifter of foot than any ever in the world before.

Since he takes sexual selection into his own hands and scientifically breeds the fish and the fowl, the beast and the vegetable, why may he not scientifically breed his own kind? The fish and the fowl and the beast and the vegetable obey dim yearnings and vague desires and reproduce themselves. "Poor the reproduction," says Man to Mother Nature; "allow me." And Mother Nature is thrust aside and exceeded by this new creator, this Man-god.

These yearnings and desires of the beast and the vegetable are the best tools nature has succeeded in devising. Having devised them, she leaves their operation to the blindness of chance. Steps in man and controls and directs them. For the first time in the history of life conscious intelligence forms and transforms life. These yearnings and desires, promptings of the "abysmal fecundity," have in man evolved into what is called "love." They arise in instinct and sensation and culminate in sentiment and emotion. They master man, and the intellect of man, as they master the beast and all the acts of the beast. And they operate in the development of man with the same blindness of chance that they operate in the development of the beast.

Now this is the law: *Love, as a means for the perpetuation and development of the human type, is very crude and open to improvement. What the intellect of man has done with the beast, the intellect of man may do with man.*

It is a truism to say that my intellect is wiser than my emotions. So, knowing the precise value and use of this erotic phenomenon, this sexual madness, this love, I, for one, elect to choose my mate with my intellect. Thus I choose Hester. And I do truly love her, but in the intellectual sense and not the sense you fanatically demand. I am not seized with a loutish vertigo when I look upon her and touch her hand. Nor do I feel impelled to leave her presence if I would live, as did Dante the presence of Beatrice; nor the painful confusion of Rousseau, when, in the same room with Madame Goton, he seemed impelled to leap into the flaming fireplace. But I do feel for Hester what happily mated men and women, after they have lived down the passion, feel in the afternoon of life. It is the affection of man for woman, which is sanity. It is the sanity of intercourse which replaces love madness; the sanity which comes upon sparrows after the ardour of mating, when they leave off wrangling and chattering and set soberly to work to build their nest for the coming brood.

Pre-nuptial love is the madness of non-understanding and part-understanding. Post-nuptial affection is the sanity of complete understanding; it is based upon reason and service and healthy sacrifice. The first is a blind mating of the blind; the second, a clear and open-eyed union of male and female who find enough in common to warrant that union. In a word and in the fullest sense of the word, it is sex comradeship. Pre-nuptial love cannot survive marriage any considerable time. It is doomed inexorably to flicker out, and when it has flickered out it must be replaced by affection, or else the parties to it must separate. We well know that many men and women, unable to build up affection on the ruins of love, do separate, or if they do not, continue to live together in cold tolerance or bitter hatred.

Now, Hester is my mate. We have much in common. There is intellectual, spiritual, and physical affinity. The caress of her voice and the feel of her mind are pleasurable to me; likewise the touch of her hand (and you know that in the union of man and woman the higher affinities are not possible unless there first be physiological affinity). We shall go through life as comrades go, hand in hand, Hester and I; and great happiness will be ours. And because of all this I say you have no right to challenge my happiness, and vex my days, and feel for me as one dead.

My dear, bewildered Dane, come down out of the clouds. If I am wrong, I have gone over the ground. Then do you go over that ground with me and show where I am wrong. But do not pour out on me your romantic and poetic spleen. Confine yourself to the Fact, man, to the irrefragable Fact.

Herbert.

Ah, your later letter has just arrived. I can only say that I understand. But withal, I am pained that I am not nearer to you. These intellectual phantasmagoria rise up like huge amorphous ghosts and hold me from you. I cannot get through the mists and glooms to press your hand and tell you how dear I hold you. Do, Dane, do let us cease from this. Let us discuss no further. Let me care for Hester in my own way so long as I do no sin and harm no one; and be you father to us, and bless us who else must go unblessed. For Hester, also, is fatherless and motherless, and you must be to her as you are to me.

Herbert.

XII. FROM DANE KEMPTON TO HERBERT WACE

London,

3a Queen's Road, Chelsea, S.W.

February 10, 19—.

So we have got into an argument! I have been poring over your last two or three letters, and they read like a set of briefs for a debate. Doubtless mine have the same forensic quality. Our letters have become rebuttals, pure and simple. This discovery gave my pen pause for a week. It occurred to me that Walt Whitman must have meant didactic letters too, when he said of the fretters of our little world, "They make me sick talking of their duty to God." Yet friend should speak to friend, should utter the word than which nothing is more sacred. "Let there be light, and there was light"—a ripple of light, and a flash, then the darkness broke and dispersed from the face of the waters. It was a trumpet-call of words bringing drama into a nebulous creation. Let the Word break up our night and let us not only grant, but avow the conviction it brings us, no matter what the consequence. Let us worship the irrefragable Fact.

You hold that marriage is an institution having for its purpose the perpetuation of the species, and that respect and affection are sufficient to bring two people into this most intimate possible relation. You also hold that the business of the world, pressing hard upon men, makes "love from their lives a thing apart," and that this is as it should be. Your letters are an exposition and a defence of what I may loosely call the practical theory. You show that the world is for work and workers, and that life is for results as seen in institutions and visible achievements. I, on the other hand, maintain that it takes a greater dowry to marry upon than affection, and that men love as intensely and with as much abandon as women. People love in proportion to the depth of their natures, and the finest man in the world has an infinite capacity for giving and receiving love store. The spell is strongest upon the finest.

This, briefly, is what we have been saying to each other. You attack my idealism, call me dreamer, and accuse me of being out of joint with the time, which itself is rigorously in joint with the laws of growth. And I class you with the Philistine because of your exaggeration of practical values. I hold that it is gross to respect the fact tangible at the expense of the feeling ineffable.

In your last letter you exploit the theory of Nutrition and Reproduction with a charm and warmth which helps me see you as I have so long known you, and which tells me again that you are worth fighting for and saving. But to trace love to its biologic beginning is not to deny its existence. Love has a history as significant as that of life. When, eons ago, the primitive man looked at his neighbour and recognised him as a fellow to himself, consciousness of kind awoke and a cell was exploded which functioned love. When, through the ages, economic forces taught men the need of mutual aid, when everywhere in life the law of development charged men with leanings and desires and outreachings, then the sway of love began in life. What was subconscious became conscious, what, back in the past, was a mere adumbration gloried out in Aurora splendours. The love of a Juliet is the outgrowth of natural processes manifesting themselves everywhere down the scale, but it is also the gift of the last evolution, and it speaks to us from the topmost notch in the scale. The charm of morning rests on a Juliet's love because its hour is young and yet old, striking the time of the past and the future. It is thus that the hunger of the race and the passion of the race become in the individual the need for happiness. The need of the race and the need of the individual are at once the same and different.

What was the point of your letter? That sexual selection obtains? I grant it. That it is incumbent upon us as intelligent men and women to call to the aid of instinct our social wisdom? I grant and avow it. But our social wisdom insists that we obey the choices of instinct; our social wisdom is only another phase of our refinement, which, in impelling us to a love of the beautiful, does not the less impel us to love. Our social wisdom educates our taste without lessening our taste for the thing. "Love a beautiful person nobly, but be sure you love her," says our social wisdom with interesting tautology. Besides, you are a heretic to your own breed, Herbert. It is you who would forsake our present social wisdom, ruling modern men by laws which obtained in primitive life. It is you who steadily hark back to the past, and to states of consciousness which were but can never be again. The early facts of biology cannot include that which transcends them. To borrow from Ernest Seton Thompson, man is evolved with the lower orders in the same way that water is changed into steam, and the nature of the change, when it is effected, is as radical. Add a number of degrees of heat to water and it is still water. Let one degree be wanting to the necessary number, and the substance is still intact. Add the last degree, and water is no longer water. From water to steam is a radical change and a transformation.

You agree to improve upon the beasts of the fields and upon our own race in the past, and in this you go farther than you have need if marriage is for nothing else than to serve the instinct for perpetuation. You shew some respect for what is natural and instinctive, yet you say that all would be as well if individual choice had not prevailed, and men and women were "shuffled about." You draw up a cold programme for action in affairs of the spirit and formulate a code of procedure in matters of the heart.

I have a programme too. Mine does not break with nature. On the contrary, it obeys every instinct and listens to every call on the senses. My love begins in my biologic self, grows with my growth, takes its hues from visioned sunsets in corn-flower skies, its grace from swaying rivers of grain seen in dreams. It is for me what it is for fish and fowl, beast and vegetable. It is my passion for perpetuation, but it is also something as different from this as I am different from beast and vegetable. My love is "blind, unreasoning, and compelling," and for that I trust it. I do not conceive myself Man-god, therefore I do not say to Nature, "Allow me." I cannot be sure that when I say it in the case of the horse, who obeys like me "dim yearning and vague desires," I do not sacrifice him to a lust of my own. The lust for owning and spoiling is hard to cope with. Perhaps a purer time is near, when, upborne by a sense of the dignity of romance and the sacredness of life, man will refrain from laying rough hands on his mute brothers.

The romance which is my proof of the good of being does not rest on passion. The unclean fires that consume the loutish and degenerate are not of

56

love. You quote instances of the hyperphysical and hysterical. The feeling that I would have you obey for your soul's sake and without which you are but half alive, is not the blind passion of an oversexed sentimentalism. Rousseau was never in love in his life, though to say it were to accuse him of perjury.

One word more. Do you wish to know why I care? I care because I know you to be of those who are capable of love. Probably it was one little twist in your development that has turned you into alien ways of thinking and living. Yes, and more than for this I care because you are the fulfilment of a sacred past. You are the son of my sacrifice and your mother's love.

I care very much indeed. I do not wish you to awake some terrible night to find that you had ended your romance before you had begun it. I vex your days and call you dead? It is because I know the life that is by the grace of God yours, and because I cannot bear to let you coffin it. Herbert, there is misery when the blood pales, and the tears dry up, and the flame of the heart sinks, and all that is left is a memory of a thought—a memory of very long ago when one was young and might have chosen to live.

I am sorry we darken the days for each other.

Your friend always,

Dane Kempton.

XIII. FROM THE SAME TO THE SAME

London,

3a Queen's Road, Chelsea, S.W.

February 12, 19—.

Barbara and Earl celebrated their anniversary yesterday. Invitations were sent out, the guests consisting of Melville and myself. "Anniversary of what?" we asked. For answer we received inscrutable smiles. Birthdays are accidents of fate. You may regret the accident or you may be thick enough in illusion to rejoice over it, but you cannot in decency celebrate an occurrence wholly independent of personal control and yet concerning itself with you! Leave the merrymaking for appreciative friends. So rules Barbara. Not a birthday, then, nor the date of their marriage. The occasion was in some flash struck from Being, the memory of which enriches them,—in a mood that for an hour held them in strong grasp, in the utterance of a word charged with destiny, in the avowal of their love if their love awaited avowal. Whatever the cause, they honoured it with a will.

Barbara's eyes flashed, her cheeks were sweetly suffused, and her voice was vibrant. Earl, too, was at his best. My heart loved this man who had lain all his life with death. His health is at its bad worst this winter, which fact made of the "Celebration" a rather heart-rending affair. He has been obliged to abandon the *Journal*, but we hope he can stay with the school. Meanwhile, his chronic invalidism of body and purse does not too much affect him. He keeps his charm of tenderness and strength. He rivets his pupils to him almost as he riveted his Barbara.

I have discovered my proof of this couple's happiness. It is that I have always taken it for granted. Simple, is it not? And absolute. Often in their presence I catch myself imagining their mutual lives and seeing vaguely the graces that each brings to each. "How she must delight him!" I say. "How his eyes speak to her!" "They can never come to the end of each other," and so on. The ordinary married couple so often brings a sense of distressed surprise: "How can these two foot it together?" "How did it happen?" "How can it go on?"

Last night counted to me. Your father and I have had such evenings, but I did not think I could do it all over again. We spoke with the fire (and conceit) of young students, exciting ourselves with expired theories, hoping old hopes, smarting under blows that perhaps had long ceased to fall. What then? What if we were ill-read in the facts? We could not have been wrong in the feeling. For the old hope that has been proven vain, a new; for the ancient hurt, a modern wrong, as great and as crying. It was good to feel that we had not grown too wise to harbour thoughts of change and redress, or too much ironed out with doctrine to be resigned. I confess it is long since I have eaten my heart in fury, in impatience, in wildness, but last night we awoke the radical in one another. We condemned the system. We placed ourselves outside the régime, refusing aught at its hands, registering our protest, hating the inordinate scheme of things only as hotly as we loved the juster Hand of a future time.

It is curious that we, offsprings of parvenue success, should be capable of such repudiation. Barbara accepts the Management without the trouble of a question. "What do you know? What do you know?" the girl demands, a radiant little angel in white, and a conservative. "You must know yourselves in the wrong, else would you smite your way through the world."

Ah, Barbara has yet to learn that it is hard to live. It is not so hard to fight, and it is easy to rest neutral, but to be fighter and bearer both, to stand staunch, holding ever to the issue, and yet, without tameness, to take rebuff and wait, there's the true course and the heroic. It is difficult when one has been conquered to know it. It is difficult to honour an outgrown ideal, which cost us, nevertheless, comfort and prestige—prizes which youth scorns and which oncoming age, pathetically enough, holds dear. It is difficult to pull up when driving too fast and too far, when galloping towards fanaticism, and it is impossible to whip oneself into passion and martyrdom. It is difficult to live, little Barbara.

For me it is also difficult to report a social function. At this one Browning presided, for Melville took up "Caponsacchi" and read it to us. That voice of his is in itself an interpretation, but Browning needs interpreting less than any other man who wrote great poems, because he wrote the greatest. It was four in the morning when the "O great, just, good God! Miserable me!" of the soldier-saint fell upon our ears. How we had listened! Earl steadily paced the floor, Barbara leaned her cheek upon my hand. Her soul was doing battle, and so was mine. We were all fighting the gallant fight. Read "Pompilia" and you are filled with reverence, read "Caponsacchi" and you are caught up by the spirit of action. You must rise and forth to burn your way like he, though you may have been too weary in spirit before to answer to your name when opportunity called roll.

It was Earl who broke the silence caused by the inner tumult. In a dreamy voice, his eyes very eager and intent, he told us how at one time he had gone up a hill that faced the house in which he lived. A hard rain was driving, he fell at every step up the slippery steepness, but at every step the beauty of it became more and more wondrous, hardly bearable. The little village sank lower and lower, and about him were soft hills, graceful and verdant, a stretch of water lying dark under the clouded sky, and the mountain gray and watchful in the distance. It was then, in the chill of a January rain, on an oak-clad hill of a western spot, that he recognised the dear features of the Mother, knew her his as hers he was, and loved her with passion. The sea is vast and wondrous, but it is alien. It holds you apart; it is not of you. But the gentle earth with her undulating form and the growing life in her lap, soothes with wordless harmonies. It was then that he forgave the fate which deformed him. A twisted oak, that is all—no less a tree and no less beautiful in the landscape! And it was sufficient to live. In the bosom of so much beauty sufficient also to die. As he stood, thinking it out, feeling the wonder and the glory, at times sorry for those who can see no longer the slanting sheets of rain and the grass at the feet, at times feeling that since this is good, in some impalpable way oblivion to all this may be also good, as he stood there, flushed with the climbing and sad with great joy, the thought came: With whom? It cannot be lived alone. With whom? He turned at the touch of an arm at his shoulder to meet the smile and the look and the quick breath of her who had sent herself his Eve.

In the dawn stealing over the world of London, Earl told the story, and there and then we saw it all—the hill in the heart of the hills, the reconciled boy who had climbed its brow, the rain-drenched woman hurrying to overtake him, with the gift of all of herself in her eyes. We looked neither at Barbara nor at Earl. Possessed of the secret, we spoke a few words and left. Our host had divulged what the anniversary sought to celebrate. We understood and were glad.

Good night, lad. Would you could have shared our heyday at the dawning!

Dane.

XIV. FROM HERBERT WACE TO DANE KEMPTON

The Ridge,

Berkeley, California.

February 31, 19—.

Love is a something that begins in sensation and ends in sentiment. Thanks to beautiful and permissible hyperbole, you have begun with sensation in your description of love, and have ended with sentiment. You have told me about love, in terms of love, which is a vain performance and unscientific. Now let me make you a definition. *Love is a disorder of mind and body, and is produced by passion under the stimulus of imagination.*

Love is a phase of the operation of the function of reproduction, and it occurs solely in man. Love, adhering to the common understanding of the term, is an emotional excitement which does not obtain among the lower animals. The lower animals lack the stimulus of imagination, and with them the passion for perpetuation remains a mere passion. But man has developed imagination. The pure sexual passion is glossed over and obscured by a cloud of fancies, mistaken yearnings, and distorted dreams. And so well is the real intent of the function obscured, that it is actually lost to him, especially during the period of love madness, so that there seems an apparent divorce between the parts which go to make up love, between passion and imagination.

The romantic lover of to-day (expressing sensation in terms of sentiment, and fondly imagining that he is reasoning) cannot reconcile his soul-exaltation with bodily grossness, cannot conceive that soul can turn body, and in the embrace of body tell out all the wonder of soul. To all sensitive and spiritual men and women come times of anguish and tears and self-revolt, when they are confounded and heart-broken by the physical aspect of love. Poor men and women! they suffer keenly and sincerely through lack of something more than a sentimental concept of love. To them, body and soul appear things apart, to be kept apart, lest the one contaminate the other. And in the end, loving well and truly, they prove their love by enduring, though unable ever quite to shake off the sense of sin and shame and personal degradation. They do not understand life, that is the trouble. The beast, lacking imagination, needs no rational rightness for the various acts of living, such as they need, and which they do not possess. Because of their unchecked and unbalanced imagination they mistake the half of life for the whole, and when forced to face the whole are affrighted and shocked. They do not reason that the need for perpetuation is the cause of passion; and that human passion, working through imagination and worked upon by imagination, becomes love.

And while I am in this vein, I may as well deny that a greater spiritual dowry than affection is required for marriage. (For that matter, I fail to see anything so spiritual in erotic phenomena.) If a man may achieve affection for a woman, without undergoing pre-nuptial madness,—if a man may take the short cut, as it were,—then I see no reason why he should not marry that woman. He is certainly justified, since affection is what romantic love must evolve into after marriage. But do not mistake me, Dane. I do not intend this sweepingly. It will not do for the whole human herd; for at once enters that abhorrent thing you rightly fear, the marriage for convenience. Alas, it too often masquerades under the guise of romantic love. Certainly, every man is not capable of taking this short cut and at the same time of avoiding a violation of true sexual selection. Having little brain, the average man can only act in line with sexual selection by undergoing the romantic love malady. But for some few of us, and I dare to include myself, the short cut is permissible. This short cut I shall take, and far be it from any worldly sense of stocks and bonds and comfortable housekeeping.

Marriage means less to man than to woman? Yes, by all means, at least to the normal man or woman. As surely as reproduction is woman's peculiar function, and nutrition man's, just so surely does marriage sum up more to woman than to man. It becomes the whole life of the woman, while to the man it is rather an episode, rather a mere side to his many-sided life. Natural selection has made it so. The countless men of the past, even from before the time they swung down out of the trees, who devoted more time and energy to their love-affairs than to the winning of food and shelter, died from innutrition in various ways. Only the men, normal men, with a proper respect for the mechanism of life, survived and perpetuated their kind. The chance was large that the abnormal lover did not win a wife at all. At least it is so to-day. The abnormal lover is not a successful bidder for women, and is usually passed by.

But while we are on this topic, do not let us forget Dante Alighieri, your prince of lovers. Has a suitable explanation ever occurred to you concerning how he came to marry Gemma, daughter of Manetto Donati, who bore him seven children, and was never once mentioned in the "Divina Commedia?" You remember what he said of his first meeting with Beatrice, "At that moment I saw most truly that the spirit of life which hath its dwelling in the secretest chambers of the heart began to tremble so violently that the least pulses of my body shook therewith." And he later had seven children by Gemma, daughter of Manetto Donati, and whom, as the historian has recorded, "there was no reason to suppose other than a good wife."

As for the primitive, I hark back to it because we are still very primitive. How many thousands years of culture, think you, have rubbed and polished at our raw edges? One, probably; at the best, not more than two. And that takes us back to screaming savagery, when, gross of body and deed, we drank blood from the skulls of our enemies, and hailed as highest paradise the orgies and carnage of Valhalla. And before that time, think you, how many thousands of years of savagery did we endure? and how many myriads of thousands in the long procession of life up from the first vitalised inorganic? Two thousand years are an extremely thin veneer with which to cover the many millions.

And further, our much-vaunted two thousand years of culture is a thing of the mind, an acquired character. We are not born with it. Each must gather it for himself after he is born, from the spoken and written words of his fellow and forerunners. Isolate a babe from all of its kind and it will never learn to speak, and without speech words, it can never think save in the concretest possible way. Yet it will possess all the brute instincts and passions—the raw edges which do constantly shove through the culture varnish of the civilised man.

Our culture is the last to come, the first to go. I have seen it go from a man in an hour, nay, on the instant. Our culture is nothing more than the accumulated wisdom of the race. It is not part of us, not a thing or attribute handed down from father to son. It is a something acquired in varying degree by each individual for himself. Yes, I do well to hark back to the primitive. It tells me where I am to-day and describes to me the world I am living in. You, Dane, are hyper-refined, or refined beyond the times. You are like the idealistic and advanced zealots, who, when such action would mean destruction, advise these United States to disarm in the face of the war-harnessed world.

But no more of this jerky letter. Soon I shall proceed to make my contention good. I shall show the higher part intellect plays in conjugal love, the control, restraint, forbearance, sacrifice. And I shall show that conjugal love is higher and finer than romantic love.

Herbert.

XV. FROM DANE KEMPTON TO HERBERT WACE

London,

3a Queen's Road, Chelsea, S.W.

March 15, 19—.

Clyde Stebbins was here an hour after your theories and definitions reached me. The fact that I had been reading treason against his sister made me pick my subjects a little too carefully for smooth conversation. Your letter, partly open, was on the table before us, and my eyes fell upon it often as I wondered what it would mean to Hester's brother—if he could read it. I no longer think only of you.

I reject your definition of love. It is not a disorder of the mind and body, nor is it solely the instrument of reproduction. I reject and resent your distinction between the pre-nuptial and post-nuptial states of feelings. Further, I hold that marriage may not be based on affection alone, and I disagree with you that population is better than principle. Children need not be brought into the world at any cost.

Love is not a disorder, but a growth. There is spiritual as well as physical growth. Some men and women never grow up strong enough to love. Their development is arrested, or they are, from the beginning, poor creatures born of starvelings, and perhaps fated to give birth to pale, sapless beings like themselves. Others there are who love, and this is no ill chance, no disease of the mind and body calling for psychiater and physician. It is a strength, a becoming, a fulfilment. Let us reason from the effect to the cause. How does this madness manifest itself? Not in weakness. You never saw a man or woman in love who was the worse for it. The lover carries all things before him, and not for himself alone, but for a larger world than ever had been his. He who loves one must perforce love all the world and all the unborn worlds. This is the way life goes, which is another way of saying it is a scientific fact. That which makes men capable of consecration is not a disorder of the mind and body. It is the greatest of all forces, and it turns the wrangling and grabbing human creature into an inspired poet.

And the cause? The passion for perpetuation and the imagination. We agree. But there are other and more immediate needs than the need of perpetuation that call out love, needs that are peculiarly of the present, being bound up with the steady outreaching for help, for fellowship in the jerky journey through the universe. If love were no more than an instrument of reproduction, you would be right in maintaining that the fastidiousness I insist on is unnecessary and unnatural. If love were that and that alone, there would be no love, which is a paradox indeed.

> "Because of our souls' yearning that we meet
>
> And mix in soul through flesh, which yours and mine
>
> Wear and impress, and make their visible selves,—
>
> All which means, for the love of you and me,
>
> Let us become one flesh, being one soul."

I dare a formula: In the beginning love arose in the passion for perpetuation; to-day, the passion for perpetuation arises in love. Just as we put ourselves in the way of natural selection, pitting the microcosm against the macrocosm in a passion of ethical feeling, just so do we reverse for ourselves processes that seem indeed to have all the force of law. This reversal is civilisation.

The lover is impelled to perpetuate himself in the Here and the Now. The law of life exacts from him the tribute of love. Imagination gives the lover the key to the object of his love. He enters and he beholds only the ideal which is hers; for him her clay self and the mere facts of her do not exist. The conditions of love are inherent in civilisation. When purpose is high and feeling rich, when "the everlasting possession of the good" is desired, then is heard the I Am of love.

Now to my definition. Negatively, love is not a disorder of the mind and body, not a madness, since it arises in the eternally most valuable, since it is the culmination of high processes, and since it makes for sanity of vision and strength and happiness. Positively, love is the awakening of the personality to the beauty and worth of some one being, caused by the passion for perpetuation and by imagination. It is a desire to hold to the good everlastingly, and to merge with it.

Aristotle proved to the satisfaction of his time that women have fewer teeth than men. Aristotle was a great man, and besides being a philosopher was the foremost scientist of his day. I cannot help thinking of this prodigious blunder. Perhaps (who knows?) the same famous fate which a sexual classification of teeth enjoys awaits a definition calling love a disorder.

I will continue to-morrow. A note has just been given me calling me to Earl, who is ill, but not seriously. Barbara has prescribed for him a game of chess. The desire to see you again has got into my blood. I think I shall be in the new West and with you before long.

Your friend always,

Dane Kempton.

XVI. FROM THE SAME TO THE SAME

London.

Sunday morning.

I must proceed with the three other points of my letter, so I shall stay here and write, though there is a sharp breeze this morning and a coquettishly escaping sunlight, and something tugs at me to go out upon the city streets. It is not restlessness, but the love of the open. I am fain to leave a walled house, and, better still, to get outside of the walls within and join the city in friendship and let the city join me. I never feel greater fellowship than when I walk—

Except when I write to you. Then do I greaten with the pride of life. My sympathies quicken and I grow young again. I constitute myself advocate of the world, and enthusiasm does not fail me in this high calling. It is but natural that in the face of scepticism which I cannot share I should feel greater faith, that in the face of revilement a sense of the glory of the thing belittled should settle upon me. I turn zealot and spend myself in long-drawn praising. I lay myself under a spell of harmony because I am serving and defending and approving what I hold to be good.

So when you insist that romantic love is pre-nuptial and that it dies at marriage as others suppose it to die at the approach of poverty, I grow glad with the knowledge that this is not true. I scrutinize facts which I hitherto took for granted, and become doubly sure. You dogmatise when you say that the lover and the husband are mutually exclusive. If there was love in the beginning, it will be at the end. Love doubles upon itself. Propinquity tightens bonds and there is a steady blossoming of the character in a radiant atmosphere. The marriages that fail are the unions which are based on liking. In these, weariness must set in, for marriage demands that men and women be all in all to each other, and unless it be so with them, the lives of the "contracting parties" are, by the laws of logic, and by the force of the laws of delicacy in the art of living, forever spoilt.

Yes, and people who truly love come to regret their married love, these too. But these have at least begun well. Their lives are infinitely richer for this fact. Their failure itself is made by it more bearable than the failure of those others who act the vulgarian and demand so little of life that even that little escapes them. No world-stains on these who are, at least, would-be lovers. They stand mistaken but irreproachable. It was neither their fault nor love's, and "life more abundant" comes to them even with the mistake.

You are consistent. Just as you maintain that love is passion, so do you think that it is no more than a preliminary thrill. You note a change; the flutter and the excitement felt in the presence of the unknown go, and you do not know that they give place to the steadier joys of the unknown, that after the promise comes the fulfilment, that the hope is not more beautiful than the realisation, that there is divinity in both, and that love does not disappoint.

Tell me, are the placid marriages of affection you are preparing to describe so very placid? Do these jog along so well? Is the control, restraint, forbearance, sacrifice, of which you speak, as readily practised for the person who is that to you which twenty others may quite as easily be, as it is for the one beyond all whom you love and deify, whom the laws of your being command that you serve, living and dying? God knows, the average marriage does not exhibit a striking picture of the practice of these virtues! Rather are such phrases ideals on stilts on which suffering marital partners attempt to hobble across their extremity. On the other hand, to some extent everybody practises restraint and sacrifice since everybody is to some extent moral. But it goes very hard with your average man and woman in your average marriage, and there is a decided setting of the mouth and narrowing of the eyes with the effort.

Whatever placidity there is is attained by means of vampirism. Diderot, the husband of a stupid seamstress, had no right to the love of a Mlle. Voland. It was vampirism and sin to take all from this woman, and to return her favour with so much less than all, as surely as cowardice and selfishness are sin. But the illicit relation will exist because custom cannot rid men and women of subtle sympathies and dear yearnings, because men and women will love though the world consider it cheap and mad. Individually, we have no difficulty in finding our happiness, but we are made advance toward it through the twisted byways of an unfrank world. "No straight road! Keep turning!" has been the scream of convention since convention began.

So for every commonplace marriage there is a canonised love, and the story is told in the old Greek civilisation by the Hetairæ. You remember how it reads in the history: "The low position generally assigned the wife in the home had a most disastrous effect upon Greek morals. She could exert no such elevating or refining influence as she casts over the modern home. The men were led to seek social and intellectual sympathy and companionship outside the family circle, among a class of women known as Hetairæ, who were esteemed chiefly for their brilliancy of intellect. As the most noted representative of this class stands Aspasia, the friend of Pericles. The influence of the Hetairæ was most harmful to social morality." And the practice persisted through many a renaissance where Lauras and Beatrices were besung, down to the brilliant encyclopædists of the eighteenth century with their avowed loves, down to our Goethe and John Stuart Mill. All of these loves rose in very different motives and environments, yet were they the same fundamentally,—strong, sweet love between man and woman, very much spoiled by the fact that custom permitted the loveless marriage at the same time, but yet love which was good since it was the best that could be had. And when the historian permits himself to say, "The influence of the Hetairæ was most harmful to social morality," it is evident that he also thinks that a marriage which compels husband or wife to seek soul's help elsewhere than in their union is bad and wrong.

To-day there is a change in attitude. Woman is new-born in strength and dignity, and the highest chivalry the world has ever known is in blossom. She is an equal, a comrade, a right regal person. She is no longer a means but an end in herself, not alone fit to mother men but fit to live in equality with men. I repeat, she is not a means but an individual, with a soul of her own to rear. Because of the greater and more general emancipation of woman the subtlety of modern love has become possible.

Now for the last point, the question of perpetuation. Just as function precedes organ, so the love of life is inherent in the living for the maintenance of life. But even the primitive man, in whom instinct is strongest, proves himself capable of death. Some men have always been able to give up their lives for some cause. (Indeed there is thought to be suicide amongst animals.) And to-day we certainly no longer say a man must live. Quite as often must he die. Men have found it wise to die at the stake or on the gallows. If this be true of our relation to the life which courses through us, how much more true is it of our instinct to perpetuate ourselves, which pertains to the love of life biologically only, which is often, in the social manifestation of that instinct, a cold intellectual concept and never a dominating thought! We are not driven to procreate. In fact, every child born into the world competes hard for its morsel. Under our unimaginable economic régime all increase in population is a menace.

I call bringing children into the world a codfish act which causes an overflux of vulgar little earthlings, if the process be not humanised and spiritualised. If the child is conceived not in lust but in love, it is rightly born. If it is the child of your ideal, the offspring of that which is your truest life, then is your progeny your immortality, and then, and then only, have you reason for pride and joy in that which you have caused to be.

My dear, dear Herbert, my love has not failed. This you must come to understand. Love never fails. The children that might have been mine are better unborn, since I could not give them a mother whom I loved. You remind me that Dante married Gemma, daughter of Manetto Donati, and she bore him seven children. Yet, Herbert, was this wife not mentioned in the "Commedia," nor in "La Vita Nuova," nor anywhere else in his writings. Dante was a Conformist. He was not in all respects above his time; witness his theology. Convention permitted the dispassionate marriage side by side with love. He was conventional, and the infinite moment of meeting in paradise with his Lady was embittered by her "cold, lessoned smiles."

"Ah, from what agonies of heart and brain,

What exultations trampling on despair,

72

What tenderness, what tears, what hate of wrong,

What passionate outcry of a soul in pain,

Uprose this poem of the earth and air,

This mediaeval miracle of song!"

It was for Beatrice that this man vexed his spirit with immortal effort and raised a Titan voice which yet is heard in charmed echoes. It was for Beatrice that he descended into the dead regions and climbed the hills of purgatory and soared towards the Rose of Paradise,—"And 'She, where is She?' instantly I cried."

Dante, our prince of lovers, might have lived better, but he loved well.

This in answer to your letter. To meet your argument I have found it best to employ something of your own method, but I cannot rid myself of the feeling that I have vulgarised the subject by saying so much about it. I fear my letter would provoke a smile from those who know love and the wonder of its simplicity through all the subtlety. "We, in loving, have no cause to speak so much!" would be their unanswerable criticism. It is easier to live than to argue about life.

The thought has suddenly assailed me that what I have said may sound derogatory to Hester. Know, then, that I do not think there is a woman in the world who is not capable of inspiring true and abiding love in the heart of some man. Besides, Hester to me looms up as a heroine. Not a hair's breadth of what I know of her that is not beautiful. My regret is that she, who could be "a vision eterne," should be doomed to receive episodically your considerate affection. She does not know your programme. She is a girl who takes your love for granted in the same way as she gives hers, without niggardliness. It is the woman who cannot be content with less than all that is slowly starved to death on a bread-and-water diet and who does not find it out until the end.

Until the carnival time when you and Hester come to love each other, if that time is to be, you two must be as separate in deed as you are in fact. Forgive me and write soon.

Yours ever,

Dane.

XVII. FROM HERBERT WACE TO DANE KEMPTON

The Ridge,

Berkeley, California.

April 2, 19—.

So you have met Hester's brother? Well, I have had an outing with Hester. She loves me well, I know, and I cannot but confess a thrill at the thought. On the other hand, well do I know the significance of that love, the significance and the cause. Notwithstanding that wonderful soul of hers, she is in no wise constituted differently from her millions of sisters on the planet to-day. She loves—she knows not why; she knows—only that she loves. In other words, she does not reason her emotions.

But let us reason, we men, after the manner of men. And be thou patient, Dane, and follow me down and under the phenomena of love to things sexless and loveless. And from there, as the proper point of departure, let us return and chart love, its phases and occurrences, from its first beginnings to its last manifestations.

Things sexless and loveless! Yes, and as such may be classed the drops of life known as unicellular organisms. Such a creature is a tiny cell, capable of performing in itself all the functions of life. That one pulsating morsel of matter is invested with an irritability which, as Herbert Spencer says, enables it "to adjust the inner relations with outer relations," to correspond to its environment—in short, to live. That single cell contracts and recoils from the things in its environment uncongenial to its constitution, and the things congenial it draws to itself and absorbs. It has no mouth, no stomach, no alimentary canal. It is all mouth, all stomach, all alimentary canal.

But at that low plane the functions of life are few and simple. This bit of vitalised inorganic has no sex, and because of that it cannot love. Reproduction is growth. When it grows over-large it splits in half, and where was one cell there are two. Nor can the parent cell be called *mother* or *father*.

and for that matter, the parent cell cannot be determined. The original cell split into two cells; one has as much claim to parenthood as the other.

It lives dimly, to be sure, this mote of life and light; but before it is a vast evolution, Dane, on the pinnacle of which are to be found men and women, Hester Stebbins, my mother, you!

A step higher we find the cell cluster, and with it begins that differentiation which has continued to this day and which still continues. Simplicity has yielded to complexity and a new epoch of life been inaugurated. The outer cells of the cluster are more exposed to environmental forces than are the inner cells; they cohere more tenaciously and a rudimentary skin is formed. Through the pores of this skin food is absorbed, and in these food-absorbing pores is foreshadowed the mouth. Division of labour has set in, and groups of cells specialise in the performance of functions. Thus, a cell group forms the skinny covering of the cluster, another cell group the mouth. And likewise, internally, the stomach, a sac for the reception and digestion of food, takes shape; and the juices of the body begin to circulate with greater definiteness, breaking channels in their passage and keeping those channels open. And, as the generations pass, still more groups of cells segregate themselves from the mass, and the heart, the lungs, the liver, and other internal organs are formed. The jelly-like organism develops a bony structure, muscles by which to move itself, and a nervous system—

Be not bored, Dane, and be not offended. These are our ancestors, and their history is our history. Remember that as surely as we one day swung down out of the trees and walked upright, just so surely, on a far earlier day, did we crawl up out of the sea and achieve our first adventure on land.

But to be brief. In the course of specialisation of function, as I have outlined, just as other organs arose, so arose sex-differentiation. Previous to that time there was no sex. A single organism realised all potentialities, fulfilled all functions. Male and female, the creative factors, were incoherently commingled. Such an individual was both male and female. It was complete in itself,—mark this, Dane, for here individual completeness ends.

The labour of reproduction was divided, and male and female, as separate entities, came into the world. They shared the work of reproduction between them. Neither was complete alone. Each was the complement of the other. In times and seasons each felt a vital need for the other. And in the satisfying of this vital need, of this yearning for completeness, we have the first manifestation of love. Male and female loved they one another—but dimly, Dane. We would not to-day call it love, yet it foreshadowed love as the food-absorbing pore foreshadowed the mouth.

As long and tedious as has been the development of this rudimentary love to the highly evolved love of to-day, just so long and tedious would be my sketch of that development. However, the factors may be hinted. The increasing correspondence of life with its environment brought about wider and wider generalisations upon that environment and the relations of the individual to it. There is no missing link to the chain that connects the first and lowest life to the last and the highest. There is no gap between the physical and psychical. From *simple reflex action*, on and up through *compound reflex action*, *instinct*, and *memory*, the passage is made, without break, to *reason*. And hand in hand with these, all acting and reacting upon one another, comes the development of the imagination and of the higher passions, feelings, and emotions. But all of this is in the books, and there is no need for me to go over the ground.

So let me sum up with an analysis of that most exquisite of poets' themes, a maiden in love. In the first place, this maiden must come of an ancestry mastered by the passion for perpetuation. It is only through those so mastered that the line comes down. The individual perishes, you know; for it is the race that lives. In this maiden is incorporated all the experience of the race. This race experience is her heritage. Her function is to pass it on to posterity. If she is disobedient, she is unfruitful; her line ceases with her; and she is without avail among the generations to come. And, be it not forgotten, there are many obedient whose lines *will* pass down.

But this maiden is obedient. By her acts she will link the past to the future, bind together the two eternities. But she is incomplete, this maiden, and being immature she is unaware of her incompleteness. Nevertheless she is the creature of the law of the race, and from her infancy she prepares herself for the task she is to perform. Hers is a certain definite organism, somewhat different from all other female organisms. Consequently there is one male in all the world whose organism is most nearly the complement of hers; one male for whom she will feel the greatest, intensest, and most vital need; one male who of all males is the fittest, organically, to be the father of her children. And so, in pinafores and pigtails, she plays with little boys and likes and dislikes according to her organic need. She comes in contact with all manner of boys, from the butcher's boy to the son of her father's friend; and likewise with men, from the gardener to her father's associates. And she is more or less attracted by those who, in greater or less degree, answer to her organic demand, or, as it were, organic ideal.

And upon creatures male she early proceeds to generalise. This kind of man she likes, that she does not like; and this kind she likes more than that kind. She does not know why she does this; nor, with the highest probability, does she know she is doing it. She simply has her likes and dislikes, that is all. She is the slave of the law, unwittingly generalising upon sex-impressions against the day when she must identify the male who most nearly completes her.

She drifts across the magic borderland to womanhood, where dreams and fancies rise and intermingle and the realities of life are lost. A dissatisfaction and a restlessness come upon her. There seems no sanity in things, and life is topsy-turvy. She is filled with vague, troubled yearnings, and the woman in her quickens and cries out for unity. It is an organic cry, old as the race, and she cannot shut out the sound of it or still the clamour in her blood.

But there is one male in all the world who is most nearly her complement, and he may be over on the other side of the world where she may not find him. So propinquity determines her fate. Of the males she is in contact with, the one who can more nearly give her the completeness she craves will be the one she loves.

All of which is well and good in its way, but let us analyze further. What is all this but the symptoms of an extreme over-excitation and nervous disorder? The equilibrium of the organism has been overthrown and there is a wild scrambling for the restoration of that equilibrium. The choice made may be good or ill, as chance and time may dictate, but the impelling excitement forces a choice. What if it be ill? What if to-morrow a male who is a far better complement should appear? The time is now. Nature is not neglectful, and well she knows the disaster of delay. She is prodigal of the individual and is satisfied with one match out of many mismatches, just as she is satisfied that of a million cod eggs one only should develop into a full-grown cod. And so this love of the human in no wise differs from that of the sparrow which forgets preservation in procreation. Thus nature tricks her creatures and the race lives on.

For the lesser creatures the trick serves the purpose well. There is need for a compelling madness, else would self-preservation overcome procreation and there be no lesser creatures. And man is content to rest coequal with the beast in the matter of mating. Notwithstanding his intelligence, which has made him the master of matter and enabled him to enslave the great blind forces, he is unable to perpetuate his species without the aid of the impelling madness. Nay, men will not have it otherwise; and when an individual urges that his reason has placed him above the beast, and that, without the impelling madness, he can mate with greater wisdom and potency, then the poets and singers rise up and fling potsherds at him. To improve upon nature by draining a malarial swamp is permitted him; to improve upon nature's methods and breed swifter carrier-pigeons and finer horses than she has ever bred is also permitted; but to improve upon nature in the breeding of the human, that is a sacrilege which cannot be condoned! Down with him! He is a brute to question our divine Love, God-given and glorious!

Ah, Dane, remember the first dim yearning of divided life, and the soils and smirches and frenzies put upon it by the spawn of multitudinous generations. There is your love, the whole history of it. There is no intrinsic shame in the thing itself, but the shame lies in that we are not greater than it.

Herbert.

XVIII. FROM THE SAME TO THE SAME

The Ridge,

Berkeley, California.

April 4, 19—.

There were several things in your letter which I forgot to answer. Much of beauty and wonder is there in what you have said, and unrelated facts without end. Many of those facts I endorse heartily, but it seems to me you fail to embody them in a coherent argument.

I have stated, in so many words, that there are two functions common to all life—nutrition and reproduction. Of this you have missed the significance in your rejection of my definition of love, so I must explain further. Unless these two functions be carried on, life must perish from the planet. Therefore they are the most essential concerns of life. The individual must preserve its own life and the life of its kind. It is more prone to preserve its own life than the life of its kind, less prone to sacrifice itself for its species. So natural selection has developed a passion of madness which forces the individual to make the sacrifice. In all forms of life below man the struggle for existence is keen and merciless. The least weakness in an individual is the signal for its destruction. Therefore it is counter to the welfare of the individual to do aught that will tend to weaken it. On the other hand, the law is that the individual must procreate. But procreation means a weakening and a temporary state of helplessness. Problem: How may the individual be brought to procreate? to do that which is inimical to its welfare? Answer: It must be forced by something deeper than reason, and that something is unreasoning passion. Did the individual reason on the matter, it would certainly abstain. It is because the passion is not rational that life has persisted to this day. Man, coming up from the walks of lower life, brought with him this most necessary passion. Developing imagination, he commingled the two; love was the product.

Now, because of our imagination, do not let us confuse the issue. The great task demanded of man is reproduction. He is urged by passion to perform this task. Passion, working through the imagination, produces love. Passion is the impelling factor, imagination the disturbing factor; and the disturbance of passion by imagination produces love.

Stripped of all its superfluities, what function does love serve in the scheme of life? That of reproduction. Nay, now, do not object, Dane; for you state the same thing, though less clearly, in your own definition of love. You say, "Love is the awakening of the personality to the beauty and worth of some one being" and is a desire to merge the life with that of the beloved being. In other words, your definition tells that the passion for perpetuation is the cause of love, and perpetuation the end to be accomplished. Thus nature tricks her creatures and the race lives on.

Then you say negatively, "Love is not a disorder of mind and body, not a madness, since it arises in the eternally most valuable, since it is the culmination of high processes, and since it makes for strength and sanity of vision and happiness." I have shown the value of passion, and the processes of which love is the culmination, and I have shown that both are unreasoning and why they are unreasoning. Do you demonstrate where I am wrong.

Then again, you dare a formula: "In the beginning love arose in the passion for perpetuation; to-day the passion for perpetuation arises in love." It is clever, but is it true? Yes, as true as this formula I dare to pattern after yours: In the beginning man ate because he was hungry; to-day he is hungry because he eats.

There are many things more I should like to answer, but I am writing this 'twixt breakfast and lecture hour, and time presses and students will not wait.

Herbert.

XIX. FROM DANE KEMPTON TO HERBERT WACE

London,

3a, Queen's Road, Chelsea, S.W.

April 22, 19—.

Nature tricks her creatures and the race lives on, and I, overcivilised, decadent dreamer that I am, rejoice that the past binds us, am proud of a history so old and so significant and of an heritage so marvellous. Nature tricks her creatures and the race lives on, and I am prayerfully grateful. The difference between us is that you are not. You are suffering from what has been well called, the sadness of science. You accept the thesis of a common origin only to regret it. You discover that romance has a history, and lo! romance has vanished! You are a Werther of science, sad to the heart with a melancholy all your own and dropping inert tears on the shrine of your accumulated facts.

In this you are with your generation. Just as every age has its prevailing disease of the body so has it its characteristic spiritual ailment. To-day we are in the throes of travail. In our arms is the child of our ever-delving intellect, but another deliverance is about to be and the suffering is great. After science comes the philosophy of science. Our eyes are bathed in Revelation, but upon our ears the music of the Word has not yet fallen. Until that time when the meaning of it all shall flash out upon the world, the race will be hidebound in callousness and in faint-hearted melancholy. As yet we do not know what to do with all which we know, and we are afflicted with the pessimism of inertia and the pessimism of dyspepsia. Intellectually, we have been living too high the last hundred years or so. In this is the secret of our difference. You insist upon cheapening life for yourself because it has become evident to you that the phenomenon is common, and I, on the other hand, shout its glory because it is universal. To myself I am breathless with wonder, but to you and in my work I needs must shout it.

Here let me be clear. I take it that you are under the sway of a contemporary mood, that your position is an accidental phase of to-day's materialism. Broadly, our quarrel is that of pessimism and optimism, only your pessimism is unconscious, which makes it the more dangerous to yourself. You are too sad to know that you are not happy or to care. Does my diagnosis surprise you? Analyze the argument of your last letter. You trace the growth of the emotion of love from protoplasm to man. You follow the progress of the force which is stronger than hunger and cold and swifter and more final than death, from its potential state in the unicellular stage where life goes on by division, up through the multifarious forms of instinctive animal mating, till you reach the love of the sexes in the human world. And the exploring leads you to the belief that nothing has been reserved for the human worth his cherishing, to the conviction that the plan of life is simple and unvaried and therefore unacceptable.

You raise the wail of Ecclesiastes, "All is vanity and a striving after wind, and there is no profit under the sun." The Preacher and Omar and Swinburne are pathetically human, and we who are also human respond to their finality, to their quizzical indifference and their stinging resentment. We also say, "Vanity of vanities," and bow our heads murmuring "Ilicet," and stretch out our hands to "turn down an empty glass," but all this in twilight moods when a dimness as of dying rests upon the soul. There are a few with whom it is always morning, and others who remember something of the radiance of the young day even in the heart of midnight. These disprove the postulates of sameness and satiety, these are not smitten by the seen fact as are you of the microscopic retina, these "see life steadily and see it whole."

We need not fear the label of an idea. When I say that your position is that of the pessimist, it is not more of an accusation than if I said it was that of the optimist. The thing to concern oneself with is the question, "which of these makes the nearer approach to the truth?" You have been asking me, "What is love worth?" And you have answered your question often enough and to your satisfaction, "In itself it is worth nothing, being but the catspaw to scheming forces." With your denial of any intrinsic beauty in the emotion, with your acceptance of it as an unfortunate incident in human affairs, comes a vague hope that the race will outgrow this force. Here is your rift in the cloud. You picture a scientific Utopia where there are no lovers and no back-harkings to the primitive passion, and you appoint yourself pioneer to the promised land of the children of biology.

Ah! I speak as if I were vexed instead of simply being sure I am in the right. I wish to help you to see that there is another reading to your facts. If love is essentially the same from protoplasm to man, it does not for this reason become worthless. By virtue of being universal it is enhanced and most divinely humanly binding. You tell me that love is involuntary, compelled by external forces as old as time and as binding as instinct, and I say that because of this, life is finally for love. What! The cavemen, and the birds, too, and the fish and the plants, forsooth! What! The inorganic, perhaps, as well as the organic, swayed by this force which is wholly physical and yet wholly psychical! And does it not fire you? You are not caught up and held by this giant fact? You find that love is not sporadic, not individual, that it does not begin with you or end with you, that it does not dissociate you, and you do not warm to the world-organic kinship, you do not hear the overword of the poets and philosophers of all times, you do not see the visions that gladdened the star-forgotten nights of saints?

The same surprise sweeps over the mind in reading Ecclesiastes. Is it a sorry scheme of things that one generation goes and another comes and the world abides forever? If the same generation peopled the earth for a million years, the dignity of life would not be increased. It is not necessary to have the assurance of eternal life as the dole for having come to be, in order to live under the aspect of eternity. It is larger to be short-lived, to be but a wave of the sea rolling for one sunful day and starry night towards a great inclusiveness. It is a higher majesty to be inalien and a part—a ringed ripple in the Vastness—than to lie broad and smiling in meaningless endlessness.

So it is a strange thing that men who are schooled by evolution to relate themselves to all that exists, and to seek for new kinships, should lament that there is no new thing under the sun. And whose eye would be satisfied with seeing and whose ear with hearing? Who would rather have the truth than the power to seek it? There is a way of reading Ecclesiastes and Schopenhauer with a triumphant lilt in the voice. After all, it is the modulation that carries the message of the text. When you write the history of love, I find it fair reading. When you tell me love is primal and engrossing, I hold it the more a sin to crouch away from its fires.

"Love is the assertion of the will to live as a definitely determined individual." This is Schopenhauer's thesis and (unnecessarily enough) he apologises for it, as if it belittled love to say that it affects man in his *essentia æterna*. The genius of the race takes the lover conscript and makes him a soldier in life's battalions.

"The genius of the race," a metaphysical term, but meaning what you do when you speak of the function of love. Schopenhauer is a pessimist consciously, you, unconsciously; and you have both missed the living value of your facts. "Love is ruled by race welfare," says Schopenhauer. "It (the race welfare) alone corresponds to the profoundness with which it is felt, to the seriousness with which it appears, to the importance which it attributes even to the trifling details of its sphere and occasion." Love concerns itself with "The composition of the next generation," therefore you find it common as the commonplace, therefore Schopenhauer regards it as a force treacherous to happiness, since to live is to be miserable. "These lovers are the traitors who seek to perpetuate the whole want and drudgery which would otherwise speedily reach an end; this they wish to frustrate as others like them have frustrated it before."

Because love frustrates the death of the race, it is the joy of my senses and the goal of my striving.

Says Schopenhauer: "Through love man shows that the species lies closer to him than the individual, and he lives more immediately in the former than in the latter. Why does the lover hang with complete abandon on the eyes of his chosen one, and is ready to make every sacrifice for her? *Because it is his immortal part that longs after her, while it is merely his mortal part that desires everything else.*" Because this is so, love is the God of my faith.

You see where our subject takes us! And all the while I care nothing for the points of argument except where they prick you from your position. One must scale the skies and swim the seas in order to reach you. Well, have I approached within your hearing?

I was sitting amongst the fennel in Barbara's garden when your letter was brought, and I read it twice to make sure I understood. When the sun lies warm on waving fennel and a city is before you, mysterious in a veil of mist, it is easier to feel love than to think about it. For a while, it was difficult to see the bearing of the data which you marshalled so well in defence of your denial. You went far in order to answer why you are content to marry a woman you do not love. Your methods are not the methods of the practical mind. I am glad for that. You idealise your attitude, you go far back in time, you enmesh yourself in theories and generalisations, you ride your imagination proudly, in order to reconcile yourself to something which suggests itself as more ideal than that for which the unreasoning heart hungers. You are sad, but you are not practical and you are not blasé.

Of Barbara, of myself, and of London doings, this is no time to write. Tell Hester your friend thinks of her.

Yours with great memories and greater hopes,

Dane Kempton.

XX. FROM HERBERT WACE TO DANE KEMPTON

The Ridge,

Berkeley, California.

May 18, 19—.

I stand aloof and laugh at myself and you. Oh, believe me, I see it very clearly myself in the heyday and cocksureness of youth, flinging at you, with much energy and little skill, my immature generalisations from science; and you with an elderly beneficence and tolerance, smiling shrewdly and affectionately upon me, secure in the knowledge that sooner or later I am sure to get through with it all and join you in your broad and placid philosophy. It is the penalty age exacts from youth. Well, I accept it.

So I am suffering from the sadness of science. I had been prone to ascribe my feelings to the passion of science. But it does not matter in the least— only, somehow, I would rather you did not misunderstand me so dreadfully. I do not raise the wail of Ecclesiastes. I am not sad, but glad. I discover romance has a history, and in history I am quicker to read the romance. I accept the thesis of a common origin, not to regret it, but to make the best of it. That is the key to my life—to make the best of it, but not drearily, with the passiveness of a slave, but passionately and with desire. Invention is an artifice man employs to overcome the roundabout. It is the short cut to satisfaction. It makes man potent, so that he can do more things in a span. I am a worker and doer. The common origin is not a despair to me; it has a value, and it strengthens my arm in the work to be done.

The play and interplay of force and matter we call "evolution." The more man understands force and matter, and the play and interplay, the more is he enabled to direct the trend of evolution, at least in human affairs. Here is a great and weltering mass of individuals which we call society. The problem is: How may it be directed so that the sum of its happiness greatens? This is my work. I would invent, overcome the roundabout, seek the short cut. And I consider all matter, all force, all factors, so that I may invent wisely and justly. And considering all factors, I consider romance, and I consider you. I weigh your value in the scheme of things, and your necessity, and I find that you are both valuable and necessary.

But the history of progress is the history of the elimination of waste. One boy, running twenty-five machines, turns out a thousand pairs of socks a day. His granny toiled a thousand days to do the same. Waste has been eliminated, the roundabout overcome. And so with romance. I strive not to be blinded by its beauty, but to give it exact appraisal. Oftentimes it is the roundabout, the wasteful, and must needs be eliminated. Thus chivalry and its romance vanished before the chemist and the engineer, before the man who mixed gunpowder and the man who dug ditches.

I melancholy? Sir, I have not the time—so may I model my answer after the great Agassiz. I am not a Werther of science, but rather you are a John Ruskin of these latter days. He wept at the profanation of the world, at the steam-launches violating the sanctity of the Venetian canals and the electric cars running beneath the shadow of the pyramids; and you weep at the violation of like sanctities in the spiritual world. A gondola is more beautiful, but the steam-launch takes one places, and an electric car is more comfortable than the hump of a camel. It is too bad, but waste romance, as waste energy, must be eliminated.

Enough. I shall go on with the argument. I have drawn the line between pre-nuptial love and post-nuptial love. The former, which is the real sexual love, the love of which the poets sing and which "makes the world go round," I have called romantic love. The latter, which in actuality is sex comradeship, I call conjugal affection or friendship. To be more definite, I shall call the one "love," the other "affection" or "friendship." Now love is not affection or friendship, yet they are ofttimes mistaken, one for the other, for it so happens that the friendship, which is akin to conjugal affection, is in many instances pre-nuptial in its development—a token, I take it, of the higher evolution of the human, an audaciousness which dares to shake off the blind passion and evade nature's trick as man evaded when he harnessed steam and rested his feet. It is of common occurrence that a man and woman, through long and tried friendship, reach a fine appreciation of each other and marry; and the run of such marriages is the happiest. Neither blinded nor frenzied by the unreasoned passion of love, they have weighed each other,—faults, virtues, and all,—and found a compatibility strong enough to withstand the strain of years and misfortune, and wise enough to compromise the individual clashes which must inevitably arise when soul shares never ending bed and board with soul. They have achieved before marriage what the love-impelled man and woman must achieve after marriage if they would continue to live together; that is, they have sought and found compatibility before binding themselves, instead of binding themselves first and then seeking if there be compatibility or not.

Let me apparently digress for the moment and bring all clear and straight. The emotions have no basis in reason. We smile or are sad at the manifestation of jealousy in another. We smile or are sad because of the unreasonableness of it. Likewise we smile at the antics of the lover. The absurdities he is guilty of, the capers he cuts, excite our philosophic risibility. We say he is mad as a March hare. (Have you ever wondered, Dane, why a March hare is deemed mad? The saying is a pregnant one.) However, love, as you have tacitly agreed, is unreasonable. In fact, in all the walks of animal life no rational sanction can be found for the love-acts of the individual. Each love act is a hazarding of the individual's life; this we know, and it is only impelled to perform such acts because of the madness of the trick, which, though it strikes at the particular life, makes for the general life.

So I think there is no discussion over the fact that this emotion of love has no basis in reason. As the old French proverb runs, "The first sigh of love is the last of wisdom." On the other hand, the individual not yet afflicted by love, or recovered from it, conducts his life in a rational manner. Every act he performs has a basis in reason—so long as it is not some other of the emotional acts. The stag, locking horns with a rival over the possession of a doe, is highly irrational; but the same stag, hiding its trail from the hounds by taking to water, is performing a highly rational act. And so with the human. We model our lives on a basis of reason—of the best reason we possess. We do not put the scullery in the drawing-room, nor do we repair our bicycles in the bedchamber. We strive not to exceed our income, and we deliberate long before investing our savings. We demand good recommendations from our cook, and take letters of introduction with us when we go abroad. We overlook the petulant manner of our friend who rowed in the losing barges at the race, and we forgive on the moment the sharp answer of the man who has sat three nights by a sick-bed. And we do all this because our acts have a basis in reason.

Comes the lover, tricked by nature, blind of passion, impelled madly toward the loved one. He is as blind to her salient imperfections as he is to her petty vices. He does not interrogate her disposition and temperament, or speculate as to how they will coördinate with his for two score years and odd. He questions nothing, desires nothing, save to possess her. And this is the paradox: *By nature he is driven to contract a temporary tie, which, by social observance and demand, must endure for a lifetime.* Too much stress cannot be laid upon this, Dane, for herein lies the secret of the whole difficulty.

But we go on with our lover. In the throes of desire—for desire is pain, whether it be heart hunger or belly hunger—he seeks to possess the loved one. The desire is a pain which seeks easement through possession. Love cannot in its very nature be peaceful or content. It is a restlessness, an unsatisfaction. I can grant a lasting love just as I can grant a lasting satisfaction; but the lasting love cannot be coupled with possession, for love is pain and desire, and possession is easement and fulfilment. Pursuit and possession are accompanied by states of consciousness so wide apart that they can never be united. What is true of pursuit cannot be true of possession, no more than the child, grasping the bright ball, can deem it the most wonderful thing in the world—an appraisement which it certainly made when the ball was beyond reach.

Let us suppose the loved one is as madly impelled toward the lover. In a few days, in an hour, nay, in an instant—for there is such a thing as love at first sight—this man and woman, two unrelated individuals, who may never have seen each other before, conceive a passion, greater, intenser, than all other affections, friendships, and social relations. So great, so intense is it, that the world could crumble to star-dust so long as their souls rushed together. If necessary, they would break all ties, forsake all friends, abandon all blood kin, run away from all moral responsibilities. There can be no discussion, Dane. We see it every day, for love is the most perfectly selfish thing in the universe.

But this is easily reconcilable with the scheme of things. The true lover is the child of nature. Natural selection has determined that exogamy produces fitter progeny than endogamy. Cross fertilisation has made stronger individuals and types, and likewise it has maintained them. On the other hand, were family affection stronger than love, there would be much intermarriage of blood relations and a consequent weakening of the breed. And in such cases it would be stamped out by the stronger-breeding exogamists. Here and there, even of old time, the wise men recognised it; and we so recognise it to-day, as witness our bars against consanguineous marriage.

But be not misled into the belief that love is finer and higher than affection and friendship, that the yielding to its blandishments is higher wisdom on the part of our lovers. Not so; they are puppets and know and think nothing about it. They come of those who yielded likewise in the past. They obey forces beyond them, greater than they, their kind, and all life, great as the great forces of the physical universe. Our lovers are children of nature, natural and uninventive. Duty and moral responsibility are less to them than passion. They will obey and procreate, though the heavens roll up as a scroll and all things come to judgment. And they are right if this is what we understand to be "the bloom, the charm, the smile of life."

Yet man is man because he chanced to develop intelligence instead of instinct; otherwise he would to this day have remained among the anthropoid apes. He has turned away from nature, become unnatural, as it were, disliked the earth upon which he found himself, and changed the face of it somewhat to his liking. His trend has been, and still is, to perform more and more acts with a rational sanction. He has developed a moral nature, made laws, and by the sheer force of his will and reason curbed his lyings and his lusts.

However, our lovers are natural and uninventive. They get married. Pursuit, with all its Tantalus delights, its sighings and its songs, is gone, never to return. And in its place is possession, which is satisfaction, familiarity, knowledge. It heralds the return of rationality, the return to duty of the weighing and measuring qualities of the mind. Our lovers discover each other to be mere man and woman after all. That ethereal substance which the man took for the body of the loved one becomes flesh and blood, prone to the common weaknesses and ills of flesh and blood. He, on the other hand, betrays little petulancies of disposition, little faults and predispositions of which she never dreamed in the pre-nuptial days, and which she now finds eminently distasteful. But at first these things are not openly unpleasant. There are no scenes. One or the other gives in on the instant, without self-betrayal, and one or the other retires to have a secret cry or to ruminate about it over a cigar—the first faint hints, I may slyly suggest, of the return of rationality. *They are beginning to think.*

Ah, these are little things, you say. Precisely; wherefore I lay emphasis upon them. The sum of the innumerable little things becomes a mighty thing to test the human soul. Moreover, many a home has been broken because of disagreement as to the uses or abuses of couch cushions, and more than one divorce induced by the lingering of tobacco odours in the curtains.

If the marriage of our lovers conform to the majority of marriages, the first year of their wedded life will determine whether they are able to share bed and board through the lengthening years. For this first year—often the first months of it—marks the transition from love to conjugal affection, or witnesses a rupture which nothing less than omnipotence can ever mend. In the first year a serious readjustment must take place. Unreason, as a basis for the relation, must give way to reason; blind, ignorant, selfish little love must flutter away, so that friendship, clear-eyed and wise, may step in. There will come moments when wills clash and desires do not chime; these must be moments of sober thought and compromise, when one or the other sacrifices self on the altar of their nascent friendship. Upon this ability to compromise depends their married happiness. Returning to the rationality which they forsook during mating-time, they cannot live a joint rational existence without compromising. If they be compatible, they will gradually grow to fit, each with the other, into the common life; compromise, on certain definite points, will become automatic; and for the rest they will exhibit a tacit and reasoned recognition of the imperfections and frailties of life.

All this reason will dictate. If they be incapable of rising to compromise, sacrifice, and unselfishness, reason will dictate separation. In such cases, when they will have become rational once more, they will reason the impossibility of a continued relation and give it up. In which case the true-love disciple may contend that there was no real love in the beginning. But he is wrong. It was just as real as that of any marriage, only it failed in the post-nuptial quest after compatibility. In all marriages love—passionate, romantic love—must disappear, to be replaced by conjugal affection or by nothing. The former are the happy marriages, the latter the mistaken ones.

As I close, the saying of La Bruyère comes to me, "The love which arises suddenly takes longest to cure." This generalisation upon all the love-affairs within the scope of a single lifetime cannot but be true, and it is quite in line with the general argument. I have shown that the love (so called) which grows slowly is akin to friendship, that it is friendship, in fact, conjugal friendship. On the other hand, the more sudden a love the more intense it must be; also the less rationality can it have. And because of its intensity and unreasonableness, the longer period must elapse ere its frenzy dies out and cool, calm thought comes in.

Herbert.

P.S.—My book is out—"The Economic Man." I send it to you. I cannot imagine you will care for the thing.

XXI. FROM THE SAME TO THE SAME

The Ridge,

Berkeley, California.

May 26, 19—.

"Pretty nineteen-year-old Louisa Naveret, because her slower-minded fiancé, Charles J. Johnson, could not understand a joke, is dying with a bullet in her brain, and he, her murderer, lies dead at the morgue. They were to have been married to-day."

From to-day's paper I quote the above introduction to a column murder-sensation in simple life. Simple it was, and elemental—the man loving steadily and doggedly and madly, after the manner of the male before possession; the woman fluttering, and teasing, and tantalising, after the manner of the female courting possession. They had been engaged for some time. The woman loved the man and fully intended to marry him. The engagement neared its close, and on the day before that of the wedding, the man, slow minded, loving intensely, procured the marriage licence. The woman read the document, and with the last coy flutter before surrender told him that she would not marry him.

"I meant it as a jest," she said as she lay on a cot at the receiving hospital; but four bullets were in her body, and Charles J. Johnson, clumsy and natural lover, lay dead in an adjoining room with the fifth bullet in his brain.

In this pitiful little tragedy appear two of the most salient characteristics of love; namely, madness and selfishness. Let us analyze Charles J. Johnson's condition. He was a lineman for a telegraph company, healthy and strong, used to open-air life and hard work. He had steady employment and good wages. Can't you see the man, content with a good digestion, unailing body, and mild pleasures, and enjoying life with bovine placidity? But pretty Louisa Naveret entered his life. The "abysmal fecundity" was stirred and life clamoured to be created. Peacefulness and content vanished. All the forces of his existence impelled him to seize upon and possess "nineteen-year-old" Louisa Naveret. He was afflicted with a disorder of mind and body, a madness so great, a delusion so powerful, a pain and unrest so pressing, that the possession of that particular "nineteen-year-old" woman became the dearest thing in the world, dearer than life itself and more potent than the "will to live."

I do well to call love a madness. Any departure from rationality is madness, and for a man of Charles J. Johnson's calibre, suicide is an extremely irrational act. But he also killed Louisa Naveret, wherein he was as selfish as he was mad. Convinced that he was not to possess her, he was determined that no other man should possess her.

While on this matter of love considered as a disorder of mind and body, I recall a recent magazine article of Mr. Finck's, in which he analyzes Sappho's conception of love. "In that famous poem of Sappho," he says, "that has been so often declared a compendium of all the emotions that make up love, I have not been able to find anything but a comic catalogue of such feelings as might overwhelm a woman if she met a bear in the woods—'deadly pallor,' 'a cold sweat,' 'a fluttering heart,' 'tongue paralyzed,' 'trembling all over,' 'a fainting fit.'"

Dante suffered similarly from the disorder of love, if you will recollect. In this connection may be cited the following passage from Diderot's "Paradox of Acting ":—

"Take two lovers, both of whom have their declarations to make. Who will come out of it best? Not I, I promise you. I remember that I approached the beloved object with fear and trembling; my heart beat, my ideas grew confused, my voice failed me, I mangled all I said; I cried *yes* for *no*; I made a thousand blunders; I was illimitably inept; I was absurd from top to toe, and the more I saw it the more absurd I became. Meanwhile, under my very eyes, a gay rival, light hearted and agreeable, master of himself, pleased with himself, losing no opportunity for the finest flattery, made himself entertaining and agreeable, enjoyed himself; he implored the touch of a hand which was at once given him, he sometimes caught it without asking leave, he kissed it once and again. I, the while, alone in a corner, avoided a sight which irritated me; stifling my sighs, cracking my fingers with grasping my wrists, plunged in melancholy, covered with a cold sweat, I could neither show nor conceal my vexation."

Oh, the clamour of life to be born is a masterful thing, and so far as the individual is concerned, a most irrational thing; and so far as the world of beasts and emotional men and women is concerned, it is a most necessary thing. That life may live and continue to live, a driving force is needed that is greater than the puny will of life. And in the disorder produced by the passion for perpetuation, whether or not assisted by imagination, is found this driving force. As Ernest Haeckel, that brave old hero of Jena, explains:—

"The irresistible passion that draws Edward to the sympathetic Otillia, or Paris to Helen, and leaps all bounds of reason and morality, is the same *powerful, unconscious*, attractive force which impels the living spermatozoon to force an entrance into the ovum in the fertilisation of the egg of the animal or plant—the same impetuous movement which unites two atoms of hydrogen to one atom of oxygen for the formation of a molecule of water."

But with the advent of intellectual man, there is no longer need for obeying blind and irresistible compulsion. Intellectual man, changing the face of life with his inventions and artifices, performing telic actions, adjusting himself and his concerns to remote ends and ultimate compensations, will grapple with the problem of perpetuation as he has grappled with that of gravitation. As he controls and directs the great natural forces so that, instead of menacing, they are made to labour for his safety and comfort, so will he control and direct the operation of the reproductive force so that life will not only be perpetuated but developed and made higher and finer. This is not more impossible than is the steam-engine impossible or democracy impossible.

Herbert.

XXII. FROM DANE KEMPTON TO HERBERT WACE

London,

3a, Queen's Road, Chelsea, S.W.

June 12, 19——.

Please remember that these letters are written to you alone. I do not think that there is less love in the world than ever before. I make you representative of a class, which, in turn, is characteristic of the modern scientific type, but I do not make you representative of all that to-day's world has lived up to and lived down. So I do not join my Ruskin in lamenting the past. To be sure, you are contemporary and you are parvenu. What then? You are few, nevertheless, and like the parvenu rich, you must pass into something quite unlike yourself. It is the law of growth. I ask you to account for yourself as an individual. The thing is fiercely personal. But you choose the roundabout method of answering me. For a view of what in your eyes is pertinent to this matter, you stretch a canvas wide as the world. You are resolved that your course should dramatise the whole play and interplay of force and matter. It is ideally ambitious of you and I am glad. It puts you in the ranks with the students of the ideal tendencies. It shows that you are not always impatient for short cuts, and that you begin to be of those who harness "horses of the sun to plough in earth's rough furrows."

Your letter sounds conclusive. Romance is waste, love is unreasoning; compatibility alone is worth while. You think this, and are ready to encrust yourself with what is conventional and practical. Ah, no, it is not even decently conventional! The formal world pretends, at least, to love. It also reaches for the fires that thrill and thaw, whereas you stand before a cold hearth and think the chill well and welcome, since you understand its cause. You have grasped part of a truth, and though my mind complete your arc into the perfection of a circle, I cannot place it about your head as a halo. My confusion comes from thinking of you more than of my creed. A pregnant factor in our debate is the debater. The Hafiz of the Hafiz maxims, the philosopher of your philosophy happens to interest me. You have been building yourself up before my eyes, and for watching I cannot speak.

With what does romance interfere? If it implied a waste of vital force, a giving up, a postponement of life, it were a roundabout path to development and happiness. But we live most when we are most under its sway, and it is for such self-promised sparks that we live at all. Romance quickens and controls as does nothing else, and because of this it is not only a means but an end in itself. It is stirred-up life. We live most when we love most. The love of romance and the romance of love is the only coin for which the heart-hurt sell their death. A trick? Perhaps. The love of life is a trick to save the races from self-murder. Nature makes legitimate her tricks. Let the Genius of the Race lure us with passion and dreaming! We are not the losers by it. And if the dream fades and we grow gray despite what has been lived, then it is something to remember that soul and sense have leapt and pulsed. I am thankful that romance has an aftermath, and that old men and women can prattle about days that were robust. I am thankful that the soldiers of life are at the end given a furlough in which to fondle the arms they wielded with clumsiness and with spirit, and in which to pass themselves in review before their pension expires and their days are over. Youth has the romance of loving, and age the romance of remembering.

Lovers are not always compatible, you say, and, before all, you insist upon good partnership. How will you insure yourself against unfitness? Surely not by a registering and weighing of qualities, not by bargaining and speculating. We do not choose our wives as we do our saddle-horses; we do not plan our marriages as we plan our houses. It may sound paradoxical, but there is a higher compatibility than that of quality and degree. It is not whether people can live together, but whether they should live together. "It is an awkward thing to play with souls,"—you override the fastidiousness of the soul in marrying your companion. Unless you are an automaton, you cannot rest happy in the fact that you and she do not disagree. For comfort's sake you would have a negative dimension to your cosmos, forgetting that your longings and your needs and, it may be, your dreams, are positive. If sex-comradeship and affection were not as accidental and as dependent on mood as love itself, your position would have much in its favour. You could then arrange for compatibility in marriage.

You speak of the methods in economics that conserve energy and capital, such as the employ of the machine-guiding boy, which saves the labour power of a hundred men, and you hold that in the realm of personal life like methods may obtain with value and dignity. I can see how natural it has become for you to take this viewpoint. One can be a zealot in matters frigid. The law behind the fact has you in its coil, and your passion goes to ice. You burn for that cold thing, compatibility. You, too, are in the market-place bound to a stake—it is not for such as you to escape the fire. If you look to compatibility and want it intensely, as others want love, then you suffer, and from your standpoint (not mine) you raise a vain cry; for compatibility, like everything else, is illusory. The illusions of love are a strength, and the ways of love are divine; through them we come to that feeling of completion which is compatibility and which is as ineffable as the white-lipped promise of waves heard by those who have also listened to weeping. Love is not responsible for institutionalism. There would be no fewer marriages if people married for convenience, nor would the law make such unions less binding. It is not the fault of love that the great social paradox exists. In the precipitancy of feeling, you say, the lover fastens upon an unsuitable mate, and, with possession, love dies. Here I attack your facts. If an awakening comes, it is not for either of these reasons. Love is not essentially rational, but then it is love. There is some consistency in affairs natural, and the esoteric draught that enchanted at one time cannot poison at another.

Love is not essentially rational, and it will not of a sudden become so at the possession of the loved one. People who marry from convenience may wake to find their union most inconvenient. "There are more things in heaven and earth," and there are more intricacies of feeling and more sloughs and depths, than are dreamed of in your philosophy. A definite understanding as to sofa cushions and tobacco smoke does not always insure unwearied forbearance and devotion. With love, on the other hand, disappointment is very much less likely to spring up, for the reason that it is free from calculation. Love is a sympathy. It takes hold, it grows upon the soul and the senses, and it does not flee before argument and explanation.

Still less can I admit that possession kills love. Do we give up living because the world is based on Will and Idea? Yet to will is to want, Schopenhauer tells us, and to want is to be in pain. Do we know ourselves in pain every minute of our lives? Hardly. This applies. You hold that, with the fulfilled hope and the appeased hunger, indifference takes the place of desire. It reads so in logic, but not in life. If what is in our possession be good, we prize it more highly for its being within reach. The good in our keeping does not sate; it pains with divine hungers. We do not tire of what we have; we rise to it. We do not know the sweetness of being steadfast until we are so impelled by the love with which we have grown great. The lover may well say: "She was not my ideal; before I knew her I was not great enough to think her. She taught me."

Besides, an acquaintance with your wife's faults does not kill your love. You cannot turn from your brother or your friend if he commit even a lurid act; you cannot turn from a stranger; much less can you turn from your beloved. Herbert, when men set themselves to judge, they are invariably ridiculous and an offence to high heaven. Believe me, it is artificial. The true judge cares not for the fact of the deed, but for its motive. And the lover knows the motive. He has the key to the life. He knows his beloved, not as she is, but "as she was born to be." His lips press and his arms enfold not her so much as the ideal of her, and unless she unmake herself, he cannot unlove her. "To judge a man by the fruit of his actions," says Professor Edward Howard Griggs, "it is necessary to know all of the fruit, which is impossible. You can only know what he eternally must be if you catch the aspect of his soul and grow to understand his aspirations and his loves." To idealise, therefore, is not to be blind, but to be far-seeing.

There is another way of looking on this question of the paradox. Granted that it is caused by romantic love, romantic love is still exclusively the best thing in the world. You cannot pay too dearly for the good of life. I know that the misery of being in the intimacy of wedlock with one who is not loved is unutterable. It is to become degraded and unrecognisable, it is to wear the brand of liar before God! The man whose outer life belies the inner is an enforced suicide. There is something of majesty on "laying one's self down with a will," and there is something of strength in cloistering the body for the spirit's health's sake, but to die when all within is warm and clamorous for life is terrible. Such a death they die who are held together, not by the bonds of the spirit, but by those of convention. They who would go from each other and dare not, die the ignominious death of fear. The suicide is contemptible, besides being pitiable, when he is hounded out of life despite himself, when he is a little embezzler of a clerk who rushes from the music hall to the Thames and thinks of the unfinished glass with his last breath. No, I do not underestimate the tragedy of the paradox. Yet I say that if love were accountable for it (which it is not), it would still be folly to forswear love. Do you ask why? Because its dangers are the dangers common to all life, and we are so made that we cannot be frightened away from our portion of experience. We are as loth to give up our nights as our days. The winters as the summers, all the seasons and all the climes, the fears as the hopes, all the travail of deepest, fullest living, we claim as our own forever. We guard jealously our heritage of feeling. Would you for all the world sleep rather than wake, forget rather than remember? Then cease the requiem of your speech about the dangers of disillusion!

Madness and selfishness were the cause of Louisa Naveret's death, and the man who was mad and selfish was her lover. The poor man had not the strength to renounce when he thought he found himself face to face with the necessity of renouncing. But all lovers are not too weak to cope with love. John Ruskin, if you remember, loved his wife, and he shot neither himself, nor her, nor Millais. Charles J. Johnson is not a Ruskin, and Ruskin's love was not a madness.

And, Herbert, to me there is nothing comic in a stress of feeling. Let the lover pale and flutter and faint; in the presence of his deity it is an acceptable form of worship. The very self-possessed lover is more preposterous!

Your book has not yet reached me. To-morrow I shall write again, providing I remember how to write a natural letter.

Yours,

Dane Kempton.

XXIII. FROM THE SAME TO THE SAME

London.

June 20, 19—.

There are impersonal hours when the things of the day drop below consciousness and the spirit grows devotional and wends a pilgrimage to larger spheres, there to sit apart. Such a respite was mine to-day. There had been a call to rouse and put forth work, and I wrought with all the puniness of my might (woe is me!), and earned my post at the window that looks out upon the large things. The best of nights and days of toil is that there comes a twilight in which fatigued eyes see clear. I said it did not matter how you do about your marriage. Time may right you in a way I cannot know. I said it did not matter if you are not righted in this, there being so much that never rights itself. Both hope and despair were followed by a calm of neutrality. The inquiry waited no solution. The stress no longer touched me, and my twilight became luminous. I saw things as from a height and forms dropped out of my range, when Barbara came tugging at me, and my pale while of abstraction was at an end.

She wanted to know what troubled me. She made her way to me, hurried but resolved, and stated her demand. "You catechised me yesterday; to-night you shall answer."

She had come to defend herself. My talk having of late taken on the sameness of that of the man of one idea, Barbara was aroused. I was gauging her because she distressed me, was her thought. (I had been trying to find whether it is possible to live differently from her and live happily and well.) "You think I am not close enough to Earl, because I mourn for my little one, perhaps. You think me not sufficiently happy to be wifely." Could I suppose aught else from such an utterance but that there was an estrangement and hidden pain? How, unless there were sorrow, could the woman see herself sorrowed for? My mind leapt to possibilities. Little Barbara on the rack was more than I could bear. I groped for her hands. It was a fault in her to be so much on her guard. She had no sorrow to confess, and spoke—only to ward off what was not directed toward her.

"The tenour of your talk led me on to believe—" she stammered with hot cheeks. It is a standing offence of hers to imagine herself accused, and she admits it is a weakness born of lack of poise. "But I took all for granted, I thought you fortunate beyond any other woman," I protested. At this the radiance broke forth. I forgave the chill that her first words on entering the room struck to my heart, and she forgot what she had imagined.

There is nothing more important than the play and interplay of feeling. Were Barbara "unwifely," I could not blame her, but neither could I have at hand my proof of dear miracles. My proof remained to me, for there she stood, her face lifted toward mine, her mouth tremulous, her grey eyes swimming. The mate woman was stirred. Barbara is twenty-six and has been married seven years, and she still vibrates with the old wonder to find herself loving and beloved.

I meant to tell you of what we spoke later, in the hope that I could show you a little better what I hold dear and why. But my hand grows nerveless. The twilight of abstraction has set in. A little while ago this hand was quick to rest on Barbara's as I called her my heroine. She is that, not alone because she is pure and good and strong, but because she can accept the test of her instincts. It takes both faith and strength to obey oneself. "When shows break up, what but one's Self remains?" asks Whitman. The shows are but shows for Barbara. Will I look into your eyes on the morrow and find them, like hers, clear? Grant that it be!

Dane.

XXIV. FROM HERBERT WACE TO DANE KEMPTON

The Ridge,

Berkeley, California.

July 1, 19—.

Somewhere in Ward you may read, "It must constantly be borne in mind that all progress consists in the arbitrary alteration, by human efforts and devices, of the normal course of nature, so that civilisation is wholly an artificial product." Why, Dane, this is large enough to base a sociology upon. And I must ask you first, is it true? Second, do you understand, do you appreciate, the tremendous significance of it? And third, how can you bring your philosophy of love in accord with it?

Romantic love is certainly not natural. It is an artifice, blunderingly and unwittingly introduced by man into the natural order. Is this audacious? Let us see. In a state of nature the love which obtains is merely the passion for perpetuation devoid of all imagination. The male possesses the prehensile organs and the superior strength. Beyond the ardour of pursuit the female has no charms for him. But he is driven irresistibly to pursuit. And by virtue of his prehensile organs and superior strength he ravishes the females of his species and goes his way. But life creeps slowly upward, increasing in complexity and necessarily in intelligence. When some forgotten inventor of the older world smote his rival or enemy with a branch of wood and found that it was good and thereafter made a practice of smiting rivals and enemies with branches of wood, then, and on that day, artificiality may be said to have begun. Then, and on that day, was begun a revolution destined to change the history of life. Then, and on that day, was laid the cornerstone of that most tremendous of artifices, CIVILISATION!

Trace it up. Our ape-like and arboreal ancestors entered upon the first of many short cuts. To crack a marrow-bone with a rock was the act which fathered the tool, and between the cracking of a marrow-bone and the riding down town in an automobile lies only a difference of degree. The one is crudely artificial, the other consummately artificial. That is all. There have been improvements. The first inventors grasped that truthful paradox, "the longest way round is the shortest way home," and forsook the direct pursuit of happiness for the indirect pursuit of happiness. If the happiness of a savage depended upon his crossing an extensive body of water, he did not directly proceed to swim it, but turned his back upon it, selected a tree from the forest, shaped it with his rude tools and hollowed it out with fire, then launched it in the water and paddled toward where his happiness lay.

Now concerning love. In the state of nature it is a brutal passion, nothing more. There is no romance attached. But life creeps upward, and the gregarious human forms social groups the like of which never existed before. Consider the family group, for instance. Such a group becomes in itself an entity. By means of the group man is better enabled to pursue happiness. But to maintain the group it must be regulated; so man formulates rules, codes, dim ethical laws for the conduct of the group members. Sexual ties are made less promiscuous and more orderly. A greater privacy is observed. And out of order and privacy spring respect and sacredness.

But life creeps upward, and the family group itself becomes but a unit of greater and greater groups. And rules and codes change in accordance, until the marriage tie becomes possessed of a history and takes to itself traditions. This history and these traditions form a great fund, to which changing conditions and growing imagination constantly add. And the traditions, more especially, bear heavily upon the individual, overmastering his natural expression of the love instinct and forcing him to an artificial expression of that love instinct. He loves, not as his savage forebears loved, but as his group loves. And the love method of his group is determined by its love traditions. Does the individual compare his beloved's eyes to the stars—it is a trick of old time which has come down to him. Does he serenade under her window or compose an ode to her beauty or virtue—his father did it before him. In his lover's voice throb the voices of myriads of lovers all dead and dust. The singers of a thousand songs are the ghostly chorus to the song of love he sings. His ideas, his very feelings are not his, but the ideas and feelings of countless lovers who lived and loved and whose lives and loves are remembered. Their mistaken facts and foolish precepts are his, and likewise their imaginative absurdities and sentimental philanderings. Without an erotic literature, a history of great loves and lovers, a garland of love songs and ballads, a sheaf of spoken love tales and adventures—without all this, which is the property of his group, he could not possibly love in the way he does.

To illustrate: Isolate a boy babe and a girl babe of cultured breed upon a desert isle. Let them feed and grow strong on shell-fish and fruit; but let them see none other of their species; hear no speech of mouth, nor acquire knowledge in any way of their kind and the things their kind has done. Well, and what then? They will grow to man and woman and mate as the beasts mate, without romance and without imagination. Does the woman oppose her will to that of the man—he will beat her. Does he become over-violent in the manifestation of his regard, she will flee away, if she can, to secret hiding-places. He will not compare her eyes to the stars; nor will she dream that he is Apollo; nor will the pair moon in the twilight over the love of Hero and Leander. And the many monogamic generations out of which he has descended would fail to prevent polygamy did another woman chance to strand on that particular isle.

It is the common practice of the man of the London slum to kick his wife to death when she has offended him. And the man of the London slum is a very natural beast who expresses himself in a very natural manner. He has never heard of Hero and Leander, and the comparison of the missus' eyes to the stars would to him be arrant bosh. The gentle, tender, considerate male is an artificial product. And so is the romantic lover, who is fashioned by the love traditions which come down to him and by the erotic literature to which he has access.

And now to the point. Romantic love being an artificial product, you cannot base its retention upon the claim that it is natural. Your only claim can be that it is the best possible artifice for the perpetuation of life, or that it is the only perfect, all-sufficient, and all-satisfying artifice that man can devise. On the one hand, for the perpetuation of life, man demonstrates the inefficiency of romantic love by his achievements in the domestic selection of animals.

And on the other hand, the very irrationality of romantic love will tend to its gradual elimination as the human grows wiser and wiser. Also, because it is such a crude artifice, it forces far too many to contract the permanent marriage tie without possessing compatibility. During the time romantic love runs its course in an individual, that individual is in a diseased, abnormal, irrational condition. Mental or spiritual health, which is rationality, makes for progress, and the future demands greater and greater mental or spiritual health, greater and greater rationality. The brain must dominate and direct both the individual and society in the time to come, not the belly and the heart. Granted that the function romantic love has served has been necessary; that is no reason to conclude that it must always be necessary, that it is eternally necessary. There is such a thing as rudimentary organs which served functions long since fallen in disuse and now unremembered.

The world has changed, Dane. Sense delights are no longer the sole end of existence. The brain is triumphing over the belly and the heart. The intellectual joy of living is finer and higher than the mere sexual joy of living. Darwin, at the conclusion of his "Origin of Species," experienced a nobler and more exquisite pleasure than did ever Solomon with his thousand concubines and wives. And while our sense delights themselves have become refined, their very refinement has been due to the increasing dominion over them of the intellect. Our canons of art are not founded on the heart. No emotion elaborated the laws of composition. We cannot experience a sense of delight in any art object unless it satisfies our intellectual discrimination. "He is a *natural* singer," we say of the poet who works unscientifically; "but he is lame, his numbers halt, and he has no knowledge of technique."

The intellect, not the heart, made man, and is continuing to make him— ah, slowly, Dane, for life creeps slowly upward. The "Advanced Margin" is a favourite shibboleth of yours. And I take it that the Advanced Margin is that portion of our race which is more dominated by intellect than the race proper. And I, as a member of that group, propose to order my affairs in a rational manner. My reason tells me that the mere passion of begetting and the paltry romance of pursuit are not the greatest and most exquisite delights of living. Intellectual delight is my bribe for living, and though the bargain be a hard one, I shall endeavour to exact the last shekel which is my due.

Wherefore I marry Hester Stebbins. I am not impelled by the archaic sex madness of the beast, nor by the obsolescent romance madness of later-day man. I contract a tie which my reason tells me is based upon health and sanity and compatibility. My intellect shall delight in that tie. My life shall be free and broad and great, and I will not be the slave to the sense delights which chained my ancient ancestry. I reject the heritage. I break the entail. And who are you to say I am unwise?

Herbert Wace.

XXV. FROM THE SAME TO THE SAME

The Ridge,

Berkeley, California.

July 5, 19—.

I had not intended to answer your letter critically, but, on re-reading, find I am forced to speak if for no other reason than your epithet "parvenu." The word has no reproach. It was ever thus that the old and perishing recognised the vigorous and new. Parvenu, upstart—the term is replete with significance and health. I doubt not Elijah himself was dubbed parvenu when he fluttered with his golden harp into that bright-browed throng, pride-swollen for that they had fought with Michael when Lucifer was hurled into hell.

"We do not choose our wives as we buy our saddle-horses; we do not plan our marriages as we do the building of our houses,"—so you say, and it is said excellently. No better indictment of romantic love do I ask. And oh, how many good men and women have I heard bitterly arraign society in that in the begetting of children it does not exercise the judgment which it exercises in breeding its horses and its dogs! Marriage is something more than the mere pulsating to romance, the thrilling to vague-sweet strains, the singing idly in empty days, the sating of self with pleasure—what of the children?

"Never mind the children," says selfish little Love. "It has been our wont never to give any thought to the children; they were incidental. Always have we sought our own pleasure; let us continue to seek our own pleasure." So Society continues to breed its horses and dogs with judgment and forethought and to trust to luck for its children.

But it won't do, Dane. Life, in a sense, is living and surviving. And all that makes for living and surviving is good. He who follows the fact cannot go astray, while he who has no reverence for the fact wanders afar. Chivalry went mad over an idea. It idealised, if you please. It made of love a fine art, and countless knights-errant devoted themselves to the service of the little god. It sentimentalised over ladies' gloves and forgot to make for living and surviving. And while chivalry committed suicide over its ladies' gloves, the stout, wooden-headed burghers, with an eye to the facts of life, dickered and bickered in trade. And on the wreck and ruin of chivalry they flaunted their parvenu insolence. God, how they triumphed! The children and cobblers and shop-keepers buying with the yellow gold the "thousand years old names!" buying with their yellow gold the proud flesh and blood of their lords to breed with them and theirs! patronising the arts, speaking a kind word to science, and patting God on the back! But they triumphed, that is the point. They reverenced the fact and made for living and surviving.

Love is life, you say, and you seem to hold it the achievement of existence. But I cannot say that life is love. Life? It is a toy, i' faith, given to us, we know not why, to play with as we chance to please. Some elect to dream, some to love, and some to fight. Some choose immediate happiness, and some ultimate happiness. One stakes the Here and Now upon the Hereafter; another takes the Here and Now and lets the Hereafter go. But each grasps the toy and does with it according to his fancy And while none may know the end of life, all know that life is the end of love. Love, poor little, crude little, love, is the means to life—and so we complete the circle. Life? It is a toy, i' faith, given us, we know not why, to play with as we chance to please.

But this we know, that love is the means to life, and it is subject to inevitable improvement. By our intellect will we improve upon it. Life abundant! finer life! higher life! fuller life! When we scientifically breed our race-horses and our draught-horses, we make for life abundant. And when we come scientifically to breed the human, we shall make for life abundant, for humanity abundant.

You say an acquaintance with the petty vices of one's wife does not kill one's love. Oh yes, it does, and out of the ashes of that love rises affection, comradeship, in kind somewhat similar to the affection and comradeship which I have for my brother. I do not *love* my brother, and it is because I do not love him, and because I do have *affection* and *comradeship* for him, that I do not turn away when he commits even a lurid act. Love, you will remember, takes its rise in the emotions, and is unstable and wanton and capricious. But affection takes its rise in the intellect, is based upon judgment of the brain. Love is unyielding tyranny; affection is compromise. Love never compromises, no more than does the mad little mating sparrow compromise.

My brother?—I played with him as a boy. His weaknesses and faults incensed and hurt me, as mine incensed and hurt him. Many were our quarrels. But he had also good qualities which pleased me, and at times performed gracious acts and even sacrifices. And I likewise. And with my brain I weighed his weaknesses and faults against his gracious acts and sacrifices, and I achieved a judgment upon him. The ethics of the family group also contributed to this judgment. The duties of kinship and the responsibilities of blood ties were impressed upon me. We grew up at our mother's knee, and she and our father became factors in determining what my conduct should be. They, too, taught me that my brother was my brother, and that in so far as he was my brother, my relations with him must be different from my relations with those who were not my brothers. And all went to crystallise an intellectual judgment, or a set of criteria, as it were, to guide all sane, unemotional acts and even to control and repress any emotional acts. These criteria, I say, became crystallised, became automatic in my thought processes.

And now, in manhood, my brother commits a lurid act, an act repulsive to me, one capable of arousing emotions of anger, of bitterness, of hatred. I experience an emotional impulse to pour my wrath upon him, to be bitter toward him, to hate him. Then I experience an intellectual impulse. Whatever way I may act, I must first settle with my crystallised criteria. The personal bonds of my boyhood and manhood press upon me—the gracious acts and sacrifices and compromises, our father and our mother, the duties of kinship and the responsibilities of blood. Thus two counter-impulses strive with me. I desire to do two counter things. Heart and head the fight is waged, and heart or head I shall act according to which is the stronger impulse. And if my affection be stronger, I shall not turn away, but clasp my brother in my arms.

I fear I have not made myself clear. It is difficult to write hurriedly of things psychological, when the extreme demand is made upon intellect and vocabulary; but at least you may roughly catch my drift. What I have striven to say is, that I forgive my brother, not because I *love* him, but because of the *affection* I bear him; also that this affection is the product of reason, is the sum of the judgments I have achieved.

Herbert.

XXVI. FROM DANE KEMPTON TO HERBERT WACE

London,

3a, Queen's Road, Chelsea, S.W.

July 21, 19—.

"Progress is an arbitrary alteration, by human efforts and devices, of the normal course of nature, so that civilisation is wholly an artificial product." You ask me to consider this refracted bit of sociology and by its light to cast out my exalted notion of love. As if you have proven that love is incompatible with civilisation! We make over life with each successive step, but we do not give over living. In developing new forms and in establishing more and more subtle social relations we are only building upon what we find ready to hand. The paradox of creature and creator does not exist. When your sociologist speaks of arbitrary alterations, he has reference to polities and governments and criteria, to the material and ideal forces which a progressive society may wield for itself. He cannot include under progress an alteration of those needs of existence which make up the quality of existence. Speak of a community which equally distributes the products of labour and I will grant that there has been an arbitrary alteration, the normal course of nature being that the stronger, openly, and even with the common assent, takes to the repletion of his desire from the weaker. But speak of a condition so progressive that it subverts the need, so that where in the one case hunger was equitably gratified, in the other, hunger was done away with, and I will say that you are giving an Arabian Nights' entertainment.

Love is of a piece with life, like hunger, like joy, like death. Your progress cannot leave it behind; your civilisation must become the exponent of it.

Your last letter is formal and elaborate, and—equivocal. In it you remind me, menacingly, of the possibilities of progress, you posit that love is at best artificial, and you apotheosise the brain. As an emancipated rationality, you say you cut yourself loose from the convention of feeling. Progress cannot affect the need and the power to love. This I have already stated. "How is it under our control to love or not to love?" Life is elaborate or it is simple (it depends upon the point of view), and you may call love the paraphernalia of its wedding-feast or you may call it more—the Blood and Body of all that quickens, a Transubstantiation which all accept, reverently or irreverently, as the case may be.

I can more readily conceive the existence of a central committee elected for the purpose of regulating the marriages of a community, than of a community satisfied with such a committee. There is no logic in social events. The world persists in not taking the next step, and what to the social scout looked a dusty bypath may prove to be the highway of progress for the hoboing millions. Side issues are constantly cropping up to knock out the main issues of the stump orator; so let us be humble. For this reason I refuse to discuss possibilities in infinity. You and I cannot have become products of an environment which is not in existence. It is safe to suppose that our needs are like those of the race and that in us nothing is vestigial that is active in others. You cannot have become too rational to love. The device has not yet been formed.

You think I should take your word for it? But why? Have you never found yourself in the wrong, never disobeyed your best promptings never meant to take the good and grasped the bad? Is it not possible that you are not yet awake, or, God pity you, that you are hidebound in the dogmatism of your bit of thinking.

It is for the second point of your letter that I called you equivocal. Earlier in our discussion, I remember, you laid stress on the fact that love is an instinct common to all forms of life; now you go to great lengths in order to show that it is artificial.

How do you differentiate between the artificial and nature? Surely a development is not artificial because it is recent! Surely man is as integral to life as his progenitors! When we come to civilisation, we are face to face with the largest and subtlest thing in life, and the civilisation of human society is not artificial. It is the fulfilment of the nature of man, the promise made

114

good, the career established, the influence sent out. A universe of mind-stuff and a civilising force constantly causing change, for change is growth, constantly compelling expression of that change—to conceive it is to conceive infinitude. And the purpose? Development, always development. To that end the individual perishes, to that end the race is conserved, to that end the peril and the sacrifice, and the agony of triumph in the overcharged heart at its last bound. And what is this refining of the type, this goal for which we all make with such tragic directness, but the gaining in the power to love? We begin with love to end with greater love, and that is progress. To write the epic of civilisation is a task for some giant artist who shall combine in himself Homer and Shakespeare, and the work will be a love story.

We do not throw away the grain and keep the chaff, nor do we transmit the "absurdities" and "philanderings" alone. If in the lover's voice throb the voices of myriads of lovers, it is because he is stirred even as they. If a ballad wakes a response in him, it is because its motif has been singing itself of its own accord in his heart, and its rhythm was the dream nightingale to which he bade Her hearken. Behind the tradition lies the fact. The expression may be ephemeral, the song flat, the motto conventional, but the feeling which prompted it is true. Else it could not have survived. And it has more than survived. It has grown with growth. For centuries it lodged in the nature of man, lulled in acquiescence, then, when the sense of recognition awoke, back in those wondrous young days, it wakened to pale life, and now the feeling is man's whole support, giving him courage to work and purpose to live.

But the half brute of the London slums kicks his wife when she offends him and knows nothing of love. Well for the honour of love that it is so! The half brute of the London slums had not food enough when a child, and malnutrition is deadly. Later, he stole and lied in order to eat, and he was bullied and kicked for it out of human shape. The trick was passed on to him. The unfortunate of the London slums will push us all from heaven's gate, because we do not do battle with the conditions that make him. It is not such as he that should lead you to scorn love, for he is a mistake and a crime.

In your example of the isolated boy babe and girl babe we meet with a different condition. The individual repeats the history of the race, and as these have been left out by the civilising forces, they revert to past racial states. For these it is natural to live stolidly—is it therefore natural for us? The point I make is that our refinement, crying in us with great voice, is as much a part of us as are the simple few hungers of the racial infant. We are not the less natural for being subtle. And can it not be that the face of romance reveals itself even to savage eyes? According to the need is the power, and the early man needs must hope and desire; he is curbed by waiting and taught by loss in the hunting, he is hungry, and he dreams that he is feasting. This dream is his romance—a red flicker in the dawn, then still the gray. To suppose this is not to be unscientific, for what is true of us must have had a beginning, and feeling, as well as being, cannot have been spontaneously generated.

There is an absolute gravitation to justice in nature. This was the creed preached by Huxley to Kingsley a week after his boy's death. Grief had turned the mind upon itself, and in the upheaval he formulated a philosophy of faith and joy!

Our reward is meted out according to our obedience to all of the law, spiritual and physical. Nature keeps a ledger paying glad life's arrears each minute of time. And the creed rises to my lips when I hear you cry shame upon the delight of love. It must be good, this thing which is so fraught with joy! You brand it sense delight, but all delight is of the senses, and Darwin at the conclusion of "The Descent of Man," if he was not overtaken by a feeling of incompleteness in the work and a consuming fever for the further task, was glad in a human way, with the senses and through the emotions. Darwin's supreme moment may have come at quite a different time. What can we know of the moments of repletion that fall into another's life? With Huxley we may only know that our hearts bound high when we strike a chord of harmony and prove ourselves obedient to "all of the law," and our hearts bound high when we love. It is nature's way of showing her approval. Oh, the strength of love and the miracles of its compensations! The sense of becoming that it gives, even in its defeats, the gladness that ripples in its sob-strangled throat!

The day for asceticism is gone, or shall we say the night? We are not afraid of sense delights. We are intent upon living on all sides of our natures, roundly and naturally. You have a fine gospel of work and I congratulate you upon it, but you make no mention of the purpose of it all. It must not be work for work's sake. "When I heard the learned astronomer—" says Whitman. Do you remember? He caught in one hour the whole majesty, caught to himself the wonder that was unseen by the watching astronomers. Somehow you feel the learned ones had made a mistake in calculating so long that they had no time to see with personal eyes the glory of the stars, and that Whitman had been philosopher and had gained where they failed. The inspiration of the poet, of the painter, of the economist, and biologist, is in the revelation which they receive of what to do and why to do. For this reason philosophy, which treats of the life and works of man, is in the highest sense sociological. The generalisations of philosophy go to improve our methods so that we may have greater proneness for sense of delight and greater possibility for sense delight. Why, what else is there? You are a poet, and you give an unrestorable day, when the sun is shining and the hills lie purple in the distance, to writing a sonnet. If you do so merely to employ yourself, it must be that the wolf of despair is at your being's door. You have come to the end, and the sun and the hills do not matter. You and they have parted company. But if you write, impelled by the wish that others should read and recognise, read and remember, and grow to know and feel better, and perhaps to love the sun and hills better, then is yours a work of love, and it will be made good to you, so that for the day which you have not seen, your night shall be instinct with light. And if your labours are more especially in the service of art, then, also, with each approach toward expression, you are warmed through with the delight of achievement.

Is my meaning quite dashed away by this torrent of speech? It is simply this: Before we think we feel, and the end of thinking is feeling. The century of Voltaire and Dr. Johnson held that man is rational, the century of James, Ribot, Lange, and Wundt is thrilled to the heart with the doctrine that first, last, and always man is emotional. To speak loosely, the dimensions of the human cosmos are feeling, emotion, and sensation.

Build your fine structures. We like to see the foundations laid well and the thick walls go up. Keep to your wizard inventions. We like to live in a magic world. And ah, the indomitable machines with their austere promise of free days for weary hands, and ah, the locomotives and the ships steaming their ways toward intercourse, toward comity, toward fellowship! We like the intricacy and the vastness of the world in which we live. But "an unconsidered life is not fit to be lived by any man," says Aristotle. We must consider the phenomenon, civilisation, searching down for the nucleus of its worth. We will find that the stone structure without hope were a pitiable thing, that the making of compacts and the banking of capital, without hope, were pitiable. This hope that is the life germane, the immortal flash of mortality, the most keenly human point in all humanity, is the hope for greater and greater social happiness. Our world is an ever unfinished house which we are employed in building. If we are imbued with the spirit of the architect and not of the hod-carrier, we will hope sweetly for the work. The house beautiful will begin to mean our life, and each night we will consult our drawings, looking to it that on the house built of our days the sun shall wester, and that within shall be intimacy, and laughter, great speech and close love, looking to it that the home be such as to better to-day's tenant so that he be more loving and lovable than the one of yesterday.

We are wrong, perhaps. Long ago we were no less than now. When we reached a hand in the darkness and grasped that of our fellow, the love and the strongly frail human abandon were no less. We have not grown in heart's munificence, perhaps. It is one of the illusions only. But the hope is ours. For what do you hope?

Dane.

XXVII. FROM THE SAME TO THE SAME

London.

July 22, 19—.

Your birthday, Herbert, and for greeting I state that I walk your length with you. A truce to quarrelling! It is now a year since you informed me you were going to be married, and since then the gods have thundered their laughter at the sight of two muttering men who sat themselves on the axes of earth to dangle their legs into orbit vastness. Chronic somnambulists that they are, they took their monopolist way thither in their sleep.

I cannot tell you how full of vagary the correspondence we have fallen into seems to me. I deliberately attempted to write you into passion and for months you deliberately continued to convict yourself out of your own mouth, and we did not see that it was tragic and comic and preposterous. Could we personify this our dealing, we would do well to call it a kind of Caliban. And the tentacles we threw out, clawing at everything, stealing for prop to our little theory all of man and God! It is the conceit of us that I find utterly hopeless of grace. So I drop my rôle of omniscience. I take my form off the hub, believing the system will maintain its gravity though I go my private way, and I promise to let you alone. Forgive me, and God bless you. Ah, yes, and many happy returns of the day. All my heart in the blessing and the wish.

I did some remembering to-day, dear lad. When you were born, I was five years younger than you are now, yet I felt myself old. "If we were as old as we feel, we would die of old age at twenty-one." My life seemed all behind me, long, turbulent, packed with pain, useless. I spoke of myself as if all were over. "It had been full of purpose, but what came of it? A few rhymes and a spoilt hope." To my morbid fancy your having come to be was a signal for me to go. I had no thought of dying, yet I accepted you as the proof of my failure. In the exacting eyes of the genius of the race I was insolvent. You were not mine. I looked into Time, and saw none of me there.

Yet the letter I wrote to your parents was sincere,—how else? And that night and the next and the next, I wrote "Gentleman Adventurers," which the critics called the epitome of all that is balladesque. One pitied the dead because they could go forth no more on water and under sky. This poem, written in a mood which beneficent nature sends on the too-sick spirit, has served for more than a quarter of a century as the complete and accepted catalogue of the reasons for living. Well, I must not laugh at it. It may be true that the passion of my heart incarnated itself in it beyond the rest, that my one song sang itself out those first three days of your life. If so, it is true that love is never cheated of its fruit, and that the joy which might have been for the individual oozes out of him to the race, that the strength which would have settled upon itself in the calm of satisfied hope, filters through him outwards.

Good night, lad. My hand is on your shoulder and I am loath to take it off. For a while I would like what cannot be, to travel with you the red-brown country-roads fragrant with hay, to cross the stiles and knock upon the cabin doors, and enter where sorrow and where gladness is, big with greeting and sure of welcome. I have often pleased myself with the fancy that the outer aspects of life are patterned after the inner, so that in the map of the spirit are to be found city and country, wood, desert, and sea, so that we know these outer worlds through having travelled the worlds within. Though I stay behind, my eyes can follow you from this night's landmark along the stretch, on to the city avenues, up the highways, tracing the twists of the bypaths, clambering untrod trails of wilderness and mountain, on, on, till out upon the sea.

In one of the near turnings a woman with waiting face smiles subtly. Her hands beckon you to the tryst. Godspeed, my son.

Dane.

XXVIII. FROM HERBERT WACE TO DANE KEMPTON

The Ridge,

Berkeley, California.

August 6, 19—.

As I have constantly insisted, our difference is temperamental. The common words we lay hold of mean one thing to you and another thing to me. I do not equivocate when I say that love is instinctive, and that the latter-day expression of love is artificial. "Art," as I understand the term in its broadness, contradistinguishes from nature. Whatever man contrives or devises is an artifice, a thing of art not of nature, and therefore artificial.

As for ourselves, among animals we are the only real inventors and artificers. Instead of hair and hide, we have soft skins, and we weave cunning textures and wear wondrous garments. In cold weather, in place of eating much fat meat, we keep ourselves warm by grate fires and steam heat. We cut up our blood-dripping meat chunks with pieces of iron hardened by fire and sharpened by stone, and we eat fish with a fork instead of our fingers. We put a roof over our heads to keep out storm and sunshine, sleep in pent rooms, and are afraid of the good night air and the open sky. In short, we are consummately artificial.

As I recollect, I have shown that the natural expression of the love instinct is bestial and brutal and violent. I have shown how imagination entered into the development of the expression of this love instinct till it became *romantic*. And, in turn, I have shown how artificial was the romantic expression of this love instinct, by isolating a boy babe and a girl babe in a natural state wherein they expressed their love instinct bestially and brutally and violently. As you say, they have simply been "left out by the civilising force." And this civilising, or socialising force is simply the sum of our many inventions. The isolated pair merely expressed their instincts in the unartificial, natural way. They had not been taught a certain particular fashion in which to express those instincts as have you and I and all artificial beings been taught.

As Mr. Finck has said, "Not till Dante's 'Vita Nuova' appeared was the gospel of modern love—the romantic adoration of a maiden by a youth—revealed for the first time in definite language."

Dante, and the men who foreshadowed and followed him, were inventors. They introduced an artifice for protracting one of our most vital pleasures. Well, they succeeded. And what of it? There are artifices and artifices, and some are better than others. The automobile is a more cunning artifice than the ox-cart, the subway than a palanquin. Devices come and devices go. Change is the essence of progress. All is development. The end of rapes and romances is the same—perpetuation. There may be head love as well as heart love. And in the time to come, when the brain ceases to be the servant of the belly, the head the lackey of the heart, in that time stirpiculture, which is scientific perpetuation, will take the place of romantic love. And in the present there may be men ready for that time. There must be a beginning, else would we still be jolting in ox-carts. And I am ready for that time now.

You say, "Love is of a piece with life, like hunger, like joy, like death." Quite true. And civilisation is merely the expression of life—a variform utterance which includes love, and hunger, and joy, and death. Else what is this civilisation for? How did it happen to be? And I answer: It is the sum of the many inventions we have made to aid us in our pursuit of life and love and joy. It helps us to live more abundantly, to love more fruitfully, to joy more intelligently, and to get grim old Death by his knotty throat and hold him at arm's length as long as possible.

I stated that "all progress consists in the arbitrary alteration, by human efforts and devices, of the normal course of nature." This sociological concept comes inevitably into accord with my philosophy of love. It is the law of development, and all things of human life (which includes love) come inside of it. Wherefore, certainly, I am not outside our province when I demand of you to bring your philosophy of love into like accord.

Incidentally, I will state that I *have* fallen in love. I have grown feverish with desire, gone mad with dumb yearning. I have felt my intellect lose dominion, and learned that I was only a garmented beast, for all the many inventions very like the other beasts ungarmented. Nay, I am no cold-blooded theorist, no thick-hided dogmatist; nor am I a chastely simple young man mooning in virginal innocence. My generalisations have been tempered in the heats of passion, and what I know I know, and without hearsay.

I have seen a learned man, drunk with wine, interrogate the new states of consciousness of his unwonted condition, and so doing, gain a more comprehensive psychological insight. So I, with my loves. I was impelled toward the women I shall presently particularise. I asked why the impulsion. I reasoned to see if there were a difference between these illicit passions of mine and the illicit passions of my respectable and respected friends. And I found no difference. Separated from codes and conventions, shorn of imagination, divested of romance, stripped naked down to the core of the matter, it was old Mother Nature crying through us, every man and woman of us, for progeny. Her one unceasing and eternal cry—Progeny! Progeny! Progeny!

Just as little girls, instinctively foreshadowing motherhood, play with dolls, so children feel vague sex promptings, and in sweetly ridiculous ways love and quarrel and make up after the approved fashion of lovers. You loved little girls in pigtails and pinafores. We all did. And in our lives there is nothing fairer and more joyful to look back upon than those same little pigtails and pinafores. But I shall pass the child loves by, and instance first my calf love.

Do you remember the incident of the torn jacket and the blackened eyes?—so inexplicable at the time. Try as you would, neither you nor Waring could get anything out of me. Oh, believe me, it was tragic! I was fifteen. Fifteen, and athrill with a strange new pulse; flushed, as the dawn, with the promise of day. And, of course, I thought it was the day, that I loved as a man loved, and that no man ever loved more. Well, well, I laugh now. I was only fifteen—a young calf who went out and butted heads with another calf in the back pasture.

She was a demure little coquette, Celia Genoine, Professor Genoine's daughter, if you will recollect. "Ah," I hear you remonstrate, "but she was a woman." Just so. Fifteen and twenty-two is usually the way of calf loves. I invested her with all the glow and colour of first youth, and in her presence became a changed being. I blushed if she looked at me; trembled at the touch of her hand or the scent of her hair. To be in her presence was to be closeted with the awfulness and splendour of God. I read immortality in her eyes. A smile from her blinded me, a gentle word or caressing look and I went faint and dizzy, and I was content to lurk in some corner and gaze upon her secretly with all my soul. And I took long, solitary walks, with book of verse beneath my arm, and learned to love as lovers had loved before me.

Sufficient romance was engendered for me to pass more than one night worshipping beneath her window. I mooned and sentimentalised and fell into a gentle melancholy, until you and Waring began to worry over an early decline, to consult specialists, and by trick and stratagem to entice me into eating more and reading less. But she married—ah, I have forgotten whom. Anyway, she married, and there was trouble about it, too, and I bade adieu to love forever.

Then came the love of my whelpage. I was twenty, and she a mad, wanton creature, wonderful and unmoral and filled with life to the brim. My blood pounds hot even now as I conjure her up. The ungarmented beast, my dear Dane, the great primordial ungarmented beast, mighty to procreate, indomitable in battle, invincible in love. Love? Do I not know it? Can I not understand how that splendid fighting animal, Antony, quartered the globe with his sword and pillowed his head between the slim breasts of Egyptian Cleopatra while that hard-won world crashed to wrack and ruin?

As I say, This was the love of my whelpage, and it was vigorous, masterful, masculine. There was no sentimentalising, no fond foolishness of youth; nor was there that cool, calm poise which comes of the calculation and discretion of age. Man and woman, we were in full tide, strong, simple, and elemental. Life rioted in our veins; we were a-bubble with the ferment; and it is out of such abundance that Mother Nature has always exacted her progeny. From the strictly emotional and naturalistic viewpoint, I must consider it, even now, the perfect love. But it was decreed that I should develop into an intellectual animal, and be something more than a mere unconscious puppet of the reproductive forces. So head mastered my heart, and I laid the grip of my will over the passion and went my way.

And then came another man's wife, a proud-breasted woman, the perfect mother, made pre-eminently to know the lip clasp of a child. You know the kind, the type. "The mothers of men," I call them. And so long as there are such women on this earth, that long may we keep faith in the breed of men. The wanton was the Mate Woman, but this was the Mother Woman, the last and highest and holiest in the hierarchy of life. In her all criteria were satisfied, and I reasoned my need of her.

And by this I take it that I was passing out of my blind puppetdom. I was becoming a conscious selective factor in the scheme of reproduction, choosing a mate, not in the lust of my eyes, but in the desire of my fatherhood. Oh, Dane, she was glorious, but she was another man's wife. Had I been living unartificially, in a state of nature, I would certainly have brained her husband (a really splendid fellow), and dragged her off with me shameless under the sky. Or had her husband not been a man, or had he been but half a man, I doubt not that I would have wrested her from him. As it was, I yearned dumbly and observed the conventions.

Nor are these experiences heart soils and smirches. They have educated me, fitted me for that which is yet to be. And I have written of them to show you that I am no closet naturalist, that I speak authoritatively out of adequate understanding. Since the end of love, when all is said and done, is progeny; and since the love of to-day is crude and wasteful; as an inventor and artificer I take it upon myself to substitute reasoned foresight and selection for the short-sighted and blundering selection of Mother Nature. What would you? The old dame would have made a mess of it had I let her have her way. She tried hard to mate me with the wanton, for it was not her method to look into the future to see if a better mother for my progeny awaited me.

And now comes Hester. I approach her, not with the milk-and-water ardours of first youth, nor with the lusty love madness of young manhood, but as an intellectual man, seeking for self and mate the ripe and rounded manhood and womanhood which comes only through the having of children—children which must be properly born and bred. In this way, and in this way only, can we fully express ourselves and the life that is in us. We shall utter ourselves in the finest speech in the world, and, our children being properly born and bred, it shall be in the finest terms of the finest speech in the world. To do this is to have lived.

Herbert.

XXIX. FROM DANE KEMPTON TO HERBERT WACE

London,

3a, Queen's Road, Chelsea, S.W.

August 26, 19—.

You insist that the question is not on the value of love but on the significance of the artificial. Be that as it may. To me love is integral with life, and to speak of civilising it away, seems, in point of fact, as preposterous and as anomalous as a Hamletless play of Hamlet. You forget that in developing you carry yourself along; you change, yet you remain racial and natural. Else there were too many missing links in all your departments. We read Homer to-day—telling proof that the chain of sympathy stretches unbroken through epochs of inventions and discoveries and revolutions. Truism that it is, it presents itself with particular force at this stage.

With how much force? We stand in danger of exaggerating these vociferous thoughts. This question of naturalness as opposed to artificiality is not immediately pertinent to our problem, nor is the matter of optimism and pessimism, nor the biologic idea of survival. We should have looked more to the way of love in the lives of men and women and become historians of the method and conduct of the force. There would have been less confusion. So I write, "Be that as it may," and go back to more immediate considerations. And yet we were not far wrong! The little flower in the crannied wall could tell what God and man is. This is of all thoughts the most charged with truth. Let me understand one of your conclusions, root and all, and all in all, and such is the gracious plan of oneness in the branching and leafage and uptowering, that I must know and name the tree. Your winding bypath, could I but follow it to the end, must bring me to the highway of your thought, every step tell-tale of the journey's destination. But soon I shall be with you (the fifth of next month, after all; the arrangements as planned). Then we will begin to know each other, and we will no longer be tormented by the irksomeness of writing. Therefore, until easier and more fluent times, to the heart of the subject straight.

Your love-affairs—how well you have outgrown them and how ably you criticise them! They have not withstood the test of time, for you bear them no loyalty. Calfdom and whelpage, vagaries of adolescence, you call them. You do not show them much respect! For this reason your examples lose what weight they might have borne. They belong so wholly to the past, they are mere wraiths of bygone stirrings, they cannot clothe you with knowledge of love. Cold now, what boots it that you have been afire? You cannot be taught by what is utterly over.

You are catching what I aim to say, I hope, for I aim to say much. Put it that instead of a girl whom you idealised, it was a principle—some scheme of reform which you honoured with all the passion of young hope and dream, and which knit your alert being into a Laocoon of striving. Your maturer eyes see this ideal impossible and narrow. In no wise can it satisfy your bolder reach and larger sympathy. But you do not laugh at what has been. If you strove for it sincerely at any time, no matter how remote, you could never again deride it. Because once you loved it you are eternal keeper of the key to its good. What has been wholly yours you never quite desert. Nothing has remained to you of your love-affairs, therefore your recital of them is empty of meaning. If you were in love to-day, and because of your philosophy you determined to do battle with your feeling, your experience would be more authoritative.

You have known love, and having known you refuse it. Henceforth, it must be reason and not feeling. "What is your objection?" you ask. This merely, that the thing cannot be. Marriage to be marriage must come through love, through the reddest romance of love, through fire of the spirit, yes, even through the love of calfdom and whelpage. Else it is a mockery. Where is the woman of character who would sell the be-all and end-all of her existence for a neat catalogue of possible advantages? Where is the man who would frankly and without embellishment dare make such proposal? You point to yourself. But you have never explained yourself to Hester, and even to me you are embellishing the matter with all the might in your persuasive pen.

The ardours of calfdom and whelpage that you smile at I would have you throb with. You underrate the firstlings of the heart, the rose and white blossoming, the call upon the senses and the readiness to respond and to fulfil, to give and to take, to be and make happy—the great pride and utter abandon which is young love. At fifteen, fortunately for the development of mind and character, hope is placed where hope must pine. Love, then, is doomed to be tragic. The youth "attains to be denied." But he sounds his depth. Thereafter, he knows what to expect of himself. He has a precedent. After this he will count it a sin to forget, and to accept the solace of mediocrity. In this lies the value of the tragedy.

I sometimes think that whatever is youngest is best. It is the young that, timid and bold, pay greatest reverence to knowledge, receiving without chill of prejudice and shameful cowardice of quibbling the brave new thought. Wisdom may be of age, but passion for scholarships, trail-breaking, and hardy prospecting in the treasure mines of research, is of young pioneerhood alone. It is a youth who dares be radical, who dares, in splendid largess, build mistake upon mistake, bleeding his life out in service. And it is a youth, standing tiptoe upon the earth, now waiting in unperturbed ease, now searching with unbridled zeal, who is lover and mystic. "The best is yet to be," says Rabbi Ben Ezra, "the last of life, for which the first is made." Yes, the last of life will be good, but only if it is like youth, beating with its pulse and instinct with its spirit.

The unhappy youth is left on the battle-field but not to die. The sword-thrusts challenge him to put forth greater strength in fiercer wars. He learns hard and well.

Indeed, I cannot leave this subject of first love. How do you know it was not good for you to love as you did? It is strange you should resolve to love no more because at one time you loved deeply enough almost to remain in love. It cannot be that you have grown old and that nature is resolving for you. You tell me of your experiences in order that I may be convinced that you know whereof you speak and I listen in wonder. Your conclusions are unwonted.

Then something was amiss, for you have outgrown and forgotten, but how is it with you in the present when your indifference waits not upon time? You approach your future wife clothed in indifference as in mail, and you do violence. How can I show you? I speak as I would to a child to whom it is necessary to explain that it is bad to abandon an education. Life is a school, and to me it seems that you are about to resign long before diploma and degree, so I interpose. I was taught by first love, and I honour that time beyond any other. I was Ellen's. I have been lonely. For the mere human need, for the sake of that which to the lonely is very dear, I have thought of marriage, but I remembered and I refused to do violence to myself remembering. Long ago my standard was established. I learned how deeply I could feel, and I refuse to acknowledge myself bankrupt, I refuse to approach an honourable human being with less than my all. Until my soul flower out again, until suns flame about my head as in that dear yoretime, I shall keep teeming with dreams and make no affront. I who have seen love, dare not live without love.

I would not give in to fate, Herbert. I would assert my manhood. I would abide in the strength of the first output, going with the flush of the first glow into the gloom. I would spurn the calm of compromise and mediocrity and register a high claim. I would keep the peace with Romance and fly her colours to the last. You have lived? It is well, and it might have been better, but do not give over and talk of stirpiculture. You are not wiser than the laws which made you.

Dane.

XXX. FROM HERBERT WACE TO DANE KEMPTON

The Ridge,

Berkeley, California.

September 18, 19—.

How abominable I must seem to you, Dane! For certainly a creature is abominable that lays rough hands on one's dearest possessions. I doubt if even you realise how deeply you are stirred by my conduct towards love. My marriage with Hester, considering the quality and degree of the contracting parties, must appear as terrible to you as the sodomies that caused God's ancient wrath to destroy cities. You see, I take your side for the time, see with your eyes, live your thoughts, suffer what you suffer; and then I become myself again and steel myself to continue in what I think is the right.

After all, mine is the harder part. There are easier tasks than those of the illusion-shatterer. That which is established is hard to overthrow. It has the nine points of possession, and woe to him who attempts its disestablishment; for it will persist till it be drowned and washed away in the blood of the reformers and radicals.

Love is a convention. Men and women are attached to it as they are attached to material things, as a king is attached to his crown or an old family to its ancestral home. We have all been led to believe that love is splendid and wonderful, and the greatest thing in the world, and it pains us to part with it. Faith, we will not part with it. The man who would bid us put it by is a knave and a fool, a vile, degraded wretch, who will receive pardon neither in this world nor the next.

This is nothing new. It is the attitude of the established whenever its conventions are attacked. It was the attitude of the Jew toward Christ, of the Roman toward the Christian, of the Christian toward the infidel and the heretic. And it is sincere and natural. All things desire to endure, and they die hard. Love will die hard, as died the idolatries of our forefathers, the geocentric theory of the universe, and the divine right of kings.

So, I say, the rancour and warmth of the established when attacked is sincere. The world is mastered by the convention of love, and when one profanes love's Holy of Holies the world is unutterably shocked and hurt. Love is a thing for lovers only. It must not be approached by the sacrilegious scientist. Let him keep to his physics and chemistry, things definite and solid and gross. Love is for ardent speculation, not laboratory analysis. Love is (as the reverend prior and the learned bodies told brother Lippo of man's soul):—

"—a fire, smoke ... no, it's not ...

It's vapour done up like a new-born babe—

(In that shape when you die it leaves your mouth)

It's ... well, what matters talking, it's the soul!"

I thoroughly understand the popular sentimental repugnance to a scientific discussion of love. Because I dissect love, and weigh and calculate, it is denied that I am capable of experiencing love. It is too radiant and glorious a thing for a dull clod like me to know. And because I cannot experience love and be made mad by it, my fitness to describe its phenomena is likewise denied. Only the lover may describe love. And only the lunatic, I suppose, may compose a medical brochure on insanity.

Herbert.

XXXI. FROM DANE KEMPTON TO HERBERT WACE

London,

October 7, 19—.

It is true that you have a hard task before you, but it is not because you are fighting convention and shattering illusion; it is because you are assailing a good. Love has never acquired the prestige of the established, and the run of marriages are prompted by advantage, routine, or passion. So you are no innovator, Herbert. The idolatry of love will not be overthrown by a drawn battle between those of the Faith and those of the Reformation. Nothing so spectacular awaits us.

I have a friend who has undertaken to translate "Inferno" into English, keeping to the *terza rima*. "It is like climbing the Matterhorn," he says gravely. "I get to places where I feel I can go neither forward nor back. The task is prodigious." And it is. But whom will it concern if he succeeds in going forward? There are few who will read his book. The translation is of more importance to the translator than to anyone else. Yet the professor's *magnum opus* confers a degree upon us all. Because a standard is upheld and a man is willing and able to climb a Matterhorn of thought, we can ourselves stride forward with better courage. The work will be an output of heroism, and it will ennoble even those who will not know of it.

I have another friend who ruined his life for love, so says the world that you think steeped in the idolatry of love. A priest, who by a few strokes was able to quell in America a strong and bitter movement, a gifted orator, a man of giant powers, and who was won away at the age of forty from his career by a mere girl. The girl planned nothing. She found herself a force in his life almost despite herself. The mere fact that she lived was enough to wrest this Titan from the arms of the Church. He told me that she criticised him with the directness of a simple nature, and that he came to understand her truths better than she herself. I think she must have loved him at first, but she did not go to him when all grew calm. I wish it could have been otherwise, and that she could have brought him a woman's heart.

The priest, as the professor, is a hero. Both made great outputs.

There are few who can live like these. But because there are a few who can love and work, the game is saved. And because there are a few of these, we must ever quarrel with the many who are not like them.

> "Give all to love;
>
> Obey thy heart;
>
> Friends, kindred, days,
>
> Estate, good fame,
>
> Plans, credit, and the Muse,—
>
> Nothing refuse."

Does this really seem such poor philosophy to you? And when, Herbert, will you marry?

Dane Kempton.

XXXII. FROM THE SAME TO THE SAME

Stanford University.

November 20, 19—.

Hester met me at the station, and we walked through the Arboretum to her home on the campus. Then followed an evening together in the dormitory parlour. I have just left her. Her face was tumultuously joyous when I murmured my "At last!" Her tearful excitement was like Barbara's. You did not tell me she is so young. You must have made her feel our closeness, or she may have found a bit of my verse that all expressed her, and presto, the whole-hearted one is my friend. Her poet is now her father, brother, comrade,—what she chooses, and all she chooses.

At one time, before we were well out of the Arboretum, our eyes met, and there was something so sad and mild and strange in the burn of her gaze that I felt her frank spirit was unveiling itself in an utterness of speech. But I have become too much spoilt by mere length of living to be able to remember back and recognise what young eyes mean when they look like that. From London to Palo Alto is a short trip, if at the end of it you meet a Hester. Yet I am sad. The mood crept on me the moment we grew aware that evening had come, and we stopped a little in front of the arch to observe the night-look of the foot-hills. Lights had begun to appear in the corridors of the quadrangle, and here and there in a professor's office, while Roble and Encina looked like lit-up ferries. There was a spell of mystery and promise in the quiet which was deeper for being suggestive of the seething student-life just subsided. It was a silence that seemed to echo with bells and recitations, and babble and laughter and heartache. I fell into thought. One generation cometh and another passeth away. There is no respite. March with time and find death, mayhap, before it has found you. As years ago the flamelet of the street-lamp, so now these outposts of the colossal embryo of a world derided me and seemed to point me out and away. The evening grew chill with "a greeting in which no kindness is."

"Your coming has been announced in every class, and your lecture is on the bulletin-boards. After that, can you be depressed?"

The light words were spoken low, as if doubtful whether they could be taken in good part, and they came with something that was like music. Was it the voice or some inexplicable feeling? I turned in wonder. Her head was raised, and in the indistinctness I caught that sweet look of hers which besought me, and which I answered without knowing to what question.

I owe you a great happiness. Good-night.

Dane Kempton.

XXXIII. FROM THE SAME TO THE SAME

Stanford University.

Wednesday.

Last night I delivered my address to the student body. Behold the chapel crowded to the doors, aisles and window-seats crammed, and faces peering in from without, those of boys and girls who had perched themselves on the outer sills. A student audience is at the same time most critical and the most generous. I spoke on Literature and Democracy.

Hester approved my effort. "How does it feel to be great?" she laughed. "How does it feel to be cruel?" I retorted. "But think, Mr. Kempton, when you visited the English classes you were just so much text for us. It should count us a unit merely to have seen you."

A memory stood up and had its revenge on me. It taunted me for the half-expressed thought, for the fled insight, for the swelling note that midmost broke. Praise the artist, and he feels himself betrayer. Blear-eyed, the poet recalls the poem's sunrise, straightens himself with the old pride, is held again by the splendour which forecasts the about-to-be-steadier glory of day, and even with the recalling he shrinks together before what he knows was a false dawn. There was never a day. The song's note never sang itself at all.

Hester looked up with that wistfulness which so draws me. Her look said: "I pity you. I wish you were as happy as I." And a thought leaped out in answer to her look which would have smote her had it spoken. It was, "You, too, are awakened by a false dawning." Why is she so sure of herself and of you? Is she sure? The puny bit of writing had a vigorous rising. The ragged author was clad in it as in ermine. So the seeming love makes a strong call, for a while holding the girl intent upon a splendour of unfolding, her nature roused, her being expectant. But later, for poet and lover, the failure and the waste! Were it otherwise with your feeling for your betrothed, the comparison would not hold.

Hester does not think these things, and she is beautiful and happy.

Yours devotedly,

Dane Kempton.

XXXIV. FROM THE SAME TO THE SAME

Stanford University.

Saturday.

Her happiness wrung it from me. Before I could intervene, the question asked itself, "How will it be with you in after years?"

Straight the answer came, "There will be Herbert."

Hester is proud. To-night I saw it in the lift of her chin, in the set of her neck, in the brilliance of her cheek. She knows herself endowed. So when she prattled with abandon of all you both meant to be and do, her form erect before me, her hands eloquent with excitement, her voice pleading for the right to her very conscious self-esteem, I asked her to look still further. Further she saw you, and was content.

That was before dinner. Later we were walking. "I have a friend in Orion," she said. The witchery of starshine played in her eyes and about her mouth. Where were you, Herbert? This night will never return. Yet what has been was for you—the more, perhaps, that you seemed away. So it is with lovers. She thinks you love her.

"I am sorry for your mood," she said. "You are holding yourself to account these days in a way I know." Then she spoke, and I learned with new heaviness of spirit that she does know the way of it. You never thought Hester had much to struggle with?

"I am difficult," she said. And again, "There are times when no power can hold me." Then she quoted Browning:—

> "Already how am I so far
>
> Out of that minute? Must I go

Still like the thistle-ball, no bar,

Onward, whenever light winds blow,

Fixed by no friendly star?"

"Are you unhappy, Hester?" I asked.

"Yes, but with no more reason than you for your unhappiness. Since you have come here, you have renewed your demands upon yourself. You wish to go to school with the youngest and find you cannot. You suffer because more seems behind you than before." Her voice rose as if she were fighting tears. It was different with her, I told her. Nothing was behind her.

"You test your work and I test my love. When you are sad, it is because the soul of the song spent itself to gain body—" She did not finish. Why is she sad? Because the soul of her love is narrower than she hoped?

On our return from our walk she sank on the seat under the '95 oak. "Did you think I meant I was always unhappy?" she asked. Her words seem always to say more than her meaning. She imparts something of her own elaborateness to them. I laughed.

"How could I with the 'Herbert is' in my ears?" Then her love became voluble. I forgot what I knew of your theories and grew aflame with her ardour. I anticipated as largely as she. She was again possessed by her hopes.

There, under the shadow of the quadrangle which her young strides measured, she spoke of what, with you in her life, the years must be. Beyond words you are blessed, Herbert. But if she mistakes?

D.K.

XXXV. FROM THE SAME TO THE SAME

Stanford University.

November 27, 19—.

Be outspoken! What will happen I can only surmise, but you must tell her what she is to you. Set her right.

This is the fourth letter in seven days about Hester. I am endeavouring to make you acquainted with her. I had no need if you loved her. How she loves you! Yet she thinks that your calm is depth, your silence prayer. Her pride protects her, but she strains for the word which does not come. She has never been quite sure, and I thank God for that. Hester has been fearing somewhat, and she has been doubting, and it is this that may save her when the night sets in and the storm breaks over her head.

You, too, are thankful that her instincts served her true and that she never quite accepted the gift that seemed to have been proffered?

You have a right to demand the reason for my renewed attack. It is because I have learned the strength of her love. "You are blessed beyond words," I said two days ago, but as you reject the blessing, Hester must know it and you must tell her. Herbert, I am your friend.

Dane Kempton.

XXXVI. FROM HERBERT WACE TO DANE KEMPTON

The Ridge,

Berkeley, California.

November 29, 19—.

What a flutter of letters! And what a fluttery Dane Kempton it is! The wine of our western sunshine has bitten into your blood and you are grown over-warm. I am glad that you and Hester have found each other so quickly and intimately; glad that you are under her charm, as I know her to be under yours; but I am not glad when you spell yourself into her and write out your heart's forebodings on her heart. For you are strangely morbid, and you are certainly guilty of reading your own doubts and fears into her unspoken and unguessed thoughts.

Believe me, rather than the soul of her love seeming narrower than she hopes, the truth is she gives her love little thought at all. She is too busy—and too sensible. Like me, she has not the time. We are workers, not dreamers; and the minutes are too full for us to lavish them on an eternal weighing and measuring of heart throbs.

Besides, Hester is too large for that sort of stuff. She is the last woman in the world to peer down at the scales to see if she is getting full value. We leave that to the lesser creatures, who spend their courtship loudly protesting how unutterable, immeasurable, and inextinguishable is their love, as though, forsooth, each dreaded lest the other deem it a bad bargain. We do not bargain and chaffer over our feelings, Hester and I. Surely you mistake, and stir storms in teacups.

"Be outspoken," you say. If my conscience were not clear, I should be troubled by that. As it is, what have I hidden? What sharp business have I driven? And who is it that cried "cheated!"? Be outspoken—about what, pray?

You bid me tell her what she is to me. Which is to bid me tell her what she already knows, to tell her that she is the Mother Woman; that of all women she is dearest to me; that of all the walks of life, that one is pleasantest wherein I may walk with her; that with her I shall find the supreme expression of myself and the life that is in me; that in all this I honour her in the finest, loftiest fashion that man can honour woman. Tell her this, Dane. By all means tell her.

"Ah, I do not mean that," I hear you say. Well, let me tell you what you mean, in my own way, and bid you tell her for me. In the lust of my eyes she is nothing to me. She is not a mere sense delight, a toy for the debauchery of my intellect and the enthronement of emotion. She is not the woman to make my pulse go fevered and me go mad. Nor is she the woman to make me forget my manhood and pride, to tumble me down doddering at her feet and gibbering like an ape. She is not the woman to put my thoughts out of joint and the world out of gear, and so to befuddle and make me drunk with the beast that is in me, that I am ready to sacrifice truth, honesty, duty, and purpose for the sake of possession. She is not the woman ever to make me swamp honour and poise and right conduct in the vortex of blind sex passion. She is not the woman to arouse in me such uncontrolled desire that for gratification I would do one ill deed, or put the slightest hurt upon the least of human creatures. She is not the most beautiful woman God Almighty ever planted on His footstool. (There have been and are many women as true and pure and noble). She is not the woman for whose bedazzlement I must advertise the value of my goods by sweating sonnets to her, or shivering serenades at her, or perpetuating follies for her. In short, she is not anything to me that the woman of conventional love is to the man.

And again, what *is* she to me? She is my other self, as it were, my good comrade, and fellow-worker and joy-sharer. With her woman she complements my man and makes us one, and this is the highest civilised sense of union. She is to me the culmination of the thousands of generations of women. It took civilisation to make her, as it takes civilisation to make our marriage. She is to me the partner in a marriage of the gods, for we become gods, we half brutes, when we muzzle the beast and are not menaced by his growls. Under heaven she is my wife and the mother of my children.

Tell her, then, tell her all you wish, you dear old fluttery, mothery poet father—as though it made any difference.

Herbert.

XXXVII. FROM DANE KEMPTON TO HERBERT WACE

Stanford University.

December 3, 19—.

Not three weeks ago you were sitting opposite me and speaking of Hester. You admitted many things that night, amongst them that the girl never carried you off your feet. You stated over again with precision all you had written. You betrothed yourself, not because Hester is different from everybody else in the world, but because she is like. You took her for what is typical in her, not for what is individual. You preferred to walk toward her before your steps were impelled, because you feared that impulsion would preclude rational choice. With the hope of out-tricking nature, you reached for Hester Stebbins, in order that there might be a wall between your heart's fancy and yourself, should your heart become rebellious. I was to understand that this is the new school, that so live the masters of matter and of self.

And as you spoke, I wondered about the woman Hester and the form of love-making which existed between you, and whether she was simple and without any charm despite her culture and her gift of song. "She either loves him too well to know or to have the strength to care, or she is, like him, of the new school," I thought. I sat and watched you, noting your youth, surprised by the scorn in your eyes and the sadness on your lips. You seemed hopeless and helpless. I closed my eyes. "What has he left himself?" I kept asking. "How will he tread 'The paths gray heads abhor?'" My own head bowed itself as before an irreparable loss. I had rejoined the child of my care only to find him blasted as by grief, the first sunshine smitten from his face and his heart weighted. One word, one ray lighting your looks in a wonted way, one uncontrolled movement of the hand, one little silence following the mention of her, would have led me to believe that I had not understood and that all was well. The night grew old with your plans and analyses. We parted with a sense of shame upon us that we should have written and spoken so long and with such heat, and to such little purpose.

You do not see how this answers your last letter. I will tell you. It shows you that you have explained yourself fully the night we spoke face to face.

You say that Hester is the woman to complement your man. This sounds like a lover, only I happen to know that she is not the irresistible woman. I found it out quite by accident—a few words dropped into a letter, a corroboration of the fact and further committal, a protracted defence of your position, running through a correspondence of over a year, and, finally, a face-to-face declaration. What boots it now that you write prettily? You do not love Hester. You want her to mother your children, and you install her in your life for the purpose before the need.

Love is not lust, and it is good. The irresistible marriage, alone, is the right one. Upon it, alone, does the sacrament rest. The chivalry of your last letter refers less to the girl than to your own ends. It is not because Hester is what she is, that "of all the walks in life that one is pleasantest wherein you may walk with her," but because that walk is the one you choose beyond any other for your wife to follow. The mother woman is legion, and you refuse to specialise.

Hester does not peer down at the scales to see if she is getting full value, yet she does look to her dignity, and, being poor, will not account herself rich. Hester has felt since you made known to her that you wished her to be yours, that she counted punily in your scheme, that you placed little of yourself in charge of her. She loved you and avowed it, but she has never been happy. The tragedy of love is not (what it is thought to be) the unreciprocated love, but the meagerly returned love. It is better to be rejected, equal turned from equal, than to be held with slim desire for slight purpose. Can you see this, Herbert? You are hurting the girl's life. She will ask for what you withhold, though not a word rise to her lips; will thirst for it through the years, will herself grow cramped with your denial till her own love seem a thing of dream, unstable and vague and illusive. And all the time you are gentle. You are devoted to her interests, furthering her happiness to the best in your power; but your power cannot touch her happiness. It is not what you do; it is the motive to your acts, and Hester would know that she has left you unmoved. You respect the function of motherhood, but you do not love Hester. Tell her this, and prevent her from entering a union in which she must feel herself half useful, half wifely, half happy, and therefore all unhappy.

It is not Hester's fault that you cannot love her, and perhaps it is not her misfortune. There is no need for panic. Of two persons, one loving and one loath, the indifferent one is in the right. Can a tree defend itself from the hewer's axe? What would avail it, then, to feel pain at the blows? It is beyond our control to love or not to love, and no effort that we may put forth can draw love to us when it is denied. It does not avail us to suffer from unrequited love.

This which I have just said is an article of faith which the doctrine of experience often contradicts, for there may be mistake, and the one who does not love may be in the wrong. If only you could wait to see the beauty which is she before you call her! A year later and Hester may flower for you in a passionate blossoming; her face may challenge you to live. A year later and you may find that she is indeed the woman to guide you and to follow you; her voice a song; her eyes a light in the day. As yet, you have not gauged her, and you would put her to small uses. Stand aside, dear Herbert. It will be better.

I have played a surly part. I may be accused of having been to you both a Dmitri Roudin and an Iago. I beg you to believe that it has not been easy for me. I have uttered the earnest word, have driven you on by the goad of friendship, which drives far. I looked upon the days that came tripping toward you out of the blue-white horizon of time and saw them gray for a dear woman, gray and silent as the tomb over a dead love, and heavy hearted for a man who is my son.

Ever wholly yours,

Dane Kempton.

XXXVIII. FROM HESTER STEBBINS TO HERBERT WACE

Stanford University.

December 15, 19—.

Over and ended. It shall be as I said last night. Herbert, there is no call for anger; believe me, there is not. I am doing what I cannot help doing. You have not changed, but my faith in you has, and I cannot pretend to a happiness I do not feel.

Oh, but I laugh, my very dear one, I laugh that I could seem to choose to wrest myself from you. Did you at one time love me? That morning of wild sunshine when you took my hand and asked me to be your wife seems very long ago. I should have understood—the blame is all mine—I should have known you did not love me, I should have been filled with anger and shame instead of happiness. The blame is all mine.

Last night, while you were speaking, I was standing in the window wondering what all the trouble was about. I could afford to be calm since I knew I was not hurting you very deeply. At most I was disappointing a very self-sufficient man. How do women find courage, O God, to take from men who love them the love they gave? No such ordeal mine?

Farewell, Herbert. Let us think calmly of each other since we have helped each other for so long a stretch of life. Farewell, dear.

Always your friend,

Hester Stebbins.

XXXIX. FROM HESTER STEBBINS TO DANE KEMPTON

Stanford University.

December 18, 19—.

Herbert has analyzed the situation and has arrived at the conclusion that my dissatisfaction arises in an inordinate desire for happiness. You should not care so much about yourself, he says. Poor, dear, young Herbert! He is very young and cannot as yet conceive how much there is about oneself that demands care. I thought it out in the hills to-day. It was gray and there was a fitful wind. What is this selfishness but a prompting to make much of life? You and I and people of our kind are old before our time, that is the reason we are not reckless. Our dreams mature us. I was a mere girl when Herbert said he wished to marry me, but I was old enough to grasp the full meaning of the pact, as he could not grasp it. In a moment I had travelled my way to the grave and back. I looked at the sheer, quick clouds that flitted past the blue, and I felt that I had caught up with life; I had overtaken the wonders that hung in the sky of my dreaming. Then I looked at him and the sunshine got in my face and made me laugh (or cry)—I was so more than happy, being so much too sure of his need of me. I am glad I walked to-day. The view from the hills was beautiful. (You see I am not unhappy!) I stood on a rock and looked about me, thinking of you, of Barbara,—I feel I know her,—and of Herbert. He and I had often come to these spots. Oh, the hungry memories! Yet what were we but a young man and a young woman, who, without being battered into apathy by misfortune, without being wearied or ill, were taking each other for better or for worse because they seemed compatible? We were doing just that, to Herbert's certain knowledge! I failed him; he hoped for more complaisance. Marriage is a hazard, Mr. Kempton, confess it is, and a man does much when he binds himself to make a woman the mother of his children—nay, the grandmother of theirs, even that. What else and what more? I would never have been wholly in my husband's life, comrade and fellow to it. Herbert knew this clearly, and I vaguely but I acted with clearness on my vagueness. It was hard to do. It has left me breathless and a little afraid to be myself,—as if I had killed a dear thing,—and tearful, too, and spasmodic for your sympathy and sanction.

I told him that for a long time I did not understand, supposing myself beloved and desired and chosen for him by God, thinking he yearned for the subtlety and mystery of me, thinking all of him needed me and cleaved earths and parted seas to come to me. Later, when I became oppressed by a lack and was made to hear the stillness that followed my unechoed words, I became grave and still myself. He had unloved me, I said, and I waited. Something seemed pending, and meanwhile I could love! I made much of every word of comfort that he dropped me, and dwelt with hope on the future. All this I told Herbert the night when I explained, and he turned pale. "You people fly away with yourselves. I cannot follow you. What is wrong, Hester?" He smiled in his distress. Yet was there in his softness an imperiousness, commanding me to be other than I am, forbidding me the right to crave in secret what I had made bold to ask for openly. His man was stronger than my woman, and I leapt to him again. "My husband," I whispered, my hands in his. This, even after I understood, dearest Mr. Kempton.

It is a sorry tangle. If only one could suit feeling to theory! It is not for a theory that I refuse to be Herbert's wife. Yet if I loved him enough, I could give up love itself for him. He hinted it, looking as from a distance at me in my attitude of protest and restraint. If I loved him enough, I could forego love itself for him. Somewhere there is a fault, it would seem, somewhere in my abandon is restraint, in my love, self-seeking. Remorse overcame me just as he was about to leave, and I schooled myself to think that there had been no affront, that it honours a woman to be wanted no matter for what end, that every use is a noble use, that we die the same, loved or used. If Herbert Wace wants a wife and thinks me fitting, why, it is well. I thought all this and aged as I thought. Nevertheless, my hand did not put itself out a second time to detain the man who had forced me to face this.

There is a youth here who loves me. If Herbert's face could shine like his for one hour, I believe I would be happier than I have ever been. And it would not spoil that happiness if this love were toward another than myself. Say you believe me. You must know it of me that before everything else in the world I pray that knowledge of love come to the man over whom the love of my girlhood was spilled.

Do you ask what is left me, dear friend? Work and tears and the intact dream. Believe me, I am not pitiable.

Hester.

THE MUTINY OF THE
ELSINORE

CHAPTER I

From the first the voyage was going wrong. Routed out of my hotel on a bitter March morning, I had crossed Baltimore and reached the pier-end precisely on time. At nine o'clock the tug was to have taken me down the bay and put me on board the *Elsinore*, and with growing irritation I sat frozen inside my taxicab and waited. On the seat, outside, the driver and Wada sat hunched in a temperature perhaps half a degree colder than mine. And there was no tug.

Possum, the fox-terrier puppy Galbraith had so inconsiderately foisted upon me, whimpered and shivered on my lap inside my greatcoat and under the fur robe. But he would not settle down. Continually he whimpered and clawed and struggled to get out. And, once out and bitten by the cold, with equal insistence he whimpered and clawed to get back.

His unceasing plaint and movement was anything but sedative to my jangled nerves. In the first place I was uninterested in the brute. He meant nothing to me. I did not know him. Time and again, as I drearily waited, I was on the verge of giving him to the driver. Once, when two little girls—evidently the wharfinger's daughters—went by, my hand reached out to the door to open it so that I might call to them and present them with the puling little wretch.

A farewell surprise package from Galbraith, he had arrived at the hotel the night before, by express from New York. It was Galbraith's way. Yet he might so easily have been decently like other folk and sent fruit . . . or flowers, even. But no; his affectionate inspiration had to take the form of a yelping, yapping two months' old puppy. And with the advent of the terrier the trouble had begun. The hotel clerk judged me a criminal before the act I had not even had time to meditate. And then Wada, on his own initiative and out of his own foolish stupidity, had attempted to smuggle the puppy into his room and been caught by a house detective. Promptly Wada had forgotten all his English and lapsed into hysterical Japanese, and the house detective remembered only his Irish; while the hotel clerk had given me to understand in no uncertain terms that it was only what he had expected of me.

Damn the dog, anyway! And damn Galbraith too! And as I froze on in the cab on that bleak pier-end, I damned myself as well, and the mad freak that had started me voyaging on a sailing-ship around the Horn.

By ten o'clock a nondescript youth arrived on foot, carrying a suit-case, which was turned over to me a few minutes later by the wharfinger. It belonged to the pilot, he said, and gave instructions to the chauffeur how to find some other pier from which, at some indeterminate time, I should be taken aboard the *Elsinore* by some other tug. This served to increase my irritation. Why should I not have been informed as well as the pilot?

An hour later, still in my cab and stationed at the shore end of the new pier, the pilot arrived. Anything more unlike a pilot I could not have imagined. Here was no blue-jacketed, weather-beaten son of the sea, but a soft-spoken gentleman, for all the world the type of successful business man one meets in all the clubs. He introduced himself immediately, and I invited him to share my freezing cab with Possum and the baggage. That some change had been made in the arrangements by Captain West was all he knew, though he fancied the tug would come along any time.

And it did, at one in the afternoon, after I had been compelled to wait and freeze for four mortal hours. During this time I fully made up my mind that I was not going to like this Captain West. Although I had never met him, his treatment of me from the outset had been, to say the least, cavalier. When the *Elsinore* lay in Erie Basin, just arrived from California with a cargo of barley, I had crossed over from New York to inspect what was to be my home for many months. I had been delighted with the ship and the cabin accommodation. Even the stateroom selected for me was satisfactory and far more spacious than I had expected. But when I peeped into the captain's room I was amazed at its comfort. When I say that it opened directly into a bath-room, and that, among other things, it was furnished with a big brass bed such as one would never suspect to find at sea, I have said enough.

Naturally, I had resolved that the bath-room and the big brass bed should be mine. When I asked the agents to arrange with the captain they seemed non-committal and uncomfortable. "I don't know in the least what it is worth," I said. "And I don't care. Whether it costs one hundred and fifty dollars or five hundred, I must have those quarters."

Harrison and Gray, the agents, debated silently with each other and scarcely thought Captain West would see his way to the arrangement. "Then he is the first sea captain I ever heard of that wouldn't," I asserted confidently. "Why, the captains of all the Atlantic liners regularly sell their quarters."

"But Captain West is not the captain of an Atlantic liner," Mr. Harrison observed gently.

"Remember, I am to be on that ship many a month," I retorted. "Why, heavens, bid him up to a thousand if necessary."

"We'll try," said Mr. Gray, "but we warn you not to place too much dependence on our efforts. Captain West is in Searsport at the present time, and we will write him to-day."

To my astonishment Mr. Gray called me up several days later to inform me that Captain West had declined my offer. "Did you offer him up to a thousand?" I demanded. "What did he say?"

"He regretted that he was unable to concede what you asked," Mr. Gray replied.

A day later I received a letter from Captain West. The writing and the wording were old-fashioned and formal. He regretted not having yet met me, and assured me that he would see personally that my quarters were made comfortable. For that matter he had already dispatched orders to Mr. Pike, the first mate of the *Elsinore*, to knock out the partition between my state-room and the spare state-room adjoining. Further—and here is where my dislike for Captain West began—he informed me that if, when once well at sea, I should find myself dissatisfied, he would gladly, in that case, exchange quarters with me.

157

Of course, after such a rebuff, I knew that no circumstance could ever persuade me to occupy Captain West's brass bed. And it was this Captain Nathaniel West, whom I had not yet met, who had now kept me freezing on pier-ends through four miserable hours. The less I saw of him on the voyage the better, was my decision; and it was with a little tickle of pleasure that I thought of the many boxes of books I had dispatched on board from New York. Thank the Lord, I did not depend on sea captains for entertainment.

I turned Possum over to Wada, who was settling with the cabman, and while the tug's sailors were carrying my luggage on board I was led by the pilot to an introduction with Captain West. At the first glimpse I knew that he was no more a sea captain than the pilot was a pilot. I had seen the best of the breed, the captains of the liners, and he no more resembled them than did he resemble the bluff-faced, gruff-voiced skippers I had read about in books. By his side stood a woman, of whom little was to be seen and who made a warm and gorgeous blob of colour in the huge muff and boa of red fox in which she was well-nigh buried.

"My God!—his wife!" I darted in a whisper at the pilot. "Going along with him? . . . "

I had expressly stipulated with Mr. Harrison, when engaging passage, that the one thing I could not possibly consider was the skipper of the *Elsinore* taking his wife on the voyage. And Mr. Harrison had smiled and assured me that Captain West would sail unaccompanied by a wife.

"It's his daughter," the pilot replied under his breath. "Come to see him off, I fancy. His wife died over a year ago. They say that is what sent him back to sea. He'd retired, you know."

Captain West advanced to meet me, and before our outstretched hands touched, before his face broke from repose to greeting and the lips moved to speech, I got the first astonishing impact of his personality. Long, lean, in his face a touch of race I as yet could only sense, he was as cool as the day was cold, as poised as a king or emperor, as remote as the farthest fixed star, as neutral as a proposition of Euclid. And then, just ere our hands met, a twinkle of—oh—such distant and controlled geniality quickened the many tiny wrinkles in the corner of the eyes; the clear blue of the eyes was suffused by an almost colourful warmth; the face, too, seemed similarly to suffuse; the thin lips, harsh-set the instant before, were as gracious as Bernhardt's when she moulds sound into speech.

So curiously was I affected by this first glimpse of Captain West that I was aware of expecting to fall from his lips I knew not what words of untold beneficence and wisdom. Yet he uttered most commonplace regrets at the delay in a voice provocative of fresh surprise to me. It was low and gentle, almost too low, yet clear as a bell and touched with a faint reminiscent twang of old New England.

"And this is the young woman who is guilty of the delay," he concluded my introduction to his daughter. "Margaret, this is Mr. Pathurst."

Her gloved hand promptly emerged from the fox-skins to meet mine, and I found myself looking into a pair of gray eyes bent steadily and gravely upon me. It was discomfiting, that cool, penetrating, searching gaze. It was not that it was challenging, but that it was so insolently business-like. It was much in the very way one would look at a new coachman he was about to engage. I did not know then that she was to go on the voyage, and that her curiosity about the man who was to be a fellow-passenger for half a year was therefore only natural. Immediately she realized what she was doing, and her lips and eyes smiled as she spoke.

As we moved on to enter the tug's cabin I heard Possum's shivering whimper rising to a screech, and went forward to tell Wada to take the creature in out of the cold. I found him hovering about my luggage, wedging my dressing-case securely upright by means of my little automatic rifle. I was startled by the mountain of luggage around which mine was no more than a fringe. Ship's stores, was my first thought, until I noted the number of trunks, boxes, suit-cases, and parcels and bundles of all sorts. The initials on what looked suspiciously like a woman's hat trunk caught my eye—"M.W." Yet Captain West's first name was Nathaniel. On closer investigation I did find several "N.W's." but everywhere I could see "M.W's." Then I remembered that he had called her Margaret.

159

I was too angry to return to the cabin, and paced up and down the cold deck biting my lips with vexation. I had so expressly stipulated with the agents that no captain's wife was to come along. The last thing under the sun I desired in the pet quarters of a ship was a woman. But I had never thought about a captain's daughter. For two cents I was ready to throw the voyage over and return on the tug to Baltimore.

By the time the wind caused by our speed had chilled me bitterly, I noticed Miss West coming along the narrow deck, and could not avoid being struck by the spring and vitality of her walk. Her face, despite its firm moulding, had a suggestion of fragility that was belied by the robustness of her body. At least, one would argue that her body must be robust from her fashion of movement of it, though little could one divine the lines of it under the shapelessness of the furs.

I turned away on my heel and fell moodily to contemplating the mountain of luggage. A huge packing-case attracted my attention, and I was staring at it when she spoke at my shoulder.

"That's what really caused the delay," she said.

"What is it?" I asked incuriously.

"Why, the *Elsinore's* piano, all renovated. When I made up my mind to come, I telegraphed Mr. Pike—he's the mate, you know. He did his best. It was the fault of the piano house. And while we waited to-day I gave them a piece of my mind they'll not forget in a hurry."

She laughed at the recollection, and commenced to peep and peer into the luggage as if in search of some particular piece. Having satisfied herself, she was starting back, when she paused and said:

"Won't you come into the cabin where it's warm? We won't be there for half an hour."

"When did you decide to make this voyage?" I demanded abruptly.

So quick was the look she gave me that I knew she had in that moment caught all my disgruntlement and disgust.

"Two days ago," she answered. "Why?"

Her readiness for give and take took me aback, and before I could speak she went on:

"Now you're not to be at all silly about my coming, Mr. Pathurst. I probably know more about long-voyaging than you do, and we're all going to be comfortable and happy. You can't bother me, and I promise you I won't bother you. I've sailed with passengers before, and I've learned to put up with more than they ever proved they were able to put up with. So there. Let us start right, and it won't be any trouble to keep on going right. I know what is the matter with you. You think you'll be called upon to entertain me. Please know that I do not need entertainment. I never saw the longest voyage that was too long, and I always arrive at the end with too many things not done for the passage ever to have been tedious, and . . . I don't play *Chopsticks*."

CHAPTER II

The *Elsinore*, fresh-loaded with coal, lay very deep in the water when we came alongside. I knew too little about ships to be capable of admiring her lines, and, besides, I was in no mood for admiration. I was still debating with myself whether or not to chuck the whole thing and return on the tug. From all of which it must not be taken that I am a vacillating type of man. On the contrary.

The trouble was that at no time, from the first thought of it, had I been keen for the voyage. Practically the reason I was taking it was because there was nothing else I was keen on. For some time now life had lost its savour. I was not jaded, nor was I exactly bored. But the zest had gone out of things. I had lost taste for my fellow-men and all their foolish, little, serious endeavours. For a far longer period I had been dissatisfied with women. I had endured them, but I had been too analytic of the faults of their primitiveness, of their almost ferocious devotion to the destiny of sex, to be enchanted with them. And I had come to be oppressed by what seemed to me the futility of art—a pompous legerdemain, a consummate charlatanry that deceived not only its devotees but its practitioners.

161

In short, I was embarking on the *Elsinore* because it was easier to than not; yet everything else was as equally and perilously easy. That was the curse of the condition into which I had fallen. That was why, as I stepped upon the deck of the *Elsinore*, I was half of a mind to tell them to keep my luggage where it was and bid Captain West and his daughter good-day.

I almost think what decided me was the welcoming, hospitable smile Miss West gave me as she started directly across the deck for the cabin, and the knowledge that it must be quite warm in the cabin.

Mr. Pike, the mate, I had already met, when I visited the ship in Erie Basin. He smiled a stiff, crack-faced smile that I knew must be painful, but did not offer to shake hands, turning immediately to call orders to half-a-dozen frozen-looking youths and aged men who shambled up from somewhere in the waist of the ship. Mr. Pike had been drinking. That was patent. His face was puffed and discoloured, and his large gray eyes were bitter and bloodshot.

I lingered, with a sinking heart watching my belongings come aboard and chiding my weakness of will which prevented me from uttering the few words that would put a stop to it. As for the half-dozen men who were now carrying the luggage aft into the cabin, they were unlike any concept I had ever entertained of sailors. Certainly, on the liners, I had observed nothing that resembled them.

One, a most vivid-faced youth of eighteen, smiled at me from a pair of remarkable Italian eyes. But he was a dwarf. So short was he that he was all sea-boots and sou'wester. And yet he was not entirely Italian. So certain was I that I asked the mate, who answered morosely:

"Him? Shorty? He's a dago half-breed. The other half's Jap or Malay."

One old man, who I learned was a bosun, was so decrepit that I thought he had been recently injured. His face was stolid and ox-like, and as he shuffled and dragged his brogans over the deck he paused every several steps to place both hands on his abdomen and execute a queer, pressing, lifting movement. Months were to pass, in which I saw him do this thousands of times, ere I learned that there was nothing the matter with him and that his action was purely a habit. His face reminded me of the Man with the Hoe, save that it was unthinkably and abysmally stupider. And his name, as I was to learn, of all names was Sundry Buyers. And he was bosun of the fine American sailing-ship *Elsinore*—rated one of the finest sailing-ships afloat!

Of this group of aged men and boys that moved the luggage along I saw only one, called Henry, a youth of sixteen, who approximated in the slightest what I had conceived all sailors to be like. He had come off a training ship, the mate told me, and this was his first voyage to sea. His face was keen-cut, alert, as were his bodily movements, and he wore sailor-appearing clothes with sailor-seeming grace. In fact, as I was to learn, he was to be the only sailor-seeming creature fore and aft.

The main crew had not yet come aboard, but was expected at any moment, the mate vouchsafed with a snarl of ominous expectancy. Those already on board were the miscellaneous ones who had shipped themselves in New York without the mediation of boarding-house masters. And what the crew itself would be like God alone could tell—so said the mate. Shorty, the Japanese (or Malay) and Italian half-caste, the mate told me, was an able seaman, though he had come out of steam and this was his first sailing voyage.

"Ordinary seamen!" Mr. Pike snorted, in reply to a question. "We don't carry Landsmen!—forget it! Every clodhopper an' cow-walloper these days is an able seaman. That's the way they rank and are paid. The merchant service is all shot to hell. There ain't no more sailors. They all died years ago, before you were born even."

I could smell the raw whiskey on the mate's breath. Yet he did not stagger nor show any signs of intoxication. Not until afterward was I to know that his willingness to talk was most unwonted and was where the liquor gave him away.

"It'd a-ben a grace had I died years ago," he said, "rather than to a-lived to see sailors an' ships pass away from the sea."

"But I understand the *Elsinore* is considered one of the finest," I urged.

"So she is . . . to-day. But what is she?—a damned cargo-carrier. She ain't built for sailin', an' if she was there ain't no sailors left to sail her. Lord! Lord! The old clippers! When I think of 'em!—*The Gamecock, Shootin' Star, Flyin' Fish, Witch o' the Wave, Staghound, Harvey Birch, Canvas-back, Fleetwing, Sea Serpent, Northern Light!* An' when I think of the fleets of the tea-clippers that used to load at Hong Kong an' race the Eastern Passages. A fine sight! A fine sight!"

I was interested. Here was a man, a live man. I was in no hurry to go into the cabin, where I knew Wada was unpacking my things, so I paced up and down the deck with the huge Mr. Pike. Huge he was in all conscience, broad-shouldered, heavy-boned, and, despite the profound stoop of his shoulders, fully six feet in height.

"You are a splendid figure of a man," I complimented.

"I was, I was," he muttered sadly, and I caught the whiff of whiskey strong on the air.

I stole a look at his gnarled hands. Any finger would have made three of mine. His wrist would have made three of my wrist.

"How much do you weigh?" I asked.

"Two hundred an' ten. But in my day, at my best, I tipped the scales close to two-forty."

"And the *Elsinore* can't sail," I said, returning to the subject which had roused him.

"I'll take you even, anything from a pound of tobacco to a month's wages, she won't make it around in a hundred an' fifty days," he answered. "Yet I've come round in the old *Flyin' Cloud* in eighty-nine days—eighty-nine days, sir, from Sandy Hook to 'Frisco. Sixty men for'ard that *was* men, an' eight boys, an' drive! drive! drive! Three hundred an' seventy-four miles for a day's run under t'gallantsails, an' in the squalls eighteen knots o' line not enough to time her. Eighty-nine days—never beat, an' tied once by the old *Andrew Jackson* nine years afterwards. Them was the days!"

"When did the *Andrew Jackson* tie her?" I asked, because of the growing suspicion that he was "having" me.

"In 1860," was his prompt reply.

"And you sailed in the *Flying Cloud* nine years before that, and this is 1913—why, that was sixty-two years ago," I charged.

"And I was seven years old," he chuckled. "My mother was stewardess on the *Flyin' Cloud*. I was born at sea. I was boy when I was twelve, on the *Herald o' the Morn*, when she made around in ninety-nine days—half the crew in irons most o' the time, five men lost from aloft off the Horn, the points of our sheath-knives broken square off, knuckle-dusters an' belayin'-pins flyin', three men shot by the officers in one day, the second mate killed dead an' no one to know who done it, an' drive! drive! drive! ninety-nine days from land to land, a run of seventeen thousand miles, an' east to west around Cape Stiff!"

"But that would make you sixty-nine years old," I insisted.

"Which I am," he retorted proudly, "an' a better man at that than the scrubby younglings of these days. A generation of 'em would die under the things I've been through. Did you ever hear of the *Sunny South*?—she that was sold in Havana to run slaves an' changed her name to *Emanuela*?"

"And you've sailed the Middle Passage!" I cried, recollecting the old phrase.

"I was on the *Emanuela* that day in Mozambique Channel when the *Brisk* caught us with nine hundred slaves between-decks. Only she wouldn't a-caught us except for her having steam."

I continued to stroll up and down beside this massive relic of the past, and to listen to his hints and muttered reminiscences of old man-killing and man-driving days. He was too real to be true, and yet, as I studied his shoulder-stoop and the age-drag of his huge feet, I was convinced that his years were as he asserted. He spoke of a Captain Sonurs.

"He was a great captain," he was saying. "An' in the two years I sailed mate with him there was never a port I didn't jump the ship goin' in an' stay in hiding until I sneaked aboard when she sailed again."

"But why?"

"The men, on account of the men swearin' blood an' vengeance and warrants against me because of my ways of teachin' them to be sailors. Why, the times I was caught, and the fines the skipper paid for me—and yet it was my work that made the ship make money."

He held up his huge paws, and as I stared at the battered, malformed knuckles I understood the nature of his work.

"But all that's stopped now," he lamented. "A sailor's a gentleman these days. You can't raise your voice or your hand to them."

At this moment he was addressed from the poop-rail above by the second mate, a medium-sized, heavily built, clean-shaven, blond man.

"The tug's in sight with the crew, sir," he announced.

The mate grunted an acknowledgment, then added, "Come on down, Mr. Mellaire, and meet our passenger."

I could not help noting the air and carriage with which Mr. Mellaire came down the poop-ladder and took his part in the introduction. He was courteous in an old-world way, soft-spoken, suave, and unmistakably from south of Mason and Dixon.

"A Southerner," I said.

"Georgia, sir." He bowed and smiled, as only a Southerner can bow and smile.

His features and expression were genial and gentle, and yet his mouth was the cruellest gash I had ever seen in a man's face. It was a gash. There is no other way of describing that harsh, thin-lipped, shapeless mouth that uttered gracious things so graciously. Involuntarily I glanced at his hands. Like the mate's, they were thick-boned, broken-knuckled, and malformed. Back into his blue eyes I looked. On the surface of them was a film of light, a gloss of gentle kindness and cordiality, but behind that gloss I knew resided neither sincerity nor mercy. Behind that gloss was something cold and terrible, that lurked and waited and watched—something catlike, something inimical and deadly. Behind that gloss of soft light and of social sparkle was the live, fearful thing that had shaped that mouth into the gash it was. What I sensed behind in those eyes chilled me with its repulsiveness and strangeness.

As I faced Mr. Mellaire, and talked with him, and smiled, and exchanged amenities, I was aware of the feeling that comes to one in the forest or jungle when he knows unseen wild eyes of hunting animals are spying upon him. Frankly I was afraid of the thing ambushed behind there in the skull of Mr. Mellaire. One so as a matter of course identifies form and feature with the spirit within. But I could not do this with the second mate. His face and form and manner and suave ease were one thing, inside which he, an entirely different thing, lay hid.

I noticed Wada standing in the cabin door, evidently waiting to ask for instructions. I nodded, and prepared to follow him inside. Mr. Pike looked at me quickly and said:

"Just a moment, Mr. Pathurst."

He gave some orders to the second mate, who turned on his heel and started for'ard. I stood and waited for Mr. Pike's communication, which he did not choose to make until he saw the second mate well out of ear-shot. Then he leaned closely to me and said:

"Don't mention that little matter of my age to anybody. Each year I sign on I sign my age one year younger. I am fifty-four, now, on the articles."

"And you don't look a day older," I answered lightly, though I meant it in all sincerity.

"And I don't feel it. I can outwork and outgame the huskiest of the younglings. And don't let my age get to anybody's ears, Mr. Pathurst. Skippers are not particular for mates getting around the seventy mark. And owners neither. I've had my hopes for this ship, and I'd a-got her, I think, except for the old man decidin' to go to sea again. As if he needed the money! The old skinflint!"

"Is he well off?" I inquired.

"Well off! If I had a tenth of his money I could retire on a chicken ranch in California and live like a fighting cock—yes, if I had a fiftieth of what he's got salted away. Why, he owns more stock in all the Blackwood ships . . . and they've always been lucky and always earned money. I'm getting old, and it's about time I got a command. But no; the old cuss has to take it into his head to go to sea again just as the berth's ripe for me to fall into."

Again I started to enter the cabin, but was stopped by the mate.

"Mr. Pathurst? You won't mention about my age?"

"No, certainly not, Mr. Pike," I said.

CHAPTER III

Quite chilled through, I was immediately struck by the warm comfort of the cabin. All the connecting doors were open, making what I might call a large suite of rooms or a whale house. The main-deck entrance, on the port side, was into a wide, well-carpeted hallway. Into this hallway, from the port side, opened five rooms: first, on entering, the mate's; next, the two state-rooms which had been knocked into one for me; then the steward's room; and, adjoining his, completing the row, a state-room which was used for the slop-chest.

Across the hall was a region with which I was not yet acquainted, though I knew it contained the dining-room, the bath-rooms, the cabin proper, which was in truth a spacious living-room, the captain's quarters, and, undoubtedly, Miss West's quarters. I could hear her humming some air as she bustled about with her unpacking. The steward's pantry, separated by crosshalls and by the stairway leading into the chart-room above on the poop, was placed strategically in the centre of all its operations. Thus, on the starboard side of it were the state-rooms of the captain and Miss West, for'ard of it were the dining-room and main cabin; while on the port side of it was the row of rooms I have described, two of which were mine.

I ventured down the hall toward the stern, and found it opened into the stern of the *Elsinore*, forming a single large apartment at least thirty-five feet from side to side and fifteen to eighteen feet in depth, curved, of course, to the lines of the ship's stern. This seemed a store-room. I noted wash-tubs, bolts of canvas, many lockers, hams and bacon hanging, a step-ladder that led up through a small hatch to the poop, and, in the floor, another hatch.

I spoke to the steward, an old Chinese, smooth-faced and *brisk* of movement, whose name I never learned, but whose age on the articles was fifty-six.

"What is down there?" I asked, pointing to the hatch in the floor.

"Him lazarette," he answered.

"And who eats there?" I indicated a table with two stationary sea-chairs.

"Him second table. Second mate and carpenter him eat that table."

When I had finished giving instructions to Wada for the arranging of my things I looked at my watch. It was early yet, only several minutes after three so I went on deck again to witness the arrival of the crew.

The actual coming on board from the tug I had missed, but for'ard of the amidship house I encountered a few laggards who had not yet gone into the forecastle. These were the worse for liquor, and a more wretched, miserable, disgusting group of men I had never seen in any slum. Their clothes were rags. Their faces were bloated, bloody, and dirty. I won't say they were villainous. They were merely filthy and vile. They were vile of appearance, of speech, and action.

"Come! Come! Get your dunnage into the fo'c's'le!"

Mr. Pike uttered these words sharply from the bridge above. A light and graceful bridge of steel rods and planking ran the full length of the *Elsinore*, starting from the poop, crossing the amidship house and the forecastle, and connecting with the forecastle-head at the very bow of the ship.

169

At the mate's command the men reeled about and glowered up at him, one or two starting clumsily to obey. The others ceased their drunken yammerings and regarded the mate sullenly. One of them, with a face mashed by some mad god in the making, and who was afterwards to be known by me as Larry, burst into a guffaw, and spat insolently on the deck. Then, with utmost deliberation, he turned to his fellows and demanded loudly and huskily:

"Who in hell's the old stiff, anyways?"

I saw Mr. Pike's huge form tense convulsively and involuntarily, and I noted the way his huge hands strained in their clutch on the bridge-railing. Beyond that he controlled himself.

"Go on, you," he said. "I'll have nothing out of you. Get into the fo'c's'le."

And then, to my surprise, he turned and walked aft along the bridge to where the tug was casting off its lines. So this was all his high and mighty talk of kill and drive, I thought. Not until afterwards did I recollect, as I turned aft down the deck, that I saw Captain West leaning on the rail at the break of the poop and gazing for'ard.

The tug's lines were being cast off, and I was interested in watching the manoeuvre until she had backed clear of the ship, at which moment, from for'ard, arose a queer babel of howling and yelping, as numbers of drunken voices cried out that a man was overboard. The second mate sprang down the poop-ladder and darted past me along the deck. The mate, still on the slender, white-painted bridge, that seemed no more than a spider thread, surprised me by the activity with which he dashed along the bridge to the 'midship house, leaped upon the canvas-covered long-boat, and swung outboard where he might see. Before the men could clamber upon the rail the second mate was among them, and it was he who flung a coil of line overboard.

What impressed me particularly was the mental and muscular superiority of these two officers. Despite their age—the mate sixty-nine and the second mate at least fifty—their minds and their bodies had acted with the swiftness and accuracy of steel springs. They were potent. They were iron. They were perceivers, willers, and doers. They were as of another species compared with the sailors under them. While the latter, witnesses of the happening and directly on the spot, had been crying out in befuddled helplessness, and with slow wits and slower bodies been climbing upon the rail, the second mate had descended the steep ladder from the poop, covered two hundred feet of deck, sprung upon the rail, grasped the instant need of the situation, and cast the coil of line into the water.

And of the same nature and quality had been the actions of Mr. Pike. He and Mr. Mellaire were masters over the wretched creatures of sailors by virtue of this remarkable difference of efficiency and will. Truly, they were more widely differentiated from the men under them than were the men under them differentiated from Hottentots—ay, and from monkeys.

I, too, by this time, was standing on the big hawser-bitts in a position to see a man in the water who seemed deliberately swimming away from the ship. He was a dark-skinned Mediterranean of some sort, and his face, in a clear glimpse I caught of it, was distorted by frenzy. His black eyes were maniacal. The line was so accurately flung by the second mate that it fell across the man's shoulders, and for several strokes his arms tangled in it ere he could swim clear. This accomplished, he proceeded to scream some wild harangue and once, as he uptossed his arms for emphasis, I saw in his hand the blade of a long knife.

Bells were jangling on the tug as it started to the rescue. I stole a look up at Captain West. He had walked to the port side of the poop, where, hands in pockets, he was glancing, now for'ard at the struggling man, now aft at the tug. He gave no orders, betrayed no excitement, and appeared, I may well say, the most casual of spectators.

The creature in the water seemed now engaged in taking off his clothes. I saw one bare arm, and then the other, appear. In his struggles he sometimes sank beneath the surface, but always he emerged, flourishing the knife and screaming his addled harangue. He even tried to escape the tug by diving and swimming underneath.

I strolled for'ard, and arrived in time to see him hoisted in over the rail of the *Elsinore*. He was stark naked, covered with blood, and raving. He had cut and slashed himself in a score of places. From one wound in the wrist the blood spurted with each beat of the pulse. He was a loathsome, non-human thing. I have seen a scared orang in a zoo, and for all the world this bestial-faced, mowing, gibbering thing reminded me of the orang. The sailors surrounded him, laying hands on him, withstraining him, the while they guffawed and cheered. Right and left the two mates shoved them away, and dragged the lunatic down the deck and into a room in the 'midship house. I could not help marking the strength of Mr. Pike and Mr. Mellaire. I had heard of the superhuman strength of madmen, but this particular madman was as a wisp of straw in their hands. Once into the bunk, Mr. Pike held down the struggling fool easily with one hand while he dispatched the second mate for marlin with which to tie the fellow's arms.

"Bughouse," Mr. Pike grinned at me. "I've seen some bughouse crews in my time, but this one's the limit."

"What are you going to do?" I asked. "The man will bleed to death."

"And good riddance," he answered promptly. "We'll have our hands full of him until we can lose him somehow. When he gets easy I'll sew him up, that's all, if I have to ease him with a clout of the jaw."

I glanced at the mate's huge paw and appreciated its anæsthetic qualities. Out on deck again, I saw Captain West on the poop, hands still in pockets, quite uninterested, gazing at a blue break in the sky to the north-east. More than the mates and the maniac, more than the drunken callousness of the men, did this quiet figure, hands in pockets, impress upon me that I was in a different world from any I had known.

Wada broke in upon my thoughts by telling me he had been sent to say that Miss West was serving tea in the cabin.

CHAPTER IV

The contrast, as I entered the cabin, was startling. All contrasts aboard the *Elsinore* promised to be startling. Instead of the cold, hard deck my feet sank into soft carpet. In place of the mean and narrow room, built of naked iron, where I had left the lunatic, I was in a spacious and beautiful apartment. With the bawling of the men's voices still in my ears, and with the pictures of their drink-puffed and filthy faces still vivid under my eyelids, I found myself greeted by a delicate-faced, prettily-gowned woman who sat beside a lacquered oriental table on which rested an exquisite tea-service of Canton china. All was repose and calm. The steward, noiseless-footed, expressionless, was a shadow, scarcely noticed, that drifted into the room on some service and drifted out again.

Not at once could I relax, and Miss West, serving my tea, laughed and said:

"You look as if you had been seeing things. The steward tells me a man has been overboard. I fancy the cold water must have sobered him."

I resented her unconcern.

"The man is a lunatic," I said. "This ship is no place for him. He should be sent ashore to some hospital."

"I am afraid, if we begin that, we'd have to send two-thirds of our complement ashore—one lump?"

"Yes, please," I answered. "But the man has terribly wounded himself. He is liable to bleed to death."

She looked at me for a moment, her gray eyes serious and scrutinizing, as she passed me my cup; then laughter welled up in her eyes, and she shook her head reprovingly.

"Now please don't begin the voyage by being shocked, Mr. Pathurst. Such things are very ordinary occurrences. You'll get used to them. You must remember some queer creatures go down to the sea in ships. The man is safe. Trust Mr. Pike to attend to his wounds. I've never sailed with Mr. Pike, but I've heard enough about him. Mr. Pike is quite a surgeon. Last voyage, they say, he performed a successful amputation, and so elated was he that he turned his attention on the carpenter, who happened to be suffering from some sort of indigestion. Mr. Pike was so convinced of the correctness of his diagnosis that he tried to bribe the carpenter into having his appendix removed." She broke off to laugh heartily, then added: "They say he offered the poor man just pounds and pounds of tobacco to consent to the operation."

"But is it safe . . . for the . . . the working of the ship," I urged, "to take such a lunatic along?"

She shrugged her shoulders, as if not intending to reply, then said:

"This incident is nothing. There are always several lunatics or idiots in every ship's company. And they always come aboard filled with whiskey and raving. I remember, once, when we sailed from Seattle, a long time ago, one such madman. He showed no signs of madness at all; just calmly seized two boarding-house runners and sprang overboard with them. We sailed the same day, before the bodies were recovered."

Again she shrugged her shoulders.

"What would you? The sea is hard, Mr. Pathurst. And for our sailors we get the worst type of men. I sometimes wonder where they find them. And we do our best with them, and somehow manage to make them help us carry on our work in the world. But they are low . . . low."

As I listened, and studied her face, contrasting her woman's sensitivity and her soft pretty dress with the brute faces and rags of the men I had noticed, I could not help being convinced intellectually of the rightness of her position. Nevertheless, I was hurt sentimentally,—chiefly, I do believe, because of the very hardness and unconcern with which she enunciated her view. It was because she was a woman, and so different from the sea-creatures, that I resented her having received such harsh education in the school of the sea.

"I could not help remarking your father's—er, er *sang froid* during the occurrence." I ventured.

"He never took his hands from his pockets!" she cried.

Her eyes sparkled as I nodded confirmation.

"I knew it! It's his way. I've seen it so often. I remember when I was twelve years old—mother was alone—we were running into San Francisco. It was in the *Dixie*, a ship almost as big as this. There was a strong fair wind blowing, and father did not take a tug. We sailed right through the Golden Gate and up the San Francisco water-front. There was a swift flood tide, too; and the men, both watches, were taking in sail as fast as they could.

"Now the fault was the steamboat captain's. He miscalculated our speed and tried to cross our bow. Then came the collision, and the *Dixie's* bow cut through that steamboat, cabin and hull. There were hundreds of passengers, men, women, and children. Father never took his hands from his pockets. He sent the mate for'ard to superintend rescuing the passengers, who were already climbing on to our bowsprit and forecastle-head, and in a voice no different from what he'd use to ask some one to pass the butter he told the second mate to set all sail. And he told him which sails to begin with."

"But why set more sails?" I interrupted.

"Because he could see the situation. Don't you see, the steamboat was cut wide open. All that kept her from sinking instantly was the bow of the *Dixie* jammed into her side. By setting more sail and keeping before the wind, he continued to keep the bow of the *Dixie* jammed.

"I was terribly frightened. People who had sprung or fallen overboard were drowning on each side of us, right in my sight, as we sailed along up the water-front. But when I looked at father, there he was, just as I had always known him, hands in pockets, walking slowly up and down, now giving an order to the wheel—you see, he had to direct the *Dixie's* course through all the shipping—now watching the passengers swarming over our bow and along our deck, now looking ahead to see his way through the ships at anchor. Sometimes he did glance at the poor, drowning ones, but he was not concerned with them.

"Of course, there were numbers drowned, but by keeping his hands in his pockets and his head cool he saved hundreds of lives. Not until the last person was off the steamboat—he sent men aboard to make sure—did he take off the press of sail. And the steamboat sank at once."

She ceased, and looked at me with shining eyes for approbation.

"It was splendid," I acknowledged. "I admire the quiet man of power, though I confess that such quietness under stress seems to me almost unearthly and beyond human. I can't conceive of myself acting that way, and I am confident that I was suffering more while that poor devil was in the water than all the rest of the onlookers put together."

"Father suffers!" she defended loyally. "Only he does not show it."

I bowed, for I felt she had missed my point.

CHAPTER V

I came out from tea in the cabin to find the tug *Britannia* in sight. She was the craft that was to tow us down Chesapeake Bay to sea. Strolling for'ard I noted the sailors being routed out of the forecastle by Sundry Buyers, for ever tenderly pressing his abdomen with his hands. Another man was helping Sundry Buyers at routing out the sailors. I asked Mr. Pike who the man was.

"Nancy—my bosun; ain't he a peach?" was the answer I got, and from the mate's manner of enunciation I was quite aware that "Nancy" had been used derisively.

Nancy could not have been more than thirty, though he looked as if he had lived a very long time. He was toothless and sad and weary of movement. His eyes were slate-coloured and muddy, his shaven face was sickly yellow. Narrow-shouldered, sunken-chested, with cheeks cavernously hollow, he looked like a man in the last stages of consumption. Little life as Sundry Buyers showed, Nancy showed even less life. And these were bosuns!— bosuns of the fine American sailing-ship *Elsinore*! Never had any illusion of mine taken a more distressing cropper.

It was plain to me that the pair of them, spineless and spunkless, were afraid of the men they were supposed to boss. And the men! Doré could never have conjured a more delectable hell's broth. For the first time I saw them all, and I could not blame the two bosuns for being afraid of them. They did not walk. They slouched and shambled, some even tottered, as from weakness or drink.

But it was their faces. I could not help remembering what Miss West had just told me—that ships always sailed with several lunatics or idiots in their crews. But these looked as if they were all lunatic or feeble-minded. And I, too, wondered where such a mass of human wreckage could have been obtained. There was something wrong with all of them. Their bodies were twisted, their faces distorted, and almost without exception they were under-sized. The several quite fairly large men I marked were vacant-faced. One man, however, large and unmistakably Irish, was also unmistakably mad. He was talking and muttering to himself as he came out. A little, curved, lop-sided man, with his head on one side and with the shrewdest and wickedest of faces and pale blue eyes, addressed an obscene remark to the mad Irishman, calling him O'Sullivan. But O'Sullivan took no notice and muttered on. On the heels of the little lop-sided man appeared an overgrown dolt of a fat youth, followed by another youth so tall and emaciated of body that it seemed a marvel his flesh could hold his frame together.

Next, after this perambulating skeleton, came the weirdest creature I have ever beheld. He was a twisted oaf of a man. Face and body were twisted as with the pain of a thousand years of torture. His was the face of an ill-treated and feeble-minded faun. His large black eyes were bright, eager, and filled with pain; and they flashed questioningly from face to face and to everything about. They were so pitifully alert, those eyes, as if for ever astrain to catch the clue to some perplexing and threatening enigma. Not until afterwards did I learn the cause of this. He was stone deaf, having had his ear-drums destroyed in the boiler explosion which had wrecked the rest of him.

I noticed the steward, standing at the galley door and watching the men from a distance. His keen, Asiatic face, quick with intelligence, was a relief to the eye, as was the vivid face of Shorty, who came out of the forecastle with a leap and a gurgle of laughter. But there was something wrong with him, too. He was a dwarf, and, as I was to come to know, his high spirits and low mentality united to make him a clown.

Mr. Pike stopped beside me a moment and while he watched the men I watched him. The expression on his face was that of a cattle-buyer, and it was plain that he was disgusted with the quality of cattle delivered.

"Something the matter with the last mother's son of them," he growled.

And still they came: one, pallid, furtive-eyed, that I instantly adjudged a drug fiend; another, a tiny, wizened old man, pinch-faced and wrinkled, with beady, malevolent blue eyes; a third, a small, well-fleshed man, who seemed to my eye the most normal and least unintelligent specimen that had yet appeared. But Mr. Pike's eye was better trained than mine.

"What's the matter with *you*?" he snarled at the man.

"Nothing, sir," the fellow answered, stopping immediately.

"What's your name?"

Mr. Pike never spoke to a sailor save with a snarl.

"Charles Davis, sir."

"What are you limping about?"

"I ain't limpin', sir," the man answered respectfully, and, at a nod of dismissal from the mate, marched off jauntily along the deck with a heodlum swing to the shoulders.

"He's a sailor all right," the mate grumbled; "but I'll bet you a pound of tobacco or a month's wages there's something wrong with him."

The forecastle now seemed empty, but the mate turned on the bosuns with his customary snarl.

"What in hell are you doing? Sleeping? Think this is a rest cure? Get in there an' rustle 'em out!"

Sundry Buyers pressed his abdomen gingerly and hesitated, while Nancy, his face one dogged, long-suffering bleakness, reluctantly entered the forecastle. Then, from inside, we heard oaths, vile and filthy, urgings and expostulations on the part of Nancy, meekly and pleadingly uttered.

I noted the grim and savage look that came on Mr. Pike's face, and was prepared for I knew not what awful monstrosities to emerge from the forecastle. Instead, to my surprise, came three fellows who were strikingly superior to the ruck that had preceded them. I looked to see the mate's face soften to some sort of approval. On the contrary, his blue eyes contracted to narrow slits, the snarl of his voice was communicated to his lips, so that he seemed like a dog about to bite.

But the three fellows. They were small men, all; and young men, anywhere between twenty-five and thirty. Though roughly dressed, they were well dressed, and under their clothes their bodily movements showed physical well-being. Their faces were keen cut, intelligent. And though I felt there was something queer about them, I could not divine what it was.

Here were no ill-fed, whiskey-poisoned men, such as the rest of the sailors, who, having drunk up their last pay-days, had starved ashore until they had received and drunk up their advance money for the present voyage. These three, on the other hand were supple and vigorous. Their movements were spontaneously quick and accurate. Perhaps it was the way they looked at me, with incurious yet calculating eyes that nothing escaped. They seemed so worldly wise, so indifferent, so sure of themselves. I was confident they were not sailors. Yet, as shore-dwellers, I could not place them. They were a type I had never encountered. Possibly I can give a better idea of them by describing what occurred.

As they passed before us they favoured Mr. Pike with the same indifferent, keen glances they gave me.

"What's your name—you?" Mr. Pike barked at the first of the trio, evidently a hybrid Irish-Jew. Jewish his nose unmistakably was. Equally unmistakable was the Irish of his eyes, and jaw, and upper lip.

The three had immediately stopped, and, though they did not look directly at one another, they seemed to be holding a silent conference. Another of the trio, in whose veins ran God alone knows what Semitic, Babylonish and Latin strains, gave a warning signal. Oh, nothing so crass as a wink or a nod. I almost doubted that I had intercepted it, and yet I knew he had communicated a warning to his fellows. More a shade of expression that had crossed his eyes, or a glint in them of sudden light—or whatever it was, it carried the message.

"Murphy," the other answered the mate.

"Sir!" Mr. Pike snarled at him.

Murphy shrugged his shoulders in token that he did not understand. It was the poise of the man, of the three of them, the cool poise that impressed me.

"When you address any officer on this ship you'll say 'sir,'" Mr. Pike explained, his voice as harsh as his face was forbidding. "Did you get *that*?"

"Yes . . . sir," Murphy drawled with deliberate slowness. "I gotcha."

"Sir!" Mr. Pike roared.

"Sir," Murphy answered, so softly and carelessly that it irritated the mate to further bullyragging.

"Well, Murphy's too long," he announced. "Nosey'll do you aboard this craft. Got *that*?"

"I gotcha . . . sir," came the reply, insolent in its very softness and unconcern. "Nosey Murphy goes . . . sir."

And then he laughed—the three of them laughed, if laughter it might be called that was laughter without sound or facial movement. The eyes alone laughed, mirthlessly and cold-bloodedly.

Certainly Mr. Pike was not enjoying himself with these baffling personalities. He turned upon the leader, the one who had given the warning and who looked the admixture of all that was Mediterranean and Semitic.

"What's *your* name?"

"Bert Rhine . . . sir," was the reply, in tones as soft and careless and silkily irritating as the other's.

"And *you*?"—this to the remaining one, the youngest of the trio, a dark-eyed, olive-skinned fellow with a face most striking in its cameo-like beauty. American-born, I placed him, of immigrants from Southern Italy—from Naples, or even Sicily.

"Twist . . . sir," he answered, precisely in the same manner as the others.

"Too long," the mate sneered. "The Kid'll do you. Got *that*?"

"I gotcha . . . sir. Kid Twist'll do me . . . sir."

"Kid'll do!"

"Kid . . . sir."

And the three laughed their silent, mirthless laugh. By this time Mr. Pike was beside himself with a rage that could find no excuse for action.

"Now I'm going to tell you something, the bunch of you, for the good of your health." The mate's voice grated with the rage he was suppressing. "I know your kind. You're dirt. D'ye get *that*? You're dirt. And on this ship you'll be treated as dirt. You'll do your work like men, or I'll know the reason why. The first time one of you bats an eye, or even looks like batting an eye, he gets his. D'ye get that? Now get out. Get along for'ard to the windlass."

Mr. Pike turned on his heel, and I swung alongside of him as he moved aft.

"What do you make of them?" I queried.

"The limit," he grunted. "I know their kidney. They've done time, the three of them. They're just plain sweepings of hell—"

Here his speech was broken off by the spectacle that greeted him on Number Two hatch. Sprawled out on the hatch were five or six men, among them Larry, the tatterdemalion who had called him "old stiff" earlier in the

181

afternoon. That Larry had not obeyed orders was patent, for he was sitting with his back propped against his sea-bag, which ought to have been in the forecastle. Also, he and the group with him ought to have been for'ard manning the windlass.

The mate stepped upon the hatch and towered over the man.

"Get up," he ordered.

Larry made an effort, groaned, and failed to get up.

"I can't," he said.

"Sir!"

"I can't, sir. I was drunk last night an' slept in Jefferson Market. An' this mornin' I was froze tight, sir. They had to pry me loose."

"Stiff with the cold you were, eh?" the mate grinned.

"It's well ye might say it, sir," Larry answered.

"And you feel like an old stiff, eh?"

Larry blinked with the troubled, querulous eyes of a monkey. He was beginning to apprehend he knew not what, and he knew that bending over him was a man-master.

"Well, I'll just be showin' you what an old stiff feels like, anyways." Mr. Pike mimicked the other's brogue.

And now I shall tell what I saw happen. Please remember what I have said of the huge paws of Mr. Pike, the fingers much longer than mine and twice as thick, the wrists massive-boned, the arm-bones and the shoulder-bones of the same massive order. With one flip of his right hand, with what I might call an open-handed, lifting, upward slap, save that it was the ends of the fingers only that touched Larry's face, he lifted Larry into the air, sprawling him backward on his back across his sea-bag.

The man alongside of Larry emitted a menacing growl and started to spring belligerently to his feet. But he never reached his feet. Mr. Pike, with the back of same right hand, open, smote the man on the side of the face. The loud smack of the impact was startling. The mate's strength was amazing. The blow looked so easy, so effortless; it had seemed like the lazy stroke of a good-natured bear, but in it was such a weight of bone and muscle that the man went down sidewise and rolled off the hatch on to the deck.

At this moment, lurching aimlessly along, appeared O'Sullivan. A sudden access of muttering, on his part, reached Mr. Pike's ear, and Mr. Pike, instantly keen as a wild animal, his paw in the act of striking O'Sullivan, whipped out like a revolver shot, "What's that?" Then he noted the sense-struck face of O'Sullivan and withheld the blow. "Bug-house," Mr. Pike commented.

Involuntarily I had glanced to see if Captain West was on the poop, and found that we were hidden from the poop by the 'midship house.

Mr. Pike, taking no notice of the man who lay groaning on the deck, stood over Larry, who was likewise groaning. The rest of the sprawling men were on their feet, subdued and respectful. I, too, was respectful of this terrific, aged figure of a man. The exhibition had quite convinced me of the verity of his earlier driving and killing days.

"Who's the old stiff now?" he demanded.

"'Tis me, sir," Larry moaned contritely.

"Get up!"

Larry got up without any difficulty at all.

"Now get for'ard to the windlass! The rest of you!"

And they went, sullenly, shamblingly, like the cowed brutes they were.

CHAPTER VI

I climbed the ladder on the side of the for'ard house (which house contained, as I discovered, the forecastle, the galley, and the donkey-engine room), and went part way along the bridge to a position by the foremast, where I could observe the crew heaving up anchor. The *Britannia* was alongside, and we were getting under way.

A considerable body of men was walking around with the windlass or variously engaged on the forecastle-head. Of the crew proper were two watches of fifteen men each. In addition were sailmakers, boys, bosuns, and the carpenter. Nearly forty men were they, but such men! They were sad and lifeless. There was no vim, no go, no activity. Every step and movement was an effort, as if they were dead men raised out of coffins or sick men dragged from hospital beds. Sick they were—whiskey-poisoned. Starved they were, and weak from poor nutrition. And worst of all, they were imbecile and lunatic.

I looked aloft at the intricate ropes, at the steel masts rising and carrying huge yards of steel, rising higher and higher, until steel masts and yards gave way to slender spars of wood, while ropes and stays turned into a delicate tracery of spider-thread against the sky. That such a wretched muck of men should be able to work this magnificent ship through all storm and darkness and peril of the sea was beyond all seeming. I remembered the two mates, the super-efficiency, mental and physical, of Mr. Mellaire and Mr. Pike—could they make this human wreckage do it? They, at least, evinced no doubts of their ability. The sea? If this feat of mastery were possible, then clear it was that I knew nothing of the sea.

I looked back at the misshapen, starved, sick, stumbling hulks of men who trod the dreary round of the windlass. Mr. Pike was right. These were not the *brisk*, devilish, able-bodied men who manned the ships of the old clipper-ship days; who fought their officers, who had the points of their sheath-knives broken off, who killed and were killed, but who did their work as men. These men, these shambling carcasses at the windlass—I looked, and looked, and vainly I strove to conjure the vision of them swinging aloft in rack and storm, "clearing the raffle," as Kipling puts it, "with their clasp knives in their teeth." Why didn't they sing a chanty as they hove the anchor up? In the old days, as I had read, the anchor always came up to the rollicking sailor songs of sea-chested men.

I tired of watching the spiritless performance, and went aft on an exploring trip along the slender bridge. It was a beautiful structure, strong yet light, traversing the length of the ship in three aerial leaps. It spanned from the forecastle-head to the forecastle-house, next to the 'midship house, and then to the poop. The poop, which was really the roof or deck over all the cabin space below, and which occupied the whole after-part of the ship, was very large. It was broken only by the half-round and half-covered wheel-house at the very stern and by the chart-house. On either side of the latter two doors opened into a tiny hallway. This, in turn, gave access to the chart-room and to a stairway that led down into the cabin quarters beneath.

I peeped into the chart-room and was greeted with a smile by Captain West. He was lolling back comfortably in a swing chair, his feet cocked on the desk opposite. On a broad, upholstered couch sat the pilot. Both were smoking cigars; and, lingering for a moment to listen to the conversation, I grasped that the pilot was an ex-sea-captain.

As I descended the stairs, from Miss West's room came a sound of humming and bustling, as she settled her belongings. The energy she displayed, to judge by the cheerful noises of it, was almost perturbing.

Passing by the pantry, I put my head inside the door to greet the steward and courteously let him know that I was aware of his existence. Here, in his little realm, it was plain that efficiency reigned. Everything was spotless and in order, and I could have wished and wished vainly for a more noiseless servant than he ashore. His face, as he regarded me, had as little or as much expression as the Sphinx. But his slant, black eyes were bright, with intelligence.

"What do you think of the crew?" I asked, in order to put words to my invasion of his castle.

"Buggy-house," he answered promptly, with a disgusted shake of the head. "Too much buggy-house. All crazy. You see. No good. Rotten. Down to hell."

That was all, but it verified my own judgment. While it might be true, as Miss West had said, that every ship's crew contained several lunatics and idiots, it was a foregone conclusion that our crew contained far more than several. In fact, and as it was to turn out, our crew, even in these degenerate sailing days, was an unusual crew in so far as its helplessness and worthlessness were beyond the average.

I found my own room (in reality it was two rooms) delightful. Wada had unpacked and stored away my entire outfit of clothing, and had filled numerous shelves with the library I had brought along. Everything was in order and place, from my shaving outfit in the drawer beside the wash-basin, and my sea-boots and oilskins hung ready to hand, to my writing materials on the desk, before which a swing arm-chair, leather-upholstered and screwed solidly to the floor, invited me. My pyjamas and dressing-gown were out. My slippers, in their accustomed place by the bed, also invited me.

Here, aft, all was fitness, intelligence. On deck it was what I have described—a nightmare spawn of creatures, assumably human, but malformed, mentally and physically, into caricatures of men. Yes, it was an unusual crew; and that Mr. Pike and Mr. Mellaire could whip it into the efficient shape necessary to work this vast and intricate and beautiful fabric of a ship was beyond all seeming of possibility.

Depressed as I was by what I had just witnessed on deck, there came to me, as I leaned back in my chair and opened the second volume of George Moore's *Hail and Farewell*, a premonition that the voyage was to be disastrous. But then, as I looked about the room, measured its generous space, realized that I was more comfortably situated than I had ever been on any passenger steamer, I dismissed foreboding thoughts and caught a pleasant vision of myself, through weeks and months, catching up with all the necessary reading which I had so long neglected.

Once, I asked Wada if he had seen the crew. No, he hadn't, but the steward had said that in all his years at sea this was the worst crew he had ever seen.

"He say, all crazy, no sailors, rotten," Wada said. "He say all big fools and bime by much trouble. 'You see,' he say all the time. 'You see, You see.'"

He pretty old man—fifty-five years, he say. Very smart man for Chinaman. Just now, first time for long time, he go to sea. Before, he have big business in San Francisco. Then he get much trouble—police. They say he opium smuggle. Oh, big, big trouble. But he catch good lawyer. He no go to jail. But long time lawyer work, and when trouble all finish lawyer got all his business, all his money, everything. Then he go to sea, like before. He make good money. He get sixty-five dollars a month on this ship. But he don't like. Crew all crazy. When this time finish he leave ship, go back start business in San Francisco."

Later, when I had Wada open one of the ports for ventilation, I could hear the gurgle and swish of water alongside, and I knew the anchor was up and that we were in the grip of the *Britannia*, towing down the Chesapeake to sea. The idea suggested itself that it was not too late. I could very easily abandon the adventure and return to Baltimore on the *Britannia* when she cast off the *Elsinore*. And then I heard a slight tinkling of china from the pantry as the steward proceeded to set the table, and, also, it was so warm and comfortable, and George Moore was so irritatingly fascinating.

CHAPTER VII

In every way dinner proved up beyond my expectations, and I registered a note that the cook, whoever or whatever he might be, was a capable man at his trade. Miss West served, and, though she and the steward were strangers, they worked together splendidly. I should have thought, from the smoothness of the service, that he was an old house servant who for years had known her every way.

The pilot ate in the chart-house, so that at table were the four of us that would always be at table together. Captain West and his daughter faced each other, while I, on the captain's right, faced Mr. Pike. This put Miss West across the corner on my right.

Mr. Pike, his dark sack coat (put on for the meal) bulging and wrinkling over the lumps of muscles that padded his stooped shoulders, had nothing at all to say. But he had eaten too many years at captains' tables not to have proper table manners. At first I thought he was abashed by Miss West's presence. Later, I decided it was due to the presence of the captain. For Captain West had a way with him that I was beginning to learn. Far removed as Mr. Pike and Mr. Mellaire were from the sailors, individuals as they were of an entirely different and superior breed, yet equally as different and far removed from his officers was Captain West. He was a serene and absolute aristocrat. He neither talked "ship" nor anything else to Mr. Pike.

On the other hand, Captain West's attitude toward me was that of a social equal. But then, I was a passenger. Miss West treated me the same way, but unbent more to Mr. Pike. And Mr. Pike, answering her with "Yes, Miss," and "No, Miss," ate good-manneredly and with his shaggy-browed gray eyes studied me across the table. I, too, studied him. Despite his violent past, killer and driver that he was, I could not help liking the man. He was honest, genuine. Almost more than for that, I liked him for the spontaneous boyish laugh he gave on the occasions when I reached the points of several funny stories. No man could laugh like that and be all bad. I was glad that it was he, and not Mr. Mellaire, who was to sit opposite throughout the voyage. And I was very glad that Mr. Mellaire was not to eat with us at all.

I am afraid that Miss West and I did most of the talking. She was breezy, vivacious, tonic, and I noted again that the delicate, almost fragile oval of her face was given the lie by her body. She was a robust, healthy young woman. That was undeniable. Not fat—heaven forbid!—not even plump; yet her lines had that swelling roundness that accompanies long, live muscles. She was full-bodied, vigorous; and yet not so full-bodied as she seemed. I remember with what surprise, when we arose from table, I noted her slender waist. At that moment I got the impression that she was willowy. And willowy she was, with a normal waist and with, in addition, always that informing bodily vigour that made her appear rounder and robuster than she really was.

It was the health of her that interested me. When I studied her face more closely I saw that only the lines of the oval of it were delicate. Delicate it was not, nor fragile. The flesh was firm, and the texture of the skin was firm and fine as it moved over the firm muscles of face and neck. The neck was a beautiful and adequate pillar of white. Its flesh was firm, its skin fine, and it was muscular. The hands, too, attracted me—not small, but well-shaped, fine, white and strong, and well cared for. I could only conclude that she was an unusual captain's daughter, just as her father was an unusual captain and man. And their noses were alike, just the hint-touch of the beak of power and race.

While Miss West was telling of the unexpectedness of the voyage, of how suddenly she had decided to come—she accounted for it as a whim— and while she told of all the complications she had encountered in her haste of preparation, I found myself casting up a tally of the efficient ones on board the *Elsinore*. They were Captain West and his daughter, the two mates, myself, of course, Wada and the steward, and, beyond the shadow of a doubt, the cook. The dinner vouched for him. Thus I found our total of efficients to be eight. But the cook, the steward, and Wada were servants, not sailors, while Miss West and myself were supernumeraries. Remained to work, direct, do, but three efficients out of a total ship's company of forty-five. I had no doubt that other efficients there were; it seemed impossible that my first impression of the crew should be correct. There was the carpenter. He might, at his trade, be as good as the cook. Then the two sailmakers, whom I had not yet seen, might prove up.

A little later during the meal I ventured to talk about what had interested me and aroused my admiration, namely, the masterfulness with which Mr. Pike and Mr. Mellaire had gripped hold of that woeful, worthless crew. It was all new to me, I explained, but I appreciated the need of it. As I led up to the occurrence on Number Two hatch, when Mr. Pike had lifted up Larry and toppled him back with a mere slap from the ends of his fingers, I saw in Mr. Pike's eyes a warning, almost threatening, expression. Nevertheless, I completed my description of the episode.

When I had quite finished there was a silence. Miss West was busy serving coffee from a copper percolator. Mr. Pike, profoundly occupied with cracking walnuts, could not quite hide the wicked, little, half-humorous, half-revengeful gleam in his eyes. But Captain West looked straight at me, but from oh! such a distance—millions and millions of miles away. His clear blue eyes were as serene as ever, his tones as low and soft.

189

"It is the one rule I ask to be observed, Mr. Pathurst—we never discuss the sailors."

It was a facer to me, and with quite a pronounced fellow-feeling for Larry I hurriedly added:

"It was not merely the discipline that interested me. It was the feat of strength."

"Sailors are trouble enough without our hearing about them, Mr. Pathurst," Captain West went on, as evenly and imperturbably as if I had not spoken. "I leave the handling of the sailors to my officers. That's their business, and they are quite aware that I tolerate no undeserved roughness or severity."

Mr. Pike's harsh face carried the faintest shadow of an amused grin as he stolidly regarded the tablecloth. I glanced to Miss West for sympathy. She laughed frankly, and said:

"You see, father never has any sailors. And it's a good plan, too."

"A very good plan," Mr. Pike muttered.

Then Miss West kindly led the talk away from that subject, and soon had us laughing with a spirited recital of a recent encounter of hers with a Boston cab-driver.

Dinner over, I stepped to my room in quest of cigarettes, and incidentally asked Wada about the cook. Wada was always a great gatherer of information.

"His name Louis," he said. "He Chinaman, too. No; only half Chinaman. Other half Englishman. You know one island Napoleon he stop long time and bime by die that island?"

"St. Helena," I prompted.

"Yes, that place Louis he born. He talk very good English."

At this moment, entering the hall from the deck, Mr. Mellaire, just relieved by the mate, passed me on his way to the big room in the stern

190

where the second table was set. His "Good evening, sir," was as stately and courteous as any southern gentleman of the old days could have uttered it. And yet I could not like the man. His outward seeming was so at variance with the personality that resided within. Even as he spoke and smiled I felt that from inside his skull he was watching me, studying me. And somehow, in a flash of intuition, I knew not why, I was reminded of the three strange young men, routed last from the forecastle, to whom Mr. Pike had read the law. They, too, had given me a similar impression.

Behind Mr. Mellaire slouched a self-conscious, embarrassed individual, with the face of a stupid boy and the body of a giant. His feet were even larger than Mr. Pike's, but the hands—I shot a quick glance to see—were not so large as Mr. Pike's.

As they passed I looked inquiry to Wada.

"He carpenter. He sat second table. His name Sam Lavroff. He come from New York on ship. Steward say he very young for carpenter, maybe twenty-two, three years old."

As I approached the open port over my desk I again heard the swish and gurgle of water and again realized that we were under way. So steady and noiseless was our progress, that, say seated at table, it never entered one's head that we were moving or were anywhere save on the solid land. I had been used to steamers all my life, and it was difficult immediately to adjust myself to the absence of the propeller-thrust vibration.

"Well, what do you think?" I asked Wada, who, like myself, had never made a sailing-ship voyage.

He smiled politely.

"Very funny ship. Very funny sailors. I don't know. Mebbe all right. We see."

"You think trouble?" I asked pointedly.

"I think sailors very funny," he evaded.

191

CHAPTER VIII

Having lighted my cigarette, I strolled for'ard along the deck to where work was going on. Above my head dim shapes of canvas showed in the starlight. Sail was being made, and being made slowly, as I might judge, who was only the veriest tyro in such matters. The indistinguishable shapes of men, in long lines, pulled on ropes. They pulled in sick and dogged silence, though Mr. Pike, ubiquitous, snarled out orders and rapped out oaths from every angle upon their miserable heads.

Certainly, from what I had read, no ship of the old days ever proceeded so sadly and blunderingly to sea. Ere long Mr. Mellaire joined Mr. Pike in the struggle of directing the men. It was not yet eight in the evening, and all hands were at work. They did not seem to know the ropes. Time and again, when the half-hearted suggestions of the bosuns had been of no avail, I saw one or the other of the mates leap to the rail and put the right rope in the hands of the men.

These, on the deck, I concluded, were the hopeless ones. Up aloft, from sounds and cries, I knew were other men, undoubtedly those who were at least a little seaman-like, loosing the sails.

But on deck! Twenty or thirty of the poor devils, tailed on a rope that hoisted a yard, would pull without concerted effort and with painfully slow movements. "Walk away with it!" Mr. Pike would yell. And perhaps for two or three yards they would manage to walk with the rope ere they came to a halt like stalled horses on a hill. And yet, did either of the mates spring in and add his strength, they were able to move right along the deck without stopping. Either of the mates, old men that they were, was muscularly worth half-a-dozen of the wretched creatures.

"This is what sailin's come to," Mr. Pike paused to snort in my ear. "This ain't the place for an officer down here pulling and hauling. But what can you do when the bosuns are worse than the men?"

"I thought sailors sang songs when they pulled," I said.

"Sure they do. Want to hear 'em?"

I knew there was malice of some sort in his voice, but I answered that I'd like to very much.

"Here, you bosun!" Mr. Pike snarled. "Wake up! Start a song! Topsail halyards!"

In the pause that followed I could have sworn that Sundry Buyers was pressing his hands against his abdomen, while Nancy, infinite bleakness freezing upon his face, was wetting his lips to begin.

Nancy it was who began, for from no other man, I was confident, could have issued so sepulchral a plaint. It was unmusical, unbeautiful, unlively, and indescribably doleful. Yet the words showed that it should have ripped and crackled with high spirits and lawlessness, for the words poor Nancy sang were:

> "Away, way, way, yar,
>
> We'll kill Paddy Doyle for bus boots."

"Quit it! Quit it!" Mr. Pike roared. "This ain't a funeral! Ain't there one of you that can sing? Come on, now! It's a topsail-yard—"

He broke off to leap in to the pin-rail and get the wrong ropes out of the men's hands to put into them the right rope.

"Come on, bosun! Break her out!"

Then out of the gloom arose Sundry Buyers' voice, cracked and crazy and even more lugubrious than Nancy's:

> "Then up aloft that yard must go,

193

Whiskey for my Johnny."

The second line was supposed to be the chorus, but not more than two men feebly mumbled it. Sundry Buyers quavered the next line:

"Oh, whiskey killed my sister Sue."

Then Mr. Pike took a hand, seizing the hauling-part next to the pin and lifting his voice with a rare snap and devilishness:

"And whiskey killed the old man, too,

Whiskey for my Johnny."

He sang the devil-may-care lines on and on, lifting the crew to the work and to the chorused emphasis of "Whiskey for my Johnny."

And to his voice they pulled, they moved, they sang, and were alive, until he interrupted the song to cry "Belay!"

And then all the life and lilt went out of them, and they were again maundering and futile things, getting in one another's way, stumbling and shuffling through the darkness, hesitating to grasp ropes, and, when they did take hold, invariably taking hold of the wrong rope first. Skulkers there were among them, too; and once, from for'ard of the 'midship house, I heard smacks, and curses, and groans, and out of the darkness hurriedly emerged two men, on their heels Mr. Pike, who chanted a recital of the distressing things that would befall them if he caught them at such tricks again.

The whole thing was too depressing for me to care to watch further, so I strolled aft and climbed the poop. In the lee of the chart-house Captain West and the pilot were pacing slowly up and down. Passing on aft, I saw steering at the wheel the weazened little old man I had noted earlier in the day. In the light of the binnacle his small blue eyes looked more malevolent than ever. So weazened and tiny was he, and so large was the brass-studded wheel, that they seemed of a height. His face was withered, scorched, and wrinkled, and in all seeming he was fifty years older than Mr. Pike. He was the most remarkable figure of a burnt-out, aged man one would expect to find able seaman on one of the proudest sailing-ships afloat. Later, through Wada, I was to learn that his name was Andy Fay and that he claimed no more years than sixty-three.

I leaned against the rail in the lee of the wheel-house, and stared up at the lofty spars and myriad ropes that I could guess were there. No, I decided I was not keen on the voyage. The whole atmosphere of it was wrong. There were the cold hours I had waited on the pier-ends. There was Miss West coming along. There was the crew of broken men and lunatics. I wondered if the wounded Greek in the 'midship house still gibbered, and if Mr. Pike had yet sewed him up; and I was quite sure I would not care to witness such a transaction in surgery.

Even Wada, who had never been in a sailing-ship, had his doubts of the voyage. So had the steward, who had spent most of a life-time in sailing-ships. So far as Captain West was concerned, crews did not exist. And as for Miss West, she was so abominably robust that she could not be anything else than an optimist in such matters. She had always lived; her red blood sang to her only that she would always live and that nothing evil would ever happen to her glorious personality.

Oh, trust me, I knew the way of red blood. Such was my condition that the red-blood health of Miss West was virtually an affront to me—for I knew how unthinking and immoderate such blood could be. And for five months at least—there was Mr. Pike's offered wager of a pound of tobacco or a month's wages to that effect—I was to be pent on the same ship with her. As sure as cosmic sap was cosmic sap, just that sure was I that ere the voyage was over I should be pestered by her making love to me. Please do not mistake me. My certainty in this matter was due, not to any exalted sense of my own desirableness to women, but to my anything but exalted concept of women as instinctive huntresses of men. In my experience women hunted men with quite the same blind tropism that marks the pursuit of the sun by the sunflower, the pursuit of attachable surfaces by the tendrils of the grapevine.

Call me blasé—I do not mind, if by blasé is meant the world-weariness, intellectual, artistic, sensational, which can come to a young man of thirty. For I was thirty, and I was weary of all these things—weary and in doubt. It was because of this state that I was undertaking the voyage. I wanted to get away by myself, to get away from all these things, and, with proper perspective, mull the matter over.

It sometimes seemed to me that the culmination of this world-sickness had been brought about by the success of my play—my first play, as every one knows. But it had been such a success that it raised the doubt in my own mind, just as the success of my several volumes of verse had raised doubts. Was the public right? Were the critics right? Surely the function of the artist was to voice life, yet what did I know of life?

So you begin to glimpse what I mean by the world-sickness that afflicted me. Really, I had been, and was, very sick. Mad thoughts of isolating myself entirely from the world had hounded me. I had even canvassed the idea of going to Molokai and devoting the rest of my years to the lepers—I, who was thirty years old, and healthy and strong, who had no particular tragedy, who had a bigger income than I knew how to spend, who by my own achievement had put my name on the lips of men and proved myself a power to be reckoned with—I was that mad that I had considered the lazar house for a destiny.

Perhaps it will be suggested that success had turned my head. Very well. Granted. But the turned head remains a fact, an incontrovertible fact—my sickness, if you will, and a real sickness, and a fact. This I knew: I had reached an intellectual and artistic climacteric, a life-climacteric of some sort. And I had diagnosed my own case and prescribed this voyage. And here was the atrociously healthy and profoundly feminine Miss West along—the very last ingredient I would have considered introducing into my prescription.

A woman! Woman! Heaven knows I had been sufficiently tormented by their persecutions to know them. I leave it to you: thirty years of age, not entirely unhandsome, an intellectual and artistic place in the world, and an income most dazzling—why shouldn't women pursue me? They would have pursued me had I been a hunchback, for the sake of my artistic place alone, for the sake of my income alone.

Yes; and love! Did I not know love—lyric, passionate, mad, romantic love? That, too, was of old time with me. I, too, had throbbed and sung and sobbed and sighed—yes, and known grief, and buried my dead. But it was so long ago. How young I was—turned twenty-four! And after that I had learned the bitter lesson that even deathless grief may die; and I had laughed again and done my share of philandering with the pretty, ferocious moths that fluttered around the light of my fortune and artistry; and after that, in turn, I had retired disgusted from the lists of woman, and gone on long lance-breaking adventures in the realm of mind. And here I was, on board the *Elsinore*, unhorsed by my encounters with the problems of the ultimate, carried off the field with a broken pate.

As I leaned against the rail, dismissing premonitions of disaster, I could not help thinking of Miss West below, bustling and humming as she made her little nest. And from her my thought drifted on to the everlasting mystery of woman. Yes, I, with all the futuristic contempt for woman, am ever caught up afresh by the mystery of woman.

Oh, no illusions, thank you. Woman, the love-seeker, obsessing and possessing, fragile and fierce, soft and venomous, prouder than Lucifer and as prideless, holds a perpetual, almost morbid, attraction for the thinker. What is this flame of her, blazing through all her contradictions and ignobilities?— this ruthless passion for life, always for life, more life on the planet? At times it seems to me brazen, and awful, and soulless. At times I am made petulant by it. And at other times I am swayed by the sublimity of it. No; there is no escape from woman. Always, as a savage returns to a dark glen where goblins are and gods may be, so do I return to the contemplation of woman.

Mr. Pike's voice interrupted my musings. From for'ard, on the main deck, I heard him snarl:

"On the main-topsail-yard, there!—if you cut that gasket I'll split your damned skull!"

197

Again he called, with a marked change of voice, and the Henry he called to I concluded was the training-ship boy.

"You, Henry, main-skysail-yard, there!" he cried. "Don't make those gaskets up! Fetch 'em in along the yard and make fast to the tye!"

Thus routed from my reverie, I decided to go below to bed. As my hand went out to the knob of the chart-house door again the mate's voice rang out:

"Come on, you gentlemen's sons in disguise! Wake up! Lively now!"

CHAPTER IX

I did not sleep well. To begin with, I read late. Not till two in the morning did I reach up and turn out the kerosene reading-lamp which Wada had purchased and installed for me. I was asleep immediately—perfect sleep being perhaps my greatest gift; but almost immediately I was awake again. And thereafter, with dozings and cat-naps and restless tossings, I struggled to win to sleep, then gave it up. For of all things, in my state of jangled nerves, to be afflicted with hives! And still again, to be afflicted with hives in cold winter weather!

At four I lighted up and went to reading, forgetting my irritated skin in Vernon Lee's delightful screed against William James, and his "will to believe." I was on the weather side of the ship, and from overhead, through the deck, came the steady footfalls of some officer on watch. I knew that they were not the steps of Mr. Pike, and wondered whether they were Mr. Mellaire's or the pilot's. Somebody above there was awake. The work was going on, the vigilant seeing and overseeing, that, I could plainly conclude, would go on through every hour of all the hours on the voyage.

At half-past four I heard the steward's alarm go off, instantly suppressed, and five minutes later I lifted my hand to motion him in through my open door. What I desired was a cup of coffee, and Wada had been with me through too many years for me to doubt that he had given the steward precise instructions and turned over to him my coffee and my coffee-making apparatus.

The steward was a jewel. In ten minutes he served me with a perfect cup of coffee. I read on until daylight, and half-past eight found me, breakfast in bed finished, dressed and shaved, and on deck. We were still towing, but all sails were set to a light favouring breeze from the north. In the chart-room Captain West and the pilot were smoking cigars. At the wheel I noted what I decided at once was an efficient. He was not a large man; if anything he was undersized. But his countenance was broad-browed and intelligently formed. Tom, I later learned, was his name—Tom Spink, an Englishman. He was blue-eyed, fair-skinned, well-grizzled, and, to the eye, a hale fifty years of age. His reply of "Good morning, sir" was cheery, and he smiled as he uttered the simple phrase. He did not look sailor-like, as did Henry, the training-ship boy; and yet I felt at once that he was a sailor, and an able one.

It was Mr. Pike's watch, and on asking him about Tom he grudgingly admitted that the man was the "best of the boiling."

Miss West emerged from the chart-house, with a rosy morning face and her vital, springy limb-movement, and immediately began establishing her contacts. On asking how I had slept, and when I said wretchedly, she demanded an explanation. I told her of my affliction of hives and showed her the lumps on my wrists.

"Your blood needs thinning and cooling," she adjudged promptly. "Wait a minute. I'll see what can be done for you."

And with that she was away and below and back in a trice, in her hand a part glass of water into which she stirred a teaspoonful of cream of tartar.

"Drink it," she ordered, as a matter of course.

I drank it. And at eleven in the morning she came up to my deck-chair with a second dose of the stuff. Also she reproached me soundly for permitting Wada to feed meat to Possum. It was from her that Wada and I learned how mortal a sin it was to give meat to a young puppy. Furthermore, she laid down the law and the diet for Possum, not alone to me and Wada, but to the steward, the carpenter, and Mr. Mellaire. Of the latter two, because they ate by themselves in the big after-room and because Possum played there, she was especially suspicious; and she was outspoken in voicing her suspicions to their faces. The carpenter mumbled embarrassed asseverations in broken English of past, present, and future innocence, the while he humbly scraped and shuffled before her on his huge feet. Mr. Mellaire's protestations were of the same nature, save that they were made with the grace and suavity of a Chesterfield.

In short, Possum's diet raised quite a tempest in the *Elsinore* teapot, and by the time it was over Miss West had established this particular contact with me and given me a feeling that we were the mutual owners of the puppy. I noticed, later in the day, that it was to Miss West that Wada went for instructions as to the quantity of warm water he must use to dilute Possum's condensed milk.

Lunch won my continued approbation of the cook. In the afternoon I made a trip for'ard to the galley to make his acquaintance. To all intents he was a Chinese, until he spoke, whereupon, measured by speech alone, he was an Englishman. In fact, so cultured was his speech that I can fairly say it was vested with an Oxford accent. He, too, was old, fully sixty—he acknowledged fifty-nine. Three things about him were markedly conspicuous: his smile, that embraced all of his clean-shaven Asiatic face and Asiatic eyes; his even-rowed, white, and perfect teeth, which I deemed false until Wada ascertained otherwise for me; and his hands and feet. It was his hands, ridiculously small and beautifully modelled, that led my scrutiny to his feet. They, too, were ridiculously small and very neatly, almost dandifiedly, shod.

We had put the pilot off at midday, but the *Britannia* towed us well into the afternoon and did not cast us off until the ocean was wide about us and the land a faint blur on the western horizon. Here, at the moment of leaving the tug, we made our "departure"—that is to say, technically began the voyage, despite the fact that we had already travelled a full twenty-four hours away from Baltimore.

It was about the time of casting off, when I was leaning on the poop-rail gazing for'ard, when Miss West joined me. She had been busy below all day, and had just come up, as she put it, for a breath of air. She surveyed the sky in weather-wise fashion for a full five minutes, then remarked:

"The barometer's very high—30 degrees 60. This light north wind won't last. It will either go into a calm or work around into a north-east gale."

"Which would you prefer?" I asked.

"The gale, by all means. It will help us off the land, and it will put me through my torment of sea-sickness more quickly. Oh, yes," she added, "I'm a good sailor, but I do suffer dreadfully at the beginning of every voyage. You probably won't see me for a couple of days now. That's why I've been so busy getting settled first."

"Lord Nelson, I have read, never got over his squeamishness at sea," I said.

"And I've seen father sea-sick on occasion," she answered. "Yes, and some of the strongest, hardest sailors I have ever known."

Mr. Pike here joined us for a moment, ceasing from his everlasting pacing up and down to lean with us on the poop-rail.

Many of the crew were in evidence, pulling on ropes on the main deck below us. To my inexperienced eye they appeared more unprepossessing than ever.

"A pretty scraggly crew, Mr. Pike," Miss West remarked.

"The worst ever," he growled, "and I've seen some pretty bad ones. We're teachin' them the ropes just now—most of 'em."

"They look starved," I commented.

"They are, they almost always are," Miss West answered, and her eyes roved over them in the same appraising, cattle-buyer's fashion I had marked in Mr. Pike. "But they'll fatten up with regular hours, no whiskey, and solid food—won't they, Mr. Pike?"

"Oh, sure. They always do. And you'll see them liven up when we get 'em in hand . . . maybe. They're a measly lot, though."

I looked aloft at the vast towers of canvas. Our four masts seemed to have flowered into all the sails possible, yet the sailors beneath us, under Mr. Mellaire's direction, were setting triangular sails, like jibs, between the masts, and there were so many that they overlapped one another. The slowness and clumsiness with which the men handled these small sails led me to ask:

"But what would you do, Mr. Pike, with a green crew like this, if you were caught right now in a storm with all this canvas spread?"

He shrugged his shoulders, as if I had asked what he would do in an earthquake with two rows of New York skyscrapers falling on his head from both sides of a street.

"Do?" Miss West answered for him. "We'd get the sail off. Oh, it can be done, Mr. Pathurst, with any kind of a crew. If it couldn't, I should have been drowned long ago."

"Sure," Mr. Pike upheld her. "So would I."

"The officers can perform miracles with the most worthless sailors, in a pinch," Miss West went on.

Again Mr. Pike nodded his head and agreed, and I noted his two big paws, relaxed the moment before and drooping over the rail, quite unconsciously tensed and folded themselves into fists. Also, I noted fresh abrasions on the knuckles. Miss West laughed heartily, as from some recollection.

"I remember one time when we sailed from San Francisco with a most hopeless crew. It was in the *Lallah Rookh*—you remember her, Mr. Pike?"

"Your father's fifth command," he nodded. "Lost on the West Coast afterwards—went ashore in that big earthquake and tidal wave. Parted her anchors, and when she hit under the cliff, the cliff fell on her."

"That's the ship. Well, our crew seemed mostly cow-boys, and bricklayers, and tramps, and more tramps than anything else. Where the boarding-house masters got them was beyond imagining. A number of them were shanghaied, that was certain. You should have seen them when they were first sent aloft." Again she laughed. "It was better than circus clowns.

And scarcely had the tug cast us off, outside the Heads, when it began to blow up and we began to shorten down. And then our mates performed miracles. You remember Mr. Harding—Silas Harding?"

"Don't I though!" Mr. Pike proclaimed enthusiastically. "He was some man, and he must have been an old man even then."

"He was, and a terrible man," she concurred, and added, almost reverently: "And a wonderful man." She turned her face to me. "He was our mate. The men were sea-sick and miserable and green. But Mr. Harding got the sail off the *Lallah Rookh* just the same. What I wanted to tell you was this:

"I was on the poop, just like I am now, and Mr. Harding had a lot of those miserable sick men putting gaskets on the main-lower-topsail. How far would that be above the deck, Mr. Pike?"

"Let me see . . . the *Lallah Rookh*." Mr. Pike paused to consider. "Oh, say around a hundred feet."

"I saw it myself. One of the green hands, a tramp—and he must already have got a taste of Mr. Harding—fell off the lower-topsail-yard. I was only a little girl, but it looked like certain death, for he was falling from the weather side of the yard straight down on deck. But he fell into the belly of the mainsail, breaking his fall, turned a somersault, and landed on his feet on deck and unhurt. And he landed right alongside of Mr. Harding, facing him. I don't know which was the more astonished, but I think Mr. Harding was, for he stood there petrified. He had expected the man to be killed. Not so the man. He took one look at Mr. Harding, then made a wild jump for the rigging and climbed right back up to that topsail-yard."

Miss West and the mate laughed so heartily that they scarcely heard me say:

"Astonishing! Think of the jar to the man's nerves, falling to apparent death that way."

"He'd been jarred harder by Silas Harding, I guess," was Mr. Pike's remark, with another burst of laughter, in which Miss West joined.

Which was all very well in a way. Ships were ships, and judging by what I had seen of our present crew harsh treatment was necessary. But that a young woman of the niceness of Miss West should know of such things and be so saturated in this side of ship life was not nice. It was not nice for me, though it interested me, I confess,—and strengthened my grip on reality. Yet it meant a hardening of one's fibres, and I did not like to think of Miss West being so hardened.

I looked at her and could not help marking again the fineness and firmness of her skin. Her hair was dark, as were her eyebrows, which were almost straight and rather low over her long eyes. Gray her eyes were, a warm gray, and very steady and direct in expression, intelligent and alive. Perhaps, taking her face as a whole, the most noteworthy expression of it was a great calm. She seemed always in repose, at peace with herself and with the external world. The most beautiful feature was her eyes, framed in lashes as dark as her brows and hair. The most admirable feature was her nose, quite straight, very straight, and just the slightest trifle too long. In this it was reminiscent of her father's nose. But the perfect modelling of the bridge and nostrils conveyed an indescribable advertisement of race and blood.

Hers was a slender-lipped, sensitive, sensible, and generous mouth—generous, not so much in size, which was quite average, but generous rather in tolerance, in power, and in laughter. All the health and buoyancy of her was in her mouth, as well as in her eyes. She rarely exposed her teeth in smiling, for which purpose she seemed chiefly to employ her eyes; but when she laughed she showed strong white teeth, even, not babyish in their smallness, but just the firm, sensible, normal size one would expect in a woman as healthy and normal as she.

I would never have called her beautiful, and yet she possessed many of the factors that go to compose feminine beauty. She had all the beauty of colouring, a white skin that was healthy white and that was emphasized by the darkness of her lashes, brows, and hair. And, in the same way, the darkness of lashes and brows and the whiteness of skin set off the warm gray of her eyes. The forehead was, well, medium-broad and medium high, and quite smooth.

No lines nor hints of lines were there, suggestive of nervousness, of blue days of depression and white nights of insomnia. Oh, she bore all the marks of the healthy, human female, who never worried nor was vexed in the spirit of her, and in whose body every process and function was frictionless and automatic.

"Miss West has posed to me as quite a weather prophet," I said to the mate. "Now what is your forecast of our coming weather?"

"She ought to be," was Mr. Pike's reply as he lifted his glance across the smooth swell of sea to the sky. "This ain't the first time she's been on the North Atlantic in winter." He debated a moment, as he studied the sea and sky. "I should say, considering the high barometer, we ought to get a mild gale from the north-east or a calm, with the chances in favour of the calm."

She favoured me with a triumphant smile, and suddenly clutched the rail as the *Elsinore* lifted on an unusually large swell and sank into the trough with a roll from windward that flapped all the sails in hollow thunder.

"The calm has it," Miss West said, with just a hint of grimness. "And if this keeps up I'll be in my bunk in about five minutes."

She waved aside all sympathy. "Oh, don't bother about me, Mr. Pathurst. Sea-sickness is only detestable and horrid, like sleet, and muddy weather, and poison ivy; besides, I'd rather be sea-sick than have the hives."

Something went wrong with the men below us on the deck, some stupidity or blunder that was made aware to us by Mr. Mellaire's raised voice. Like Mr. Pike, he had a way of snarling at the sailors that was distinctly unpleasant to the ear.

On the faces of several of the sailors bruises were in evidence. One, in particular, had an eye so swollen that it was closed.

"Looks as if he had run against a stanchion in the dark," I observed.

Most eloquent, and most unconscious, was the quick flash of Miss West's eyes to Mr. Pike's big paws, with freshly abraded knuckles, resting on the rail. It was a stab of hurt to me. *She knew.*

CHAPTER X

That evening the three men of us had dinner alone, with racks on the table, while the *Elsinore* rolled in the calm that had sent Miss West to her room.

"You won't see her for a couple of days," Captain West told me. "Her mother was the same way—a born sailor, but always sick at the outset of a voyage."

"It's the shaking down." Mr. Pike astonished me with the longest observation I had yet heard him utter at table. "Everybody has to shake down when they leave the land. We've got to forget the good times on shore, and the good things money'll buy, and start watch and watch, four hours on deck and four below. And it comes hard, and all our tempers are strung until we can make the change. Did it happen that you heard Caruso and Blanche Arral this winter in New York, Mr. Pathurst?"

I nodded, still marvelling over this spate of speech at table.

"Well, think of hearing them, and Homer, and Witherspoon, and Amato, every night for nights and nights at the Metropolitan; and then to give it the go-by, and get to sea and shake down to watch and watch."

"You don't like the sea?" I queried.

He sighed.

"I don't know. But of course the sea is all I know—"

"Except music," I threw in.

"Yes, but the sea and all the long-voyaging has cheated me out of most of the music I oughta have had coming to me."

"I suppose you've heard Schumann Heink?"

"Wonderful, wonderful!" he murmured fervently, then regarded me with an eager wistfulness. "I've half-a-dozen of her records, and I've got the second dog-watch below. If Captain West don't mind . . . " (Captain West nodded that he didn't mind). "And if you'd want to hear them? The machine is a good one."

And then, to my amazement, when the steward had cleared the table, this hoary old relic of man-killing and man-driving days, battered waif of the sea that he was, carried in from his room a most splendid collection of phonograph records. These, and the machine, he placed on the table. The big doors were opened, making the dining-room and the main cabin into one large room. It was in the cabin that Captain West and I lolled in big leather chairs while Mr. Pike ran the phonograph. His face was in a blaze of light from the swinging lamps, and every shade of expression was visible to me.

In vain I waited for him to start some popular song. His records were only of the best, and the care he took of them was a revelation. He handled each one reverently, as a sacred thing, untying and unwrapping it and brushing it with a fine camel's hair brush while it revolved and ere he placed the needle on it. For a time all I could see was the huge brute hands of a brute-driver, with skin off the knuckles, that expressed love in their every movement. Each touch on the discs was a caress, and while the record played he hovered over it and dreamed in some heaven of music all his own.

During this time Captain West lay back and smoked a cigar. His face was expressionless, and he seemed very far away, untouched by the music. I almost doubted that he heard it. He made no remarks between whiles, betrayed no sign of approbation or displeasure. He seemed preternaturally serene, preternaturally remote. And while I watched him I wondered what his duties were. I had not seen him perform any. Mr. Pike had attended to the loading of the ship. Not until she was ready for sea had Captain West come on board. I had not seen him give an order. It looked to me that Mr. Pike and Mr. Mellaire did the work. All Captain West did was to smoke cigars and keep blissfully oblivious of the *Elsinore's* crew.

When Mr. Pike had played the "Hallelujah Chorus" from the *Messiah*, and "He Shall Feed His Flock," he mentioned to me, almost apologetically, that he liked sacred music, and for the reason, perhaps, that for a short period, a child ashore in San Francisco, he had been a choir boy.

"And then I hit the dominie over the head with a baseball bat and sneaked off to sea again," he concluded with a harsh laugh.

And thereat he fell to dreaming while he played Meyerbeer's "King of Heaven," and Mendelssohn's "O Rest in the Lord."

When one bell struck, at quarter to eight, he carried his music, all carefully wrapped, back into his room. I lingered with him while he rolled a cigarette ere eight bells struck.

"I've got a lot more good things," he said confidentially: "Coenen's 'Come Unto Me,' and Faure's 'Crucifix'; and there's 'O Salutaris,' and 'Lead, Kindly Light' by the Trinity Choir; and 'Jesu, Lover of My Soul' would just melt your heart. I'll play 'em for you some night."

"Do you believe in them?" I was led to ask by his rapt expression and by the picture of his brute-driving hands which I could not shake from my consciousness.

He hesitated perceptibly, then replied:

"I do . . . when I'm listening to them."

* * * * *

My sleep that night was wretched. Short of sleep from the previous night, I closed my book and turned my light off early. But scarcely had I dropped into slumber when I was aroused by the recrudescence of my hives. All day they had not bothered me; yet the instant I put out the light and slept, the damnable persistent itching set up. Wada had not yet gone to bed, and from him I got more cream of tartar. It was useless, however, and at midnight, when I heard the watch changing, I partially dressed, slipped into my dressing-gown, and went up on to the poop.

I saw Mr. Mellaire beginning his four hours' watch, pacing up and down the port side of the poop; and I slipped away aft, past the man at the wheel, whom I did not recognize, and took refuge in the lee of the wheel-house.

Once again I studied the dim loom and tracery of intricate rigging and lofty, sail-carrying spars, thought of the mad, imbecile crew, and experienced premonitions of disaster. How could such a voyage be possible, with such a crew, on the huge *Elsinore*, a cargo-carrier that was only a steel shell half an inch thick burdened with five thousand tons of coal? It was appalling to contemplate. The voyage had gone wrong from the first. In the wretched unbalance that loss of sleep brings to any good sleeper, I could decide only that the voyage was doomed. Yet how doomed it was, in truth, neither I nor a madman could have dreamed.

I thought of the red-blooded Miss West, who had always lived and had no doubts but what she would always live. I thought of the killing and driving and music-loving Mr. Pike. Many a haler remnant than he had gone down on a last voyage. As for Captain West, he did not count. He was too neutral a being, too far away, a sort of favoured passenger who had nothing to do but serenely and passively exist in some Nirvana of his own creating.

Next I remembered the self-wounded Greek, sewed up by Mr. Pike and lying gibbering between the steel walls of the 'midship-house. This picture almost decided me, for in my fevered imagination he typified the whole mad, helpless, idiotic crew. Certainly I could go back to Baltimore. Thank God I had the money to humour my whims. Had not Mr. Pike told me, in reply to a question, that he estimated the running expenses of the *Elsinore* at two hundred dollars a day? I could afford to pay two hundred a day, or two thousand, for the several days that might be necessary to get me back to the land, to a pilot tug, or any inbound craft to Baltimore.

I was quite wholly of a mind to go down and rout out Captain West to tell him my decision, when another presented itself: *Then are you, the thinker and philosopher, the world-sick one, afraid to go down, to cease in the darkness?* Bah! My own pride in my life-pridelessness saved Captain West's sleep from interruption. Of course I would go on with the adventure, if adventure it

209

might be called, to go sailing around Cape Horn with a shipload of fools and lunatics—and worse; for I remembered the three Babylonish and Semitic ones who had aroused Mr. Pike's ire and who had laughed so terribly and silently.

Night thoughts! Sleepless thoughts! I dismissed them all and started below, chilled through by the cold. But at the chart-room door I encountered Mr. Mellaire.

"A pleasant evening, sir," he greeted me. "A pity there's not a little wind to help us off the land."

"What do you think of the crew?" I asked, after a moment or so.

Mr. Mellaire shrugged his shoulders.

"I've seen many queer crews in my time, Mr. Pathurst. But I never saw one as queer as this—boys, old men, cripples and—you saw Tony the Greek go overboard yesterday? Well, that's only the beginning. He's a sample. I've got a big Irishman in my watch who's going bad. Did you notice a little, dried-up Scotchman?"

"Who looks mean and angry all the time, and who was steering the evening before last?"

"The very one—Andy Fay. Well, Andy Fay's just been complaining to me about O'Sullivan. Says O'Sullivan's threatened his life. When Andy Fay went off watch at eight he found O'Sullivan stropping a razor. I'll give you the conversation as Andy gave it to me:

"'Says O'Sullivan to me, "Mr. Fay, I'll have a word wid yeh?" "Certainly," says I; "what can I do for you?" "Sell me your sea-boots, Mr. Fay," says O'Sullivan, polite as can be. "But what will you be wantin' of them?" says I. "'Twill be a great favour," says O'Sullivan. "But it's my only pair," says I; "and you have a pair of your own," says I. "Mr. Fay, I'll be needin' me own in bad weather," says O'Sullivan. "Besides," says I, "you have no money." "I'll pay for them when we pay off in Seattle," says O'Sullivan. "I'll not do it," says I; "besides, you're not tellin' me what you'll be doin' with them." "But I will

210

tell yeh," says O'Sullivan; "I'm wantin' to throw 'em over the side." And with that I turns to walk away, but O'Sullivan says, very polite and seducin'-like, still a-stroppin' the razor, "Mr. Fay," says he, "will you kindly step this way an' have your throat cut?" And with that I knew my life was in danger, and I have come to make report to you, sir, that the man is a violent lunatic.'

"Or soon will be," I remarked. "I noticed him yesterday, a big man muttering continually to himself?"

"That's the man," Mr. Mellaire said.

"Do you have many such at sea?" I asked.

"More than my share, I do believe, sir."

He was lighting a cigarette at the moment, and with a quick movement he pulled off his cap, bent his head forward, and held up the blazing match that I might see.

I saw a grizzled head, the full crown of which was not entirely bald, but partially covered with a few sparse long hairs. And full across this crown, disappearing in the thicker fringe above the ears, ran the most prodigious scar I had ever seen. Because the vision of it was so fleeting, ere the match blew out, and because of the scar's very prodigiousness, I may possibly exaggerate, but I could have sworn that I could lay two fingers deep into the horrid cleft and that it was fully two fingers broad. There seemed no bone at all, just a great fissure, a deep valley covered with skin; and I was confident that the brain pulsed immediately under that skin.

He pulled his cap on and laughed in an amused, reassuring way.

"A crazy sea cook did that, Mr. Pathurst, with a meat-axe. We were thousands of miles from anywhere, in the South Indian Ocean at the time, running our Easting down, but the cook got the idea into his addled head that we were lying in Boston Harbour, and that I wouldn't let him go ashore. I had my back to him at the time, and I never knew what struck me."

"But how could you recover from so fearful an injury?" I questioned. "There must have been a splendid surgeon on board, and you must have had wonderful vitality."

He shook his head.

"It must have been the vitality . . . and the molasses."

"Molasses!"

"Yes; the captain had old-fashioned prejudices against antiseptics. He always used molasses for fresh wound-dressings. I lay in my bunk many weary weeks—we had a long passage—and by the time we reached Hong Kong the thing was healed, there was no need for a shore surgeon, and I was standing my third mate's watch—we carried third mates in those days."

Not for many a long day was I to realize the dire part that scar in Mr. Mellaire's head was to play in his destiny and in the destiny of the *Elsinore*. Had I known at the time, Captain West would have received the most unusual awakening from sleep that he ever experienced; for he would have been routed out by a very determined, partially-dressed passenger with a proposition capable of going to the extent of buying the *Elsinore* outright with all her cargo, so that she might be sailed straight back to Baltimore.

As it was, I merely thought it a very marvellous thing that Mr. Mellaire should have lived so many years with such a hole in his head.

We talked on, and he gave me many details of that particular happening, and of other happenings at sea on the part of the lunatics that seem to infest the sea.

And yet I could not like the man. In nothing he said, nor in the manner of saying things, could I find fault. He seemed generous, broad-minded, and, for a sailor, very much of a man of the world. It was easy for me to overlook his excessive suavity of speech and super-courtesy of social mannerism. It was not that. But all the time I was distressingly, and, I suppose, intuitively aware, though in the darkness I couldn't even see his eyes, that there, behind those eyes, inside that skull, was ambuscaded an alien personality that spied upon me, measured me, studied me, and that said one thing while it thought another thing.

When I said good night and went below it was with the feeling that I had been talking with the one half of some sort of a dual creature. The other half had not spoken. Yet I sensed it there, fluttering and quick, behind the mask of words and flesh.

CHAPTER XI

But I could not sleep. I took more cream of tartar. It must be the heat of the bed-clothes, I decided, that excited my hives. And yet, whenever I ceased struggling for sleep, and lighted the lamp and read, my skin irritation decreased. But as soon as I turned out the lamp and closed my eyes I was troubled again. So hour after hour passed, through which, between vain attempts to sleep, I managed to wade through many pages of Rosny's *Le Termite*—a not very cheerful proceeding, I must say, concerned as it is with the microscopic and over-elaborate recital of Noël Servaise's tortured nerves, bodily pains, and intellectual phantasma. At last I tossed the novel aside, damned all analytical Frenchmen, and found some measure of relief in the more genial and cynical Stendhal.

Over my head I could hear Mr. Mellaire steadily pace up and down. At four the watches changed, and I recognized the age-lag in Mr. Pike's promenade. Half an hour later, just as the steward's alarm went off, instantly checked by that light-sleeping Asiatic, the *Elsinore* began to heel over on my side. I could hear Mr. Pike barking and snarling orders, and at times a trample and shuffle of many feet passed over my head as the weird crew pulled and hauled. The *Elsinore* continued to heel over until I could see the water against my port, and then she gathered way and dashed ahead at such a rate that I could hear the stinging and singing of the foam through the circle of thick glass beside me.

The steward brought me coffee, and I read till daylight and after, when Wada served me breakfast and helped me dress. He, too, complained of inability to sleep. He had been bunked with Nancy in one of the rooms in the 'midship-house. Wada described the situation. The tiny room, made of steel, was air-tight when the steel door was closed. And Nancy insisted on keeping the door closed. As a result Wada, in the upper bunk, had stifled. He told me that the air had got so bad that the flame of the lamp, no matter how high it was turned, guttered down and all but refused to burn. Nancy snored beautifully through it all, while he had been unable to close his eyes.

"He is not clean," quoth Wada. "He is a pig. No more will I sleep in that place."

On the poop I found the *Elsinore*, with many of her sails furled, slashing along through a troubled sea under an overcast sky. Also I found Mr. Mellaire marching up and down, just as I had left him hours before, and it took quite a distinct effort for me to realize that he had had the watch off between four and eight. Even then, he told me, he had slept from four until half-past seven.

"That is one thing, Mr. Pathurst, I always sleep like a baby . . . which means a good conscience, sir, yes, a good conscience."

And while he enunciated the platitude I was uncomfortably aware that that alien thing inside his skull was watching me, studying me.

In the cabin Captain West smoked a cigar and read the Bible. Miss West did not appear, and I was grateful that to my sleeplessness the curse of sea-sickness had not been added.

Without asking permission of anybody, Wada arranged a sleeping place for himself in a far corner of the big after-room, screening the corner with a solidly lashed wall of my trunks and empty book boxes.

It was a dreary enough day, no sun, with occasional splatters of rain and a persistent crash of seas over the weather rail and swash of water across the deck. With my eyes glued to the cabin ports, which gave for'ard along the main deck, I could see the wretched sailors, whenever they were given some task of pull and haul, wet through and through by the boarding seas. Several times I saw some of them taken off their feet and rolled about in the creaming foam. And yet, erect, unstaggering, with certitude of weight and strength, among these rolled men, these clutching, cowering ones, moved either Mr.

Pike or Mr. Mellaire. They were never taken off their feet. They never shrank away from a splash of spray or heavier bulk of down-falling water. They had fed on different food, were informed with a different spirit, were of iron in contrast with the poor miserables they drove to their bidding.

In the afternoon I dozed for half-an-hour in one of the big chairs in the cabin. Had it not been for the violent motion of the ship I could have slept there for hours, for the hives did not trouble. Captain West, stretched out on the cabin sofa, his feet in carpet slippers, slept enviably. By some instinct, I might say, in the deep of sleep, he kept his place and was not rolled off upon the floor. Also, he lightly held a half-smoked cigar in one hand. I watched him for an hour, and knew him to be asleep, and marvelled that he maintained his easy posture and did not drop the cigar.

After dinner there was no phonograph. The second dog-watch was Mr. Pike's on deck. Besides, as he explained, the rolling was too severe. It would make the needle jump and scratch his beloved records.

And no sleep! Another weary night of torment, and another dreary, overcast day and leaden, troubled sea. And no Miss West. Wada, too, is sea-sick, although heroically he kept his feet and tried to tend on me with glassy, unseeing eyes. I sent him to his bunk, and read through the endless hours until my eyes were tired, and my brain, between lack of sleep and over-use, was fuzzy.

Captain West is no conversationalist. The more I see of him the more I am baffled. I have not yet found a reason for that first impression I received of him. He has all the poise and air of a remote and superior being, and yet I wonder if it be not poise and air and nothing else. Just as I had expected, that first meeting, ere he spoke a word, to hear fall from his lips words of untold beneficence and wisdom, and then heard him utter mere social commonplaces, so I now find myself almost forced to conclude that his touch of race, and beak of power, and all the tall, aristocratic slenderness of him have nothing behind them.

And yet, on the other hand, I can find no reason for rejecting that first impression. He has not shown any strength, but by the same token he has not shown any weakness. Sometimes I wonder what resides behind those clear blue eyes. Certainly I have failed to find any intellectual backing. I tried him out with William James' *Varieties of Religious Experience*. He glanced at a few pages, then returned it to me with the frank statement that it did not interest him. He has no books of his own. Evidently he is not a reader. Then what is he? I dared to feel him out on politics. He listened courteously, said sometimes yes and sometimes no, and, when I ceased from very discouragement, said nothing.

Aloof as the two officers are from the men, Captain West is still more aloof from his officers. I have not seen him address a further word to Mr. Mellaire than "Good morning" on the poop. As for Mr. Pike, who eats three times a day with him, scarcely any more conversation obtains between them. And I am surprised by what seems the very conspicuous awe with which Mr. Pike seems to regard his commander.

Another thing. What are Captain West's duties? So far he has done nothing, save eat three times a day, smoke many cigars, and each day stroll a total of one mile around the poop. The mates do all the work, and hard work it is, four hours on deck and four below, day and night with never a variation. I watch Captain West and am amazed. He will loll back in the cabin and stare straight before him for hours at a time, until I am almost frantic to demand of him what are his thoughts. Sometimes I doubt that he is thinking at all. I give him up. I cannot fathom him.

Altogether a depressing day of rain-splatter and wash of water across the deck. I can see, now, that the problem of sailing a ship with five thousand tons of coal around the Horn is more serious than I had thought. So deep is the *Elsinore* in the water that she is like a log awash. Her tall, six-foot bulwarks of steel cannot keep the seas from boarding her. She has not the buoyancy one is accustomed to ascribe to ships. On the contrary, she is weighted down until she is dead, so that, for this one day alone, I am appalled at the thought of how many thousands of tons of the North Atlantic have boarded her and poured out through her spouting scuppers and clanging ports.

Yes, a depressing day. The two mates have alternated on deck and in their bunks. Captain West has dozed on the cabin sofa or read the Bible. Miss West is still sea-sick. I have tired myself out with reading, and the fuzziness of my unsleeping brain makes for melancholy. Even Wada is anything but a cheering spectacle, crawling out of his bunk, as he does at stated intervals, and with sick, glassy eyes trying to discern what my needs may be. I almost wish I could get sea-sick myself. I had never dreamed that a sea voyage could be so unenlivening as this one is proving.

CHAPTER XII

Another morning of overcast sky and leaden sea, and of the *Elsinore*, under half her canvas, clanging her deck ports, spouting water from her scuppers, and dashing eastward into the heart of the Atlantic. And I have failed to sleep half-an-hour all told. At this rate, in a very short time I shall have consumed all the cream of tartar on the ship. I never have had hives like these before. I can't understand it. So long as I keep my lamp burning and read I am untroubled. The instant I put out the lamp and drowse off the irritation starts and the lumps on my skin begin to form.

Miss West may be sea-sick, but she cannot be comatose, because at frequent intervals she sends the steward to me with more cream of tartar.

I have had a revelation to-day. I have discovered Captain West. He is a Samurai.—You remember the Samurai that H. G. Wells describes in his *Modern Utopia*—the superior breed of men who know things and are masters of life and of their fellow-men in a super-benevolent, super-wise way? Well, that is what Captain West is. Let me tell it to you.

We had a shift of wind to-day. In the height of a south-west gale the wind shifted, in the instant, eight points, which is equivalent to a quarter of the circle. Imagine it! Imagine a gale howling from out of the south-west.

And then imagine the wind, in a heavier and more violent gale, abruptly smiting you from the north-west. We had been sailing through a circular storm, Captain West vouchsafed to me, before the event, and the wind could be expected to box the compass.

Clad in sea-boots, oilskins and sou'wester, I had for some time been hanging upon the rail at the break of the poop, staring down fascinated at the poor devils of sailors, repeatedly up to their necks in water, or submerged, or dashed like straws about the deck, while they pulled and hauled, stupidly, blindly, and in evident fear, under the orders of Mr. Pike.

Mr. Pike was with them, working them and working with them. He took every chance they took, yet somehow he escaped being washed off his feet, though several times I saw him entirely buried from view. There was more than luck in the matter; for I saw him, twice, at the head of a line of the men, himself next to the pin. And twice, in this position, I saw the North Atlantic curl over the rail and fall upon them. And each time he alone remained, holding the turn of the rope on the pin, while the rest of them were rolled and sprawled helplessly away.

Almost it seemed to me good fun, as at a circus, watching their antics. But I did not apprehend the seriousness of the situation until, the wind screaming higher than ever and the sea a-smoke and white with wrath, two men did not get up from the deck. One was carried away for'ard with a broken leg—it was Iare Jacobson, a dull-witted Scandinavian; and the other, Kid Twist, was carried away, unconscious, with a bleeding scalp.

In the height of the gusts, in my high position, where the seas did not break, I found myself compelled to cling tightly to the rail to escape being blown away. My face was stung to severe pain by the high-driving spindrift, and I had a feeling that the wind was blowing the cobwebs out of my sleep-starved brain.

And all the time, slender, aristocratic, graceful in streaming oilskins, in apparent unconcern, giving no orders, effortlessly accommodating his body to the violent rolling of the *Elsinore*, Captain West strolled up and down.

218

It was at this stage in the gale that he unbent sufficiently to tell me that we were going through a circular storm and that the wind was boxing the compass. I did notice that he kept his gaze pretty steadily fixed on the overcast, cloud-driven sky. At last, when it seemed the wind could not possibly blow more fiercely, he found in the sky what he sought. It was then that I first heard his voice—a sea-voice, clear as a bell, distinct as silver, and of an ineffable sweetness and volume, as it might be the trump of Gabriel. That voice!—effortless, dominating! The mighty threat of the storm, made articulate by the resistance of the *Elsinore*, shouted in all the stays, bellowed in the shrouds, thrummed the taut ropes against the steel masts, and from the myriad tiny ropes far aloft evoked a devil's chorus of shrill pipings and screechings. And yet, through this bedlam of noise, came Captain West's voice, as of a spirit visitant, distinct, unrelated, mellow as all music and mighty as an archangel's call to judgment. And it carried understanding and command to the man at the wheel, and to Mr. Pike, waist-deep in the wash of sea below us. And the man at the wheel obeyed, and Mr. Pike obeyed, barking and snarling orders to the poor wallowing devils who wallowed on and obeyed him in turn. And as the voice was the face. This face I had never seen before. It was the face of the spirit visitant, chaste with wisdom, lighted by a splendour of power and calm. Perhaps it was the calm that smote me most of all. It was as the calm of one who had crossed chaos to bless poor sea-worn men with the word that all was well. It was not the face of the fighter. To my thrilled imagination it was the face of one who dwelt beyond all strivings of the elements and broody dissensions of the blood.

The Samurai had arrived, in thunders and lightnings, riding the wings of the storm, directing the gigantic, labouring *Elsinore* in all her intricate massiveness, commanding the wisps of humans to his will, which was the will of wisdom.

And then, that wonderful Gabriel voice of his, silent (while his creatures laboured his will), unconcerned, detached and casual, more slenderly tall and aristocratic than ever in his streaming oilskins, Captain West touched my shoulder and pointed astern over our weather quarter. I looked, and all that I could see was a vague smoke of sea and air and a cloud-bank of sky that tore at the ocean's breast. And at the same moment the gale from the south-west ceased. There was no gale, no moving zephyrs, nothing but a vast quietude of air.

"What is it?" I gasped, out of equilibrium from the abrupt cessation of wind.

"The shift," he said. "There she comes."

And it came, from the north-west, a blast of wind, a blow, an atmospheric impact that bewildered and stunned and again made the *Elsinore* harp protest. It forced me down on the rail. I was like a windle-straw. As I faced this new abruptness of gale it drove the air back into my lungs, so that I suffocated and turned my head aside to breathe in the lee of the draught. The man at the wheel again listened to the Gabriel voice; and Mr. Pike, on the deck below, listened and repeated the will of the voice; and Captain West, in slender and stately balance, leaned into the face of the wind and slowly paced the deck.

It was magnificent. Now, and for the first time, I knew the sea, and the men who overlord the sea. Captain West had vindicated himself, exposited himself. At the height and crisis of storm he had taken charge of the *Elsinore*, and Mr. Pike had become, what in truth was all he was, the foreman of a gang of men, the slave-driver of slaves, serving the one from beyond—the Samurai.

A minute or so longer Captain West strolled up and down, leaning easily into the face of this new and abominable gale or resting his back against it, and then he went below, pausing for a moment, his hand on the knob of the chart-room door, to cast a last measuring look at the storm-white sea and wrath-sombre sky he had mastered.

Ten minutes later, below, passing the open cabin door, I glanced in and saw him. Sea-boots and storm-trappings were gone; his feet, in carpet slippers, rested on a hassock; while he lay back in the big leather chair smoking dreamily, his eyes wide open, absorbed, non-seeing—or, if they saw, seeing things beyond the reeling cabin walls and beyond my ken. I have developed an immense respect for Captain West, though now I know him less than the little I thought I knew him before.

CHAPTER XIII

Small wonder that Miss West remains sea-sick on an ocean like this, which has become a factory where the veering gales manufacture the selectest and most mountainous brands of cross-seas. The way the poor *Elsinore* pitches, plunges, rolls, and shivers, with all her lofty spars and masts and all her five thousand tons of dead-weight cargo, is astonishing. To me she is the most erratic thing imaginable; yet Mr. Pike, with whom I now pace the poop on occasion, tells me that coal is a good cargo, and that the *Elsinore* is well-loaded because he saw to it himself.

He will pause abruptly, in the midst of his interminable pacing, in order to watch her in her maddest antics. The sight is very pleasant to him, for his eyes glisten and a faint glow seems to irradiate his face and impart to it a hint of ecstasy. The *Elsinore* has a snug place in his heart, I am confident. He calls her behaviour admirable, and at such times will repeat to me that it was he who saw to her loading.

It is very curious, the habituation of this man, through a long life on the sea, to the motion of the sea. There *is* a rhythm to this chaos of crossing, buffeting waves. I sense this rhythm, although I cannot solve it. But Mr. Pike *knows* it. Again and again, as we paced up and down this afternoon, when to me nothing unusually antic seemed impending, he would seize my arm as I lost balance, and as the *Elsinore* smashed down on her side and heeled over and over with a colossal roll that seemed never to end, and that always ended with an abrupt, snap-of-the-whip effect as she began the corresponding roll to windward. In vain I strove to learn how Mr. Pike forecasts these antics, and I am driven to believe that he does not consciously forecast them at all. He *feels* them; he knows them. They, and the sea, are ingrained in him.

Toward the end of our little promenade I was guilty of impatiently shaking off a sudden seizure of my arm in his big paw. If ever, in an hour, the *Elsinore* had been less gymnastic than at that moment, I had not noticed it. So I shook off the sustaining clutch, and the next moment the *Elsinore* had smashed down and buried a couple of hundred feet of her starboard rail beneath the sea, while I had shot down the deck and smashed myself breathless against the wall of the chart-house. My ribs and one shoulder are sore from it yet. Now how did he know?

And he never staggers nor seems in danger of being rolled away. On the contrary, such a surplus of surety of balance has he that time and again he lent his surplus to me. I begin to have more respect, not for the sea, but for the men of the sea, and not for the sweepings of seamen that are as slaves on our decks, but for the real seamen who are their masters—for Captain West, for Mr. Pike, yes, and for Mr. Mellaire, dislike him as I do.

As early as three in the afternoon the wind, still a gale, went back to the south-west. Mr. Mellaire had the deck, and he went below and reported the change to Captain West.

"We'll wear ship at four, Mr. Pathurst," the second mate told me when he came back. "You'll find it an interesting manoeuvre."

"But why wait till four?" I asked.

"The Captain's orders, sir. The watches will be changing, and we'll have the use of both of them, without working a hardship on the watch below by calling it out now."

And when both watches were on deck Captain West, again in oilskins, came out of the chart-house. Mr. Pike, out on the bridge, took charge of the many men who, on deck and on the poop, were to manage the mizzen-braces, while Mr. Mellaire went for'ard with his watch to handle the fore-and main-braces. It was a pretty manoeuvre, a play of leverages, by which they eased the force of the wind on the after part of the *Elsinore* and used the force of the wind on the for'ard part.

Captain West gave no orders whatever, and, to all intents, was quite oblivious of what was being done. He was again the favoured passenger, taking a stroll for his health's sake. And yet I knew that both his officers were uncomfortably aware of his presence and were keyed to their finest seamanship. I know, now, Captain West's position on board. He is the brains of the *Elsinore*. He is the master strategist. There is more in directing a ship on the ocean than in standing watches and ordering men to pull and haul. They are pawns, and the two officers are pieces, with which Captain West plays the game against sea, and wind, and season, and ocean current. He is the knower. They are his tongue, by which he makes his knowledge articulate.

* * * * *

A bad night—equally bad for the *Elsinore* and for me. She is receiving a sharp buffeting at the hands of the wintry North Atlantic. I fell asleep early, exhausted from lack of sleep, and awoke in an hour, frantic with my lumped and burning skin. More cream of tartar, more reading, more vain attempts to sleep, until shortly before five, when the steward brought me my coffee, I wrapped myself in my dressing-gown, and like a being distracted prowled into the cabin. I dozed in a leather chair and was thrown out by a violent roll of the ship. I tried the sofa, sinking to sleep immediately, and immediately thereafter finding myself precipitated to the floor. I am convinced that when Captain West naps on the sofa he is only half asleep. How else can he maintain so precarious a position?—unless, in him, too, the sea and its motion be ingrained.

I wandered into the dining-room, wedged myself into a screwed chair, and fell asleep, my head on my arms, my arms on the table. And at quarter past seven the steward roused me by shaking my shoulders. It was time to set table.

Heavy with the brief heaviness of sleep I had had, I dressed and stumbled up on to the poop in the hope that the wind would clear my brain. Mr. Pike had the watch, and with sure, age-lagging step he paced the deck. The man is a marvel—sixty-nine years old, a life of hardship, and as sturdy as a lion. Yet of the past night alone his hours had been: four to six in the afternoon on deck; eight to twelve on deck; and four to eight in the morning on deck. In a few minutes he would be relieved, but at midday he would again be on deck.

I leaned on the poop-rail and stared for'ard along the dreary waste of deck. Every port and scupper was working to ease the weight of North Atlantic that perpetually fell on board. Between the rush of the cascades, streaks of rust showed everywhere. Some sort of a wooden pin-rail had carried away on the starboard-rail at the foot of the mizzen-shrouds, and an amazing raffle of ropes and tackles washed about. Here Nancy and half-a-dozen men worked sporadically, and in fear of their lives, to clear the tangle.

The long-suffering bleakness was very pronounced on Nancy's face, and when the walls of water, in impending downfall, reared above the *Elsinore's* rail, he was always the first to leap for the life-line which had been stretched fore and aft across the wide space of deck.

The rest of the men were scarcely less backward in dropping their work and springing to safety—if safety it might be called, to grip a rope in both hands and have legs sweep out from under, and be wrenched full-length upon the boiling surface of an ice-cold flood. Small wonder they look wretched. Bad as their condition was when they came aboard at Baltimore, they look far worse now, what of the last several days of wet and freezing hardship.

From time to time, completing his for'ard pace along the poop, Mr. Pike would pause, ere he retraced his steps, and snort sardonic glee at what happened to the poor devils below. The man's heart is callous. A thing of iron, he has endured; and he has no patience nor sympathy with these creatures who lack his own excessive iron.

I noticed the stone-deaf man, the twisted oaf whose face I have described as being that of an ill-treated and feeble-minded faun. His bright, liquid, pain-filled eyes were more filled with pain than ever, his face still more lean and drawn with suffering. And yet his face showed an excess of nervousness, sensitiveness, and a pathetic eagerness to please and do. I could not help observing that, despite his dreadful sense-handicap and his wrecked, frail body, he did the most work, was always the last of the group to spring to the life-line and always the first to loose the life-line and slosh knee-deep or waist-deep through the churning water to attack the immense and depressing tangle of rope and tackle.

I remarked to Mr. Pike that the men seemed thinner and weaker than when they came on board, and he delayed replying for a moment while he stared down at them with that cattle-buyer's eye of his.

"Sure they are," he said disgustedly. "A weak breed, that's what they are—nothing to build on, no stamina. The least thing drags them down. Why, in my day we grew fat on work like that—only we didn't; we worked so hard there wasn't any chance for fat. We kept in fighting trim, that was all. But as for this scum and slum—say, you remember, Mr. Pathurst, that man I spoke to the first day, who said his name was Charles Davis?"

"The one you thought there was something the matter with?"

"Yes, and there was, too. He's in that 'midship room with the Greek now. He'll never do a tap of work the whole Voyage. He's a hospital case, if there ever was one. Talk about shot to pieces! He's got holes in him I could shove my fist through. I don't know whether they're perforating ulcers, or cancers, or cannon-shot wounds, or what not. And he had the nerve to tell me they showed up after he came on board!"

"And he had them all the time?" I asked.

"All the time! Take my word, Mr. Pathurst, they're years old. But he's a wonder. I watched him those first days, sent him aloft, had him down in the fore-hold trimming a few tons of coal, did everything to him, and he never showed a wince. Being up to the neck in the salt water finally fetched him, and now he's reported off duty—for the voyage. And he'll draw his wages for the whole time, have all night in, and never do a tap. Oh, he's a hot one to have passed over on us, and the *Elsinore's* another man short."

"Another!" I exclaimed. "Is the Greek going to die?"

"No fear. I'll have him steering in a few days. I refer to the misfits. If we rolled a dozen of them together they wouldn't make one real man. I'm not saying it to alarm you, for there's nothing alarming about it; but we're going to have proper hell this voyage." He broke off to stare reflectively at his broken knuckles, as if estimating how much drive was left in them, then sighed and concluded, "Well, I can see I've got my work cut out for me."

225

Sympathizing with Mr. Pike is futile; the only effect is to make his mood blacker. I tried it, and he retaliated with:

"You oughta see the bloke with curvature of the spine in Mr. Mellaire's watch. He's a proper hobo, too, and a land lubber, and don't weigh more'n a hundred pounds, and must be fifty years old, and he's got curvature of the spine, and he's able seaman, if you please, on the Elsinore. And worse than all that, he puts it over on you; he's nasty, he's mean, he's a viper, a wasp. He ain't afraid of anything because he knows you dassent hit him for fear of croaking him. Oh, he's a pearl of purest ray serene, if anybody should slide down a backstay and ask you. If you fail to identify him any other way, his name is Mulligan Jacobs."

* * * * *

After breakfast, again on deck, in Mr. Mellaire's watch, I discovered another efficient. He was at the wheel, a small, well-knit, muscular man of say forty-five, with black hair graying on the temples, a big eagle-face, swarthy, with keen, intelligent black eyes.

Mr. Mellaire vindicated my judgment by telling me the man was the best sailor in his watch, a proper seaman. When he referred to the man as the Maltese Cockney, and I asked why, he replied:

"First, because he is Maltese, Mr. Pathurst; and next, because he talks Cockney like a native. And depend upon it, he heard Bow Bells before he lisped his first word."

"And has O'Sullivan bought Andy Fay's sea-boots yet?" I queried.

It was at this moment that Miss West emerged upon the poop. She was as rosy and vital as ever, and certainly, if she had been sea-sick, she flew no signals of it. As she came toward me, greeting me, I could not help remarking again the lithe and springy limb-movement with which she walked, and her fine, firm skin. Her neck, free in a sailor collar, with white sweater open at the throat, seemed almost redoubtably strong to my sleepless, jaundiced eyes. Her hair, under a white knitted cap, was smooth and well-groomed. In fact, the totality of impression she conveyed was of a well-groomedness one would not expect of a sea-captain's daughter, much less of a woman who had been sea-sick. Life!—that is the key of her, the essential note of her—life and health. I'll wager she has never entertained a morbid thought in that practical, balanced, sensible head of hers.

"And how have you been?" she asked, then rattled on with sheer exuberance ere I could answer. "Had a lovely night's sleep. I was really over my sickness yesterday, but I just devoted myself to resting up. I slept ten solid hours—what do you think of that?"

"I wish I could say the same," I replied with appropriate dejection, as I swung in beside her, for she had evinced her intention of promenading.

"Oh, then you've been sick?"

"On the contrary," I answered dryly. "And I wish I had been. I haven't had five hours' sleep all told since I came on board. These pestiferous hives. . ."

I held up a lumpy wrist to show. She took one glance at it, halted abruptly, and, neatly balancing herself to the roll, took my wrist in both her hands and gave it close scrutiny.

"Mercy!" she cried; and then began to laugh.

I was of two minds. Her laughter was delightful to the ear, there was such a mellowness, and healthiness, and frankness about it. On the other hand, that it should be directed at my misfortune was exasperating. I suppose my perplexity showed in my face, for when she had eased her laughter and looked at me with a sobering countenance, she immediately went off into more peals.

"You poor child," she gurgled at last. "And when I think of all the cream of tartar I made you consume!"

It was rather presumptuous of her to poor-child me, and I resolved to take advantage of the data I already possessed in order to ascertain just how many years she was my junior. She had told me she was twelve years old the time the *Dixie* collided with the river steamer in San Francisco Bay. Very well, all I had to do was to ascertain the date of that disaster and I had her. But in the meantime she laughed at me and my hives.

"I suppose it is—er—humorous, in some sort of way," I said a bit stiffly, only to find that there was no use in being stiff with Miss West, for it only set her off into more laughter.

"What you needed," she announced, with fresh gurglings, "was an exterior treatment."

"Don't tell me I've got the chicken-pox or the measles," I protested.

"No." She shook her head emphatically while she enjoyed another paroxysm. "What you are suffering from is a severe attack . . . "

She paused deliberately, and looked me straight the eyes.

"Of bedbugs," she concluded. And then, all seriousness and practicality, she went on: "But we'll have that righted in a jiffy. I'll turn the *Elsinore*'s after-quarters upside down, though I know there are none in father's room or mine. And though this is my first voyage with Mr. Pike I know he's too hard-bitten" (here I laughed at her involuntary pun) "an old sailor not to know that his room is clean. Yours" (I was perturbed for fear she was going to say that I had brought them on board) "have most probably drifted in from for'ard. They always have them for'ard.

"And now, Mr. Pathurst, I am going down to attend to your case. You'd better get your Wada to make up a camping kit for you. The next couple of nights you'll spend in the cabin or chart-room. And be sure Wada removes all silver and metallic tarnishable stuff from your rooms. There's going to be all sorts of fumigating, and tearing out of woodwork, and rebuilding. Trust me. I know the vermin."

CHAPTER XIV

Such a cleaning up and turning over! For two nights, one in the chart-room and one on the cabin sofa, I have soaked myself in sleep, and I am now almost stupid with excess of sleep. The land seems very far away. By some strange quirk, I have an impression that weeks, or months, have passed since I left Baltimore on that bitter March morning. And yet it was March 28, and this is only the first week in April.

I was entirely right in my first estimation of Miss West. She is the most capable, practically masterful woman I have ever encountered. What passed between her and Mr. Pike I do not know; but whatever it was, she was convinced that he was not the erring one. In some strange way, my two rooms are the only ones which have been invaded by this plague of vermin. Under Miss West's instructions bunks, drawers, shelves, and all superficial woodwork have been ripped out. She worked the carpenter from daylight till dark, and then, after a night of fumigation, two of the sailors, with turpentine and white lead, put the finishing touches on the cleansing operations. The carpenter is now busy rebuilding my rooms. Then will come the painting, and in two or three more days I expect to be settled back in my quarters.

Of the men who did the turpentining and white-leading there have been four. Two of them were quickly rejected by Miss West as not being up to the work. The first one, Steve Roberts, which he told me was his name, is an interesting fellow. I talked with him quite a bit ere Miss West sent him packing and told Mr. Pike that she wanted a real sailor.

This is the first time Steve Roberts has ever seen the sea. How he happened to drift from the western cattle-ranges to New York he did not explain, any more than did he explain how he came to ship on the *Elsinore*. But here he is, not a sailor on horseback, but a cowboy on the sea. He is a small man, but most powerfully built. His shoulders are very broad, and his muscles bulge under his shirt; and yet he is slender-waisted, lean-limbed, and hollow-cheeked. This last, however, is not due to sickness or ill-health. Tyro as he is on the sea, Steve Roberts is keen and intelligent . . . yes, and crooked. He has a way of looking straight at one with utmost frankness while he talks, and yet it is at such moments I get most strongly the impression of crookedness. But he is a man, if trouble should arise, to be reckoned with. In ways he suggests a kinship with the three men Mr. Pike took so instant a prejudice against—Kid Twist, Nosey Murphy, and Bert Rhine. And I have already noticed, in the dog-watches, that it is with this trio that Steve Roberts chums.

The second sailor Miss West rejected, after silently watching him work for five minutes, was Mulligan Jacobs, the wisp of a man with curvature of the spine. But before she sent him packing other things occurred in which I was concerned. I was in the room when Mulligan Jacobs first came in to go to work, and I could not help observing the startled, avid glance he threw at my big shelves of books. He advanced on them in the way a robber might advance on a secret hoard of gold, and as a miser would fondle gold so Mulligan Jacobs fondled these book-titles with his eyes.

And such eyes! All time bitterness and venom Mr. Pike had told me the man possessed was there in his eyes. They were small, pale-blue, and gimlet-pointed with fire. His eyelids were inflamed, and but served to ensanguine the bitter and cold-blazing intensity of the pupils. The man was constitutionally a hater, and I was not long in learning that he hated all things except books.

"Would you care to read some of them?" I said hospitably.

All the caress in his eyes for the books vanished as he turned his head to look at me, and ere he spoke I knew that I, too, was hated.

"It's hell, ain't it?—you with a strong body and servants to carry for you a weight of books like this, and me with a curved spine that puts the pot-hooks of hell-fire into my brain?"

How can I possibly convey the terrible venomousness with which he uttered these words? I know that Mr. Pike, dragging his feet down the hall past my open door, gave me a very gratifying sense of safety. Being alone in the room with this man seemed much the same as if I were locked in a cage with a tiger-cat. The devilishness, the wickedness, and, above all, the pitch of glaring hatred with which the man eyed me and addressed me, were most unpleasant. I swear I knew fear—not calculated caution, not timid apprehension, but blind, panic, unreasoned terror. The malignancy of the creature was blood curdling; nor did it require words to convey it: it poured from him, out of his red-rimmed, blazing eyes, out of his withered, twisted, tortured face, out of his broken-nailed, crooked talons of hands. And yet, in that very moment of instinctive startle and repulsion, the thought was in my mind that with one hand I could take the throat of the weazened wisp of a crippled thing and throttle the malformed life out of it.

But there was little encouragement in such thought—no more than a man might feel in a cave of rattlesnakes or a pit of centipedes, for, crush them with his very bulk, nevertheless they would first sink their poison into him. And so with this Mulligan Jacobs. My fear of him was the fear of being infected with his venom. I could not help it; for I caught a quick vision of the black and broken teeth I had seen in his mouth sinking into my flesh, polluting me, eating me with their acid, destroying me.

One thing was very clear. In the creature was no fear. Absolutely, he did not know fear. He was as devoid of it as the fetid slime one treads underfoot in nightmares. Lord, Lord! that is what the thing was, a nightmare.

"You suffer pain often?" I asked, attempting to get myself in hand by the calculated use of sympathy.

"The hooks are in me, in the brain, white-hot hooks that burn an' burn," was his reply. "But by what damnable right do you have all these books, and time to read 'em, an' all night in to read 'em, an' soak in them, when me brain's on fire, and I'm watch and watch, an' me broken spine won't let me carry half a hundredweight of books about with me?"

Another madman, was my conclusion; and yet I was quickly compelled to modify it, for, thinking to play with a rattle-brain, I asked him what were the books up to half a hundredweight he carried, and what were the writers he preferred. His library, he told me, among other things included, first and fore-most, a complete Byron. Next was a complete Shakespeare; also a complete Browning in one volume. A full hall-dozen he had in the forecastle of Renan, a stray volume of Lecky, Winwood Reade's *Martyrdom of Man*, several of Carlyle, and eight or ten of Zola. Zola he swore by, though Anatole France was a prime favourite.

He might be mad, was my revised judgment, but he was most differently mad from any madman I had ever encountered. I talked on with him about books and bookmen. He was most universal and particular. He liked O. Henry. George Moore was a cad and a four—flusher. Edgar Saltus' *Anatomy of Negation* was profounder than Kant. Maeterlinck was a mystic frump. Emerson was a charlatan. Ibsen's *Ghosts* was the stuff, though Ibsen was a bourgeois lickspittler. Heine was the real goods. He preferred Flaubert to de Maupassant, and Turgenieff to Tolstoy; but Gorky was the best of the Russian boiling. John Masefield knew what he was writing about, and Joseph Conrad was living too fat to turn out the stuff he first turned out.

And so it went, the most amazing running commentary on literature I had ever heard. I was hugely interested, and I quizzed him on sociology. Yes, he was a Red, and knew his Kropotkin, but he was no anarchist. On the other hand, political action was a blind-alley leading to reformism and quietism. Political socialism had gone to pot, while industrial unionism was the logical culmination of Marxism. He was a direct actionist. The mass strike was the thing. Sabotage, not merely as a withdrawal of efficiency, but as a keen destruction-of-profits policy, was the weapon. Of course he believed in the propaganda of the deed, but a man was a fool to talk about it. His job was to do it and keep his mouth shut, and the way to do it was to shoot the evidence. Of course, *he* talked; but what of it? Didn't he have curvature of the spine? He didn't care when he got his, and woe to the man who tried to give it to him.

And while he talked he hated me. He seemed to hate the things he talked about and espoused. I judged him to be of Irish descent, and it was patent that he was self-educated. When I asked him how it was he had come to sea, he replied that the hooks in his brain were as hot one place as another. He unbent enough to tell me that he had been an athlete, when he was a young man, a professional foot-racer in Eastern Canada. And then his disease had come upon him, and for a quarter of a century he had been a common tramp and vagabond, and he bragged of a personal acquaintance with more city prisons and county jails than any man that ever existed.

It was at this stage in our talk that Mr. Pike thrust his head into the doorway. He did not address me, but he favoured me with a most sour look of disapprobation. Mr. Pike's countenance is almost petrified. Any expression seems to crack it—with the exception of sourness. But when Mr. Pike wants to look sour he has no difficulty at all. His hard-skinned, hard-muscled face just flows to sourness. Evidently he condemned my consuming Mulligan Jacobs's time. To Mulligan Jacobs he said in his customary snarl:

"Go on an' get to your work. Chew the rag in your watch below."

And then I got a sample of Mulligan Jacobs. The venom of hatred I had already seen in his face was as nothing compared with what now was manifested. I had a feeling that, like stroking a cat in cold weather, did I touch his face it would crackle electric sparks.

"Aw, go to hell, you old stiff," said Mulligan Jacobs.

If ever I had seen murder in a man's eyes, I saw it then in the mate's. He lunged into the room, his arm tensed to strike, the hand not open but clenched. One stroke of that bear's paw and Mulligan Jacobs and all the poisonous flame of him would have been quenched in the everlasting darkness. But he was unafraid. Like a cornered rat, like a rattlesnake on the trail, unflinching, sneering, snarling, he faced the irate giant. More than that. He even thrust his face forward on its twisted neck to meet the blow.

It was too much for Mr. Pike; it was too impossible to strike that frail, crippled, repulsive thing.

"It's me that can call you the stiff," said Mulligan Jacobs. "I ain't no Larry. G'wan an' hit me. Why don't you hit me?"

And Mr. Pike was too appalled to strike the creature. He, whose whole career on the sea had been that of a bucko driver in a shambles, could not strike this fractured splinter of a man. I swear that Mr. Pike actually struggled with himself to strike. I saw it. But he could not.

"Go on to your work," he ordered. "The voyage is young yet, Mulligan. I'll have you eatin' outa my hand before it's over."

And Mulligan Jacobs's face thrust another inch closer on its twisted neck, while all his concentrated rage seemed on the verge of bursting into incandescence. So immense and tremendous was the bitterness that consumed him that he could find no words to clothe it. All he could do was to hawk and guttural deep in his throat until I should not have been surprised had he spat poison in the mate's face.

And Mr. Pike turned on his heel and left the room, beaten, absolutely beaten.

* * * * *

I can't get it out of my mind. The picture of the mate and the cripple facing each other keeps leaping up under my eyelids. This is different from the books and from what I know of existence. It is revelation. Life is a profoundly amazing thing. What is this bitter flame that informs Mulligan Jacobs? How dare he—with no hope of any profit, not a hero, not a leader of a forlorn hope nor a martyr to God, but a mere filthy, malignant rat—how dare he, I ask myself, be so defiant, so death-inviting? The spectacle of him makes me doubt all the schools of the metaphysicians and the realists. No philosophy has a leg to stand on that does not account for Mulligan Jacobs. And all the midnight oil of philosophy I have burned does not enable me to account for Mulligan Jacobs . . . unless he be insane. And then I don't know.

Was there ever such a freight of human souls on the sea as these humans with whom I am herded on the *Elsinore*?

* * * * *

And now, working in my rooms, white-leading and turpentining, is another one of them. I have learned his name. It is Arthur Deacon. He is the pallid, furtive-eyed man whom I observed the first day when the men were routed out of the forecastle to man the windlass—the man I so instantly adjudged a drug-fiend. He certainly looks it.

I asked Mr. Pike his estimate of the man.

"White slaver," was his answer. "Had to skin outa New York to save his skin. He'll be consorting with those other three larrakins I gave a piece of my mind to."

"And what do you make of them?" I asked.

"A month's wages to a pound of tobacco that a district attorney, or a committee of some sort investigating the New York police is lookin' for 'em right now. I'd like to have the cash somebody's put up in New York to send them on this get-away. Oh, I know the breed."

"Gangsters?" I queried.

"That's what. But I'll trim their dirty hides. I'll trim 'em. Mr. Pathurst, this voyage ain't started yet, and this old stiff's a long way from his last legs. I'll give them a run for their money. Why, I've buried better men than the best of them aboard this craft. And I'll bury some of them that think me an old stiff."

He paused and looked at me solemnly for a full half minute.

"Mr. Pathurst, I've heard you're a writing man. And when they told me at the agents' you were going along passenger, I made a point of going to see your play. Now I'm not saying anything about that play, one way or the other. But I just want to tell you, that as a writing man you'll get stuff in plenty to write about on this voyage. Hell's going to pop, believe me, and right here before you is the stiff that'll do a lot of the poppin'. Some several and plenty's going to learn who's an old stiff."

CHAPTER XV

How I have been sleeping! This relief of renewed normality is delicious—thanks to Miss West. Now why did not Captain West, or Mr. Pike, both experienced men, diagnose my trouble for me? And then there was Wada. But no; it required Miss West. Again I contemplate the problem of woman. It is just such an incident among a million others that keeps the thinker's gaze fixed on woman. They truly are the mothers and the conservers of the race.

Rail as I will at Miss West's red-blood complacency of life, yet I must bow my head to her life-giving to me. Practical, sensible, hard-headed, a comfort-maker and a nest-builder, possessing all the distressing attributes of the blind-instinctive race-mother, nevertheless I must confess I am most grateful that she is along. Had she not been on the *Elsinore*, by this time I should have been so overwrought from lack of sleep that I would be biting my veins and howling—as mad a hatter as any of our cargo of mad hatters. And so we come to it—the everlasting mystery of woman. One may not be able to get along with her; yet is it patent, as of old time, that one cannot get along without her. But, regarding Miss West, I do entertain one fervent hope, namely, that she is not a suffragette. That would be too much.

Captain West may be a Samurai, but he is also human. He was really a bit fluttery this morning, in his reserved, controlled way, when he regretted the plague of vermin I had encountered in my rooms. It seems he has a keen sense of hospitality, and that he is my host on the *Elsinore*, and that, although he is oblivious of the existence of the crew, he is not oblivious of my comfort. By his few expressions of regret it appears that he cannot forgive himself for his careless acceptance of the erroneous diagnosis of my affliction. Yes; Captain West is a real human man. Is he not the father of the slender-faced, strapping-bodied Miss West?

"Thank goodness that's settled," was Miss West's exclamation this morning, when we met on the poop and after I had told her how gloriously I had slept.

And then, that nightmare episode dismissed because, forsooth, for all practical purposes—it was settled, she next said:

"Come on and see the chickens."

And I accompanied her along the spidery bridge to the top of the 'midship-house, to look at the one rooster and the four dozen fat hens in the ship's chicken-coop.

As I accompanied her, my eyes dwelling pleasurably on that vital gait of hers as she preceded me, I could not help reflecting that, coming down on the tug from Baltimore, she had promised not to bother me nor require to be entertained.

Come and see the chickens!—Oh, the sheer female possessiveness of that simple invitation! For effrontery of possessiveness is there anything that can exceed the nest-making, planet-populating, female, human woman?—*Come and see the chickens!* Oh, well, the sailors for'ard may be hard-bitten, but I can promise Miss West that here, aft, is one male passenger, unmarried and never married, who is an equally hard-bitten adventurer on the sea of matrimony. When I go over the census I remember at least several women, superior to Miss West, who trilled their song of sex and failed to shipwreck me.

As I read over what I have written I notice how the terminology of the sea has stolen into my mental processes. Involuntarily I think in terms of the sea. Another thing I notice is my excessive use of superlatives. But then, everything on board the *Elsinore* is superlative. I find myself continually combing my vocabulary in quest of just and adequate words. Yet am I aware of failure. For example, all the words of all the dictionaries would fail to approximate the exceeding terribleness of Mulligan Jacobs.

But to return to the chickens. Despite every precaution, it was evident that they had had a hard time during the past days of storm. It was equally evident that Miss West, even during her sea-sickness, had not neglected them. Under her directions the steward had actually installed a small oil-stove in the big coop, and she now beckoned him up to the top of the house as he was passing for'ard to the galley. It was for the purpose of instructing him further in the matter of feeding them.

Where were the grits? They needed grits. He didn't know. The sack had been lost among the miscellaneous stores, but Mr. Pike had promised a couple of sailors that afternoon to overhaul the lazarette.

"Plenty of ashes," she told the steward. "Remember. And if a sailor doesn't clean the coop each day, you report to me. And give them only clean food—no spoiled scraps, mind. How many eggs yesterday?"

The steward's eyes glistened with enthusiasm as he said he had got nine the day before and expected fully a dozen to-day.

237

"The poor things," said Miss West—to me. "You've no idea how bad weather reduces their laying." She turned back upon the steward. "Mind now, you watch and find out which hens don't lay, and kill them first. And you ask me each time before you kill one."

I found myself neglected, out there on top the draughty house, while Miss West talked chickens with the Chinese ex-smuggler. But it gave me opportunity to observe her. It is the length of her eyes that accentuates their steadiness of gaze—helped, of course, by the dark brows and lashes. I noted again the warm gray of her eyes. And I began to identify her, to locate her. She is a physical type of the best of the womanhood of old New England. Nothing spare nor meagre, nor bred out, but generously strong, and yet not quite what one would call robust. When I said she was strapping-bodied I erred. I must fall back on my other word, which will have to be the last: Miss West is vital-bodied. That is the key-word.

When we had regained the poop, and Miss West had gone below, I ventured my customary pleasantry with Mr. Mellaire of:

"And has O'Sullivan bought Andy Fay's sea-boots yet?"

"Not yet, Mr. Pathurst," was the reply, "though he nearly got them early this morning. Come on along, sir, and I'll show you."

Vouchsafing no further information, the second mate led the way along the bridge, across the 'midship-house and the for'ard-house. From the edge of the latter, looking down on Number One hatch, I saw two Japanese, with sail-needles and twine, sewing up a canvas-swathed bundle that unmistakably contained a human body.

"O'Sullivan used a razor," said Mr. Mellaire.

"And that is Andy Fay?" I cried.

"No, sir, not Andy. That's a Dutchman. Christian Jespersen was his name on the articles. He got in O'Sullivan's way when O'Sullivan went after the boots. That's what saved Andy. Andy was more active. Jespersen couldn't get out of his own way, much less out of O'Sullivan's. There's Andy sitting over there."

238

I followed Mr. Mellaire's gaze, and saw the burnt-out, aged little Scotchman squatted on a spare spar and sucking a pipe. One arm was in a sling and his head was bandaged. Beside him squatted Mulligan Jacobs. They were a pair. Both were blue-eyed, and both were malevolent-eyed. And they were equally emaciated. It was easy to see that they had discovered early in the voyage their kinship of bitterness. Andy Fay, I knew, was sixty-three years old, although he looked a hundred; and Mulligan Jacobs, who was only about fifty, made up for the difference by the furnace-heat of hatred that burned in his face and eyes. I wondered if he sat beside the injured bitter one in some sense of sympathy, or if he were there in order to gloat.

Around the corner of the house strolled Shorty, flinging up to me his inevitable clown-grin. One hand was swathed in bandages.

"Must have kept Mr. Pike busy," was my comment to Mr. Mellaire.

"He was sewing up cripples about all his watch from four till eight."

"What?" I asked. "Are there any more?"

"One more, sir, a sheeny. I didn't know his name before, but Mr. Pike got it—Isaac B. Chantz. I never saw in all my life at sea as many sheenies as are on board the *Elsinore* right now. Sheenies don't take to the sea as a rule. We've certainly got more than our share of them. Chantz isn't badly hurt, but you ought to hear him whimper."

"Where's O'Sullivan?" I inquired.

"In the 'midship-house with Davis, and without a mark. Mr. Pike got into the rumpus and put him to sleep with one on the jaw. And now he's lashed down and talking in a trance. He's thrown the fear of God into Davis. Davis is sitting up in his bunk with a marlin-spike, threatening to brain O'Sullivan if he starts to break loose, and complaining that it's no way to run a hospital. He'd have padded cells, straitjackets, night and day nurses, and violent wards, I suppose—and a convalescents' home in a Queen Anne cottage on the poop.

"Oh dear, oh dear," Mr. Mellaire sighed. "This is the funniest voyage and the funniest crew I've ever tackled. It's not going to come to a good end. Anybody can see that with half an eye. It'll be dead of winter off the Horn, and a fo'c's'le full of lunatics and cripples to do the work.—Just take a look at that one. Crazy as a bedbug. He's likely to go overboard any time."

I followed his glance and saw Tony the Greek, the one who had sprung overboard the first day. He had just come around the corner of the house, and, beyond one arm in a sling, seemed in good condition. He walked easily and with strength, a testimonial to the virtues of Mr. Pike's rough surgery.

My eyes kept returning to the canvas-covered body of Christian Jespersen, and to the Japanese who sewed with sail-twine his sailor's shroud. One of them had his right hand in a huge wrapping of cotton and bandage.

"Did he get hurt, too?" I asked.

"No, sir. He's the sail-maker. They're both sail-makers. He's a good one, too. Yatsuda is his name. But he's just had blood-poisoning and lain in hospital in New York for eighteen months. He flatly refused to let them amputate. He's all right now, but the hand is dead, all except the thumb and fore-finger, and he's teaching himself to sew with his left hand. He's as clever a sail-maker as you'll find at sea."

"A lunatic and a razor make a cruel combination," I remarked.

"It's put five men out of commission," Mr. Mellaire sighed. "There's O'Sullivan himself, and Christian Jespersen gone, and Andy Fay, and Shorty, and the sheeny. And the voyage not started yet. And there's Lars with the broken leg, and Davis laid off for keeps—why, sir, we'll soon be that weak it'll take both watches to set a staysail."

Nevertheless, while I talked in a matter-of-fact way with Mr. Mellaire, I was shocked—no; not because death was aboard with us. I have stood by my philosophic guns too long to be shocked by death, or by murder. What affected me was the utter, stupid bestiality of the affair. Even murder—murder for cause—I can understand. It is comprehensible that men should kill one another in the passion of love, of hatred, of patriotism, of religion.

But this was different. Here was killing without cause, an orgy of blind-brutishness, a thing monstrously irrational.

Later on, strolling with Possum on the main deck, as I passed the open door of the hospital I heard the muttering chant of O'Sullivan, and peeped in. There he lay, lashed fast on his back in the lower bunk, rolling his eyes and raving. In the top bunk, directly above, lay Charles Davis, calmly smoking a pipe. I looked for the marlin-spike. There it was, ready to hand, on the bedding beside him.

"It's hell, ain't it, sir?" was his greeting. "And how am I goin' to get any sleep with that baboon chattering away there. He never lets up—keeps his chin-music goin' right along when he's asleep, only worse. The way he grits his teeth is something awful. Now I leave it to you, sir, is it right to put a crazy like that in with a sick man? And I am a sick man."

While he talked the massive form of Mr. Pike loomed beside me and halted just out of sight of the man in the bunk. And the man talked on.

"By rights, I oughta have that lower bunk. It hurts me to crawl up here. It's inhumanity, that's what it is, and sailors at sea are better protected by the law than they used to be. And I'll have you for a witness to this before the court when we get to Seattle."

Mr. Pike stepped into the doorway.

"Shut up, you damned sea-lawyer, you," he snarled. "Haven't you played a dirty trick enough comin' on board this ship in your condition? And if I have anything more out of you . . . "

Mr. Pike was so angry that he could not complete the threat. After spluttering for a moment he made a fresh attempt.

"You . . . you . . . well, you annoy me, that's what you do."

"I know the law, sir," Davis answered promptly. "I worked full able seaman on this here ship. All hands can testify to that. I was aloft from the start. Yes, sir, and up to my neck in salt water day and night. And you had me below trimmin' coal. I did full duty and more, until this sickness got me—"

"You were petrified and rotten before you ever saw this ship," Mr. Pike broke in.

"The court'll decide that, sir," replied the imperturbable Davis.

"And if you go to shoutin' off your sea-lawyer mouth," Mr. Pike continued, "I'll jerk you out of that and show you what real work is."

"An' lay the owners open for lovely damages when we get in," Davis sneered.

"Not if I bury you before we get in," was the mate's quick, grim retort. "And let me tell you, Davis, you ain't the first sea-lawyer I've dropped over the side with a sack of coal to his feet."

Mr. Pike turned, with a final "Damned sea-lawyer!" and started along the deck. I was walking behind him when he stopped abruptly.

"Mr. Pathurst."

Not as an officer to a passenger did he thus address me. His tone was imperative, and I gave heed.

"Mr. Pathurst. From now on the less you see aboard this ship the better. That is all."

And again he turned on his heel and went his way.

CHAPTER XVI

No, the sea is not a gentle place. It must be the very hardness of the life that makes all sea-people hard. Of course, Captain West is unaware that his crew exists, and Mr. Pike and Mr. Mellaire never address the men save to give commands. But Miss West, who is more like myself, a passenger, ignores the men. She does not even say good-morning to the man at the wheel when she first comes on deck. Nevertheless I shall, at least to the man at the wheel. Am I not a passenger?

Which reminds me. Technically I am not a passenger. The *Elsinore* has no licence to carry passengers, and I am down on the articles as the third mate and am supposed to receive thirty-five dollars a month. Wada is down as cabin boy, although I paid a good price for his passage and he is my servant.

Not much time is lost at sea in getting rid of the dead. Within an hour after I had watched the sail-makers at work Christian Jespersen was slid overboard, feet first, a sack of coal to his feet to sink him. It was a mild, calm day, and the *Elsinore*, logging a lazy two knots, was not hove to for the occasion. At the last moment Captain West came for'ard, prayer-book in hand, read the brief service for burial at sea, and returned immediately aft. It was the first time I had seen him for'ard.

I shall not bother to describe the burial. All I shall say of it is that it was as sordid as Christian Jespersen's life had been and as his death had been.

As for Miss West, she sat in a deck-chair on the poop busily engaged with some sort of fancy work. When Christian Jespersen and his coal splashed into the sea the crew immediately dispersed, the watch below going to its bunks, the watch on deck to its work. Not a minute elapsed ere Mr. Mellaire was giving orders and the men were pulling and hauling. So I returned to the poop to be unpleasantly impressed by Miss West's smiling unconcern.

"Well, he's buried," I observed.

"Oh," she said, with all the tonelessness of disinterest, and went on with her stitching.

She must have sensed my frame of mind, for, after a moment, she paused from her sewing and looked at me.

Your first sea funeral, Mr. Pathurst?

"Death at sea does not seem to affect you," I said bluntly.

"Not any more than on the land." She shrugged her shoulders. "So many people die, you know. And when they are strangers to you . . . well, what do you do on the land when you learn that some workers have been killed in a factory you pass every day coming to town? It is the same on the sea."

"It's too bad we are a hand short," I said deliberately.

It did not miss her. Just as deliberately she replied:

"Yes, isn't it? And so early in the voyage, too." She looked at me, and when I could not forbear a smile of appreciation she smiled back.

"Oh, I know very well, Mr. Pathurst, that you think me a heartless wretch. But it isn't that it's . . . it's the sea, I suppose. And yet, I didn't know this man. I don't remember ever having seen him. At this stage of the voyage I doubt if I could pick out half-a-dozen of the sailors as men I had ever laid eyes on. So why vex myself with even thinking of this stupid stranger who was killed by another stupid stranger? As well might one die of grief with reading the murder columns of the daily papers."

"And yet, it seems somehow different," I contended.

"Oh, you'll get used to it," she assured me cheerfully, and returned to her sewing.

I asked her if she had read Moody's *Ship of Souls*, but she had not. I searched her out further. She liked Browning, and was especially fond of *The Ring and the Book*. This was the key to her. She cared only for healthful literature—for the literature that exposits the vital lies of life.

For instance, the mention of Schopenhauer produced smiles and laughter. To her all the philosophers of pessimism were laughable. The red blood of her would not permit her to take them seriously. I tried her out with a conversation I had had with De Casseres shortly before leaving New York. De Casseres, after tracing Jules de Gaultier's philosophic genealogy back to Schopenhauer and Nietzsche, had concluded with the proposition that out of their two formulas de Gaultier had constructed an even profounder formula. The "Will-to-Live" of the one and the "Will-to-Power" of the other were, after all, only parts of de Gaultier's supreme generalization, the "Will-to-Illusion."

I flatter myself that even De Casseres would have been pleased with the way I repeated his argument. And when I had concluded it, Miss West

244

promptly demanded if the realists might not be fooled by their own phrases as often and as completely as were the poor common mortals with the vital lies they never questioned.

And there we were. An ordinary young woman, who had never vexed her brains with ultimate problems, hears such things stated for the first time, and immediately, and with a laugh, sweeps them all away. I doubt not that De Casseres would have agreed with her.

"Do you believe in God?" I asked rather abruptly. She dropped her sewing into her lap, looked at me meditatively, then gazed on and away across the flashing sea and up into the azure dome of sky. And finally, with true feminine evasion, she replied:

"My father does."

"But you?" I insisted.

"I really don't know. I don't bother my head about such things. I used to when I was a little girl. And yet . . . yes, surely I believe in God. At times, when I am not thinking about it at all, I am very sure, and my faith that all is well is just as strong as the faith of your Jewish friend in the phrases of the philosophers. That's all it comes to, I suppose, in every case—faith. But, as I say, why bother?"

"Ah, I have you now, Miss West!" I cried. "You are a true daughter of Herodias."

"It doesn't sound nice," she said with a *moue*.

"And it isn't," I exulted. "Nevertheless, it is what you are. It is Arthur Symon's poem, *The Daughters of Herodias*. Some day I shall read it to you, and you will answer. I know you will answer that you, too, have looked often upon the stars."

We had just got upon the subject of music, of which she possesses a surprisingly solid knowledge, and she was telling me that Debussy and his school held no particular charm for her, when Possum set up a wild yelping.

245

The puppy had strayed for'ard along the bridge to the 'midship-house, and had evidently been investigating the chickens when his disaster came upon him. So shrill was his terror that we both stood up. He was dashing along the bridge toward us at full speed, yelping at every jump and continually turning his head back in the direction whence he came.

I spoke to him and held out my hand, and was rewarded with a snap and clash of teeth as he scuttled past. Still with head turned back, he went on along the poop. Before I could apprehend his danger, Mr. Pike and Miss West were after him. The mate was the nearer, and with a magnificent leap gained the rail just in time to intercept Possum, who was blindly going overboard under the slender railing. With a sort of scooping kick Mr. Pike sent the animal rolling half across the poop. Howling and snapping more violently, Possum regained his feet and staggered on toward the opposite railing.

"Don't touch him!" Mr. Pike cried, as Miss West showed her intention of catching the crazed little animal with her hands. "Don't touch'm! He's got a fit."

But it did not deter her. He was half-way under the railing when she caught him up and held him at arm's length while he howled and barked and slavered.

"It's a fit," said Mr. Pike, as the terrier collapsed and lay on the deck jerking convulsively.

"Perhaps a chicken pecked him," said Miss West. "At any rate, get a bucket of water."

"Better let me take him," I volunteered helplessly, for I was unfamiliar with fits.

"No; it's all right," she answered. "I'll take charge of him. The cold water is what he needs. He got too close to the coop, and a peck on the nose frightened him into the fit."

"First time I ever heard of a fit coming that way," Mr. Pike remarked, as he poured water over the puppy under Miss West's direction. "It's just a plain puppy fit. They all get them at sea."

"I think it was the sails that caused it," I argued. "I've noticed that he is very afraid of them. When they flap, he crouches down in terror and starts to run. You noticed how he ran with his head turned back?"

"I've seen dogs with fits do that when there was nothing to frighten them," Mr. Pike contended.

"It was a fit, no matter what caused it," Miss West stated conclusively. "Which means that he has not been fed properly. From now on I shall feed him. You tell your boy that, Mr. Pathurst. Nobody is to feed Possum anything without my permission."

At this juncture Wada arrived with Possum's little sleeping box, and they prepared to take him below.

"It was splendid of you, Miss West," I said, "and rash, as well, and I won't attempt to thank you. But I tell you what-you take him. He's your dog now."

She laughed and shook her head as I opened the chart-house door for her to pass.

"No; but I'll take care of him for you. Now don't bother to come below. This is my affair, and you would only be in the way. Wada will help me."

And I was rather surprised, as I returned to my deck chair and sat down, to find how affected I was by the little episode. I remembered, at the first, that my pulse had been distinctly accelerated with the excitement of what had taken place. And somehow, as I leaned back in my chair and lighted a cigarette, the strangeness of the whole voyage vividly came to me. Miss West and I talk philosophy and art on the poop of a stately ship in a circle of flashing sea, while Captain West dreams of his far home, and Mr. Pike and Mr. Mellaire stand watch and watch and snarl orders, and the slaves of men pull and haul, and Possum has fits, and Andy Fay and Mulligan Jacobs burn with hatred unconsumable, and the small-handed half-caste Chinese cooks for all, and Sundry Buyers perpetually presses his abdomen, and O'Sullivan raves in the steel cell of the 'midship-house, and Charles Davis lies about him nursing a marlin-spike, and Christian Jespersen, miles astern, is deep sunk in the sea with a sack of coal at his feet.

CHAPTER XVII

Two weeks out to-day, on a balmy sea, under a cloud-flecked sky, and slipping an easy eight knots through the water to a light easterly wind. Captain West said he was almost convinced that it was the north-east trade. Also, I have learned that the *Elsinore*, in order to avoid being jammed down on Cape San Roque, on the Brazil coast, must first fight eastward almost to the coast of Africa. On occasion, on this traverse, the Cape Verde Islands are raised. No wonder the voyage from Baltimore to Seattle is reckoned at eighteen thousand miles.

I found Tony, the suicidal Greek, steering this morning when I came on deck. He seemed sensible enough, and quite rationally took off his hat when I said good morning to him. The sick men are improving nicely, with the exceptions of Charles Davis and O'Sullivan. The latter still is lashed to his bunk, and Mr. Pike has compelled Davis to attend on him. As a result, Davis moves about the deck, bringing food and water from the galley and grumbling his wrongs to every member of the crew.

Wada told me a strange thing this morning. It seems that he, the steward, and the two sail-makers foregather each evening in the cook's room—all being Asiatics—where they talk over ship's gossip. They seem to miss little, and Wada brings it all to me. The thing Wada told me was the curious conduct of Mr. Mellaire. They have sat in judgment on him and they do not approve of his intimacy with the three gangsters for'ard.

"But, Wada," I said, "he is not that kind of a man. He is very hard and rough with all the sailors. He treats them like dogs. You know that."

"Sure," assented Wada. "Other sailors he do that. But those three very bad men he make good friends. Louis say second mate belong aft like first mate and captain. No good for second mate talk like friend with sailors. No good for ship. Bime by trouble. You see. Louis say Mr. Mellaire crazy do that kind funny business."

248

All of which, if it were true, and I saw no reason to doubt it, led me to inquire. It seems that the gangsters, Kid Twist, Nosey Murphy, and Bert Rhine, have made themselves cocks of the forecastle. Standing together, they have established a reign of terror and are ruling the forecastle. All their training in New York in ruling the slum brutes and weaklings in their gangs fits them for the part. As near as I could make out from Wada's tale, they first began on the two Italians in their watch, Guido Bombini and Mike Cipriani. By means I cannot guess, they have reduced these two wretches to trembling slaves. As an instance, the other night, according to the ship's gossip, Bert Rhine made Bombini get out of bed and fetch him a drink of water.

Isaac Chantz is likewise under their rule, though he is treated more kindly. Herman Lunkenheimer, a good-natured but simple-minded dolt of a German, received a severe beating from the three because he refused to wash some of Nosey Murphy's dirty garments. The two bosuns are in fear of their lives with this clique, which is growing; for Steve Roberts, the ex-cowboy, and the white-slaver, Arthur Deacon, have been admitted to it.

I am the only one aft who possesses this information, and I confess I don't know what to do with it. I know that Mr. Pike would tell me to mind my own business. Mr. Mellaire is out of the question. And Captain West hasn't any crew. And I fear Miss West would laugh at me for my pains. Besides, I understand that every forecastle has its bully, or group of bullies; so this is merely a forecastle matter and no concern of the afterguard. The ship's work goes on. The only effect I can conjecture is an increase in the woes of the unfortunates who must bow to this petty tyranny for'ard.

—Oh, and another thing Wada told me. The gangster clique has established its privilege of taking first cut of the salt-beef in the meat-kids. After that, the rest take the rejected pieces. But I will say, contrary to my expectations, the *Elsinore's* forecastle is well found. The men are not on whack. They have all they want to eat. A barrel of good hardtack stands always open in the forecastle. Louis bakes fresh bread for the sailors three times a week. The variety of food is excellent, if not the quality. There is no restriction in the amount of water for drinking purposes. And I can only say that in this good weather the men's appearance improves daily.

249

Possum is very sick. Each day he grows thinner. Scarcely can I call him a perambulating skeleton, because he is too weak to walk. Each day, in this delightful weather, Wada, under Miss West's instructions, brings him up in his box and places him out of the wind on the awninged poop. She has taken full charge of the puppy, and has him sleep in her room each night. I found her yesterday, in the chart-room, reading up the *Elsinore*'s medical library. Later on she overhauled the medicine-chest. She is essentially the life-giving, life-conserving female of the species. All her ways, for herself and for others, make toward life.

And yet—and this is so curious it gives me pause—she shows no interest in the sick and injured for'ard.

They are to her cattle, or less than cattle. As the life-giver and race-conserver, I should have imagined her a Lady Bountiful, tripping regularly into that ghastly steel-walled hospital room of the midship-house and dispensing gruel, sunshine, and even tracts. On the contrary, as with her father, these wretched humans do not exist.

And still again, when the steward jammed a splinter under his nail, she was greatly concerned, and manipulated the tweezers and pulled it out. The Elsinore reminds me of a slave plantation before the war; and Miss West is the lady of the plantation, interested only in the house-slaves. The field slaves are beyond her ken or consideration, and the sailors are the Elsinore's field slaves. Why, several days back, when Wada suffered from a severe headache, she was quite perturbed, and dosed him with aspirin. Well, I suppose this is all due to her sea-training. She has been trained hard.

We have the phonograph in the second dog-watch every other evening in this fine weather. On the alternate evenings this period is Mr. Pike's watch on deck. But when it is his evening below, even at dinner, he betrays his anticipation by an eagerness ill suppressed. And yet, on each such occasion, he punctiliously waits until we ask if we are to be favoured with music. Then his hard-bitten face lights up, although the lines remain hard as ever, hiding his ecstasy, and he remarks gruffly, off-handedly, that he guesses he can play over a few records. And so, every other evening, we watch this killer and driver, with lacerated knuckles and gorilla paws, brushing and caressing his beloved discs, ravished with the music of them, and, as he told me early in the voyage, at such moments believing in God.

A strange experience is this life on the Elsinore. I confess, while it seems that I have been here for long months, so familiar am I with every detail of the little round of living, that I cannot orient myself. My mind continually strays from things non-understandable to things incomprehensible—from our Samurai captain with the exquisite Gabriel voice that is heard only in the tumult and thunder of storm; on to the ill-treated and feeble-minded faun with the bright, liquid, pain-filled eyes; to the three gangsters who rule the forecastle and seduce the second mate; to the perpetually muttering O'Sullivan in the steel-walled hole and the complaining Davis nursing the marlin-spike in the upper bunk; and to Christian Jespersen somewhere adrift in this vastitude of ocean with a coal-sack at his feet. At such moments all the life on the *Elsinore* becomes as unreal as life to the philosopher is unreal.

I am a philosopher. Therefore, it is unreal to me. But is it unreal to Messrs. Pike and Mellaire? to the lunatics and idiots? to the rest of the stupid herd for'ard? I cannot help remembering a remark of De Casseres. It was over the wine in Mouquin's. Said he: "The profoundest instinct in man is to war against the truth; that is, against the Real. He shuns facts from his infancy. His life is a perpetual evasion. Miracle, chimera and to-morrow keep him alive. He lives on fiction and myth. It is the Lie that makes him free. Animals alone are given the privilege of lifting the veil of Isis; men dare not. The animal, awake, has no fictional escape from the Real because he has no imagination. Man, awake, is compelled to seek a perpetual escape into Hope, Belief, Fable, Art, God, Socialism, Immortality, Alcohol, Love. From Medusa-Truth he makes an appeal to Maya-Lie."

Ben will agree that I have quoted him fairly. And so, the thought comes to me, that to all these slaves of the *Elsinore* the Real is real because they fictionally escape it. One and all they are obsessed with the belief that they are free agents. To me the Real is unreal, because I have torn aside the veils of fiction and myth. My pristine fictional escape from the Real, making

251

me a philosopher, has bound me absolutely to the wheel of the Real. I, the super-realist, am the only unrealist on board the *Elsinore*. Therefore I, who penetrate it deepest, in the whole phenomena of living on the *Elsinore* see it only as phantasmagoria.

Paradoxes? I admit it. All deep thinkers are drowned in the sea of contradictions. But all the others on the *Elsinore*, sheer surface swimmers, keep afloat on this sea—forsooth, because they have never dreamed its depth. And I can easily imagine what Miss West's practical, hard-headed judgment would be on these speculations of mine. After all, words are traps. I don't know what I know, nor what I think I think.

This I do know: I cannot orient myself. I am the maddest and most sea-lost soul on board. Take Miss West. I am beginning to admire her. Why, I know not, unless it be because she is so abominably healthy. And yet, it is this very health of her, the absence of any shred of degenerative genius, that prevents her from being great . . . for instance, in her music.

A number of times, now, I have come in during the day to listen to her playing. The piano is good, and her teaching has evidently been of the best. To my astonishment I learn that she is a graduate of Bryn Mawr, and that her father took a degree from old Bowdoin long ago. And yet she lacks in her music.

Her touch is masterful. She has the firmness and weight (without sharpness or pounding) of a man's playing—the strength and surety that most women lack and that some women know they lack. When she makes a slip she is ruthless with herself, and replays until the difficulty is overcome. And she is quick to overcome it.

Yes, and there is a sort of temperament in her work, but there is no sentiment, no fire. When she plays Chopin, she interprets his sureness and neatness. She is the master of Chopin's technique, but she never walks where Chopin walks on the heights. Somehow, she stops short of the fulness of music.

I did like her method with Brahms, and she was not unwilling, at my suggestion, to go over and over the Three Rhapsodies. On the Third Intermezzo she was at her best, and a good best it was.

"You were talking of Debussy," she remarked. "I've got some of his stuff here. But I don't get into it. I don't understand it, and there is no use in trying. It doesn't seem altogether like real music to me. It fails to get hold of me, just as I fail to get hold of it."

"Yet you like MacDowell," I challenged.

"Y . . . es," she admitted grudgingly. "His New England Idylls and Fireside Tales. And I like that Finnish man's stuff, Sibelius, too, although it seems to me too soft, too richly soft, too beautiful, if you know what I mean. It seems to cloy."

What a pity, I thought, that with that noble masculine touch of hers she is unaware of the deeps of music. Some day I shall try to get from her just what Beethoven, say, and Chopin, mean to her. She has not read Shaw's *Perfect Wagnerite*, nor had she ever heard of Nietzsche's *Case of Wagner*. She likes Mozart, and old Boccherini, and Leonardo Leo. Likewise she is partial to Schumann, especially Forest Scenes. And she played his Papillons most brilliantly. When I closed my eyes I could have sworn it was a man's fingers on the keys.

And yet, I must say it, in the long run her playing makes me nervous. I am continually led up to false expectations. Always, she seems just on the verge of achieving the big thing, the super-big thing, and always she just misses it by a shade. Just as I am prepared for the culminating flash and illumination, I receive more perfection of technique. She is cold. She must be cold . . . Or else, and the theory is worth considering, she is too healthy.

I shall certainly read to her *The Daughters of Herodias*.

CHAPTER XVIII

Was there ever such a voyage! This morning, when I came on deck, I found nobody at the wheel. It was a startling sight—the great *Elsinore*, by the wind, under an Alpine range of canvas, every sail set from skysails to try-sails and spanker, slipping across the surface of a mild trade-wind sea, and no hand at the wheel to guide her.

No one was on the poop. It was Mr. Pike's watch, and I strolled for'ard along the bridge to find him. He was on Number One hatch giving some instructions to the sail-makers. I awaited my chance, until he glanced up and greeted me.

"Good morning," I answered. "And what man is at the wheel now?"

"That crazy Greek, Tony," he replied.

"A month's wages to a pound of tobacco he isn't," I offered.

Mr. Pike looked at me with quick sharpness.

"Who is at the wheel?"

"Nobody," I replied.

And then he exploded into action. The age-lag left his massive frame, and he bounded aft along the deck at a speed no man on board could have exceeded; and I doubt if very many could have equalled it. He went up the poop-ladder three steps at a time and disappeared in the direction of the wheel behind the chart-house.

Next came a promptitude of bellowed orders, and all the watch was slacking away after braces to starboard and pulling on after braces to port. I had already learned the manoeuvre. Mr. Pike was wearing ship.

As I returned aft along the bridge Mr. Mellaire and the carpenter emerged from the cabin door. They had been interrupted at breakfast, for they were wiping their mouths. Mr. Pike came to the break of the poop, called down instructions to the second mate, who proceeded for'ard, and ordered the carpenter to take the wheel.

As the *Elsinore* swung around on her heel Mr. Pike put her on the back track so as to cover the water she had just crossed over. He lowered the glasses through which he was scanning the sea and pointed down the hatchway that opened into the big after-room beneath. The ladder was gone.

"Must have taken the lazarette ladder with him," said Mr. Pike.

Captain West strolled out of the chart-room. He said good morning in his customary way, courteously to me and formally to the mate, and strolled on along the poop to the wheel, where he paused to glance into the binnacle. Turning, he went on leisurely to the break of the poop. Again he came back to us. Fully two minutes must have elapsed ere he spoke.

"What is the matter, Mr. Pike? Man overboard?"

"Yes, sir," was the answer.

"And took the lazarette ladder along with him?" Captain West queried.

"Yes, sir. It's the Greek that jumped over at Baltimore."

Evidently the affair was not serious enough for Captain West to be the Samurai. He lighted a cigar and resumed his stroll. And yet he had missed nothing, not even the absence of the ladder.

Mr. Pike sent look-outs aloft to every skysail-yard, and the *Elsinore* slipped along through the smooth sea. Miss West came up and stood beside me, searching the ocean with her eyes while I told her the little I knew. She evidenced no excitement, and reassured me by telling me how difficult it was to lose a man of Tony's suicidal type.

"Their madness always seems to come upon them in fine weather or under safe circumstances," she smiled, "when a boat can be lowered or a tug is alongside. And sometimes they take life—preservers with them, as in this case."

At the end of an hour Mr. Pike wore the *Elsinore* around, and again retraced the course she must have been sailing when the Greek went over. Captain West still strolled and smoked, and Miss West made a brief trip below to give Wada forgotten instructions about Possum. Andy Pay was called to the wheel, and the carpenter went below to finish his breakfast.

It all seemed rather callous to me. Nobody was much concerned for the man who was overboard somewhere on that lonely ocean. And yet I had to admit that everything possible was being done to find him. I talked a little with Mr. Pike, and he seemed more vexed than anything else. He disliked to have the ship's work interrupted in such fashion.

Mr. Mellaire's attitude was different.

"We are short-handed enough as it is," he told me, when he joined us on the poop. "We can't afford to lose him even if he is crazy. We need him. He's a good sailor most of the time."

The hail came from the mizzen-skysail-yard. The Maltese Cockney it was who first sighted the man and called down the information. The mate, looking to windwards, suddenly lowered his glasses, rubbed his eyes in a puzzled way, and looked again. Then Miss West, using another pair of glasses, cried out in surprise and began to laugh.

"What do you make of it, Miss West?" the mate asked.

"He doesn't seem to be in the water. He's standing up."

Mr. Pike nodded.

"He's on the ladder," he said. "I'd forgotten that. It fooled me at first. I couldn't understand it." He turned to the second mate. "Mr. Mellaire, will you launch the long boat and get some kind of a crew into it while I back the main-yard? I'll go in the boat. Pick men that can pull an oar."

"You go, too," Miss West said to me. "It will be an opportunity to get outside the *Elsinore* and see her under full sail."

Mr. Pike nodded consent, so I went along, sitting near him in the stern-sheets where he steered, while half a dozen hands rowed us toward the suicide, who stood so weirdly upon the surface of the sea. The Maltese Cockney pulled the stroke oar, and among the other five men was one whose name I had but recently learned—Ditman Olansen, a Norwegian. A good seaman, Mr. Mellaire had told me, in whose watch he was; a good seaman, but "crank-eyed." When pressed for an explanation Mr. Mellaire had said that he was the sort of man who flew into blind rages, and that one never could tell what little thing would produce such a rage. As near as I could grasp it, Ditman Olansen was a Berserker type. Yet, as I watched him pulling in good time at the oar, his large, pale-blue eyes seemed almost bovine—the last man in the world, in my judgment, to have a Berserker fit.

As we drew close to the Greek he began to scream menacingly at us and to brandish a sheath-knife. His weight sank the ladder until the water washed his knees, and on this submerged support he balanced himself with wild writhing and outflinging of arms. His face, grimacing like a monkey's, was not a pretty thing to look upon. And as he continued to threaten us with the knife I wondered how the problem of rescuing him would be solved.

But I should have trusted Mr. Pike for that. He removed the boat-stretcher from under the Maltese Cockney's feet and laid it close to hand in the stern-sheets. Then he had the men reverse the boat and back it upon the Greek. Dodging a sweep of the knife, Mr. Pike awaited his chance, until a passing wave lifted the boat's stern high, while Tony was sinking toward the trough. This was the moment. Again I was favoured with a sample of the lightning speed with which that aged man of sixty-nine could handle his body. Timed precisely, and delivered in a flash and with weight, the boat-stretcher came down on the Greek's head. The knife fell into the sea, and the demented creature collapsed and followed it, knocked unconscious. Mr. Pike scooped him out, quite effortlessly it seemed to me, and flung him into the boat's bottom at my feet.

The next moment the men were bending to their oars and the mate was steering back to the *Elsinore*. It was a stout rap Mr. Pike had administered with the boat-stretcher. Thin streaks of blood oozed on the damp, plastered hair from the broken scalp. I could but stare at the lump of unconscious flesh that dripped sea-water at my feet. A man, all life and movement one moment, defying the universe, reduced the next moment to immobility and the blackness and blankness of death, is always a fascinating object for the contemplative eye of the philosopher. And in this case it had been accomplished so simply, by means of a stick of wood brought sharply in contact with his skull.

If Tony the Greek be accounted an *appearance*, what was he now?—a *disappearance*? And if so, whither had he disappeared? And whence would he journey back to reoccupy that body when what we call consciousness returned to him? The first word, much less the last, of the phenomena of personality and consciousness yet remains to be uttered by the psychologists.

Pondering thus, I chanced to lift my eyes, and the glorious spectacle of the *Elsinore* burst upon me. I had been so long on board, and in board of her, that I had forgotten she was a white-painted ship. So low to the water was her hull, so delicate and slender, that the tall, sky-reaching spars and masts and the hugeness of the spread of canvas seemed preposterous and impossible, an insolent derision of the law of gravitation. It required effort to realize that that slim curve of hull inclosed and bore up from the sea's bottom five thousand tons of coal. And again, it seemed a miracle that the mites of men had conceived and constructed so stately and magnificent an element-defying fabric—mites of men, most woefully like the Greek at my feet, prone to precipitation into the blackness by means of a rap on the head with a piece of wood.

Tony made a struggling noise in his throat, then coughed and groaned. From somewhere he was reappearing. I noticed Mr. Pike look at him quickly, as if apprehending some recrudescence of frenzy that would require more boat-stretcher. But Tony merely fluttered his big black eyes open and stared at me for a long minute of incurious amaze ere he closed them again.

"What are you going to do with him?" I asked the mate.

"Put 'm back to work," was the reply. "It's all he's good for, and he ain't hurt. Somebody's got to work this ship around the Horn."

When we hoisted the boat on board I found Miss West had gone below. In the chart-room Captain West was winding the chronometers. Mr. Mellaire had turned in to catch an hour or two of sleep ere his watch on deck at noon. Mr. Mellaire, by the way, as I have forgotten to state, does not sleep aft. He shares a room in the 'midship-house with Mr. Pike's Nancy.

Nobody showed sympathy for the unfortunate Greek. He was bundled out upon Number Two hatch like so much carrion and left there unattended, to recover consciousness as he might elect. Yes, and so inured have I become that I make free to admit I felt no sympathy for him myself. My eyes were still filled with the beauty of the *Elsinore*. One does grow hard at sea.

CHAPTER XIX

One does not mind the trades. We have held the north-east trade for days now, and the miles roll off behind us as the patent log whirls and tinkles on the taffrail. Yesterday, log and observation approximated a run of two hundred and fifty-two miles; the day before we ran two hundred and forty, and the day before that two hundred and sixty-one. But one does not appreciate the force of the wind. So balmy and exhilarating is it that it is so much atmospheric wine. I delight to open my lungs and my pores to it. Nor does it chill. At any hour of the night, while the cabin lies asleep, I break off from my reading and go up on the poop in the thinnest of tropical pyjamas.

I never knew before what the trade wind was. And now I am infatuated with it. I stroll up and down for an hour at a time, with whichever mate has the watch. Mr. Mellaire is always full-garmented, but Mr. Pike, on these delicious nights, stands his first watch after midnight in his pyjamas. He is a fearfully muscular man. Sixty-nine years seem impossible when I see his single, slimpsy garments pressed like fleshings against his form and bulged by heavy bone and huge muscle. A splendid figure of a man! What he must have been in the hey-day of youth two score years and more ago passes comprehension.

The days, so filled with simple routine, pass as in a dream. Here, where time is rigidly measured and emphasized by the changing of the watches, where every hour and half-hour is persistently brought to one's notice by the striking of the ship's bells fore and aft, time ceases. Days merge into days, and weeks slip into weeks, and I, for one, can never remember the day of the week or month.

The *Elsinore* is never totally asleep. Day and night, always, there are the men on watch, the look-out on the forecastle head, the man at the wheel, and the officer of the deck. I lie reading in my bunk, which is on the weather side, and continually over my head during the long night hours impact the footsteps of one mate or the other, pacing up and down, and, as I well know, the man himself is for ever peering for'ard from the break of the poop, or glancing into the binnacle, or feeling and gauging the weight and direction of wind on his cheek, or watching the cloud-stuff in the sky adrift and a-scud across the stars and the moon. Always, always, there are wakeful eyes on the *Elsinore*.

Last night, or this morning, rather, about two o'clock, as I lay with the printed page swimming drowsily before me, I was aroused by an abrupt outbreak of snarl from Mr. Pike. I located him as at the break of the poop; and the man at whom he snarled was Larry, evidently on the main deck beneath him. Not until Wada brought me breakfast did I learn what had occurred.

Larry, with his funny pug nose, his curiously flat and twisted face, and his querulous, plaintive chimpanzee eyes, had been moved by some unlucky whim to venture an insolent remark under the cover of darkness on the main deck. But Mr. Pike, from above, at the break of the poop, had picked the offender unerringly. This was when the explosion occurred. Then the unfortunate Larry, truly half-devil and all child, had waxed sullen and retorted still more insolently; and the next he knew, the mate, descending upon him like a hurricane, had handcuffed him to the mizzen fife-rail.

Imagine, on Mr. Pike's part, that this was one for Larry and at least ten for Kid Twist, Nosey Murphy, and Bert Rhine. I'll not be so absurd as to say that the mate is afraid of those gangsters. I doubt if he has ever experienced fear. It is not in him. On the other hand, I am confident that he apprehends trouble from these men, and that it was for their benefit he made this example of Larry.

Larry could stand no more than an hour in irons, at which time his stupid brutishness overcame any fear he might have possessed, because he bellowed out to the poop to come down and loose him for a fair fight. Promptly Mr. Pike was there with the key to the handcuffs. As if Larry had the shred of a chance against that redoubtable aged man! Wada reported that Larry, amongst other things, had lost a couple of front teeth and was laid up in his bunk for the day. When I met Mr. Pike on deck after eight o'clock I glanced at his knuckles. They verified Wada's tale.

I cannot help being amused by the keen interest I take in little events like the foregoing. Not only has time ceased, but the world has ceased. Strange it is, when I come to think of it, in all these weeks I have received no letter, no telephone call, no telegram, no visitor. I have not been to the play. I have not read a newspaper. So far as I am concerned, there are no plays nor newspapers. All such things have vanished with the vanished world. All that exists is the *Elsinore*, with her queer human freightage and her cargo of coal, cleaving a rotund of ocean of which the skyline is a dozen miles away.

I am reminded of Captain Scott, frozen on his south-polar venture, who for ten months after his death was believed by the world to be alive. Not until the world learned of his death was he anything but alive to the world. By the same token, was he not alive? And by the same token, here on the *Elsinore*, has not the land-world ceased? May not the pupil of one's eye be, not merely the centre of the world, but the world itself? Truly, it is tenable that the world exists only in consciousness. "The world is my idea," said Schopenhauer. Said Jules de Gaultier, "The world is my invention." His dogma was that imagination created the Real. Ah, me, I know that the practical Miss West would dub my metaphysics a depressing and unhealthful exercise of my wits.

To-day, in our deck chairs on the poop, I read *The Daughters of Herodias* to Miss West. It was superb in its effect—just what I had expected of her. She hemstitched a fine white linen handkerchief for her father while I read. (She is never idle, being so essentially a nest-maker and comfort-producer and race-conserver; and she has a whole pile of these handkerchiefs for her father.)

261

She smiled, how shall I say?—oh, incredulously, triumphantly, oh, with all the sure wisdom of all the generations of women in her warm, long gray eyes, when I read:

"But they smile innocently and dance on,

Having no thought but this unslumbering thought:

'Am I not beautiful? Shall I not be loved?'

Be patient, for they will not understand,

Not till the end of time will they put by

The weaving of slow steps about men's hearts."

"But it is well for the world that it is so," was her comment.

Ah, Symons knew women! His perfect knowledge she attested when I read that magnificent passage:

"They do not understand that in the world

There grows between the sunlight and the grass

Anything save themselves desirable.

It seems to them that the swift eyes of men

Are made but to be mirrors, not to see

Far-off, disastrous, unattainable things.

'For are not we,' they say, 'the end of all?

Why should you look beyond us? If you look

Into the night, you will find nothing there:

We also have gazed often at the stars.'"

"It is true," said Miss West, in the pause I permitted in order to see how she had received the thought. "We also have gazed often at the stars."

It was the very thing I had predicted to her face that she would say.

"But wait," I cried. "Let me read on." And I read:

"'We, we alone among all beautiful things,

We only are real: for the rest are dreams.

Why will you follow after wandering dreams

When we await you? And you can but dream

Of us, and in our image fashion them.'"

"True, most true," she murmured, while all unconsciously pride and power mounted in her eyes.

"A wonderful poem," she conceded—nay, proclaimed—when I had done.

"But do you not see . . ." I began impulsively, then abandoned the attempt. For how could she see, being woman, the "far-off, disastrous, unattainable things," when she, as she so stoutly averred, had gazed often on the stars?

She? What could she see, save what all women see—that they only are real, and that all the rest are dreams.

"I am proud to be a daughter of Herodias," said Miss West.

"Well," I admitted lamely, "we agree. You remember it is what I told you-you were."

"I am grateful for the compliment," she said; and in those long gray eyes of hers were limned and coloured all the satisfaction, and self-certitude and answering complacency of power that constitute so large a part of the seductive mystery and mastery that is possessed by woman.

CHAPTER XX

Heavens!—how I read in this fine weather. I take so little exercise that my sleep need is very small; and there are so few interruptions, such as life teems with on the land, that I read myself almost stupid. Recommend me a sea-voyage any time for a man who is behind in his reading. I am making up years of it. It is an orgy, a debauch; and I am sure the addled sailors adjudge me the queerest creature on board.

At times, so fuzzy do I get from so much reading, that I am glad for any diversion. When we strike the doldrums, which lie between the north-east and the south-east trades, I shall have Wada assemble my little twenty-two automatic rifle and try to learn how to shoot. I used to shoot, when I was a wee lad. I can remember dragging a shot-gun around with me over the hills. Also, I possessed an air-rifle, with which, on great occasion, I was even able to slaughter a robin.

While the poop is quite large for promenading, the available space for deck-chairs is limited to the awnings that stretch across from either side of the chart-house and that are of the width of the chart-house. This space again is restricted to one side or the other according to the slant of the morning and afternoon sun and the freshness of the breeze. Wherefore, Miss West's chair and mine are most frequently side by side. Captain West has a chair, which he infrequently occupies. He has so little to do in the working of the ship, taking his regular observations and working them up with such celerity, that he is rarely in the chart-room for any length of time. He elects to spend his hours in the main cabin, not reading, not doing anything save dream with eyes wide open in the draught of wind that pours through the open ports and door from out the huge crojack and the jigger staysails.

Miss West is never idle. Below, in the big after-room, she does her own laundering. Nor will she let the steward touch her father's fine linen. In the main cabin she has installed a sewing-machine. All hand-stitching, and embroidering, and fancy work she does in the deck-chair beside me. She avers that she loves the sea and the atmosphere of sea-life, yet, verily, she has brought her home-things and land-things along with her—even to her pretty china for afternoon tea.

Most essentially is she the woman and home-maker. She is a born cook. The steward and Louis prepare dishes extraordinary and *de luxe* for the cabin table; yet Miss West is able at a moment's notice to improve on these dishes. She never lets any of their dishes come on the table without first planning them or passing on them. She has quick judgment, an unerring taste, and is possessed of the needful steel of decision. It seems she has only to look at a dish, no matter who has cooked it, and immediately divine its lack or its surplusage, and prescribe a treatment that transforms it into something indescribably different and delicious—My, how I do eat! I am quite dumbfounded by the unfailing voracity of my appetite. Already am I quite convinced that I am glad Miss West is making the voyage.

She has sailed "out East," as she quaintly calls it, and has an enormous repertoire of tasty, spicy, Eastern dishes. In the cooking of rice Louis is a master; but in the making of the accompanying curry he fades into a blundering amateur compared with Miss West. In the matter of curry she is a sheer genius. How often one's thoughts dwell upon food when at sea!

So in this trade-wind weather I see a great deal of Miss West. I read all the time, and quite a good part of the time I read aloud to her passages, and even books, with which I am interested in trying her out. Then, too, such reading gives rise to discussions, and she has not yet uttered anything that would lead me to change my first judgment of her. She is a genuine daughter of Herodias.

And yet she is not what one would call a cute girl. She isn't a girl, she is a mature woman with all the freshness of a girl. She has the carriage, the attitude of mind, the aplomb of a woman, and yet she cannot be described as

265

being in the slightest degree stately. She is generous, dependable, sensible—yes, and sensitive; and her superabundant vitality, the vitality that makes her walk so gloriously, discounts the maturity of her. Sometimes she seems all of thirty to me; at other times, when her spirits and risibilities are aroused, she scarcely seems thirteen. I shall make a point of asking Captain West the date of the *Dixie*'s collision with that river steamer in San Francisco Bay. In a word, she is the most normal, the most healthy, natural woman I have ever known.

Yes, and she is feminine, despite, no matter how she does her hair, that it is as invariably smooth and well-groomed as all the rest of her. On the other hand, this perpetual well-groomedness is relieved by the latitude of dress she allows herself. She never fails of being a woman. Her sex, and the lure of it, is ever present. Possibly she may possess high collars, but I have never seen her in one on board. Her blouses are always open at the throat, disclosing one of her choicest assets, the muscular, adequate neck, with its fine-textured garmenture of skin. I embarrass myself by stealing long glances at that bare throat of hers and at the hint of fine, firm-surfaced shoulder.

Visiting the chickens has developed into a regular function. At least once each day we make the journey for'ard along the bridge to the top of the 'midship-house. Possum, who is now convalescent, accompanies us. The steward makes a point of being there so as to receive instructions and report the egg-output and laying conduct of the many hens. At the present time our four dozen hens are laying two dozen eggs a day, with which record Miss West is greatly elated.

Already she has given names to most of them. The cock is Peter, of course. A much-speckled hen is Dolly Varden. A slim, trim thing that dogs Peter's heels she calls Cleopatra. Another hen—the mellowest-voiced one of all—she addresses as Bernhardt. One thing I have noted: whenever she and the steward have passed death sentence on a non-laying hen (which occurs regularly once a week), she takes no part in the eating of the meat, not even when it is metamorphosed into one of her delectable curries. At such times she has a special curry made for herself of tinned lobster, or shrimp, or tinned chicken.

266

Ah, I must not forget. I have learned that it was no man-interest (in me, if you please) that brought about her sudden interest to come on the voyage. It was for her father that she came. Something is the matter with Captain West. At rare moments I have observed her gazing at him with a world of solicitude and anxiety in her eyes.

I was telling an amusing story at table yesterday midday, when my glance chanced to rest upon Miss West. She was not listening. Her food on her fork was suspended in the air a sheer instant as she looked at her father with all her eyes. It was a stare of fear. She realized that I was observing, and with superb control, slowly, quite naturally, she lowered the fork and rested it on her plate, retaining her hold on it and retaining her father's face in her look.

But I had seen. Yes; I had seen more than that. I had seen Captain West's face a transparent white, while his eyelids fluttered down and his lips moved noiselessly. Then the eyelids raised, the lips set again with their habitual discipline, and the colour slowly returned to his face. It was as if he had been away for a time and just returned. But I had seen, and guessed her secret.

And yet it was this same Captain West, seven hours later, who chastened the proud sailor spirit of Mr. Pike. It was in the second dog-watch that evening, a dark night, and the watch was pulling away on the main deck. I had just come out of the chart-house door and seen Captain West pace by me, hands in pockets, toward the break of the poop. Abruptly, from the mizzen-mast, came a snap of breakage and crash of fabric. At the same instant the men fell backward and sprawled over the deck.

A moment of silence followed, and then Captain West's voice went out:

"What carried away, Mr. Pike?"

"The halyards, sir," came the reply out of the darkness.

There was a pause. Again Captain West's voice went out.

"Next time slack away on your sheet first."

Now Mr. Pike is incontestably a splendid seaman. Yet in this instance he had been wrong. I have come to know him, and I can well imagine the hurt to his pride. And more—he has a wicked, resentful, primitive nature, and though he answered respectfully enough, "Yes, sir," I felt safe in predicting to myself that the poor devils under him would receive the weight of his resentment in the later watches of the night.

They evidently did; for this morning I noted a black eye on John Hackey, a San Francisco hoodlum, and Guido Bombini was carrying a freshly and outrageously swollen jaw. I asked Wada about the matter, and he soon brought me the news. Quite a bit of beating up takes place for'ard of the deck-houses in the night watches while we of the after-guard peacefully slumber.

Even to-day Mr. Pike is going around sullen and morose, snarling at the men more than usual, and barely polite to Miss West and me when we chance to address him. His replies are grunted in monosyllables, and his face is set in superlative sourness. Miss West who is unaware of the occurrence, laughs and calls it a "sea grouch"—a phenomenon with which she claims large experience.

But I know Mr. Pike now—the stubborn, wonderful old sea-dog. It will be three days before he is himself again. He takes a terrible pride in his seamanship, and what hurts him most is the knowledge that he was guilty of the blunder.

CHAPTER XXI

To-day, twenty-eight days out, in the early morning, while I was drinking my coffee, still carrying the north-east trade, we crossed the line. And Charles Davis signalized the event by murdering O'Sullivan. It was Boney, the lanky splinter of a youth in Mr. Mellaire's watch, who brought the news. The second mate and I had just arrived in the hospital room, when Mr. Pike entered.

O'Sullivan's troubles were over. The man in the upper bunk had completed the mad, sad span of his life with the marlin-spike.

I cannot understand this Charles Davis. He sat up calmly in his bunk, and calmly lighted his pipe ere he replied to Mr. Mellaire. He certainly is not insane. Yet deliberately, in cold blood, he has murdered a helpless man.

"What'd you do it for?" Mr. Mellaire demanded.

"Because, sir," said Charles Davis, applying a second match to his pipe, "because"—puff, puff—"he bothered my sleep." Here he caught Mr. Pike's glowering eye. "Because"—puff, puff—"he annoyed me. The next time"— puff, puff—"I hope better judgment will be shown in what kind of a man is put in with me. Besides"—puff, puff—"this top bunk ain't no place for me. It hurts me to get into it"—puff, puff—"an' I'm gem' back to that lower bunk as soon as you get O'Sullivan out of it."

"But what'd you do it for?" Mr. Pike snarled.

"I told you, sir, because he annoyed me. I got tired of it, an' so, this morning, I just put him out of his misery. An' what are you goin' to do about it? The man's dead, ain't he? An' I killed 'm in self-defence. I know the law. What right'd you to put a ravin' lunatic in with me, an' me sick an' helpless?"

"By God, Davis!" the mate burst forth. "You'll never draw your pay-day in Seattle. I'll fix you out for this, killing a crazy lashed down in his bunk an' harmless. You'll follow 'm overside, my hearty."

"If I do, you'll hang for it, sir," Davis retorted. He turned his cool eyes on me. "An' I call on you, sir, to witness the threats he's made. An' you'll testify to them, too, in court. An' he'll hang as sure as I go over the side. Oh, I know his record. He's afraid to face a court with it. He's been up too many a time with charges of man-killin' an' brutality on the high seas. An' a man could retire for life an live off the interest of the fines he's paid, or his owners paid for him—"

"Shut your mouth or I'll knock it out of your face!" Mr. Pike roared, springing toward him with clenched, up-raised fist.

Davis involuntarily shrank away. His flesh was weak, but not so his spirit. He got himself promptly in hand and struck another match.

269

"You can't get my goat, sir," he sneered, under the shadow of the impending blow. "I ain't scared to die. A man's got to die once anyway, an' it's none so hard a trick to do when you can't help it. O'Sullivan died so easy it was amazin'. Besides, I ain't goin' to die. I'm goin' to finish this voyage, an' sue the owners when I get to Seattle. I know my rights an' the law. An' I got witnesses."

Truly, I was divided between admiration for the courage of this wretched sailor and sympathy for Mr. Pike thus bearded by a sick man he could not bring himself to strike.

Nevertheless he sprang upon the man with calculated fury, gripped him between the base of the neck and the shoulders with both gnarled paws, and shook him back and forth, violently and frightfully, for a full minute. It was a wonder the man's neck was not dislocated.

"I call on you to witness, sir," Davis gasped at me the instant he was free.

He coughed and strangled, felt his throat, and made wry neck-movements indicative of injury.

"The marks'll begin to show in a few minutes," he murmured complacently as his dizziness left him and his breath came back.

This was too much for Mr. Pike, who turned and left the room, growling and cursing incoherently, deep in his throat. When I made my departure, a moment later, Davis was refilling his pipe and telling Mr. Mellaire that he'd have him up for a witness in Seattle.

* * * * *

So we have had another burial at sea. Mr. Pike was vexed by it because the *Elsinore*, according to sea tradition, was going too fast through the water for a proper ceremony. Thus a few minutes of the voyage were lost by backing the *Elsinore*'s main-topsail and deadening her way while the service was read and O'Sullivan was slid overboard with the inevitable sack of coal at his feet.

"Hope the coal holds out," Mr. Pike grumbled morosely at me five minutes later.

* * * * *

And we sit on the poop, Miss West and I, tended on by servants, sipping afternoon tea, sewing fancy work, discussing philosophy and art, while a few feet away from us, on this tiny floating world, all the grimy, sordid tragedy of sordid, malformed, brutish life plays itself out. And Captain West, remote, untroubled, sits dreaming in the twilight cabin while the draught of wind from the crojack blows upon him through the open ports. He has no doubts, no worries. He believes in God. All is settled and clear and well as he nears his far home. His serenity is vast and enviable. But I cannot shake from my eyes that vision of him when life forsook his veins, and his mouth slacked, and his eyelids closed, while his face took on the white transparency of death.

I wonder who will be the next to finish the game and depart with a sack of coal.

"Oh, this is nothing, sir," Mr. Mellaire remarked to me cheerfully as we strolled the poop during the first watch. "I was once on a voyage on a tramp steamer loaded with four hundred Chinks—I beg your pardon, sir—Chinese. They were coolies, contract labourers, coming back from serving their time.

"And the cholera broke out. We hove over three hundred of them overboard, sir, along with both bosuns, most of the Lascar crew, and the captain, the mate, the third mate, and the first and third engineers. The second and one white oiler was all that was left below, and I was in command on deck, when we made port. The doctors wouldn't come aboard. They made me anchor in the outer roads and told me to heave out my dead. There was some tall buryin' about that time, Mr. Pathurst, and they went overboard without canvas, coal, or iron. They had to. I had nobody to help me, and the Chinks below wouldn't lift a hand.

"I had to go down myself, drag the bodies on to the slings, then climb on deck and heave them up with the donkey. And each trip I took a drink. I was pretty drunk when the job was done."

"And you never caught it yourself?" I queried. Mr. Mellaire held up his left hand. I had often noted that the index finger was missing.

271

"That's all that happened to me, sir. The old man'd had a fox-terrier like yours. And after the old man passed out the puppy got real, chummy with me. Just as I was making the hoist of the last sling-load, what does the puppy do but jump on my leg and sniff my hand. I turned to pat him, and the next I knew my other hand had slipped into the gears and that finger wasn't there any more."

"Heavens!" I cried. "What abominable luck to come through such a terrible experience like that and then lose your finger!"

"That's what I thought, sir," Mr. Mellaire agreed.

"What did you do?" I asked.

"Oh, just held it up and looked at it, and said 'My goodness gracious!' and took another drink."

"And you didn't get the cholera afterwards?"

"No, sir. I reckon I was so full of alcohol the germs dropped dead before they could get to me." He considered a moment. "Candidly, Mr. Pathurst, I don't know about that alcohol theory. The old man and the mates died drunk, and so did the third engineer. But the chief was a teetotaller, and he died, too."

* * * * *

Never again shall I wonder that the sea is hard. I walked apart from the second mate and stared up at the magnificent fabric of the *Elsinore* sweeping and swaying great blotting curves of darkness across the face of the starry sky.

CHAPTER XXII

Something has happened. But nobody knows, either fore or aft, except the interested persons, and they will not say anything. Yet the ship is abuzz with rumours and guesses.

This I do know: Mr. Pike has received a fearful blow on the head. At table, yesterday, at midday, I arrived late, and, passing behind his chair, I saw a prodigious lump on top of his head. When I was seated, facing him, I noted that his eyes seemed dazed; yes, and I could see pain in them. He took no part in the conversation, ate perfunctorily, behaved stupidly at times, and it was patent that he was controlling himself with an iron hand.

And nobody dares ask him what has happened. I know I don't dare ask him, and I am a passenger, a privileged person. This redoubtable old sea-relic has inspired me with a respect for him that partakes half of timidity and half of awe.

He acts as if he were suffering from concussion of the brain. His pain is evident, not alone in his eyes and the strained expression of his face, but by his conduct when he thinks he is unobserved. Last night, just for a breath of air and a moment's gaze at the stars, I came out of the cabin door and stood on the main deck under the break of the poop. From directly over my head came a low and persistent groaning. My curiosity was aroused, and I retreated into the cabin, came out softly on to the poop by way of the chart-house, and strolled noiselessly for'ard in my slippers. It was Mr. Pike. He was leaning collapsed on the rail, his head resting on his arms. He was giving voice in secret to the pain that racked him. A dozen feet away he could not be heard. But, close to his shoulder, I could hear his steady, smothered groaning that seemed to take the form of a chant. Also, at regular intervals, he would mutter:

"Oh dear, oh dear, oh dear, oh dear, oh dear." Always he repeated the phrase five times, then returned to his groaning. I stole away as silently as I had come.

Yet he resolutely stands his watches and performs all his duties of chief officer. Oh, I forgot. Miss West dared to quiz him, and he replied that he had a toothache, and that if it didn't get better he'd pull it out.

Wada cannot learn what has happened. There were no eye-witnesses. He says that the Asiatic clique, discussing the affair in the cook's room, thinks the three gangsters are responsible. Bert Rhine is carrying a lame shoulder. Nosey Murphy is limping as from some injury in the hips. And Kid Twist has been so badly beaten that he has not left his bunk for two days. And that is all the data to build on. The gangsters are as close-mouthed as Mr. Pike. The Asiatic clique has decided that murder was attempted and that all that saved the mate was his hard skull.

Last evening, in the second dog-watch, I got another proof that Captain West is not so oblivious of what goes on aboard the *Elsinore* as he seems. I had gone for'ard along the bridge to the mizzen-mast, in the shadow of which I was leaning. From the main deck, in the alley-way between the 'midship-house and the rail, came the voices of Bert Rhine, Nosey Murphy, and Mr. Mellaire. It was not ship's work. They were having a friendly, even sociable chat, for their voices hummed genially, and now and again one or another laughed, and sometimes all laughed.

I remembered Wada's reports on this unseamanlike intimacy of the second mate with the gangsters, and tried to make out the nature of the conversation. But the gangsters were low-voiced, and all I could catch was the tone of friendliness and good-nature.

Suddenly, from the poop, came Captain West's voice. It was the voice, not of the Samurai riding the storm, but of the Samurai calm and cold. It was clear, soft, and mellow as the mellowest bell ever cast by eastern artificers of old time to call worshippers to prayer. I know I slightly chilled to it—it was so exquisitely sweet and yet as passionless as the ring of steel on a frosty night. And I knew the effect on the men beneath me was electrical. I could *feel* them stiffen and chill to it as I had stiffened and chilled. And yet all he said was:

"Mr. Mellaire."

"Yes, sir," answered Mr. Mellaire, after a moment of tense silence.

"Come aft here," came Captain West's voice.

I heard the second mate move along the deck beneath me and stop at the foot of the poop-ladder.

"Your place is aft on the poop, Mr. Mellaire," said the cold, passionless voice.

"Yes, sir," answered the second mate.

That was all. Not another word was spoken. Captain West resumed his stroll on the weather side of the poop, and Mr. Mellaire, ascending the ladder, went to pacing up and down the lee side.

I continued along the bridge to the forecastle head and purposely remained there half an hour ere I returned to the cabin by way of the main deck. Although I did not analyze my motive, I knew I did not desire any one to know that I had overheard the occurrence.

* * * * *

I have made a discovery. Ninety per cent. of our crew is brunette. Aft, with the exception of Wada and the steward, who are our servants, we are all blonds. What led me to this discovery was Woodruff's *Effects of Tropical Light on White Men*, which I am just reading. Major Woodruff's thesis is that the white-skinned, blue-eyed Aryan, born to government and command, ever leaving his primeval, overcast and foggy home, ever commands and governs the rest of the world and ever perishes because of the too-white light he encounters. It is a very tenable hypothesis, and will bear looking into.

But to return. Every one of us who sits aft in the high place is a blond Aryan. For'ard, leavened with a ten per cent, of degenerate blonds, the remaining ninety per cent, of the slaves that toil for us are brunettes. They will not perish. According to Woodruff, they will inherit the earth, not because of their capacity for mastery and government, but because of their skin-pigmentation which enables their tissues to resist the ravages of the sun.

And I look at the four of us at table—Captain West, his daughter, Mr. Pike, and myself—all fair-skinned, blue-eyed, and perishing, yet mastering and commanding, like our fathers before us, to the end of our type on the earth. Ah, well, ours is a lordly history, and though we may be doomed to pass, in our time we shall have trod on the faces of all peoples, disciplined them to obedience, taught them government, and dwelt in the palaces we have compelled them by the weight of our own right arms to build for us.

The *Elsinore* depicts this in miniature. The best of the food and all spacious and beautiful accommodation is ours. For'ard is a pig-sty and a slave-pen.

As a king, Captain West sits above all. As a captain of soldiers, Mr. Pike enforces his king's will. Miss West is a princess of the royal house. And I? Am I not an honourable, noble-lineaged pensioner on the deeds and achievements of my father, who, in his day, compelled thousands of the lesser types to the building of the fortune I enjoy?

CHAPTER XXIII

The north-west trade carried us almost into the south-east trade, and then left us for several days to roll and swelter in the doldrums.

During this time I have discovered that I have a genius for rifle-shooting. Mr. Pike swore I must have had long practice; and I confess I was myself startled by the ease of the thing. Of course, it's the knack; but one must be so made, I suppose, in order to be able to acquire the knack.

By the end of half an hour, standing on the heaving deck and shooting at bottles floating on the rolling swell, I found that I broke each bottle at the first shot. The supply of empty bottles giving out, Mr. Pike was so interested that he had the carpenter saw me a lot of small square blocks of hard wood. These were more satisfactory. A well-aimed shot threw them out of the water and spinning into the air, and I could use a single block until it had drifted out of range. In an hour's time I could, shooting quickly and at short range, empty my magazine at a block and hit it nine times, and, on occasion, ten times, out of eleven.

I might not have judged my aptitude as unusual, had I not induced Miss West and Wada to try their hands. Neither had luck like mine. I finally persuaded Mr. Pike, and he went behind the wheel-house so that none of the crew might see how poor a shot he was. He was never able to hit the mark, and was guilty of the most ludicrous misses.

"I never could get the hang of rifle-shooting," he announced disgustedly, "but when it comes to close range with a gat I'm right there. I guess I might as well overhaul mine and limber it up."

He went below and came back with a huge '44 automatic pistol and a handful of loaded clips.

"Anywhere from right against the body up to ten or twelve feet away, holding for the stomach, it's astonishing, Mr. Pathurst, what you can do with a weapon like this. Now you can't use a rifle in a mix-up. I've been down and under, with a bunch giving me the boot, when I turned loose with this. Talk about damage! It ranged them the full length of their bodies. One of them'd just landed his brogans on my face when I let'm have it. The bullet entered just above his knee, smashed the collarbone, where it came out, and then clipped off an ear. I guess that bullet's still going. It took more than a full-sized man to stop it. So I say, give me a good handy gat when something's doing."

"Ain't you afraid you'll use all your ammunition up?" he asked anxiously half an hour later, as I continued to crack away with my new toy.

He was quite reassured when I told him Wada had brought along fifty thousand rounds for me.

In the midst of the shooting, two sharks came swimming around. They were quite large, Mr. Pike said, and he estimated their length at fifteen feet. It was Sunday morning, so that the crew, except for working the ship, had its time to itself, and soon the carpenter, with a rope for a fish-line and a great iron hook baited with a chunk of salt pork the size of my head, captured first one, and then the other, of the monsters. They were hoisted in on the main deck. And then I saw a spectacle of the cruelty of the sea.

The full crew gathered about with sheath knives, hatchets, clubs, and big butcher knives borrowed from the galley. I shall not give the details, save that they gloated and lusted, and roared and bellowed their delight in the atrocities they committed. Finally, the first of the two fish was thrown back into the ocean with a pointed stake thrust into its upper and lower jaws so that it could not close its mouth. Inevitable and prolonged starvation was the fate thus meted out to it.

"I'll show you something, boys," Andy Fay cried, as they prepared to handle the second shark.

The Maltese Cockney had been a most capable master of ceremonies with the first one. More than anything else, I think, was I hardened against these brutes by what I saw them do. In the end, the maltreated fish thrashed about the deck entirely eviscerated. Nothing remained but the mere flesh-shell of the creature, yet it would not die. It was amazing the life that lingered when all the vital organs were gone. But more amazing things were to follow.

Mulligan Jacobs, his arms a butcher's to the elbows, without as much as "by your leave," suddenly thrust a hunk of meat into my hand. I sprang back, startled, and dropped it to the deck, while a gleeful howl went up from the two-score men. I was shamed, despite myself. These brutes held me in little respect; and, after all, human nature is so strange a compound that even a philosopher dislikes being held in disesteem by the brutes of his own species.

I looked at what I had dropped. It was the heart of the shark, and as I looked, there under my eyes, on the scorching deck where the pitch oozed from the seams, the heart pulsed with life.

And I dared. I would not permit these animals to laugh at any fastidiousness of mine. I stooped and picked up the heart, and while I concealed and conquered my qualms I held it in my hand and felt it beat in my hand.

At any rate, I had won a mild victory over Mulligan Jacobs; for he abandoned me for the more delectable diversion of torturing the shark that would not die. For several minutes it had been lying quite motionless. Mulligan Jacobs smote it a heavy blow on the nose with the flat of a hatchet, and as the thing galvanized into life and flung its body about the deck the little venomous man screamed in ecstasy:

"The hooks are in it!—the hooks are in it!—and burnin' hot!"

He squirmed and writhed with fiendish delight, and again he struck it on the nose and made it leap.

This was too much, and I beat a retreat—feigning boredom, or cessation of interest, of course; and absently carrying the still throbbing heart in my hand.

As I came upon the poop I saw Miss West, with her sewing basket, emerging from the port door of the chart-house. The deck-chairs were on that side, so I stole around on the starboard side of the chart-house in order to fling overboard unobserved the dreadful thing I carried. But, drying on the surface in the tropic heat and still pulsing inside, it stuck to my hand, so that it was a bad cast. Instead of clearing the railing, it struck on the pin-rail and stuck there in the shade, and as I opened the door to go below and wash my hands, with a last glance I saw it pulse where it had fallen.

When I came back it was still pulsing. I heard a splash overside from the waist of the ship, and knew the carcass had been flung overboard. I did not go around the chart-house and join Miss West, but stood enthralled by the spectacle of that heart that beat in the tropic heat.

Boisterous shouts from the sailors attracted my attention. They had all climbed to the top of the tall rail and were watching something outboard. I followed their gaze and saw the amazing thing. That long-eviscerated shark was not dead. It moved, it swam, it thrashed about, and ever it strove to escape from the surface of the ocean. Sometimes it swam down as deep as fifty or a hundred feet, and then, still struggling to escape the surface, struggled involuntarily to the surface. Each failure thus to escape fetched wild laughter from the men. But why did they laugh? The thing was sublime, horrible, but it was not humorous. I leave it to you. What is there laughable in the sight of a pain-distraught fish rolling helplessly on the surface of the sea and exposing to the sun all its essential emptiness?

I was turning away, when renewed shouting drew my gaze. Half a dozen other sharks had appeared, smaller ones, nine or ten feet long. They attacked their helpless comrade. They tore him to pieces they destroyed him, devoured him. I saw the last shred of him disappear down their maws. He was gone, disintegrated, entombed in the living bodies of his kind, and already entering into the processes of digestion. And yet, there, in the shade on the pin-rail, that unbelievable and monstrous heart beat on.

CHAPTER XXIV

The voyage is doomed to disaster and death. I know Mr. Pike, now, and if ever he discovers the identity of Mr. Mellaire, murder will be done. Mr. Mellaire is not Mr. Mellaire. He is not from Georgia. He is from Virginia. His name is Waltham—Sidney Waltham. He is one of the Walthams of Virginia, a black sheep, true, but a Waltham. Of this I am convinced, just as utterly as I am convinced that Mr. Pike will kill him if he learns who he is.

Let me tell how I have discovered all this. It was last night, shortly before midnight, when I came up on the poop to enjoy a whiff of the southeast trades in which we are now bowling along, close-hauled in order to weather Cape San Roque. Mr. Pike had the watch, and I paced up and down with him while he told me old pages of his life. He has often done this, when not "sea-grouched," and often he has mentioned with pride—yes, with reverence—a master with whom he sailed five years. "Old Captain Somers," he called him—"the finest, squarest, noblest man I ever sailed under, sir."

Well, last night our talk turned on lugubrious subjects, and Mr. Pike, wicked old man that he is, descanted on the wickedness of the world and on the wickedness of the man who had murdered Captain Somers.

"He was an old man, over seventy years old," Mr. Pike went on. "And they say he'd got a touch of palsy—I hadn't seen him for years. You see, I'd had to clear out from the coast because of trouble. And that devil of a second mate caught him in bed late at night and beat him to death. It was terrible. They told me about it. Right in San Francisco, on board the *Jason Harrison*, it happened, eleven years ago.

"And do you know what they did? First, they gave the murderer life, when he should have been hanged. His plea was insanity, from having had his head chopped open a long time before by a crazy sea-cook. And when he'd served seven years the governor pardoned him. He wasn't any good, but his people were a powerful old Virginian family, the Walthams—I guess you've heard of them—and they brought all kinds of pressure to bear. His name was Sidney Waltham."

At this moment the warning bell, a single stroke fifteen minutes before the change of watch, rang out from the wheel and was repeated by the look-out on the forecastle head. Mr. Pike, under his stress of feeling, had stopped walking, and we stood at the break of the poop. As chance would have it, Mr. Mellaire was a quarter of an hour ahead of time, and he climbed the poop-ladder and stood beside us while the mate concluded his tale.

"I didn't mind it," Mr. Pike continued, "as long as he'd got life and was serving his time. But when they pardoned him out after only seven years I swore I'd get him. And I will. I don't believe in God or devil, and it's a rotten crazy world anyway; but I do believe in hunches. And I know I'm going to get him."

"What will you do?" I queried.

"Do?" Mr. Pike's voice was fraught with surprise that I should not know. "Do? Well, what did he do to old Captain Somers? Yet he's disappeared these last three years now. I've heard neither hide nor hair of him. But he's a sailor, and he'll drift back to the sea, and some day . . . "

In the illumination of a match with which the second mate was lighting his pipe I saw Mr. Pike's gorilla arms and huge clenched paws raised to heaven, and his face convulsed and working. Also, in that brief moment of light, I saw that the second mate's hand which held the match was shaking.

"And I ain't never seen even a photo of him," Mr. Pike added. "But I've got a general idea of his looks, and he's got a mark unmistakable. I could know him by it in the dark. All I'd have to do is feel it. Some day I'll stick my fingers into that mark."

281

"What did you say, sir, was the captain's name?" Mr. Mellaire asked casually.

"Somers—old Captain Somers," Mr. Pike answered.

Mr. Mellaire repeated the name aloud several times, and then hazarded:

"Didn't he command the *Lammermoor* thirty years ago?"

"That's the man."

"I thought I recognized him. I lay at anchor in a ship next to his in Table Bay that time ago."

"Oh, the wickedness of the world, the wickedness of the world," Mr. Pike muttered as he turned and strode away.

I said good-night to the second mate and had started to go below, when he called to me in a low voice, "Mr. Pathurst!"

I stopped, and then he said, hurriedly and confusedly:

"Never mind, sir . . . I beg your pardon . . . I—I changed my mind."

Below, lying in my bunk, I found myself unable to read. My mind was bent on returning to what had just occurred on deck, and, against my will, the most gruesome speculations kept suggesting themselves.

And then came Mr. Mellaire. He had slipped down the booby hatch into the big after-room and thence through the hallway to my room. He entered noiselessly, on clumsy tiptoes, and pressed his finger warningly to his lips. Not until he was beside my bunk did he speak, and then it was in a whisper.

"I beg your pardon, sir, Mr. Pathurst . . . I—I beg your pardon; but, you see, sir, I was just passing, and seeing you awake I . . . I thought it would not inconvenience you to . . . you see, I thought I might just as well prefer a small favour . . . seeing that I would not inconvenience you, sir . . . I . . . I . . . "

282

I waited for him to proceed, and in the pause that ensued, while he licked his dry lips with his tongue, the thing ambushed in his skull peered at me through his eyes and seemed almost on the verge of leaping out and pouncing upon me.

"Well, sir," he began again, this time more coherently, "it's just a little thing—foolish on my part, of course—a whim, so to say—but you will remember, near the beginning of the voyage, I showed you a scar on my head . . . a really small affair, sir, which I contracted in a misadventure. It amounts to a deformity, which it is my fancy to conceal. Not for worlds, sir, would I care to have Miss West, for instance, know that I carried such a deformity. A man is a man, sir—you understand—and you have not spoken of it to her?"

"No," I replied. "It just happens that I have not."

"Nor to anybody else?—to, say, Captain West?—or, say, Mr. Pike?"

"No, I haven't mentioned it to anybody," I averred.

He could not conceal the relief he experienced. The perturbation went out of his face and manner, and the ambushed thing drew back deeper into the recess of his skull.

"The favour, sir, Mr. Pathurst, that I would prefer is that you will not mention that little matter to anybody. I suppose" (he smiled, and his voice was superlatively suave) "it is vanity on my part—you understand, I am sure."

I nodded, and made a restless movement with my book as evidence that I desired to resume my reading.

"I can depend upon you for that, Mr. Pathurst?" His whole voice and manner had changed. It was practically a command, and I could almost see fangs, bared and menacing, sprouting in the jaws of that thing I fancied dwelt behind his eyes.

"Certainly," I answered coldly.

"Thank you, sir—I thank you," he said, and, without more ado, tiptoed from the room.

Of course I did not read. How could I? Nor did I sleep. My mind ran on, and on, and not until the steward brought my coffee, shortly before five, did I sink into my first doze.

One thing is very evident. Mr. Pike does not dream that the murderer of Captain Somers is on board the *Elsinore*. He has never glimpsed that prodigious fissure that clefts Mr. Mellaire's, or, rather, Sidney Waltham's, skull. And I, for one, shall never tell Mr. Pike. And I know, now, why from the very first I disliked the second mate. And I understand that live thing, that other thing, that lurks within and peers out through the eyes. I have recognized the same thing in the three gangsters for'ard. Like the second mate, they are prison birds. The restraint, the secrecy, and iron control of prison life has developed in all of them terrible other selves.

Yes, and another thing is very evident. On board this ship, driving now through the South Atlantic for the winter passage of Cape Horn, are all the elements of sea tragedy and horror. We are freighted with human dynamite that is liable at any moment to blow our tiny floating world to fragments.

CHAPTER XXV

The days slip by. The south-east trade is brisk and small splashes of sea occasionally invade my open ports. Mr. Pike's room was soaked yesterday. This is the most exciting thing that has happened for some time. The gangsters rule in the forecastle. Larry and Shorty have had a harmless *fight*. The hooks continue to burn in Mulligan Jacobs's brain. Charles Davis resides alone in his little steel room, coming out only to get his food from the galley. Miss West plays and sings, doctors Possum, launders, and is for ever otherwise busy with her fancy work. Mr. Pike runs the phonograph every other evening in the second dog-watch. Mr. Mellaire hides the cleft in his head. I keep his secret. And Captain West, more remote than ever, sits in the draught of wind in the twilight cabin.

We are now thirty-seven days at sea, in which time, until to-day, we have not sighted a vessel. And to-day, at one time, no less than six vessels were visible from the deck. Not until I saw these ships was I able thoroughly to realize how lonely this ocean is.

Mr. Pike tells me we are several hundred miles off the South American coast. And yet, only the other day, it seems, we were scarcely more distant from Africa. A big velvety moth fluttered aboard this morning, and we are filled with conjecture. How possibly could it have come from the South American coast these hundreds of miles in the teeth of the trades?

The Southern Cross has been visible, of course, for weeks; the North Star has disappeared behind the bulge of the earth; and the Great Bear, at its highest, is very low. Soon it, too, will be gone and we shall be raising the Magellan Clouds.

I remember the fight between Larry and Shorty. Wada reports that Mr. Pike watched it for some time, until, becoming incensed at their awkwardness, he clouted both of them with his open hands and made them stop, announcing that until they could make a better showing he intended doing all the fighting on the *Elsinore* himself.

It is a feat beyond me to realize that he is sixty-nine years old. And when I look at the tremendous build of him and at his fearful, man-handling hands, I conjure up a vision of him avenging Captain Somers's murder.

Life is cruel. Amongst the *Elsinore*'s five thousand tons of coal are thousands of rats. There is no way for them to get out of their steel-walled prison, for all the ventilators are guarded with stout wire-mesh. On her previous voyage, loaded with barley, they increased and multiplied. Now they are imprisoned in the coal, and cannibalism is what must occur among them. Mr. Pike says that when we reach Seattle there will be a dozen or a score of survivors, huge fellows, the strongest and fiercest. Sometimes, passing the mouth of one ventilator that is in the after wall of the chart-house, I can hear their plaintive squealing and crying from far beneath in the coal.

Other and luckier rats are in the 'tween decks for'ard, where all the spare suits of sails are stored. They come out and run about the deck at night, steal food from the galley, and lap up the dew. Which reminds me that Mr. Pike will no longer look at Possum. It seems, under his suggestion, that Wada trapped a rat in the donkey-engine room. Wada swears that it was the father of all rats, and that, by actual measurement, it scaled eighteen inches from nose to the tip of tail. Also, it seems that Mr. Pike and Wada, with the door shut in the former's room, pitted the rat against Possum, and that Possum was licked. They were compelled to kill the rat themselves, while Possum, when all was over, lay down and had a fit.

Now Mr. Pike abhors a coward, and his disgust with Possum is profound. He no longer plays with the puppy, nor even speaks to him, and, whenever he passes him on the deck, glowers sourly at him.

I have been reading up the South Atlantic Sailing Directions, and I find that we are now entering the most beautiful sunset region in the world. And this evening we were favoured with a sample. I was in my quarters, overhauling my books, when Miss West called to me from the foot of the chart-house stairs:

"Mr. Pathurst!—Come quick! Oh, do come quick! You can't afford to miss it!"

Half the sky, from the zenith to the western sea-line, was an astonishing sheet of pure, pale, even gold. And through this sheen, on the horizon, burned the sun, a disc of richer gold. The gold of the sky grew more golden, then tarnished before our eyes and began to glow faintly with red. As the red deepened, a mist spread over the whole sheet of gold and the burning yellow sun. Turner was never guilty of so audacious an orgy in gold-mist.

Presently, along the horizon, entirely completing the circle of sea and sky, the tight-packed shapes of the trade wind clouds began to show through the mist; and as they took form they spilled with rose-colour at their upper edges, while their bases were a pulsing, bluish-white. I say it advisedly. All the colours of this display *pulsed*.

As the gold-mist continued to clear away, the colours became garish, bold; the turquoises went into greens and the roses turned to the red of blood. And the purple and indigo of the long swells of sea were bronzed with the colour-riot in the sky, while across the water, like gigantic serpents, crawled red and green sky-reflections. And then all the gorgeousness quickly dulled, and the warm, tropic darkness drew about us.

CHAPTER XXVI

The *Elsinore* is truly the ship of souls, the world in miniature; and, because she is such a small world, cleaving this vastitude of ocean as our larger world cleaves space, the strange juxtapositions that continually occur are startling.

For instance, this afternoon on the poop. Let me describe it. Here was Miss West, in a crisp duck sailor suit, immaculately white, open at the throat, where, under the broad collar, was knotted a man-of-war black silk neckerchief. Her smooth-groomed hair, a trifle rebellious in the breeze, was glorious. And here was I, in white ducks, white shoes, and white silk shirt, as immaculate and well-tended as she. The steward was just bringing the pretty tea-service for Miss West, and in the background Wada hovered.

We had been discussing philosophy—or, rather, I had been feeling her out; and from a sketch of Spinoza's anticipations of the modern mind, through the speculative interpretations of the latest achievements in physics of Sir Oliver Lodge and Sir William Ramsay, I had come, as usual, to De Casseres, whom I was quoting, when Mr. Pike snarled orders to the watch.

"'In this rise into the azure of pure perception, attainable only by a very few human beings, the spectacular sense is born,'." I was quoting. "'Life is no longer good or evil. It is a perpetual play of forces without beginning or end. The freed Intellect merges itself with the World-Will and partakes of its essence, which is not a moral essence but an æsthetic essence . . . "

And at this moment the watch swarmed on to the poop to haul on the port-braces of the mizzen-sky-sail, royal and topgallant-sail. The sailors passed us, or toiled close to us, with lowered eyes. They did not look at us, so far removed from them were we. It was this contrast that caught my fancy.

Here were the high and low, slaves and masters, beauty and ugliness, cleanness and filth. Their feet were bare and scaled with patches of tar and pitch. Their unbathed bodies were garmented in the meanest of clothes, dingy, dirty, ragged, and sparse. Each one had on but two garments—dungaree trousers and a shoddy cotton shirt.

And we, in our comfortable deck-chairs, our two servants at our backs, the quintessence of elegant leisure, sipped delicate tea from beautiful, fragile cups, and looked on at these wretched ones whose labour made possible the journey of our little world. We did not speak to them, nor recognize their existence, any more than would they have dared speak to us.

And Miss West, with the appraising eye of a plantation mistress for the condition of her field slaves, looked them over.

"You see how they have fleshed up," she said, as they coiled the last turns of the ropes over the pins and faded away for'ard off the poop. "It is the regular hours, the good weather, the hard work, the open air, the sufficient food, and the absence of whisky. And they will keep in this fettle until they get off the Horn. And then you will see them go down from day to day. A winter passage of the Horn is always a severe strain on the men.

"But then, once we are around and in the good weather of the Pacific, you will see them gain again from day to day. And when we reach Seattle they will be in splendid shape. Only they will go ashore, drink up their wages in several days, and ship away on other vessels in precisely the same sodden, miserable condition that they were in when they sailed with us from Baltimore."

And just then Captain West came out the chart-house door, strolled by for a single turn up and down, and with a smile and a word for us and an all-observant eye for the ship, the trim of her sails, the wind, and the sky, and the weather promise, went back through the chart-house door—the blond Aryan master, the king, the Samurai.

And I finished sipping my tea of delicious and most expensive aroma, and our slant-eyed, dark-skinned servitors carried the pretty gear away, and I read, continuing De Casseres:

"'Instinct wills, creates, carries on the work of the species. The Intellect destroys, negatives, satirizes and ends in pure nihilism, instinct creates life, endlessly, hurling forth profusely and blindly its clowns, tragedians and comedians. Intellect remains the eternal spectator of the play. It participates at will, but never gives itself wholly to the fine sport. The Intellect, freed from the trammels of the personal will, soars into the ether of perception, where Instinct follows it in a thousand disguises, seeking to draw it down to earth.'"

CHAPTER XXVII

We are now south of Rio and working south. We are out of the latitude of the trades, and the wind is capricious. Rain squalls and wind squalls vex the *Elsinore*. One hour we may be rolling sickeningly in a dead calm, and the next hour we may be dashing fourteen knots through the water and taking off sail as fast as the men can clew up and lower away. A night of calm, when sleep is well-nigh impossible in the sultry, muggy air, may be followed by a day of blazing sun and an oily swell from the south'ard, connoting great gales in that area of ocean we are sailing toward—or all day long the *Elsinore*, under an overcast sky, royals and sky sails furled, may plunge and buck under wind-pressure into a short and choppy head-sea.

And all this means work for the men. Taking Mr. Pike's judgment, they are very inadequate, though by this time they know the ropes. He growls and grumbles, and snorts and sneers whenever he watches them doing anything. To-day, at eleven in the morning, the wind was so violent, continuing in greater gusts after having come in a great gust, that Mr. Pike ordered the mainsail taken off. The great crojack was already off. But the watch could not clew up the mainsail, and, after much vain sing-songing and pull-hauling, the watch below was routed out to bear a hand.

"My God!" Mr. Pike groaned to me. "Two watches for a rag like that when half a decent watch could do it! Look at that preventer bosun of mine!"

Poor Nancy! He looked the saddest, sickest, bleakest creature I had ever seen. He was so wretched, so miserable, so helpless. And Sundry Buyers was just as impotent. The expression on his face was of pain and hopelessness, and as he pressed his abdomen he lumbered futilely about, ever seeking something he might do and ever failing to find it. He pottered. He would stand and stare at one rope for a minute or so at a time, following it aloft with his eyes through the maze of ropes and stabs and gears with all the intentness of a man working out an intricate problem. Then, holding his hand against his stomach, he would lumber on a few steps and select another rope for study.

"Oh dear, oh dear," Mr. Pike lamented. "How can one drive with bosuns like that and a crew like that? Just the same, if I was captain of this ship I'd drive 'em. I'd show 'em what drive was, if I had to lose a few of them. And when they grow weak off the Horn what'll we do? It'll be both watches all the time, which will weaken them just that much the faster."

Evidently this winter passage of the Horn is all that one has been led to expect from reading the narratives of the navigators. Iron men like the two mates are very respectful of "Cape Stiff," as they call that uttermost tip of the American continent. Speaking of the two mates, iron-made and iron-mouthed that they are, it is amusing that in really serious moments both of them curse with "Oh dear, oh dear."

In the spells of calm I take great delight in the little rifle. I have already fired away five thousand rounds, and have come to consider myself an expert. Whatever the knack of shooting may be, I've got it. When I get back I shall take up target practice. It is a neat, deft sport.

Not only is Possum afraid of the sails and of rats, but he is afraid of rifle-fire, and at the first discharge goes yelping and ki-yi-ing below. The dislike Mr. Pike has developed for the poor little puppy is ludicrous. He even told me that if it were his dog he'd throw it overboard for a target. Just the same, he is an affectionate, heart-warming little rascal, and has already crept so deep into my heart that I am glad Miss West did not accept him.

And—oh!—he insists on sleeping with me on top the bedding; a proceeding which has scandalized the mate. "I suppose he'll be using your toothbrush next," Mr. Pike growled at me. But the puppy loves my companionship, and is never happier than when on the bed with me. Yet the bed is not entirely paradise, for Possum is badly frightened when ours is the lee side and the seas pound and smash against the glass ports. Then the little beggar, electric with fear to every hair tip, crouches and snarls menacingly and almost at the same time whimpers appeasingly at the storm-monster outside.

"Father *knows* the sea," Miss West said to me this afternoon. "He understands it, and he loves it."

"Or it may be habit," I ventured.

She shook her head.

"He does know it. And he loves it. That is why he has come back to it. All his people before him were sea folk. His grandfather, Anthony West, made forty-six voyages between 1801 and 1847. And his father, Robert, sailed master to the north-west coast before the gold days and was captain of some of the fastest Cape Horn clippers after the gold discovery. Elijah West, father's great-grandfather, was a privateersman in the Revolution. He commanded the armed brig *New Defence*. And, even before that, Elijah's father, in turn, and Elijah's father's father, were masters and owners on long-voyage merchant adventures.

"Anthony West, in 1813 and 1814, commanded the *David Bruce*, with letters of marque. He was half-owner, with Gracie & Sons as the other half-owners. She was a two-hundred-ton schooner, built right up in Maine. She carried a long eighteen-pounder, two ten-pounders, and ten six-pounders, and she sailed like a witch. She ran the blockade off Newport and got away to the English Channel and the Bay of Biscay. And, do you know, though she only cost twelve thousand dollars all told, she took over three hundred thousand dollars of British prizes. A brother of his was on the *Wasp*.

"So, you see, the sea is in our blood. She is our mother. As far back as we can trace all our line was born to the sea." She laughed and went on. "We've pirates and slavers in our family, and all sorts of disreputable sea-rovers. Old Ezra West, just how far back I don't remember, was executed for piracy and his body hung in chains at Plymouth.

291

"The sea is father's blood. And he knows, well, a ship, as you would know a dog or a horse. Every ship he sails has a distinct personality for him. I have watched him, in high moments, and *seen* him think. But oh! the times I have seen him when he does not think—when he *feels* and knows everything without thinking at all. Really, with all that appertains to the sea and ships, he is an artist. There is no other word for it."

"You think a great deal of your father," I remarked.

"He is the most wonderful man I have ever known," she replied. "Remember, you are not seeing him at his best. He has never been the same since mother's death. If ever a man and woman were one, they were." She broke off, then concluded abruptly. "You don't know him. You don't know him at all."

CHAPTER XXVIII

"I think we are going to have a fine sunset," Captain West remarked last evening.

Miss West and I abandoned our rubber of cribbage and hastened on deck. The sunset had not yet come, but all was preparing. As we gazed we could see the sky gathering the materials, grouping the gray clouds in long lines and towering masses, spreading its palette with slow-growing, glowing tints and sudden blobs of colour.

"It's the Golden Gate!" Miss West cried, indicating the west. "See! We're just inside the harbour. Look to the south there. If that isn't the sky-line of San Francisco! There's the Call Building, and there, far down, the Ferry Tower, and surely that is the Fairmount." Her eyes roved back through the opening between the cloud masses, and she clapped her hands. "It's a sunset within a sunset! See! The Farallones!"—swimming in a miniature orange and red sunset all their own. "Isn't it the Golden Gate, and San Francisco, and the Farallones?" She appealed to Mr. Pike, who, leaning near, on the poop-rail, was divided between gazing sourly at Nancy pottering on the main deck and sourly at Possum, who, on the bridge, crouched with terror each time the crojack flapped emptily above him.

The mate turned his head and favoured the sky picture with a solemn stare.

"Oh, I don't know," he growled. "It may look like the Farallones to you, but to me it looks like a battleship coming right in the Gate with a bone in its teeth at a twenty-knot clip."

Sure enough. The floating Farallones had metamorphosed into a giant warship.

Then came the colour riot, the dominant tone of which was green. It was green, green, green—the blue-green of the springing year, and sere and yellow green and tawny-brown green of autumn. There were orange green, gold green, and a copper green. And all these greens were rich green beyond description; and yet the richness and the greenness passed even as we gazed upon it, going out of the gray clouds and into the sea, which assumed the exquisite golden pink of polished copper, while the hollows of the smooth and silken ripples were touched by a most ethereal pea green.

The gray clouds became a long, low swathe of ruby red, or garnet red—such as one sees in a glass of heavy burgundy when held to the light. There was such depth to this red! And, below it, separated from the main colour-mass by a line of gray-white fog, or line of sea, was another and smaller streak of ruddy-coloured wine.

I strolled across the poop to the port side.

"Oh! Come back! Look! Look!" Miss West cried to me.

"What's the use?" I answered. "I've something just as good over here."

She joined me, and as she did so I noted, a sour grin on Mr. Pike's face.

The eastern heavens were equally spectacular. That quarter of the sky was sheer and delicate shell of blue, the upper portions of which faded, changed, through every harmony, into a pale, yet warm, rose, all trembling, palpitating, with misty blue tinting into pink. The reflection of this coloured sky-shell upon the water made of the sea a glimmering watered silk, all changeable, blue, Nile-green, and salmon-pink. It was silky, silken, a wonderful silk that veneered and flossed the softly moving, wavy water.

And the pale moon looked like a wet pearl gleaming through the tinted mist of the sky-shell.

In the southern quadrant of the sky we discovered an entirely different sunset—what would be accounted a very excellent orange-and-red sunset anywhere, with grey clouds hanging low and lighted and tinted on all their under edges.

"Huh!" Mr. Pike muttered gruffly, while we were exclaiming over our fresh discovery. "Look at the sunset I got here to the north. It ain't doing so badly now, I leave it to you."

And it wasn't. The northern quadrant was a great fen of colour and cloud, that spread ribs of feathery pink, fleece-frilled, from the horizon to the zenith. It was all amazing. Four sunsets at the one time in the sky! Each quadrant glowed, and burned, and pulsed with a sunset distinctly its own.

And as the colours dulled in the slow twilight, the moon, still misty, wept tears of brilliant, heavy silver into the dim lilac sea. And then came the hush of darkness and the night, and we came to ourselves, out of reverie, sated with beauty, leaning toward each other as we leaned upon the rail side by side.

* * * * *

I never grow tired of watching Captain West. In a way he bears a sort of resemblance to several of Washington's portraits. He is six feet of aristocratic thinness, and has a very definite, leisurely and stately grace of movement. His thinness is almost ascetic. In appearance and manner he is the perfect old-type New England gentleman.

He has the same gray eyes as his daughter, although his are genial rather than warm; and his eyes have the same trick of smiling. His skin is pinker than hers, and his brows and lashes are fairer. But he seems removed beyond passion, or even simple enthusiasm. Miss West is firm, like her father; but there is warmth in her firmness. He is clean, he is sweet and courteous; but he is coolly sweet, coolly courteous. With all his certain graciousness, in cabin or on deck, so far as his social equals are concerned, his graciousness is cool, elevated, thin.

He is the perfect master of the art of doing nothing. He never reads, except the Bible; yet he is never bored. Often, I note him in a deck-chair, studying his perfect finger-nails, and, I'll swear, not seeing them at all. Miss West says he loves the sea. And I ask myself a thousand times, "But how?" He shows no interest in any phase of the sea. Although he called our attention to the glorious sunset I have just described, he did not remain on deck to enjoy it. He sat below, in the big leather chair, not reading, not dozing, but merely gazing straight before him at nothing.

* * * * *

The days pass, and the seasons pass. We left Baltimore at the tail-end of winter, went into spring and on through summer, and now we are in fall weather and urging our way south to the winter of Cape Horn. And as we double the Cape and proceed north, we shall go through spring and summer—a long summer—pursuing the sun north through its declination and arriving at Seattle in summer. And all these seasons have occurred, and will have occurred, in the space of five months.

Our white ducks are gone, and, in south latitude thirty-five, we are wearing the garments of a temperate clime. I notice that Wada has given me heavier underclothes and heavier pyjamas, and that Possum, of nights, is no longer content with the top of the bed but must crawl underneath the bed-clothes.

* * * * *

We are now off the Plate, a region notorious for storms, and Mr. Pike is on the lookout for a pampero. Captain West does not seem to be on the lookout for anything; yet I notice that he spends longer hours on deck when the sky and barometer are threatening.

Yesterday we had a hint of Plate weather, and to-day an awesome fiasco of the same. The hint came last evening between the twilight and the dark. There was practically no wind, and the *Elsinore*, just maintaining steerage way by means of intermittent fans of air from the north, floundered exasperatingly in a huge glassy swell that rolled up as an echo from some blown-out storm to the south.

Ahead of us, arising with the swiftness of magic, was a dense slate-blackness. I suppose it was cloud-formation, but it bore no semblance to clouds. It was merely and sheerly a blackness that towered higher and higher until it overhung us, while it spread to right and left, blotting out half the sea.

And still the light puffs from the north filled our sails; and still, as the *Elsinore* floundered on the huge, smooth swells and the sails emptied and flapped a hollow thunder, we moved slowly towards that ominous blackness. In the cast, in what was quite distinctly an active thunder cloud, the lightning fairly winked, while the blackness in front of us was rent with blobs and flashes of lightning.

The last puffs left us, and in the hushes, between the rumbles of the nearing thunder, the voices of the men aloft on the yards came to one's ear as if they were right beside one instead of being hundreds of feet away and up in the air. That they were duly impressed by what was impending was patent from the earnestness with which they worked. Both watches toiled under both mates, and Captain West strolled the poop in his usual casual way, and gave no orders at all, save in low conventional tones, when Mr. Pike came upon the poop and conferred with him.

Miss West, having deserted the scene five minutes before, returned, a proper sea-woman, clad in oil-skins, sou'wester, and long sea-boots. She ordered me, quite peremptorily, to do the same. But I could not bring myself to leave the deck for fear of missing something, so I compromised by having Wada bring my storm-gear to me.

And then the wind came, smack out of the blackness, with the abruptness of thunder and accompanied by the most diabolical thunder. And with the rain and thunder came the blackness. It was tangible. It drove past us in the bellowing wind like so much stuff that one could feel. Blackness as well as wind impacted on us. There is no other way to describe it than by the old, ancient old, way of saying one could not see his hand before his face.

"Isn't it splendid!" Miss West shouted into my ear, close beside me, as we clung to the railing of the break of the poop.

"Superb!" I shouted back, my lips to her ear, so that her hair tickled my face.

And, I know not why—it must have been spontaneous with both of us—in that shouting blackness of wind, as we clung to the rail to avoid being blown away, our hands went out to each other and my hand and hers gripped and pressed and then held mutually to the rail.

"Daughter of Herodias," I commented grimly to myself; but my hand did not leave hers.

"What is happening?" I shouted in her ear.

"We've lost way," came her answer. "I think we're caught aback! The wheel's up, but she could not steer!"

The Gabriel voice of the Samurai rang out. "Hard over?" was his mellow storm-call to the man at the wheel. "Hard over, sir," came the helmsman's reply, vague, cracked with strain, and smothered.

Came the lightning, before us, behind us, on every side, bathing us in flaming minutes at a time. And all the while we were deafened by the unceasing uproar of thunder. It was a weird sight—far aloft the black skeleton of spars and masts from which the sails had been removed; lower down, the sailors clinging like monstrous bugs as they passed the gaskets and furled; beneath them the few set sails, filled backward against the masts, gleaming whitely, wickedly, evilly, in the fearful illumination; and, at the bottom, the deck and bridge and houses of the *Elsinore*, and a tangled riff-raff of flying ropes, and clumps and bunches of swaying, pulling, hauling, human creatures.

It was a great moment, the master's moment—caught all aback with all our bulk and tonnage and infinitude of gear, and our heaven-aspiring masts two hundred feet above our heads. And our master was there, in sheeting flame, slender, casual, imperturbable, with two men—one of them a murderer—under him to pass on and enforce his will, and with a horde of inefficients and weaklings to obey that will, and pull, and haul, and by the sheer leverages of physics manipulate our floating world so that it would endure this fury of the elements.

What happened next, what was done, I do not know, save that now and again I heard the Gabriel voice; for the darkness came, and the rain in pouring, horizontal sheets. It filled my mouth and strangled my lungs as if I had fallen overboard. It seemed to drive up as well as down, piercing its way under my sou'wester, through my oilskins, down my tight-buttoned collar, and into my sea-boots. I was dizzied, obfuscated, by all this onslaught of thunder, lightning, wind, blackness, and water. And yet the master, near to me, there on the poop, lived and moved serenely in all, voicing his wisdom and will to the wisps of creatures who obeyed and by their brute, puny strength pulled braces, slacked sheets, dragged courses, swung yards and lowered them, hauled on buntlines and clewlines, smoothed and gasketed the huge spreads of canvas.

How it happened I know not, but Miss West and I crouched together, clinging to the rail and to each other in the shelter of the thrumming weather-cloth. My arm was about her and fast to the railing; her shoulder pressed close against me, and by one hand she held tightly to the lapel of my oilskin.

An hour later we made our way across the poop to the chart-house, helping each other to maintain footing as the *Elsinore* plunged and bucked in the rising sea and was pressed over and down by the weight of wind on her few remaining set sails. The wind, which had lulled after the rain, had risen in recurrent gusts to storm violence. But all was well with the gallant ship. The crisis was past, and the ship lived, and we lived, and with streaming faces and bright eyes we looked at each other and laughed in the bright light of the chart-room.

"Who can blame one for loving the sea?" Miss West cried out exultantly, as she wrung the rain from her ropes of hair which had gone adrift in the turmoil. "And the men of the sea!" she cried. "The masters of the sea! You saw my father . . . "

"He is a king," I said.

"He is a king," she repeated after me.

And the *Elsinore* lifted on a cresting sea and flung down on her side, so that we were thrown together and brought up breathless against the wall.

I said good-night to her at the foot of the stairs, and as I passed the open door to the cabin I glanced in. There sat Captain West, whom I had thought still on deck. His storm-trappings were removed, his sea-boots replaced by slippers; and he leaned back in the big leather chair, eyes wide open, beholding visions in the curling smoke of a cigar against a background of wildly reeling cabin wall.

It was at eleven this morning that the Plate gave us a fiasco. Last night's was a real pampero—though a mild one. To-day's promised to be a far worse one, and then laughed at us as a proper cosmic joke. The wind, during the night, had so eased that by nine in the morning we had all our topgallant-sails set. By ten we were rolling in a dead calm. By eleven the stuff began making up ominously in the south'ard.

The overcast sky closed down. Our lofty trucks seemed to scrape the cloud-zenith. The horizon drew in on us till it seemed scarcely half a mile away. The *Elsinore* was embayed in a tiny universe of mist and sea. The lightning played. Sky and horizon drew so close that the *Elsinore* seemed on the verge of being absorbed, sucked in by it, sucked up by it.

Then from zenith to horizon the sky was cracked with forked lightning, and the wet atmosphere turned to a horrid green. The rain, beginning gently, in dead calm, grew into a deluge of enormous streaming drops. It grew darker and darker, a green darkness, and in the cabin, although it was midday, Wada and the steward lighted lamps. The lightning came closer and closer, until the ship was enveloped in it. The green darkness was continually a-tremble with flame, through which broke greater illuminations of forked lightning. These became more violent as the rain lessened, and, so absolutely were we centred in this electrical maelstrom, there was no connecting any chain or flash or fork of lightning with any particular thunder-clap. The atmosphere all about us paled and flamed. Such a crashing and smashing! We looked every moment for the *Elsinore* to be struck. And never had I seen such colours in lightning. Although from moment to moment we were dazzled by the greater bolts, there persisted always a tremulous, pulsing lesser play of light, sometimes softly blue, at other times a thin purple that quivered on into a thousand shades of lavender.

And there was no wind. No wind came. Nothing happened. The *Elsinore*, naked-sparred, under only lower-topsails, with spanker and crojack furled, was prepared for anything. Her lower-topsails hung in limp emptiness from the yards, heavy with rain and flapping soggily when she rolled. The cloud mass thinned, the day brightened, the green blackness passed into gray twilight, the lightning eased, the thunder moved along away from us, and there was no wind. In half an hour the sun was shining, the thunder muttered intermittently along the horizon, and the *Elsinore* still rolled in a hush of air.

"You can't tell, sir," Mr. Pike growled to me. "Thirty years ago I was dismasted right here off the Plate in a clap of wind that come on just as that come on."

It was the changing of the watches, and Mr. Mellaire, who had come on the poop to relieve the mate, stood beside me.

"One of the nastiest pieces of water in the world," he concurred. "Eighteen years ago the Plate gave it to me—lost half our sticks, twenty hours on our beam-ends, cargo shifted, and foundered. I was two days in the boat before an English tramp picked us up. And none of the other boats ever was picked up."

"The *Elsinore* behaved very well last night," I put in cheerily.

300

"Oh, hell, that wasn't nothing," Mr. Pike grumbled. "Wait till you see a real pampero. It's a dirty stretch hereabouts, and I, for one, 'll be glad when we get across It. I'd sooner have a dozen Cape Horn snorters than one of these. How about you, Mr. Mellaire?"

"Same here, sir," he answered. "Those sou'-westers are honest. You know what to expect. But here you never know. The best of ship-masters can get tripped up off the Plate."

"'As I've found out . . .

Beyond a doubt,'

Mr. Pike hummed from Newcomb's *Celeste*, as he went down the ladder.

CHAPTER XXIX

The sunsets grow more bizarre and spectacular off this coast of the Argentine. Last evening we had high clouds, broken white and golden, flung disorderly, generously, over the western half of the sky, while in the east was painted a second sunset—a reflection, perhaps, of the first. At any rate, the eastern sky was a bank of pale clouds that shed soft, spread rays of blue and white upon a blue-grey sea.

And the evening before last we had a gorgeous Arizona riot in the west. Bastioned upon the ocean cloud-tier was piled upon cloud-tier, spacious and lofty, until we gazed upon a Grand Canyon a myriad times vaster and more celestial than that of the Colorado. The clouds took on the same stratified, serrated, rose-rock formation, and all the hollows were filled with the opal blues and purple hazes of the Painted Lands.

The Sailing Directions say that these remarkable sunsets are due to the dust being driven high into the air by the winds that blow across the pampas of the Argentine.

301

And our sunset to-night—I am writing this at midnight, as I sit propped in my blankets, wedged by pillows, while the *Elsinore* wallows damnably in a dead calm and a huge swell rolling up from the Cape Horn region, where, it does seem, gales perpetually blow. But our sunset. Turner might have perpetrated it. The west was as if a painter had stood off and slapped brushfuls of gray at a green canvas. On this green background of sky the clouds spilled and crumpled.

But such a background! Such an orgy of green! No shade of green was missing in the interstices, large and small, between the milky, curdled clouds—Nile-green high up, and then, in order, each with a thousand shades, blue-green, brown-green, grey-green, and a wonderful olive-green that tarnished into a rich bronze-green.

During the display the rest of the horizon glowed with broad bands of pink, and blue, and pale green, and yellow. A little later, when the sun was quite down, in the background of the curdled clouds smouldered a wine-red mass of colour, that faded to bronze and tinged all the fading greens with its sanguinary hue. The clouds themselves flushed to rose of all shades, while a fan of gigantic streamers of pale rose radiated toward the zenith. These deepened rapidly into flaunting rose-flame and burned long in the slow-closing twilight.

And with all this wonder of the beauty of the world still glowing in my brain hours afterward, I hear the snarling of Mr. Pike above my head, and the trample and drag of feet as the men move from rope to rope and pull and haul. More weather is making, and from the way sail is being taken in it cannot be far off.

* * * * *

Yet at daylight this morning we were still wallowing in the same dead calm and sickly swell. Miss West says the barometer is down, but that the warning has been too long, for the Plate, to amount to anything. Pamperos happen quickly here, and though the *Elsinore*, under bare poles to her upper-topsails, is prepared for anything, it may well be that they will be crowding on canvas in another hour.

Mr. Pike was so fooled that he actually had set the topgallant-sails, and the gaskets were being taken off the royals, when the Samurai came on deck, strolled back and forth a casual five minutes, then spoke in an undertone to Mr. Pike. Mr. Pike did not like it. To me, a tyro, it was evident that he disagreed with his master. Nevertheless, his voice went out in a snarl aloft to the men on the royal-yards to make all fast again. Then it was clewlines and buntlines and lowering of yards as the topgallant-sails were stripped off. The crojack was taken in, and some of the outer fore-and-aft handsails, whose order of names I can never remember.

A breeze set in from the south-west, blowing briskly under a clear sky. I could see that Mr. Pike was secretly pleased. The Samurai had been mistaken. And each time Mr. Pike glanced aloft at the naked topgallant- and royal-yards, I knew his thought was that they might well be carrying sail. I was quite convinced that the Plate had fooled Captain West. So was Miss West convinced, and, being a favoured person like myself, she frankly told me so.

"Father will be setting sail in half an hour," she prophesied.

What superior weather-sense Captain West possesses I know not, save that it is his by Samurai right. The sky, as I have said, was clear. The air was brittle—sparkling gloriously in the windy sun. And yet, behold, in a brief quarter of an hour, the change that took place. I had just returned from a trip below, and Miss West was venting her scorn on the River Plate and promising to go below to the sewing-machine, when we heard Mr. Pike groan. It was a whimsical groan of disgust, contrition, and acknowledgment of inferiority before the master.

"Here comes the whole River Plate," was what he groaned.

Following his gaze to the south-west, we saw it coming. It was a cloud-mass that blotted out the sunlight and the day. It seemed to swell and belch and roll over and over on itself as it advanced with a rapidity that told of enormous wind behind it and in it. Its speed was headlong, terrific; and, beneath it, covering the sea, advancing with it, was a gray bank of mist.

303

Captain West spoke to the mate, who bawled the order along, and the watch, reinforced by the watch below, began dewing up the mainsail and foresail and climbing into the rigging.

"Keep off! Put your wheel over! Hard over!" Captain West called gently to the helmsman.

And the big wheel spun around, and the *Elsinore's* bow fell off so that she might not be caught aback by the onslaught of wind.

Thunder rode in that rushing, rolling blackness of cloud; and it was rent by lightning as it fell upon us.

Then it was rain, wind, obscureness of gloom, and lightning. I caught a glimpse of the men on the lower-yards as they were blotted from view and as the *Elsinore* heeled over and down. There were fifteen men of them to each yard, and the gaskets were well passed ere we were struck. How they regained the deck I do not know, I never saw; for the *Elsinore*, under only upper- and lower-topsails, lay down on her side, her port-rail buried in the sea, and did not rise.

There was no maintaining an unsupported upright position on that acute slant of deck. Everybody held on. Mr. Pike frankly gripped the poop-rail with both hands, and Miss West and I made frantic clutches and scrambled for footing. But I noticed that the Samurai, poised lightly, like a bird on the verge of flight, merely rested one hand on the rail. He gave no orders. As I divined, there was nothing to be done. He waited—that was all—in tranquillity and repose. The situation was simple. Either the masts would go, or the *Elsinore* would rise with her masts intact, or she would never rise again.

In the meantime she lay dead, her lee yardarms almost touching the sea, the sea creaming solidly to her hatch-combings across the buried, unseen rail.

The minutes were as centuries, until the bow paid off and the *Elsinore*, turned tail before it, righted to an even keel. Immediately this was accomplished Captain West had her brought back upon the wind. And immediately, thereupon, the big foresail went adrift from its gaskets. The shock, or succession of shocks, to the ship, from the tremendous buffeting that followed, was fearful. It seemed she was being racked to pieces. Master and mate were side by side when this happened, and the expressions on their faces typified them. In neither face was apprehension. Mr. Pike's face bore a sour sneer for the worthless sailors who had botched the job. Captain West's face was serenely considerative.

Still, nothing was to be done, could be done; and for five minutes the *Elsinore* was shaken as in the maw of some gigantic monster, until the last shreds of the great piece of canvas had been torn away.

"Our foresail has departed for Africa," Miss West laughed in my ear.

She is like her father, unaware of fear.

"And now we may as well go below and be comfortable," she said five minutes later. "The worst is over. It will only be blow, blow, blow, and a big sea making."

* * * * *

All day it blew. And the big sea that arose made the *Elsinore*'s conduct almost unlivable. My only comfort was achieved by taking to my bunk and wedging myself with pillows buttressed against the bunk's sides by empty soap-boxes which Wada arranged. Mr. Pike, clinging to my door-casing while his legs sprawled adrift in a succession of terrific rolls, paused to tell me that it was a new one on him in the pampero line. It was all wrong from the first. It had not come on right. It had no reason to be.

He paused a little longer, and, in a casual way, that under the circumstances was ridiculously transparent, exposed what was at ferment in his mind.

First of all he was absurd enough to ask if Possum showed symptoms of sea-sickness. Next, he unburdened his wrath for the inefficients who had lost the foresail, and sympathized with the sail-makers for the extra work thrown upon them. Then he asked permission to borrow one of my books, and, clinging to my bunk, selected Buchner's *Force and Matter* from my shelf, carefully wedging the empty space with the doubled magazine I use for that purpose.

Still he was loth to depart, and, cudgelling his brains for a pretext, he set up a rambling discourse on River Plate weather. And all the time I kept wondering what was behind it all. At last it came.

"By the way, Mr. Pathurst," he remarked, "do you happen to remember how many years ago Mr. Mellaire said it was that he was dismasted and foundered off here?"

I caught his drift on the instant.

"Eight years ago, wasn't it?" I lied.

Mr. Pike let this sink in and slowly digested it, while the *Elsinore* was guilty of three huge rolls down to port and back again.

"Now I wonder what ship was sunk off the Plate eight years ago?" he communed, as if with himself. "I guess I'll have to ask Mr. Mellaire her name. You can search me for all any I can recollect."

He thanked me with unwonted elaborateness for *Force and Matter*, of which I knew he would never read a line, and felt his way to the door. Here he hung on for a moment, as if struck by a new and most accidental idea.

"Now it wasn't, by any chance, that he said eighteen years ago?" he queried.

I shook my head.

"Eight years ago," I said. "That's the way I remember it, though why I should remember it at all I don't know. But that is what he said," I went on with increasing confidence. "Eight years ago. I am sure of it."

Mr. Pike looked at me ponderingly, and waited until the *Elsinore* had fairly righted for an instant ere he took his departure down the hall.

I think I have followed the working of his mind. I have long since learned that his memory of ships, officers, cargoes, gales, and disasters is remarkable. He is a veritable encyclopædia of the sea. Also, it is patent that he has equipped himself with Sidney Waltham's history. As yet, he does not dream that Mr. Mellaire is Sidney Waltham, and he is merely wondering if Mr. Mellaire was a ship-mate of Sidney Waltham eighteen years ago in the ship lost off the Plate.

In the meantime, I shall never forgive Mr. Mellaire for this slip he has made. He should have been more careful.

CHAPTER XXX

An abominable night! A wonderful night! Sleep? I suppose I did sleep, in catnaps, but I swear I heard every bell struck until three-thirty. Then came a change, an easement. No longer was it a stubborn, loggy fight against pressures. The *Elsinore* moved. I could feel her slip, and slide, and send, and soar. Whereas before she had been flung continually down to port, she now rolled as far to one side as to the other.

I knew what had taken place. Instead of remaining hove-to on the pampero, Captain West had turned tail and was running before it. This, I understood, meant a really serious storm, for the north-east was the last direction in which Captain West desired to go. But at any rate the movement, though wilder, was easier, and I slept. I was awakened at five by the thunder of seas that fell aboard, rushed down the main deck, and crashed against the cabin wall. Through my open door I could see water swashing up and down the hall, while half a foot of water creamed and curdled from under my bunk across the floor each time the ship rolled to starboard.

The steward brought me my coffee, and, wedged by boxes and pillows, like an equilibrist, I sat up and drank it. Luckily I managed to finish it in time, for a succession of terrific rolls emptied one of my book-shelves. Possum, crawling upward from my feet under the covered way of my bed, yapped with terror as the seas smashed and thundered and as the avalanche of books descended upon us. And I could not but grin when the *Paste Board Crown* smote me on the head, while the puppy was knocked gasping with Chesterton's *What's Wrong with the World?*

"Well, what do you think?" I queried of the steward who was helping to set us and the books to rights.

He shrugged his shoulders, and his bright slant eyes were very bright as he replied:

"Many times I see like this. Me old man. Many times I see more bad. Too much wind, too much work. Rotten dam bad."

I could guess that the scene on deck was a spectacle, and at six o'clock, as gray light showed through my ports in the intervals when they were not submerged, I essayed the side-board of my bunk like a gymnast, captured my careering slippers, and shuddered as I thrust my bare feet into their chill sogginess. I did not wait to dress. Merely in pyjamas I headed for the poop, Possum wailing dismally at my desertion.

It was a feat to travel the narrow halls. Time and again I paused and held on until my finger-tips hurt. In the moments of easement I made progress. Yet I miscalculated. The foot of the broad stairway to the chart-house rested on a cross-hall a dozen feet in length. Over-confidence and an unusually violent antic of the *Elsinore* caused the disaster. She flung down to starboard with such suddenness and at such a pitch that the flooring seemed to go out from under me and I hustled helplessly down the incline. I missed a frantic clutch at the newel-post, flung up my arm in time to save my face, and, most fortunately, whirled half about, and, still falling, impacted with my shoulder muscle-pad on Captain West's door.

Youth will have its way. So will a ship in a sea. And so will a hundred and seventy pounds of a man. The beautiful hardwood door-panel splintered, the latch fetched away, and I broke the nails of the four fingers of my right hand in a futile grab at the flying door, marring the polished surface with four parallel scratches. I kept right on, erupting into Captain West's spacious room with the big brass bed.

Miss West, swathed in a woollen dressing-gown, her eyes heavy still with sleep, her hair glorious and for the once ungroomed, clinging in the doorway that gave entrance on the main cabin, met my startled gaze with an equally startled gaze.

It was no time for apologies. I kept right on my mad way, caught the foot stanchion, and was whipped around in half a circle flat upon Captain West's brass bed.

Miss West was beginning to laugh.

"Come right in," she gurgled.

A score of retorts, all deliciously inadvisable, tickled my tongue, so I said nothing, contenting myself with holding on with my left hand while I nursed my stinging right hand under my arm-pit. Beyond her, across the floor of the main cabin, I saw the steward in pursuit of Captain West's Bible and a sheaf of Miss West's music. And as she gurgled and laughed at me, beholding her in this intimacy of storm, the thought flashed through my brain:

She is a woman. She is desirable.

Now did she sense this fleeting, unuttered flash of mine? I know not, save that her laughter left her, and long conventional training asserted itself as she said:

"I just knew everything was adrift in father's room. He hasn't been in it all night. I could hear things rolling around . . . What is wrong? Are you hurt?"

"Stubbed my fingers, that's all," I answered, looking at my broken nails and standing gingerly upright.

"My, that *was* a roll," she sympathized.

"Yes; I'd started to go upstairs," I said, "and not to turn into your father's bed. I'm afraid I've ruined the door."

Came another series of great rolls. I sat down on the bed and held on. Miss West, secure in the doorway, began gurgling again, while beyond, across the cabin carpet, the steward shot past, embracing a small writing-desk that had evidently carried away from its fastenings when he seized hold of it for support. More seas smashed and crashed against the for'ard wall of the cabin; and the steward, failing of lodgment, shot back across the carpet, still holding the desk from harm.

Taking advantage of favouring spells, I managed to effect my exit and gain the newel-post ere the next series of rolls came. And as I clung on and waited, I could not forget what I had just seen. Vividly under my eyelids burned the picture of Miss West's sleep-laden eyes, her hair, and all the softness of her. *A woman and desirable* kept drumming in my brain.

But I forgot all this, when, nearly at the top, I was thrown up the hill of the stairs as if it had suddenly become downhill. My feet flew from stair to stair to escape falling, and I flew, or fell, apparently upward, until, at the top, I hung on for dear life while the stern of the *Elsinore* flung skyward on some mighty surge.

Such antics of so huge a ship! The old stereotyped "toy" describes her; for toy she was, the sheerest splinter of a plaything in the grip of the elements. And yet, despite this overwhelming sensation of microscopic helplessness, I was aware of a sense of surety. There was the Samurai. Informed with his will and wisdom, the *Elsinore* was no cat's-paw. Everything was ordered, controlled. She was doing what he ordained her to do, and, no matter what storm-Titans bellowed about her and buffeted her, she would continue to do what he ordained her to do.

I glanced into the chart-room. There he sat, leaned back in a screw-chair, his sea-booted legs, wedged against the settee, holding him in place in the most violent rolls. His black oilskin coat glistened in the lamplight with a myriad drops of ocean that advertised a recent return from deck. His sou'wester, black and glistening, was like the helmet of some legendary hero. He was smoking a cigar, and he smiled and greeted me. But he seemed very tired and very old—old with wisdom, however, not weakness. The flesh of his face, the pink pigment quite washed and worn away, was more transparent than ever; and yet never was he more serene, never more the master absolute of our tiny, fragile world. The age that showed in him was not a matter of terrestrial years. It was ageless, passionless, beyond human. Never had he appeared so great to me, so far remote, so much a spirit visitant.

And he cautioned and advised me, in silver-mellow beneficent voice, as I essayed the venture of opening the chart-house door to gain outside. He knew the moment, although I never could have guessed it for myself, and gave the word that enabled me to win the poop.

Water was everywhere. The *Elsinore* was rushing through a blurring whirr of water. Seas creamed and licked the poop-deck edge, now to starboard, now to port. High in the air, over-towering and perilously down-toppling, following-seas pursued our stern. The air was filled with spindrift like a fog or spray. No officer of the watch was in sight. The poop was deserted, save for two helmsmen in streaming oilskins under the half-shelter of the open wheel-house. I nodded good morning to them.

One was Tom Spink, the elderly but keen and dependable English sailor. The other was Bill Quigley, one of a forecastle group of three that herded uniquely together, though the other two, Frank Fitzgibbon and Richard Oiler, were in the second mate's watch. The three had proved handy with their fists, and clannish; they had fought pitched forecastle battles with the gangster clique and won a sort of neutrality of independence for themselves. They were not exactly sailors—Mr. Mellaire sneeringly called them the "bricklayers"—but they had successfully refused subservience to the gangster crowd.

To cross the deck from the chart-house to the break of the poop was no slight feat, but I managed it and hung on to the railing while the wind stung my flesh with the flappings of my pyjamas. At this moment, and for the moment, the *Elsinore* righted to an even keel, and dashed along and down the avalanching face of a wave. And as she thus righted her deck was filled with water level from rail to rail. Above this flood, or knee-deep in it, Mr. Pike and half-a-dozen sailors were bunched on the fife-rail of the mizzen-mast. The carpenter, too, was there, with a couple of assistants.

The next roll spilled half a thousand tons of water outboard sheer over the starboard-rail, while all the starboard ports opened automatically and gushed huge streams. Then came the opposite roll to port, with a clanging shut of the iron doors; and a hundred tons of sea sloshed outboard across the port-rail, while all the iron doors on that side opened wide and gushed. And all this time, it must not be forgotten, the *Elsinore* was dashing ahead through the sea.

The only sail she carried was three upper-topsails. Not the tiniest triangle of headsail was on her. I had never seen her with so little wind-surface, and the three narrow strips of canvas, bellied to the seemingness of sheet-iron with the pressure of the wind, drove her before the gale at astonishing speed.

As the water on the deck subsided the men on the fife-rail left their refuge. One group, led by the redoubtable Mr. Pike, strove to capture a mass of planks and twisted steel. For the moment I did not recognize what it was. The carpenter, with two men, sprang upon Number Three hatch and worked hurriedly and fearfully. And I knew why Captain West had turned tail to the storm. Number Three hatch was a wreck. Among other things the great timber, called the "strong-back," was broken. He had had to run, or founder. Before our decks were swept again I could make out the carpenter's emergency repairs. With fresh timbers he was bolting, lashing, and wedging Number Three hatch into some sort of tightness.

When the *Elsinore* dipped her port-rail under and scooped several hundred tons of South Atlantic, and then, immediately rolling her starboard-rail under, had another hundred tons of breaking sea fall in board upon her, all the men forsook everything and scrambled for life upon the fife-rail. In the bursting spray they were quite hidden; and then I saw them and counted them all as they emerged into view. Again they waited for the water to subside.

The mass of wreckage pursued by Mr. Pike and his men ground a hundred feet along the deck for'ard, and, as the *Elsinore's* stern sank down in some abyss, ground back again and smashed up against the cabin wall. I identified this stuff as part of the bridge. That portion which spanned from the mizzen-mast to the 'midship-house was missing, while the starboard boat on the 'midship-house was a splintered mess.

Watching the struggle to capture and subdue the section of bridge, I was reminded of Victor Hugo's splendid description of the sailor's battle with a ship's gun gone adrift in a night of storm. But there was a difference, I found that Hugo's narrative had stirred me more profoundly than was I stirred by this actual struggle before my eyes.

I have repeatedly said that the sea makes one hard. I now realized how hard I had become as I stood there at the break of the poop in my wind-shipped, spray-soaked pyjamas. I felt no solicitude for the forecastle humans who struggled in peril of their lives beneath me. They did not count. Ah—I was even curious to see what might happen, did they get caught by those crashing avalanches of sea ere they could gain the safety of the fife-rail.

And I saw. Mr. Pike, in the lead, of course, up to his waist in rushing water, dashed in, caught the flying wreckage with a turn of rope, and fetched it up short with a turn around one of the port mizzen-shrouds. The *Elsinore* flung down to port, and a solid wall of down-toppling green upreared a dozen feet above the rail. The men fled to the fife-rail. But Mr. Pike, holding his turn, held on, looked squarely into the wall of the wave, and received the downfall. He emerged, still holding by the turn the captured bridge.

The feeble-minded faun (the stone-deaf man) led the way to Mr. Pike's assistance, followed by Tony, the suicidal Greek. Paddy was next, and in order came Shorty, Henry the training-ship boy, and Nancy, last, of course, and looking as if he were going to execution.

The deck-water was no more than knee-deep, though rushing with torrential force, when Mr. Pike and the six men lifted the section of bridge and started for'ard with it. They swayed and staggered, but managed to keep going.

The carpenter saw the impending ocean-mountain first. I saw him cry to his own men and then to Mr. Pike ere he fled to the fife-rail. But Mr. Pike's men had no chance. Abreast of the 'midship-house, on the starboard side, fully fifteen feet above the rail and twenty above the deck, the sea fell on board. The top of the 'midship-house was swept clean of the splintered boat. The water, impacting against the side of the house, spouted skyward as high as the crojack-yard. And all this, in addition to the main bulk of the wave, swept and descended upon Mr. Pike and his men.

They disappeared. The bridge disappeared. The *Elsinore* rolled to port and dipped her deck full from rail to rail. Next, she plunged down by the head, and all this mass of water surged forward. Through the creaming, foaming surface now and then emerged an arm, or a head, or a back, while cruel edges of jagged plank and twisted steel rods advertised that the bridge was turning over and over. I wondered what men were beneath it and what mauling they were receiving.

And yet these men did not count. I was aware of anxiety only for Mr. Pike. He, in a way, socially, was of my caste and class. He and I belonged aft in the high place; ate at the same table. I was acutely desirous that he should not be hurt or killed. The rest did not matter. They were not of my world. I imagine the old-time skippers, on the middle passage, felt much the same toward their slave-cargoes in the fetid 'tween decks.

The *Elsinore's* bow tilted skyward while her stern fell into a foaming valley. Not a man had gained his feet. Bridge and men swept back toward me and fetched up against the mizzen-shrouds. And then that prodigious, incredible old man appeared out of the water, on his two legs, upright, dragging with him, a man in each hand, the helpless forms of Nancy and the Faun. My heart leapt at beholding this mighty figure of a man-killer and slave-driver, it is true, but who sprang first into the teeth of danger so that his slaves might follow, and who emerged with a half-drowned slave in either hand.

I knew augustness and pride as I gazed—pride that my eyes were blue, like his; that my skin was blond, like his; that my place was aft with him, and with the Samurai, in the high place of government and command. I nearly wept with the chill of pride that was akin to awe and that tingled and bristled along my spinal column and in my brain. As for the rest—the weaklings and the rejected, and the dark-pigmented things, the half-castes, the mongrel-bloods, and the dregs of long-conquered races—how could they count? My heels were iron as I gazed on them in their peril and weakness. Lord! Lord! For ten thousand generations and centuries we had stamped upon their faces and enslaved them to the toil of our will.

Again the *Elsinore* rolled to starboard and to port, while the spume spouted to our lower-yards and a thousand tons of South Atlantic surged across from rail to rail. And again all were down and under, with jagged plank and twisted steel overriding them. And again that amazing blond-skinned giant emerged, on his two legs upstanding, a broken waif like a rat in either hand. He forced his way through rushing, waist-high water, deposited his burdens with the carpenter on the fife-rail, and returned to drag Larry reeling to his feet and help him to the fife-rail. Out of the wash, Tony, the Greek, crawled on hands and knees and sank down helplessly at the fife-rail. There was nothing suicidal now in his mood. Struggle as he would, he could not lift himself until the mate, gripping his oilskin at the collar, with one hand flung him through the air into the carpenter's arms.

Next came Shorty, his face streaming blood, one arm hanging useless, his sea-boots stripped from him. Mr. Pike pitched him into the fife-rail, and returned for the last man. It was Henry, the training-ship boy. Him I had seen, unstruggling, motionless, show at the surface like a drowned man and sink again as the flood surged aft and smashed him against the cabin. Mr. Pike, shoulder-deep, twice beaten to his knees and under by bursting seas, caught the lad, shouldered him, and carried him away for'ard.

An hour later, in the cabin, I encountered Mr. Pike going into breakfast. He had changed his clothes, and he had shaved! Now how could one treat a hero such as he save as I treated him when I remarked off-handedly that he must have had a lively watch?

"My," he answered, equally off-handedly, "I did get a prime soaking."

That was all. He had had no time to see me at the poop-rail. It was merely the day's work, the ship's work, the MAN'S work—all capitals, if you please, in MAN. I was the only one aft who knew, and I knew because I had chanced to see. Had I not been on the poop at that early hour no one aft ever would have known those gray, storm-morning deeds of his.

"Anybody hurt?" I asked.

"Oh, some of the men got wet. But no bones broke. Henry'll be laid off for a day. He got turned over in a sea and bashed his head. And Shorty's got a wrenched shoulder, I think.—But, say, we got Davis into the top bunk! The seas filled him full and he had to climb for it. He's all awash and wet now, and you oughta seen me praying for more." He paused and sighed. "I'm getting old, I guess. I oughta wring his neck, but somehow I ain't got the gumption. Just the same, he'll be overside before we get in."

"A month's wages against a pound of tobacco he won't," I challenged.

"No," said Mr. Pike slowly. "But I'll tell you what I will do. I'll bet you a pound of tobacco even, or a month's wages even, that I'll have the pleasure of putting a sack of coal to his feet that never will come off."

"Done," said I.

"Done," said Mr. Pike. "And now I guess I'll get a bite to eat."

CHAPTER XXXI

The more I see of Miss West the more she pleases me. Explain it in terms of propinquity, or isolation, or whatever you will; I, at least, do not attempt explanation. I know only that she is a woman and desirable. And I am rather proud, in a way, to find that I am just a man like any man. The midnight oil, and the relentless pursuit I have endured in the past from the whole tribe of women, have not, I am glad to say, utterly spoiled me.

I am obsessed by that phrase—a *woman and desirable*. It beats in my brain, in my thought. I go out of my way to steal a glimpse of Miss West through a cabin door or vista of hall when she does not know I am looking. A woman is a wonderful thing. A woman's hair is wonderful. A woman's softness is a magic.—Oh, I know them for what they are, and yet this very knowledge makes them only the more wonderful. I know—I would stake my soul—that Miss West has considered me as a mate a thousand times to once that I have so considered her. And yet—she is a *woman and desirable*.

And I find myself continually reminded of Richard Le Gallienne's inimitable quatrain:

"Were I a woman, I would all day long

Sing my own beauty in some holy song,

Bend low before it, hushed and half afraid,

And say 'I am a woman' all day long."

Let me advise all philosophers suffering from world-sickness to take a long sea voyage with a woman like Miss West.

In this narrative I shall call her "Miss West" no more. She has ceased to be Miss West. She is Margaret. I do not think of her as Miss West. I think of her as Margaret. It is a pretty word, a woman-word. What poet must have created it! Margaret! I never tire of it. My tongue is enamoured of it. Margaret West! What a name to conjure with! A name provocative of dreams and mighty connotations. The history of our westward-faring race is written in it. There is pride in it, and dominion, and adventure, and conquest. When I murmur it I see visions of lean, beaked ships, of winged helmets, and heels iron-shod of restless men, royal lovers, royal adventurers, royal fighters. Yes, and even now, in these latter days when the sun consumes us, still we sit in the high seat of government and command.

Oh—and by the way—she is twenty-four years old. I asked Mr. Pike the date of the *Dixie's* collision with the river steamer in San Francisco Bay. This occurred in 1901. Margaret was twelve years old at the time. This is 1913. Blessings on the head of the man who invented arithmetic! She is twenty-four. Her name is Margaret, and she is desirable.

* * * * *

There are so many things to tell about. Where and how this mad voyage, with a mad crew, will end is beyond all surmise. But the *Elsinore* drives on, and day by day her history is bloodily written. And while murder is done, and while the whole floating drama moves toward the bleak southern ocean and the icy blasts of Cape Horn, I sit in the high place with the masters, unafraid, I am proud to say, in an ecstasy, I am proud to say, and I murmur over and over to *myself—Margaret, a woman; Margaret, and desirable.*

But to resume. It is the first day of June. Ten days have passed since the pampero. When the strong back on Number Three hatch was repaired Captain West came back on the wind, hove to, and rode out the gale. Since then, in calm, and fog, and damp, and storm, we have won south until to-day we are almost abreast of the Falklands. The coast of the Argentine lies to the West, below the sea-line, and some time this morning we crossed the fiftieth parallel of south latitude. Here begins the passage of Cape Horn, for so it is reckoned by the navigators—fifty south in the Atlantic to fifty south in the Pacific.

And yet all is well with us in the matter of weather. The *Elsinore* slides along with favouring winds. Daily it grows colder. The great cabin stove roars and is white-hot, and all the connecting doors are open, so that the whole after region of the ship is warm and comfortable. But on the deck the air bites, and Margaret and I wear mittens as we promenade the poop or go for'ard along the repaired bridge to see the chickens on the 'midship-house. The poor, wretched creatures of instinct and climate! Behold, as they approach the southern mid-winter of the Horn, when they have need of all their feathers, they proceed to moult, because, forsooth, this is the summer time in the land they came from. Or is moulting determined by the time of year they happen to be born? I shall have to look into this. Margaret will know.

Yesterday ominous preparations were made for the passage of the Horn. All the braces were taken from the main deck pin-rails and geared and arranged so that they may be worked from the tops of the houses.

Thus, the fore-braces run to the top of the forecastle, the main-braces to the top of the 'midship-house, and the mizzen-braces to the poop. It is evident that they expect our main deck frequently to be filled with water. So evident is it that a laden ship when in big seas is like a log awash, that fore and aft, on both sides, along the deck, shoulder-high, life-lines have been rigged. Also, the two iron doors, on port and starboard, that open from the cabin directly upon the main deck, have been barricaded and caulked. Not until we are in the Pacific and flying north will these doors open again.

And while we prepare to battle around the stormiest headland in the world our situation on board grows darker. This morning Petro Marinkovich, a sailor in Mr. Mellaire's watch, was found dead on Number One hatch. The body bore several knife-wounds and the throat was cut. It was palpably done by some one or several of the forecastle hands; but not a word can be elicited. Those who are guilty of it are silent, of course; while others who may chance to know are afraid to speak.

Before midday the body was overside with the customary sack of coal. Already the man is a past episode. But the humans for'ard are tense with expectancy of what is to come. I strolled for'ard this afternoon, and noted for the first time a distinct hostility toward me. They recognize that I belong with the after-guard in the high place. Oh, nothing was said; but it was patent by the way almost every man looked at me, or refused to look at me. Only Mulligan Jacobs and Charles Davis were outspoken.

"Good riddance," said Mulligan Jacobs. "The Guinea didn't have the spunk of a louse. And he's better off, ain't he? He lived dirty, an' he died dirty, an' now he's over an' done with the whole dirty game. There's men on board that oughta wish they was as lucky as him. Theirs is still a-coming to 'em."

"You mean . . . ?" I queried.

"Whatever you want to think I mean," the twisted wretch grinned malevolently into my face.

Charles Davis, when I peeped into his iron room, was exuberant.

"A pretty tale for the court in Seattle," he exulted. "It'll only make my case that much stronger. And wait till the reporters get hold of it! The hell-ship *Elsinore*! They'll have pretty pickin's!"

"I haven't seen any hell-ship," I said coldly.

"You've seen my treatment, ain't you?" he retorted. "You've seen the hell I've got, ain't you?"

"I know you for a cold-blooded murderer," I answered.

319

"The court will determine that, sir. All you'll have to do is to testify to facts."

"I'll testify that had I been in the mate's place I'd have hanged you for murder."

His eyes positively sparkled.

"I'll ask you to remember this conversation when you're under oath, sir," he cried eagerly.

I confess the man aroused in me a reluctant admiration. I looked about his mean, iron-walled room. During the pampero the place had been awash. The white paint was peeling off in huge scabs, and iron-rust was everywhere. The floor was filthy. The place stank with the stench of his sickness. His pannikin and unwashed eating-gear from the last meal were scattered on the floor: His blankets were wet, his clothing was wet. In a corner was a heterogeneous mass of soggy, dirty garments. He lay in the very bunk in which he had brained O'Sullivan. He had been months in this vile hole. In order to live he would have to remain months more in it. And while his rat-like vitality won my admiration, I loathed and detested him in very nausea.

"Aren't you afraid?" I demanded. "What makes you think you will last the voyage? Don't you know bets are being made that you won't?"

So interested was he that he seemed to prick up his ears as he raised on his elbow.

"I suppose you're too scared to tell me about them bets," he sneered.

"Oh, I've bet you'll last," I assured him.

"That means there's others that bet I won't," he rattled on hastily. "An' that means that there's men aboard the *Elsinore* right now financially interested in my taking-off."

At this moment the steward, bound aft from the galley, paused in the doorway and listened, grinning. As for Charles Davis, the man had missed his vocation. He should have been a land-lawyer, not a sea-lawyer.

"Very well, sir," he went on. "I'll have you testify to that in Seattle, unless you're lying to a helpless sick man, or unless you'll perjure yourself under oath."

He got what he was seeking, for he stung me to retort:

"Oh, I'll testify. Though I tell you candidly that I don't think I'll win my bet."

"You loose 'm bet sure," the steward broke in, nodding his head. "That fellow him die damn soon."

"Bet with'm, sir," David challenged me. "It's a straight tip from me, an' a regular cinch."

The whole situation was so gruesome and grotesque, and I had been swept into it so absurdly, that for the moment I did not know what to do or say.

"It's good money," Davis urged. "I ain't goin' to die. Look here, steward, how much you want to bet?"

"Five dollar, ten dollar, twenty dollar," the steward answered, with a shoulder-shrug that meant that the sum was immaterial.

"Very well then, steward. Mr. Pathurst covers your money, say for twenty. Is it a go, sir?"

"Why don't you bet with him yourself?" I demanded.

"Sure I will, sir. Here, you steward, I bet you twenty even I don't die."

The steward shook his head.

"I bet you twenty to ten," the sick man insisted. "What's eatin' you, anyway?"

"You live, me lose, me pay you," the steward explained. "You die, I win, you dead; no pay me."

Still grinning and shaking his head, he went his way.

"Just the same, sir, it'll be rich testimony," David chuckled. "An' can't you see the reporters eatin' it up?"

The Asiatic clique in the cook's room has its suspicions about the death of Marinkovich, but will not voice them. Beyond shakings of heads and dark mutterings, I can get nothing out of Wada or the steward. When I talked with the sail-maker, he complained that his injured hand was hurting him and that he would be glad when he could get to the surgeons in Seattle. As for the murder, when pressed by me, he gave me to understand that it was no affair of the Japanese or Chinese on board, and that he was a Japanese.

But Louis, the Chinese half-caste with the Oxford accent, was more frank. I caught him aft from the galley on a trip to the lazarette for provisions.

"We are of a different race, sir, from these men," he said; "and our safest policy is to leave them alone. We have talked it over, and we have nothing to say, sir, nothing whatever to say. Consider my position. I work for'ard in the galley; I am in constant contact with the sailors; I even sleep in their section of the ship; and I am one man against many. The only other countryman I have on board is the steward, and he sleeps aft. Your servant and the two sail-makers are Japanese. They are only remotely kin to us, though we've agreed to stand together and apart from whatever happens."

"There is Shorty," I said, remembering Mr. Pike's diagnosis of his mixed nationality.

"But we do not recognize him, sir," Louis answered suavely. "He is Portuguese; he is Malay; he is Japanese, true; but he is a mongrel, sir, a mongrel and a bastard. Also, he is a fool. And please, sir, remember that we are very few, and that our position compels us to neutrality."

"But your outlook is gloomy," I persisted. "How do you think it will end?"

"We shall arrive in Seattle most probably, some of us. But I can tell you this, sir: I have lived a long life on the sea, but I have never seen a crew like this. There are few sailors in it; there are bad men in it; and the rest are fools and worse. You will notice I mention no names, sir; but there are men on board whom I do not care to antagonize. I am just Louis, the cook. I do my work to the best of my ability, and that is all, sir."

"And will Charles Davis arrive in Seattle?" I asked, changing the topic in acknowledgment of his right to be reticent.

"No, I do not think so, sir," he answered, although his eyes thanked me for my courtesy. "The steward tells me you have bet that he will. I think, sir, it is a poor bet. We are about to go around the Horn. I have been around it many times. This is midwinter, and we are going from east to west. Davis' room will be awash for weeks. It will never be dry. A strong healthy man confined in it could well die of the hardship. And Davis is far from well. In short, sir, I know his condition, and he is in a shocking state. Surgeons might prolong his life, but here in a wind-jammer it is shortened very rapidly. I have seen many men die at sea. I know, sir. Thank you, sir."

And the Eurasian Chinese-Englishman bowed himself away.

CHAPTER XXXII

Things are worse than I fancied. Here are two episodes within the last seventy-two hours. Mr. Mellaire, for instance, is going to pieces. He cannot stand the strain of being on the same vessel with the man who has sworn to avenge Captain Somers's murder, especially when that man is the redoubtable Mr. Pike.

For several days Margaret and I have been remarking the second mate's bloodshot eyes and pain-lined face and wondering if he were sick. And to-day the secret leaked out. Wada does not like Mr. Mellaire, and this morning, when he brought me breakfast, I saw by the wicked, gleeful gleam in his almond eyes that he was spilling over with some fresh, delectable ship's gossip.

For several days, I learned, he and the steward have been solving a cabin mystery. A gallon can of wood alcohol, standing on a shelf in the after-room, had lost quite a portion of its contents. They compared notes and then made of themselves a Sherlock Holmes and a Doctor Watson. First, they gauged the daily diminution of alcohol. Next they gauged it several times daily, and learned that the diminution, whenever it occurred, was first apparent immediately after meal-time. This focussed their attention on two suspects—the second mate and the carpenter, who alone sat in the after-room. The rest was easy. Whenever Mr. Mellaire arrived ahead of the carpenter more alcohol was missing. When they arrived and departed together, the alcohol was undisturbed. The carpenter was never alone in the room. The syllogism was complete. And now the steward stores the alcohol under his bunk.

But wood alcohol is deadly poison. What a constitution this man of fifty must have! Small wonder his eyes have been bloodshot. The great wonder is that the stuff did not destroy him.

I have not whispered a word of this to Margaret; nor shall I whisper it. I should like to put Mr. Pike on his guard; and yet I know that the revealing of Mr. Mellaire's identity would precipitate another killing. And still we drive south, close-hauled on the wind, toward the inhospitable tip of the continent. To-day we are south of a line drawn between the Straits of Magellan and the Falklands, and to-morrow, if the breeze holds, we shall pick up the coast of Tierra del Fuego close to the entrance of the Straits of Le Maire, through which Captain West intends to pass if the wind favours.

The other episode occurred last night. Mr. Pike says nothing, yet he knows the crew situation. I have been watching some time now, ever since the death of Marinkovich; and I am certain that Mr. Pike never ventures on the main deck after dark. Yet he holds his tongue, confides in no man, and plays out the bitter perilous game as a commonplace matter of course and all in the day's work.

And now to the episode. Shortly after the close of the second dog-watch last evening I went for'ard to the chickens on the 'midship-house on an errand for Margaret. I was to make sure that the steward had carried out her orders. The canvas covering to the big chicken coop had to be down, the ventilation insured, and the kerosene stove burning properly. When I had proved to my satisfaction the dependableness of the steward, and just as I was on the verge of returning to the poop, I was drawn aside by the weird crying of penguins in the darkness and by the unmistakable noise of a whale blowing not far away.

I had climbed around the end of the port boat, and was standing there, quite hidden in the darkness, when I heard the unmistakable age-lag step of the mate proceed along the bridge from the poop. It was a dim starry night, and the *Elsinore*, in the calm ocean under the lee of Tierra del Fuego, was slipping gently and prettily through the water at an eight-knot clip.

Mr. Pike paused at the for'ard end of the housetop and stood in a listening attitude. From the main deck below, near Number Two hatch, across the mumbling of various voices, I could recognize Kid Twist, Nosey Murphy, and Bert Rhine—the three gangsters. But Steve Roberts, the cowboy, was also there, as was Mr. Mellaire, both of whom belonged in the other watch and should have been turned in; for, at midnight, it would be their watch on deck. Especially wrong was Mr. Mellaire's presence, holding social converse with members of the crew—a breach of ship ethics most grievous.

I have always been cursed with curiosity. Always have I wanted to know; and, on the *Elsinore*, I have already witnessed many a little scene that was a clean-cut dramatic gem. So I did not discover myself, but lurked behind the boat.

Five minutes passed. Ten minutes passed. The men still talked. I was tantalized by the crying of the penguins, and by the whale, evidently playful, which came so close that it spouted and splashed a biscuit-toss away. I saw Mr. Pike's head turn at the sound; he glanced squarely in my direction, but did not see me. Then he returned to listening to the mumble of voices from beneath.

Now whether Mulligan Jacobs just happened along, or whether he was deliberately scouting, I do not know. I tell what occurred. Up-and-down the side of the 'midship-house is a ladder. And up this ladder Mulligan Jacobs climbed so noiselessly that I was not aware of his presence until I heard Mr. Pike snarl:

"What the hell you doin' here?"

Then I saw Mulligan Jacobs in the gloom, within two yards of the mate.

"What's it to you?" Mulligan Jacobs snarled back. The voices below hushed. I knew every man stood there tense and listening. No; the philosophers have not yet explained Mulligan Jacobs. There is something more to him than the last word has said in any book. He stood there in the darkness, a fragile creature with curvature of the spine, facing alone the first mate, and he was not afraid.

Mr. Pike cursed him with fearful, unrepeatable words, and again demanded what he was doing there.

"I left me plug of tobacco here when I was coiling down last," said the little twisted man—no; he did not say it. He spat it out like so much venom.

"Get off of here, or I'll throw you off, you and your tobacco," raged the mate.

Mulligan Jacobs lurched closer to Mr. Pike, and in the gloom and with the roll of the ship swayed in the other's face.

"By God, Jacobs!" was all the mate could say.

"You old stiff," was all the terrible little cripple could retort.

Mr. Pike gripped him by the collar and swung him in the air.

"Are you goin' down?—or am I goin' to throw you down?" the mate demanded.

I cannot describe their manner of utterance. It was that of wild beasts.

"I ain't ate outa your hand yet, have I?" was the reply.

Mr. Pike tried to say something, still holding the cripple suspended, but he could do no more than strangle in his impotence of rage.

"You're an old stiff, an old stiff, an old stiff," Mulligan Jacobs chanted, equally incoherent and unimaginative with brutish fury.

"Say it again and over you go," the mate managed to enunciate thickly.

"You're an old stiff," gasped Mulligan Jacobs. He was flung. He soared through the air with the might of the fling, and even as he soared and fell through the darkness he reiterated:

"Old stiff! Old stiff!"

He fell among the men on Number Two hatch, and there were confusion and movement below, and groans.

Mr. Pike paced up and down the narrow house and gritted his teeth. Then he paused. He leaned his arms on the bridge-rail, rested his head on his arms for a full minute, then groaned:

"Oh dear, oh dear, oh dear, oh dear." That was all. Then he went aft, slowly, dragging his feet along the bridge.

CHAPTER XXXIII

The days grow gray. The sun has lost its warmth, and each noon, at meridian, it is lower in the northern sky. All the old stars have long since gone, and it would seem the sun is following them. The world—the only world I know—has been left behind far there to the north, and the hill of the earth is between it and us. This sad and solitary ocean, gray and cold, is the end of all things, the falling-off place where all things cease. Only it grows colder, and grayer, and penguins cry in the night, and huge amphibians moan and slubber, and great albatrosses, gray with storm-battling of the Horn, wheel and veer.

* * * * *

"Land ho!" was the cry yesterday morning. I shivered as I gazed at this, the first land since Baltimore a few centuries ago. There was no sun, and the morning was damp and cold with a brisk wind that penetrated any garment. The deck thermometer marked 30—two degrees below freezing-point; and now and then easy squalls of snow swept past.

327

All of the land that was to be seen was snow. Long, low chains of peaks, snow-covered, arose out of the ocean. As we drew closer, there were no signs of life. It was a sheer, savage, bleak, forsaken land. By eleven, off the entrance of Le Maire Straits, the squalls ceased, the wind steadied, and the tide began to make through in the direction we desired to go.

Captain West did not hesitate. His orders to Mr. Pike were quick and tranquil. The man at the wheel altered the course, while both watches sprang aloft to shake out royals and skysails. And yet Captain West knew every inch of the risk he took in this graveyard of ships.

When we entered the narrow strait, under full sail and gripped by a tremendous tide, the rugged headlands of Tierra del Fuego dashed by with dizzying swiftness. Close we were to them, and close we were to the jagged coast of Staten Island on the opposite shore. It was here, in a wild bight, between two black and precipitous walls of rock where even the snow could find no lodgment, that Captain West paused in a casual sweep of his glasses and gazed steadily at one place. I picked the spot up with my own glasses and was aware of an instant chill as I saw the four masts of a great ship sticking out of the water. Whatever craft it was, it was as large as the *Elsinore*, and it had been but recently wrecked.

"One of the German nitrate ships," said Mr. Pike. Captain West nodded, still studying the wreck, then said:

"She looks quite deserted. Just the same, Mr. Pike, send several of your best-sighted sailors aloft, and keep a good lookout yourself. There may be some survivors ashore trying to signal us."

But we sailed on, and no signals were seen. Mr. Pike was delighted with our good fortune. He was guilty of walking up and down, rubbing his hands and chuckling to himself. Not since 1888, he told me, had he been through the Straits of Le Maire. Also, he said that he knew of shipmasters who had made forty voyages around the Horn and had never once had the luck to win through the straits. The regular passage is far to the east around Staten Island, which means a loss of westing, and here, at the tip of the world, where the great west wind, unobstructed by any land, sweeps round and around the narrow girth of earth, westing is the thing that has to be fought for mile by mile and inch by inch. The Sailing Directions advise masters on the Horn passage: *Make Westing. Whatever you do, make westing.*

When we emerged from the straits in the early afternoon the same steady breeze continued, and in the calm water under the lee of Tierra del Fuego, which extends south-westerly to the Horn, we slipped along at an eight-knot clip.

Mr. Pike was beside himself. He could scarcely tear himself from the deck when it was his watch below. He chuckled, rubbed his hands, and incessantly hummed snatches from the Twelfth Mass. Also, he was voluble.

"To-morrow morning we'll be up with the Horn. We'll shave it by a dozen or fifteen miles. Think of it! We'll just steal around! I never had such luck, and never expected to. Old girl *Elsinore*, you're rotten for'ard, but the hand of God is at your helm."

Once, under the weather cloth, I came upon him talking to himself. It was more a prayer.

"If only she don't pipe up," he kept repeating. "If only she don't pipe up."

Mr. Mellaire was quite different.

"It never happens," he told me. "No ship ever went around like this. You watch her come. She always comes a-smoking out of the sou'west."

"But can't a vessel ever steal around?" I asked.

"The odds are mighty big against it, sir," he answered. "I'll give you a line on them. I'll wager even, sir, just a nominal bet of a pound of tobacco, that inside twenty-four hours we'll he hove to under upper-topsails. I'll wager ten pounds to five that we're not west of the Horn a week from now; and, fifty to fifty being the passage, twenty pounds to five that two weeks from now we're not up with fifty in the Pacific."

329

As for Captain West, the perils of Le Maire behind, he sat below, his slippered feet stretched before him, smoking a cigar. He had nothing to say whatever, although Margaret and I were jubilant and dared duets through all of the second dog-watch.

* * * * *

And this morning, in a smooth sea and gentle breeze, the Horn bore almost due north of us not more than six miles away. Here we were, well abreast and reeling off westing.

"What price tobacco this morning?" I quizzed Mr. Mellaire.

"Going up," he came back. "Wish I had a thousand bets like the one with *you*, sir."

I glanced about at sea and sky and gauged the speed of our way by the foam, but failed to see anything that warranted his remark. It was surely fine weather, and the steward, in token of the same, was trying to catch fluttering Cape pigeons with a bent pin on a piece of thread.

For'ard, on the poop, I encountered Mr. Pike. It *was* an encounter, for his salutation was a grunt.

"Well, we're going right along," I ventured cheerily.

He made no reply, but turned and stared into the gray south-west with an expression sourer than any I had ever seen on his face. He mumbled something I failed to catch, and, on my asking him to repeat it, he said:

"It's breeding weather. Can't you see it?"

I shook my head.

"What d'ye think we're taking off the kites for?" he growled.

I looked aloft. The skysails were already furled; men were furling the royals; and the topgallant-yards were running down while clewlines and buntlines bagged the canvas. Yet, if anything, our northerly breeze fanned even more gently.

"Bless me if I can see any weather," I said.

"Then go and take a look at the barometer," he grunted, as he turned on his heel and swung away from me.

In the chart-room was Captain West, pulling on his long sea-boots. That would have told me had there been no barometer, though the barometer was eloquent enough of itself. The night before it had stood at 30.10. It was now 28.64. Even in the pampero it had not been so low as that.

"The usual Cape Horn programme," Captain West smiled to me, as he stood up in all his lean and slender gracefulness and reached for his long oilskin coat.

Still I could scarcely believe.

"Is it very far away?" I inquired.

He shook his head, and forebore in the act of speaking to lift his hand for me to listen. The *Elsinore* rolled uneasily, and from without came the soft and hollow thunder of sails emptying themselves against the masts and gear.

We had chatted a bare five minutes, when again he lifted his head. This time the *Elsinore* heeled over slightly and remained heeled over, while the sighing whistle of a rising breeze awoke in the rigging.

"It's beginning to make," he said, in the good old Anglo-Saxon of the sea.

And then I heard Mr. Pike snarling out orders, and in my heart discovered a growing respect for Cape Horn—Cape Stiff, as the sailors call it.

An hour later we were hove to on the port tack under upper-topsails and foresail. The wind had come out of the south-west, and our leeway was setting us down upon the land. Captain West gave orders to the mate to stand by to wear ship. Both watches had been taking in sail, so that both watches were on deck for the manoeuvre.

It was astounding, the big sea that had arisen in so short a time. The wind was blowing a gale that ever, in recurring gusts, increased upon itself. Nothing was visible a hundred yards away. The day had become black-gray. In the cabin lamps were burning. The view from the poop, along the length of the great labouring ship, was magnificent. Seas burst and surged across her weather-rail and kept her deck half filled, despite the spouting ports and gushing scuppers.

On each of the two houses and on the poop the ship's complement, all in oilskins, was in groups. For'ard, Mr. Mellaire had charge. Mr. Pike took charge of the 'midship-house and the poop. Captain West strolled up and down, saw everything, said nothing; for it was the mate's affair.

When Mr. Pike ordered the wheel hard up, he slacked off all the mizzen-yards, and followed it with a partial slacking of the main-yards, so that the after-pressures were eased. The foresail and fore-lower- and-upper-topsails remained flat in order to pay the head off before the wind. All this took time. The men were slow, not strong, and without snap. They reminded me of dull oxen by the way they moved and pulled. And the gale, ever snorting harder, now snorted diabolically. Only at intervals could I glimpse the group on top the for'ard-house. Again and again, leaning to it and holding their heads down, the men on the 'midship-house were obliterated by the drive of crested seas that burst against the rail, spouted to the lower-yards, and swept in horizontal volumes across to leeward. And Mr. Pike, like an enormous spider in a wind-tossed web, went back and forth along the slender bridge that was itself a shaken thread in the blast of the storm.

So tremendous were the gusts that for the time the *Elsinore* refused to answer. She lay down to it; she was swept and racked by it; but her head did not pay off before it, and all the while we drove down upon that bitter, iron coast. And the world was black-gray, and violent, and very cold, with the flying spray freezing to ice in every lodgment.

We waited. The groups of men, head down to it, waited. Mr. Pike, restless, angry, his blue eyes as bitter as the cold, his mouth as much a-snarl as the snarl of the elements with which he fought, waited. The Samurai waited, tranquil, casual, remote. And Cape Horn waited, there on our lee, for the bones of our ship and us.

And then the *Elsinore's* bow paid off. The angle of the beat of the gale changed, and soon, with dreadful speed, we were dashing straight before it and straight toward the rocks we could not see. But all doubt was over. The success of the manoeuvre was assured. Mr. Mellaire, informed by messenger along the bridge from Mr. Pike, slacked off the head-yards. Mr. Pike, his eye on the helmsman, his hand signalling the order, had the wheel put over to port to check the *Elsinore's* rush into the wind as she came up on the starboard tack. All was activity. Main- and mizzen-yards were braced up, and the *Elsinore*, snugged down and hove to, had a lee of thousands of miles of Southern Ocean.

And all this had been accomplished in the stamping ground of storm, at the end of the world, by a handful of wretched weaklings, under the drive of two strong mates, with behind them the placid will of the Samurai.

It had taken thirty minutes to wear ship, and I had learned how the best of shipmasters can lose their ships without reproach. Suppose the *Elsinore* had persisted in her refusal to payoff? Suppose anything had carried away? And right here enters Mr. Pike. It is his task ever to see that every rope and block and all the myriad other things in the vast and complicated gear of the *Elsinore* are in strength not to carry away. Always have the masters of our race required henchmen like Mr. Pike, and it seems the race has well supplied those henchmen.

Ere I went below I heard Captain West tell Mr. Pike that while both watches were on deck it would be just as well to put a reef in the foresail before they furled it. The mainsail and the crojack being off, I could see the men black on the fore-yard. For half-an-hour I lingered, watching them. They seemed to make no progress with the reef. Mr. Mellaire was with them, having direct supervision of the job, while Mr. Pike, on the poop, growled and grumbled and spat endless blasphemies into the flying air.

"What's the matter?" I asked.

"Two watches on a single yardarm and unable to put a reef in a handkerchief like that!" he snorted. "What'll it be if we're off here a month?"

"A month!" I cried.

"A month isn't anything for Cape Stiff," he said grimly. "I've been off here seven weeks and then turned tail and run around the other way."

"Around the world?" I gasped.

"It was the only way to get to 'Frisco," he answered. "The Horn's the Horn, and there's no summer seas that I've ever noticed in this neighbourhood."

My fingers were numb and I was chilled through when I took a last look at the wretched men on the fore-yard and went below to warm up.

A little later, as I went in to table, through a cabin port I stole a look for'ard between seas and saw the men still struggling on the freezing yard.

The four of us were at table, and it was very comfortable, in spite of the *Elsinore*'s violent antics. The room was warm. The storm-racks on the table kept each dish in its place. The steward served and moved about with ease and apparent unconcern, although I noticed an occasional anxious gleam in his eyes when he poised some dish at a moment when the ship pitched and flung with unusual wildness.

And now and again I thought of the poor devils on the yard. Well, they belonged there by right, just as we belonged here by right in this oasis of the cabin. I looked at Mr. Pike and wagered to myself that half-a-dozen like him could master that stubborn foresail. As for the Samurai, I was convinced that alone, not moving from his seat, by a tranquil exertion of will, he could accomplish the same thing.

The lighted sea-lamps swung and leaped in their gimbals, ever battling with the dancing shadows in the murky gray. The wood-work creaked and groaned. The jiggermast, a huge cylinder of hollow steel that perforated the apartment through deck above and floor beneath, was hideously vocal with the storm. Far above, taut ropes beat against it so that it clanged like a boiler-shop. There was a perpetual thunder of seas falling on our deck and crash of water against our for'ard wall; while the ten thousand ropes and gears aloft bellowed and screamed as the storm smote them.

And yet all this was from without. Here, at this well-appointed table, was no draught nor breath of wind, no drive of spray nor wash of sea. We were in the heart of peace in the midmost centre of the storm. Margaret was in high spirits, and her laughter vied with the clang of the jiggermast. Mr. Pike was gloomy, but I knew him well enough to attribute his gloom, not to the elements, but to the inefficients futilely freezing on the yard. As for me, I looked about at the four of us—blue-eyed, gray-eyed, all fair-skinned and royal blond—and somehow it seemed that I had long since lived this, and that with me and in me were all my ancestors, and that their lives and memories were mine, and that all this vexation of the sea and air and labouring ship was of old time and a thousand times before.

CHAPTER XXXIV

"How are you for a climb?" Margaret asked me, shortly after we had left the table.

She stood challengingly at my open door, in oilskins, sou'wester, and sea-boots.

"I've never seen you with a foot above the deck since we sailed," she went on. "Have you a good head?"

I marked my book, rolled out of my bunk in which I had been wedged, and clapped my hands for Wada.

"Will you?" she cried eagerly.

"If you let me lead," I answered airily, "and if you will promise to hold on tight. Whither away?"

"Into the top of the jigger. It's the easiest. As for holding on, please remember that I have often done it. It is with you the doubt rests."

"Very well," I retorted; "do you lead then. I shall hold on tight."

"I have seen many a landsman funk it," she teased. "There are no lubber-holes in our tops."

"And most likely I shall," I agreed. "I've never been aloft in my life, and since there is no hole for a lubber."

She looked at me, half believing my confession of weakness, while I extended my arms for the oilskin which Wada struggled on to me.

On the poop it was magnificent, and terrible, and sombre. The universe was very immediately about us. It blanketed us in storming wind and flying spray and grayness. Our main deck was impassable, and the relief of the wheel came aft along the bridge. It was two o'clock, and for over two hours the frozen wretches had laid out upon the fore-yard. They were still there, weak, feeble, hopeless. Captain West, stepping out in the lee of the chart-house, gazed at them for several minutes.

"We'll have to give up that reef," he said to Mr. Pike. "Just make the sail fast. Better put on double gaskets."

And with lagging feet, from time to time pausing and holding on as spray and the tops of waves swept over him, the mate went for'ard along the bridge to vent his scorn on the two watches of a four-masted ship that could not reef a foresail.

It is true. They could not do it, despite their willingness, for this I have learned: *the men do their weak best whenever the order is given to shorten sail.* It must be that they are afraid. They lack the iron of Mr. Pike, the wisdom and the iron of Captain West. Always, have I noticed, with all the alacrity of which they are capable, do they respond to any order to shorten down. That is why they are for'ard, in that pigsty of a forecastle, because they lack the iron. Well, I can say only this: If nothing else could have prevented the funk hinted at by Margaret, the sorry spectacle of these ironless, spineless creatures was sufficient safeguard. How could I funk in the face of their weakness—I, who lived aft in the high place?

Margaret did not disdain the aid of my hand as she climbed upon the pin-rail at the foot of the weather jigger-rigging. But it was merely the recognition of a courtesy on her part, for the next moment she released her mittened hand from mine, swung boldly outboard into the face of the gale, and around against the ratlines. Then she began to climb. I followed, almost unaware of the ticklishness of the exploit to a tyro, so buoyed up was I by her example and by my scorn of the weaklings for'ard. Where men could go, I could go. What men could do, I could do. And no daughter of the Samurai could out-game me.

Yet it was slow work. In the windward rolls against the storm-gusts one was pinned helplessly, like a butterfly, against the rigging. At such times, so great was the pressure one could not lift hand nor foot. Also, there was no need for holding on. As I have said, one was pinned against the rigging by the wind.

Through the snow beginning to drive the deck grew small beneath me, until a fall meant a broken back or death, unless one landed in the sea, in which case the result would be frigid drowning. And still Margaret climbed. Without pause she went out under the overhanging platform of the top, shifted her holds to the rigging that went aloft from it, and swung around this rigging, easily, carelessly, timing the action to the roll, and stood safely upon the top.

I followed. I breathed no prayers, knew no qualms, as I presented my back to the deck and climbed out under the overhang, feeling with my hands for holds I could not see. I was in an ecstasy. I could dare anything. Had she sprung into the air, stretched out her arms, and soared away on the breast of the gale, I should have unhesitatingly followed her.

As my head outpassed the edge of the top so that she came into view, I could see she was looking at me with storm-bright eyes. And as I swung around the rigging lightly and joined her, I saw approval in her eyes that was quickly routed by petulance.

"Oh, you've done this sort of thing before," she reproached, calling loudly, so that I might hear, her lips close to my ear.

337

I shook a denial with my head that brightened her eyes again. She nodded and smiled, and sat down, dangling her sea-boots into snow-swirled space from the edge of the top. I sat beside her, looking down into the snow that hid the deck while it exaggerated the depth out of which we had climbed.

We were all alone there, a pair of storm petrels perched in mid air on a steel stick that arose out of snow and that vanished above into snow. We had come to the tip of the world, and even that tip had ceased to be. But no. Out of the snow, down wind, with motionless wings, driving fully eighty or ninety miles an hour, appeared a huge albatross. He must have been fifteen feet from wing-tip to wing-tip. He had seen his danger ere we saw him, and, tilting his body on the blast, he carelessly veered clear of collision. His head and neck were rimed with age or frost—we could not tell which—and his bright bead-eye noted us as he passed and whirled away on a great circle into the snow to leeward.

Margaret's hand shot out to mine.

"It alone was worth the climb!" she cried. And then the *Elsinore* flung down, and Margaret's hand clutched tighter for holding, while from the hidden depths arose the crash and thunder of the great west wind drift upon our decks.

Quickly as the snow-squall had come, it passed with the same sharp quickness, and as in a flash we could see the lean length of the ship beneath us—the main deck full with boiling flood, the forecastle-head buried in a bursting sea, the lookout, stationed for very life back on top the for'ard-house, hanging on, head down, to the wind-drive of ocean, and, directly under us, the streaming poop and Mr. Mellaire, with a handful of men, rigging relieving tackles on the tiller. And we saw the Samurai emerge in the lee of the chart-house, swaying with casual surety on the mad deck, as he spoke what must have been instructions to Mr. Pike.

The gray circle of the world had removed itself from us for several hundred yards, and we could see the mighty sweep of sea. Shaggy gray-beards, sixty feet from trough to crest, leapt out of the windward murky gray, and in unending procession rushed upon the *Elsinore*, one moment overtoppling her slender frailness, the next moment splashing a hundred tons of water on her deck and flinging her skyward as they passed beneath and foamed and crested from sight in the murky gray to leeward. And the great albatrosses veered and circled about us, beating up into the bitter violence of the gale and sweeping grandly away before it far faster than it blew.

Margaret forbore from looking to challenge me with eloquent, questioning eyes. With numb fingers inside my thick mitten, I drew aside the ear-flap of her sou'wester and shouted:

"It is nothing new. I have been here before. In the lives of all my fathers have I been here. The frost is on my cheek, the salt bites my nostrils, the wind chants in my ears, and it is an old happening. I know, now, that my forbears were Vikings. I was seed of them in their own day. With them I have raided English coasts, dared the Pillars of Hercules, forayed the Mediterranean, and sat in the high place of government over the soft sun-warm peoples. I am Hengist and Horsa; I am of the ancient heroes, even legendary to them. I have bearded and bitten the frozen seas, and, aforetime of that, ere ever the ice-ages came to be, I have dripped my shoulders in reindeer gore, slain the mastodon and the sabre-tooth, scratched the record of my prowess on the walls of deep-buried caves—ay, and suckled she-wolves side by side with my brother-cubs, the scars of whose fangs are now upon me."

She laughed deliciously, and a snow-squall drove upon us and cut our cheeks, and the *Elsinore* flung over and down as if she would never rise again, while we held on and swept through the air in a dizzying arc. Margaret released a hand, still laughing, and pressed aside my ear-flap.

"I don't know anything about it," she cried. "It sounds like poetry. But I believe it. It has to be, for it has been. I have heard it aforetime, when skin-clad men sang in fire-circles that pressed back the frost and night."

"And the books?" she queried maliciously, as we prepared to descend.

"They can go hang, along with all the brain-sick, world-sick fools that wrote them," I replied.

Again she laughed deliciously, though the wind tore the sound away as she swung out into space, muscled herself by her arms while she caught footholds beneath her which she could not see, and passed out of my sight under the perilous overhang of the top.

CHAPTER XXXV

"What price tobacco?" was Mr. Mellaire's greeting, when I came on deck this morning, bruised and weary, aching in every bone and muscle from sixty hours of being tossed about.

The wind had fallen to a dead calm toward morning, and the *Elsinore*, her several spread sails booming and slatting, rolled more miserably than ever. Mr. Mellaire pointed for'ard of our starboard beam. I could make out a bleak land of white and jagged peaks.

"Staten Island, the easterly end of it," said Mr. Mellaire.

And I knew that we were in the position of a vessel just rounding Staten Island preliminary to bucking the Horn. And, yet, four days ago, we had run through the Straits of Le Maire and stolen along toward the Horn. Three days ago we had been well abreast of the Horn and even a few miles past. And here we were now, starting all over again and far in the rear of where we had originally started.

* * * * *

The condition of the men is truly wretched. During the gale the forecastle was washed out twice. This means that everything in it was afloat and that every article of clothing, including mattresses and blankets, is wet and will remain wet in this bitter weather until *we are around the Horn* and well up in the good-weather latitudes. The same is true of the 'midship-house. Every room in it, with the exception of the cook's and the sail-makers' (which open for'ard on Number Two hatch), is soaking. And they have no fires in their rooms with which to dry things out.

I peeped into Charles Davis's room. It was terrible. He grinned to me and nodded his head.

"It's just as well O'Sullivan wasn't here, sir," he said. "He'd a-drowned in the lower bunk. And I want to tell you I was doing some swimmin' before I could get into the top one. And salt water's bad for my sores. I oughtn't to be in a hole like this in Cape Horn weather. Look at the ice, there, on the floor. It's below freezin' right now in this room, and my blankets are wet, and I'm a sick man, as any man can tell that's got a nose."

"If you'd been decent to the mate you might have got decent treatment in return," I said.

"Huh!" he sneered. "You needn't think you can lose me, sir. I can grow fat on this sort of stuff. Why, sir, when I think of the court doin's in Seattle I just couldn't die. An' if you'll listen to me, sir, you'll cover the steward's money. You can't lose. I'm advisin' you, sir, because you're a sort of decent sort. Anybody that bets on my going over the side is a sure loser."

"How could you dare ship on a voyage like this in your condition?" I demanded.

"Condition?" he queried with a fine assumption of innocence. "Why, that is why I did ship. I was in tiptop shape when I sailed. All this come out on me afterward. You remember seem' me aloft, an' up to my neck in water. And I trimmed coal below, too. A sick man couldn't do it. And remember, sir, you'll have to testify to how I did my duty at the beginning before I took down."

"I'll bet with you myself if you think I'm goin' to die," he called after me.

Already the sailors show marks of the hardship they are enduring. It is surprising, in so short a time, how lean their faces have grown, how lined and seamed. They must dry their underclothing with their body heat. Their outer garments, under their oilskins, are soggy. And yet, paradoxically, despite their lean, drawn faces, they have grown very stout. Their walk is a waddle, and they bulge with seaming corpulency. This is due to the amount of clothing

341

they have on. I noticed Larry, to-day, had on two vests, two coats, and an overcoat, with his oilskin outside of that. They are elephantine in their gait for, in addition to everything else, they have wrapped their feet, outside their sea-boots, with gunny sacking.

It *is* cold, although the deck thermometer stood at thirty-three to-day at noon. I had Wada weigh the clothing I wear on deck. Omitting oilskins and boots, it came to eighteen pounds. And yet I am not any too warm in all this gear when the wind is blowing. How sailors, after having once experienced the Horn, can ever sign on again for a voyage around is beyond me. It but serves to show how stupid they must be.

I feel sorry for Henry, the training-ship boy. He is more my own kind, and some day he will make a henchman of the afterguard and a mate like Mr. Pike. In the meantime, along with Buckwheat, the other boy who berths in the 'midship-house with him, he suffers the same hardship as the men. He is very fair-skinned, and I noticed this afternoon, when he was pulling on a brace, that the sleeves of his oil-skins, assisted by the salt water, have chafed his wrists till they are raw and bleeding and breaking out in sea-boils. Mr. Mellaire tells me that in another week there will be a plague of these boils with all hands for'ard.

"When do you think we'll be up with the Horn again?" I innocently queried of Mr. Pike.

He turned upon me in a rage, as if I had insulted him, and positively snarled in my face ere he swung away without the courtesy of an answer. It is evident that he takes the sea seriously. That is why, I fancy, he is so excellent a seaman.

* * * * *

The days pass—if the interval of sombre gray that comes between the darknesses can be called day. For a week, now, we have not seen the sun. Our ship's position in this waste of storm and sea is conjectural. Once, by dead reckoning, we gained up with the Horn and a hundred miles south of it. And then came another sou'west gale that tore our fore-topsail and brand new spencer out of the belt-ropes and swept us away to a conjectured longitude east of Staten Island.

Oh, I know now this Great West Wind that blows for ever around the world south of 55. And I know why the chart-makers have capitalized it, as, for instance, when I read "The Great West Wind Drift." And I know why the *Sailing Directions* advise: "*Whatever you do, make westing! make westing!*"

And the West Wind and the drift of the West Wind will not permit the *Elsinore* to make westing. Gale follows gale, always from the west, and we make easting. And it is bitter cold, and each gale snorts up with a prelude of driving snow.

In the cabin the lamps burn all day long. No more does Mr. Pike run the phonograph, nor does Margaret ever touch the piano. She complains of being bruised and sore. I have a wrenched shoulder from being hurled against the wall. And both Wada and the steward are limping. Really, the only comfort I can find is in my bunk, so wedged with boxes and pillows that the wildest rolls cannot throw me out. There, save for my meals and for an occasional run on deck for exercise and fresh air, I lie and read eighteen and nineteen hours out of the twenty-four. But the unending physical strain is very wearisome.

How it must be with the poor devils for'ard is beyond conceiving. The forecastle has been washed out several times, and everything is soaking wet. Besides, they have grown weaker, and two watches are required to do what one ordinary watch could do. Thus, they must spend as many hours on the sea-swept deck and aloft on the freezing yards as I do in my warm, dry bunk. Wada tells me that they never undress, but turn into their wet bunks in their oil-skins and sea-boots and wet undergarments.

To look at them crawling about on deck or in the rigging is enough. They are truly weak. They are gaunt-cheeked and haggard-gray of skin, with great dark circles under their eyes. The predicted plague of sea-boils and sea-cuts has come, and their hands and wrists and arms are frightfully afflicted. Now one, and now another, and sometimes several, either from being knocked down by seas or from general miserableness, take to the bunk for a day or so off. This means more work for the others, so that the men on their feet are not tolerant of the sick ones, and a man must be very sick to escape being dragged out to work by his mates.

I cannot but marvel at Andy Fay and Mulligan Jacobs. Old and fragile as they are, it seems impossible that they can endure what they do. For that matter, I cannot understand why they work at all. I cannot understand why any of them toil on and obey an order in this freezing hell of the Horn. Is it because of fear of death that they do not cease work and bring death to all of us? Or is it because they are slave-beasts, with a slave-psychology, so used all their lives to being driven by their masters that it is beyond their mental power to refuse to obey?

And yet most of them, in a week after we reach Seattle, will be on board other ships outward bound for the Horn. Margaret says the reason for this is that sailors forget. Mr. Pike agrees. He says give them a week in the southeast trades as we run up the Pacific and they will have forgotten that they have ever been around the Horn. I wonder. Can they be as stupid as this? Does pain leave no record with them? Do they fear only the immediate thing? Have they no horizons wider than a day? Then indeed do they belong where they are.

They *are* cowardly. This was shown conclusively this morning at two o'clock. Never have I witnessed such panic fear, and it was fear of the immediate thing—fear, stupid and beast-like. It was Mr. Mellaire's watch. As luck would have it, I was reading Boas's *Mind of Primitive Man* when I heard the rush of feet over my head. The *Elsinore* was hove to on the port tack at the time, under very short canvas. I was wondering what emergency had brought the watch upon the poop, when I heard another rush of feet that meant the second watch. I heard no pulling and hauling, and the thought of mutiny flashed across my mind.

Still nothing happened, and, growing curious, I got into my sea-boots, sheepskin coat, and oilskin, put on my sou'wester and mittens, and went on deck. Mr. Pike had already dressed and was ahead of me. Captain West, who in this bad weather sleeps in the chart-room, stood in the lee doorway of the house, through which the lamplight streamed on the frightened faces of the men.

Those of the 'midship-house were not present, but every man Jack of the forecastle, with the exception of Andy Fay and Mulligan Jacobs, as I afterwards learned, had joined in the flight aft. Andy Fay, who belonged in the watch below, had calmly remained in his bunk, while Mulligan Jacobs had taken advantage of the opportunity to sneak into the forecastle and fill his pipe.

"What is the matter, Mr. Pike?" Captain West asked.

Before the mate could reply, Bert Rhine snickered:

"The devil's come aboard, sir."

But his snicker was palpably an assumption of unconcern he did not possess. The more I think over it the more I am surprised that such keen men as the gangsters should have been frightened by what had occurred. But frightened they were, the three of them, out of their bunks and out of the precious surcease of their brief watch below.

So fear-struck was Larry that he chattered and grimaced like an ape, and shouldered and struggled to get away from the dark and into the safety of the shaft of light that shone out of the chart-house. Tony, the Greek, was just as bad, mumbling to himself and continually crossing himself. He was joined in this, as a sort of chorus, by the two Italians, Guido Bombini and Mike Cipriani. Arthur Deacon was almost in collapse, and he and Chantz, the Jew, shamelessly clung to each other for support. Bob, the fat and overgrown youth, was sobbing, while the other youth, Bony the Splinter, was shivering and chattering his teeth. Yes, and the two best sailors for'ard, Tom Spink and the Maltese Cockney, stood in the background, their backs to the dark, their faces yearning toward the light.

More than all other contemptible things in this world there are two that I loathe and despise: hysteria in a woman; fear and cowardice in a man. The first turns me to ice. I cannot sympathize with hysteria. The second turns my stomach. Cowardice in a man is to me positively nauseous. And this fear-smitten mass of human animals on our reeling poop raised my gorge. Truly, had I been a god at that moment, I should have annihilated the whole mass of them. No; I should have been merciful to one. He was the Faun. His bright, pain-liquid, and flashing-eager eyes strained from face to face with desire to understand. He did not know what had occurred, and, being stone-deaf, had thought the rush aft a response to a call for all hands.

I noticed Mr. Mellaire. He may be afraid of Mr. Pike, and he is a murderer; but at any rate he has no fear of the supernatural. With two men above him in authority, although it was his watch, there was no call for him to do anything. He swayed back and forth in balance to the violent motions of the *Elsinore* and looked on with eyes that were amused and cynical.

"What does the devil look like, my man?" Captain West asked.

Bert Rhine grinned sheepishly.

"Answer the captain!" Mr. Pike snarled at him.

Oh, it was murder, sheer murder, that leapt into the gangster's eyes for the instant, in acknowledgment of the snarl. Then he replied to Captain West:

"I didn't wait to see, sir. But it's one whale of a devil."

"He's as big as a elephant, sir," volunteered Bill Quigley. "I seen'm face to face, sir. He almost got me when I run out of the fo'c's'le."

"Oh, Lord, sir!" Larry moaned. "The way he hit the house, sir. It was the call to Judgment."

"Your theology is mixed, my man," Captain West smiled quietly, though I could not help seeing how tired was his face and how tired were his wonderful Samurai eyes.

He turned to the mate.

"Mr. Pike, will you please go for'ard and interview this devil? Fasten him up and tie him down and I'll take a look at him in the morning."

"Yes, sir," said Mr. Pike; and Kipling's line came to me:

"Woman, Man, or God or Devil, was there anything we feared?"

And as I went for'ard through the wall of darkness after Mr. Pike and Mr. Mellaire along the freezing, slender, sea-swept bridge—not a sailor dared to accompany us—other lines of "The Galley Slave" drifted through my brain, such as:

"Our bulkheads bulged with cotton and our masts were stepped in gold—

We ran a mighty merchandise of niggers in the hold. . . "

And:

"By the brand upon my shoulder, by the gall of clinging steel,

By the welts the whips have left me, by the scars that never heal . . . "

And:

"Battered chain-gangs of the orlop, grizzled draughts of years gone by . . . "

And I caught my great, radiant vision of Mr. Pike, galley slave of the race, and a driver of men under men greater than he; the faithful henchman, the able sailorman, battered and grizzled, branded and galled, the servant of the sweep-head that made mastery of the sea. I know him now. He can never again offend me. I forgive him everything—the whiskey raw on his breath the day I came aboard at Baltimore, his moroseness when sea and wind do not favour, his savagery to the men, his snarl and his sneer.

On top the 'midship-house we got a ducking that makes me shiver to recall. I had dressed too hastily properly to fasten my oilskin about my neck, so that I was wet to the skin. We crossed the next span of bridge through driving spray, and were well upon the top of the for'ard-house when something adrift on the deck hit the for'ard wall a terrific smash.

"Whatever it is, it's playing the devil," Mr. Pike yelled in my ear, as he endeavoured to locate the thing by the dry-battery light-stick which he carried.

The pencil of light travelled over dark water, white with foam, that churned upon the deck.

"There it goes!" Mr. Pike cried, as the *Elsinore* dipped by the head and hurtled the water for'ard.

The light went out as the three of us caught holds and crouched to a deluge of water from overside. As we emerged, from under the forecastle-head we heard a tremendous thumping and battering. Then, as the bow lifted, for an instant in the pencil of light that immediately lost it, I glimpsed a vague black object that bounded down the inclined deck where no water was. What became of it we could not see.

Mr. Pike descended to the deck, followed by Mr. Mellaire. Again, as the *Elsinore* dipped by the head and fetched a surge of sea-water from aft along the runway, I saw the dark object bound for'ard directly at the mates. They sprang to safety from its charge, the light went out, while another icy sea broke aboard.

For a time I could see nothing of the two men. Next, in the light flashed from the stick, I guessed that Mr. Pike was in pursuit of the thing. He evidently must have captured it at the rail against the starboard rigging and caught a turn around it with a loose end of rope. As the vessel rolled to windward some sort of a struggle seemed to be going on. The second mate sprang to the mate's assistance, and, together, with more loose ends, they seemed to subdue the thing.

I descended to see. By the light-stick we made it out to be a large, barnacle-crusted cask.

"She's been afloat for forty years," was Mr. Pike's judgment. "Look at the size of the barnacles, and look at the whiskers."

"And it's full of something," said Mr. Mellaire. "Hope it isn't water."

I rashly lent a hand when they started to work the cask for'ard, between seas and taking advantage of the rolls and pitches, to the shelter under the forecastle-head. As a result, even through my mittens, I was cut by the sharp edges of broken shell.

"It's liquor of some sort," said the mate, "but we won't risk broaching it till morning."

"But where did it come from?" I asked.

"Over the side's the only place it could have come from." Mr. Pike played the light over it. "Look at it! It's been afloat for years and years."

"The stuff ought to be well-seasoned," commented Mr. Mellaire.

Leaving them to lash the cask securely, I stole along the deck to the forecastle and peered in. The men, in their headlong flight, had neglected to close the doors, and the place was afloat. In the flickering light from a small and very smoky sea-lamp it was a dismal picture. No self-respecting cave-man, I am sure, would have lived in such a hole.

Even as I looked a bursting sea filled the runway between the house and rail, and through the doorway in which I stood the freezing water rushed waist-deep. I had to hold on to escape being swept inside the room. From a top bunk, lying on his side, Andy Fay regarded me steadily with his bitter blue eyes. Seated on the rough table of heavy planks, his sea-booted feet swinging in the water, Mulligan Jacobs pulled at his pipe. When he observed me he pointed to pulpy book-pages that floated about.

"Me library's gone to hell," he mourned as he indicated the flotsam. "There's me Byron. An' there goes Zola an' Browning with a piece of

Shakespeare runnin' neck an' neck, an' what's left of *Anti-Christ* makin' a bad last. An' there's Carlyle and Zola that cheek by jowl you can't tell 'em apart."

Here the *Elsinore* lay down to starboard, and the water in the forecastle poured out against my legs and hips. My wet mittens slipped on the iron work, and I swept down the runway into the scuppers, where I was turned over and over by another flood that had just boarded from windward.

I know I was rather confused, and that I had swallowed quite a deal of salt water, ere I got my hands on the rungs of the ladder and climbed to the top of the house. On my way aft along the bridge I encountered the crew coming for'ard. Mr. Mellaire and Mr. Pike were talking in the lee of the chart-house, and inside, as I passed below, Captain West was smoking a cigar.

After a good rub down, in dry pyjamas, I was scarcely back in my bunk with the *Mind of Primitive Man* before me, when the stampede over my head was repeated. I waited for the second rush. It came, and I proceeded to dress.

The scene on the poop duplicated the previous one, save that the men were more excited, more frightened. They were babbling and chattering all together.

"Shut up!" Mr. Pike was snarling when I came upon them. "One at a time, and answer the captain's question."

"It ain't no barrel this time, sir," Tom Spink said. "It's alive. An' if it ain't the devil it's the ghost of a drownded man. I see 'm plain an' clear. He's a man, or was a man once—"

"They was two of 'em, sir," Richard Giller, one of the "bricklayers," broke in.

"I think he looked like Petro Marinkovich, sir," Tom Spink went on.

"An' the other was Jespersen—I seen 'm," Giller added.

"They was three of 'em, sir," said Nosey Murphy. "O'Sullivan, sir, was the other one. They ain't devils, sir. They're drownded men. They come aboard right over the bows, an' they moved slow like drownded men. Sorensen seen the first one first. He caught my arm an' pointed, an' then I seen 'm. He was

350

on top the for'ard-house. And Olansen seen 'm, an' Deacon, sir, an' Hackey. We all seen 'm, sir . . . an' the second one; an' when the rest run away I stayed long enough to see the third one. Mebbe there's more. I didn't wait to see."

Captain West stopped the man.

"Mr. Pike," he said wearily, "will you straighten this nonsense out."

"Yes, sir," Mr. Pike responded, then turned on the man. "Come on, all of you! There's three devils to tie down this time."

But the men shrank away from the order and from him.

"For two cents . . . " I heard Mr. Pike growl to himself, then choke off utterance.

He flung about on his heel and started for the bridge. In the same order as on the previous trip, Mr. Mellaire second, and I bringing up the rear, we followed. It was a similar journey, save that we caught a ducking midway on the first span of bridge as well as a ducking on the 'midship-house.

We halted on top the for'ard-house. In vain Mr. Pike flashed his light-stick. Nothing was to be seen nor heard save the white-flecked dark water on our deck, the roar of the gale in our rigging, and the crash and thunder of seas falling aboard. We advanced half-way across the last span of bridge to the fore-castle head, and were driven to pause and hang on at the foremast by a bursting sea.

Between the drives of spray Mr. Pike flashed his stick. I heard him exclaim something. Then he went on to the forecastle-head, followed by Mr. Mellaire, while I waited by the foremast, clinging tight, and endured another ducking. Through the emergencies I could see the pencil of light, appearing and disappearing, darting here and there. Several minutes later the mates were back with me.

"Half our head-gear's carried away," Mr. Pike told me. "We must have run into something."

"I felt a jar, right after you' went below, sir, last time," said Mr. Mellaire. "Only I thought it was a thump of sea."

"So did I feel it," the mate agreed. "I was just taking off my boots. I thought it was a sea. But where are the three devils?"

"Broaching the cask," the second mate suggested.

We made the forecastle-head, descended the iron ladder, and went for'ard, inside, underneath, out of the wind and sea. There lay the cask, securely lashed. The size of the barnacles on it was astonishing. They were as large as apples and inches deep. A down-fling of bow brought a foot of water about our boots; and as the bow lifted and the water drained away, it drew out from the shell-crusted cask streamers of seaweed a foot or so in length.

Led by Mr. Pike and watching our chance between seas, we searched the deck and rails between the forecastle-head and the for'ard-house and found no devils. The mate stepped into the forecastle doorway, and his light-stick cut like a dagger through the dim illumination of the murky sea-lamp. And we saw the devils. Nosey Murphy had been right. There were three of them.

Let me give the picture: A drenched and freezing room of rusty, paint-scabbed iron, low-roofed, double-tiered with bunks, reeking with the filth of thirty men, despite the washing of the sea. In a top bunk, on his side, in sea-boots and oilskins, staring steadily with blue, bitter eyes, Andy Fay; on the table, pulling at a pipe, with hanging legs dragged this way and that by the churn of water, Mulligan Jacobs, solemnly regarding three men, sea-booted and bloody, who stand side by side, of a height and not duly tall, swaying in unison to the *Elsinore's* down-flinging and up-lifting.

But such men! I know my East Side and my East End, and I am accustomed to the faces of all the ruck of races, yet with these three men I was at fault. The Mediterranean had surely never bred such a breed; nor had Scandinavia. They were not blonds. They were not brunettes. Nor were they of the Brown, or Black, or Yellow. Their skin was white under a bronze of weather. Wet as was their hair, it was plainly a colourless, sandy hair. Yet their eyes were dark—and yet not dark. They were neither blue, nor gray, nor green, nor hazel. Nor were they black. They were topaz, pale topaz; and they gleamed and dreamed like the eyes of great cats. They regarded us like walkers in a dream, these pale-haired storm-waifs with pale, topaz eyes. They did not bow, they did not smile, in no way did they recognize our presence save that they looked at us and dreamed.

But Andy Fay greeted us.

"It's a hell of a night an' not a wink of sleep with these goings-on," he said.

"Now where did they blow in from a night like this?" Mulligan Jacobs complained.

"You've got a tongue in your mouth," Mr. Pike snarled. "Why ain't you asked 'em?"

"As though you didn't know I could use the tongue in me mouth, you old stiff," Jacobs snarled back.

But it was no time for their private feud. Mr. Pike turned on the dreaming new-comers and addressed them in the mangled and aborted phrases of a dozen languages such as the world-wandering Anglo-Saxon has had every opportunity to learn but is too stubborn-brained and wilful-mouthed to wrap his tongue about.

The visitors made no reply. They did not even shake their heads. Their faces remained peculiarly relaxed and placid, incurious and pleasant, while in their eyes floated profounder dreams. Yet they were human. The blood of their injuries stained them and clotted on their clothes.

"Dutchmen," snorted Mr. Pike, with all due contempt for other breeds, as he waved them to make themselves at home in any of the bunks.

Mr. Pike's ethnology is narrow. Outside his own race he is aware of only three races: niggers, Dutchmen, and Dagoes.

Again our visitors proved themselves human. They understood the mate's invitation, and, glancing first at one another, they climbed into three top-bunks and closed their eyes. I could swear the first of them was asleep in half a minute.

"We'll have to clean up for'ard, or we'll be having the sticks about our ears," the mate said, already starting to depart. "Get the men along, Mr. Mellaire, and call out the carpenter."

CHAPTER XXXVI

And no westing! We have been swept back three degrees of casting since the night our visitors came on board. They are the great mystery, these three men of the sea. "Horn Gypsies," Margaret calls them; and Mr. Pike dubs them "Dutchmen." One thing is certain, they have a language of their own which they talk with one another. But of our hotch-potch of nationalities fore and aft there is no person who catches an inkling of their language or nationality.

Mr. Mellaire raised the theory that they were Finns of some sort, but this was indignantly denied by our big-footed youth of a carpenter, who swears he is a Finn himself. Louis, the cook, avers that somewhere over the world, on some forgotten voyage, he has encountered men of their type; but he can neither remember the voyage nor their race. He and the rest of the Asiatics accept their presence as a matter of course; but the crew, with the exception of Andy Fay and Mulligan Jacobs, is very superstitious about the new-comers, and will have nothing to do with them.

"No good will come of them, sir," Tom Spink, at the wheel, told us, shaking his head forebodingly.

Margaret's mittened hand rested on my arm as we balanced to the easy roll of the ship. We had paused from our promenade, which we now take each day, religiously, as a constitutional, between eleven and twelve.

"Why, what is the matter with them?" she queried, nudging me privily in warning of what was coming.

"Because they ain't men, Miss, as we can rightly call men. They ain't regular men."

"It was a bit irregular, their manner of coming on board," she gurgled.

"That's just it, Miss," Tom Spink exclaimed, brightening perceptibly at the hint of understanding. "Where'd they come from? They won't tell. Of course they won't tell. They ain't men. They're spirits—ghosts of sailors that drowned as long ago as when that cask went adrift from a sinkin' ship, an' that's years an' years, Miss, as anybody can see, lookin' at the size of the barnacles on it."

"Do you think so?" Margaret queried.

"We all think so, Miss. We ain't spent our lives on the sea for nothin'. There's no end of landsmen don't believe in the Flyin' Dutchman. But what do they know? They're just landsmen, ain't they? They ain't never had their leg grabbed by a ghost, such as I had, on the *Kathleen*, thirty-five years ago, down in the hole 'tween the water-casks. An' didn't that ghost rip the shoe right off of me? An' didn't I fall through the hatch two days later an' break my shoulder?"

"Now, Miss, I seen 'em makin' signs to Mr. Pike that we'd run into their ship hove to on the other tack. Don't you believe it. There wasn't no ship."

"But how do you explain the carrying away of our head-gear?" I demanded.

"There's lots of things can't be explained, sir," was Tom Spink's answer. "Who can explain the way the Finns plays tom-fool tricks with the weather? Yet everybody *knows* it. Why are we havin' a hard passage around the Horn, sir? I ask you that. Why, sir?"

I shook my head.

"Because of the carpenter, sir. We've found out he's a Finn. Why did he keep it quiet all the way down from Baltimore?"

355

"Why did he tell it?" Margaret challenged.

"He didn't tell it, Miss—leastways, not until after them three others boarded us. I got my suspicions he knows more about 'm than he's lettin' on. An' look at the weather an' the delay we're gettin'. An' don't everybody know the Finns is regular warlocks an' weather-breeders?"

My ears pricked up.

"Where did you get *that* word *warlock?*" I questioned.

Tom Spink looked puzzled.

"What's wrong with it, sir?" he asked.

"Nothing. It's all right. But where did you get it?"

"I never got it, sir. I always had it. That's what Finns is—warlocks."

"And these three new-comers—they aren't Finns?" asked Margaret.

The old Englishman shook his head solemnly.

"No, Miss. They're drownded sailors a long time drownded. All you have to do is look at 'm. An' the carpenter could tell us a few if he was minded."

* * * * *

Nevertheless, our mysterious visitors are a welcome addition to our weakened crew. I watch them at work. They are strong and willing. Mr. Pike says they are real sailormen, even if he doesn't understand their lingo. His theory is that they are from some small old-country or outlander ship, which, hove to on the opposite tack to the *Elsinore*, was run down and sunk.

I have forgotten to say that we found the barnacled cask nearly filled with a most delicious wine which none of us can name. As soon as the gale moderated Mr. Pike had the cask brought aft and broached, and now the steward and Wada have it all in bottles and spare demijohns. It is beautifully aged, and Mr. Pike is certain that it is some sort of a mild and unheard-of brandy. Mr. Mellaire merely smacks his lips over it, while Captain West, Margaret, and I steadfastly maintain that it is wine.

The condition of the men grows deplorable. They were always poor at pulling on ropes, but now it takes two or three to pull as much as one used to pull. One thing in their favour is that they are well, though grossly, fed. They have all they want to eat, such as it is, but it is the cold and wet, the terrible condition of the forecastle, the lack of sleep, and the almost continuous toil of both watches on deck. Either watch is so weak and worthless that any severe task requires the assistance of the other watch. As an instance, we finally managed a reef in the foresail in the thick of a gale. It took both watches two hours, yet Mr. Pike tells me that under similar circumstances, with an average crew of the old days, he has seen a single watch reef the foresail in twenty minutes.

I have learned one of the prime virtues of a steel sailing-ship. Such a craft, heavily laden, does not strain her seams open in bad weather and big seas. Except for a tiny leak down in the fore-peak, with which we sailed from Baltimore and which is bailed out with a pail once in several weeks, the *Elsinore* is bone-dry. Mr. Pike tells me that had a wooden ship of her size and cargo gone through the buffeting we have endured, she would be leaking like a sieve.

And Mr. Mellaire, out of his own experience, has added to my respect for the Horn. When he was a young man he was once eight weeks in making around from 50 in the Atlantic to 50 in the Pacific. Another time his vessel was compelled to put back twice to the Falklands for repairs. And still another time, in a wooden ship running back in distress to the Falklands, his vessel was lost in a shift of gale in the very entrance to Port Stanley. As he told me:

"And after we'd been there a month, sir, who should come in but the old *Lucy Powers*. She was a sight!—her foremast clean gone out of her and half her spars, the old man killed from one of the spars falling on him, the mate with two broken arms, the second mate sick, and what was left of the crew at the pumps. We'd lost our ship, so my skipper took charge, refitted her, doubled up both crews, and we headed the other way around, pumping two hours in every watch clear to Honolulu."

The poor wretched chickens! Because of their ill-judged moulting they are quite featherless. It is a marvel that one of them survives, yet so far we have lost only six. Margaret keeps the kerosene stove going, and, though they have ceased laying, she confidently asserts that they are all layers and that we shall have plenty of eggs once we get fine weather in the Pacific.

There is little use to describe these monotonous and perpetual westerly gales. One is very like another, and they follow so fast on one another's heels that the sea never has a chance to grow calm. So long have we rolled and tossed about that the thought, say, of a solid, unmoving billiard-table is inconceivable. In previous incarnations I have encountered things that did not move, but . . . they were in previous incarnations.

We have been up to the Diego Ramirez Rocks twice in the past ten days. At the present moment, by vague dead reckoning, we are two hundred miles east of them. We have been hove down to our hatches three times in the last week. We have had six stout sails, of the heaviest canvas, furled and double-gasketed, torn loose and stripped from the yards. Sometimes, so weak are our men, not more than half of them can respond to the call for all hands.

Lars Jacobson, who had his leg broken early in the voyage, was knocked down by a sea several days back and had the leg rebroken. Ditman Olansen, the crank-eyed Norwegian, went Berserker last night in the second dog-watch and pretty well cleaned out his half of the forecastle. Wada reports that it required the bricklayers, Fitzgibbon and Gilder, the Maltese Cockney, and Steve Roberts, the cowboy, finally to subdue the madman. These are all men of Mr. Mellaire's watch. In Mr. Pike's watch John Hackey, the San Francisco hoodlum, who has stood out against the gangsters, has at last succumbed and joined them. And only this morning Mr. Pike dragged Charles Davis by the scruff of the neck out of the forecastle, where he had caught him expounding sea-law to the miserable creatures. Mr. Mellaire, I notice on occasion, remains unduly intimate with the gangster clique. And yet nothing serious happens.

And Charles Davis does not die. He seems actually to be gaining in weight. He never misses a meal. From the break of the poop, in the shelter of the weather cloth, our decks a thunder and rush of freezing water, I often watch him slip out of his room between seas, mug and plate in hand, and hobble for'ard to the galley for his food. He is a keen judge of the ship's motions, for never yet have I seen him get a serious ducking. Sometimes, of course, he may get splattered with spray or wet to the knees, but he manages to be out of the way whenever a big graybeard falls on board.

CHAPTER XXXVII

A wonderful event to-day! For five minutes, at noon, the sun was actually visible. But such a sun!—a pale and cold and sickly orb that at meridian was only 90 degrees 18 minutes above the horizon. And within the hour we were taking in sail and lying down to the snow-gusts of a fresh south-west gale.

Whatever you do, make westing! make westing!—this sailing rule of the navigators for the Horn has been bitten out of iron. I can understand why shipmasters, with a favouring slant of wind, have left sailors, fallen overboard, to drown without heaving-to to lower a boat. Cape Horn is iron, and it takes masters of iron to win around from east to west.

And we make easting! This west wind is eternal. I listen incredulously when Mr. Pike or Mr. Mellaire tells of times when easterly winds have blown in these latitudes. It is impossible. Always does the west wind blow, gale upon gale and gales everlasting, else why the "Great West Wind Drift" printed on the charts! We of the afterguard are weary of this eternal buffeting. Our men have become pulpy, washed-out, sore-corroded shadows of men. I should not be surprised, in the end, to see Captain West turn tail and run eastward around the world to Seattle. But Margaret smiles with surety, and nods her head, and affirms that her father will win around to 50 in the Pacific.

How Charles Davis survives in that wet, freezing, paint-scabbed room of iron in the 'midship-house is beyond me—just as it is beyond me that the wretched sailors in the wretched forecastle do not lie down in their bunks and die, or, at least, refuse to answer the call of the watches.

Another week has passed, and we are to-day, by observation, sixty miles due south of the Straits of Le Maire, and we are hove-to, in a driving gale, on the port tack. The glass is down to 28.58, and even Mr. Pike acknowledges that it is one of the worst Cape Horn snorters he has ever experienced.

In the old days the navigators used to strive as far south as 64 degrees or 65 degrees, into the Antarctic drift ice, hoping, in a favouring spell, to make westing at a prodigious rate across the extreme-narrowing wedges of longitude. But of late years all shipmasters have accepted the hugging of the land all the way around. Out of ten times ten thousand passages of Cape Stiff from east to west, this, they have concluded, is the best strategy. So Captain West hugs the land. He heaves-to on the port tack until the leeward drift brings the land into perilous proximity, then wears ship and heaves-to on the port tack and makes leeway off shore.

I may be weary of all this bitter movement of a labouring ship on a frigid sea, but at the same time I do not mind it. In my brain burns the flame of a great discovery and a great achievement. I have found what makes all the books go glimmering; I have achieved what my very philosophy tells me is the greatest achievement a man can make. I have found the love of woman. I do not know whether she cares for me. Nor is that the point. The point is that in myself I have risen to the greatest height to which the human male animal can rise.

I know a woman and her name is Margaret. She is Margaret, a *woman and desirable*. My blood is red. I am not the pallid scholar I so proudly deemed myself to be. I am a man, and a lover, despite the books. As for De Casseres—if ever I get back to New York, equipped as I now am, I shall confute him with the same ease that he has confuted all the schools. Love is the final word. To the rational man it alone gives the super-rational sanction for living. Like Bergson in his overhanging heaven of intuition, or like one who has bathed in Pentecostal fire and seen the New Jerusalem, so I have trod the materialistic dictums of science underfoot, scaled the last peak of philosophy, and leaped into my heaven, which, after all, is within myself. The stuff that composes me, that is I, is so made that it finds its supreme realization in the love of woman. It is the vindication of being. Yes, and it is the wages of being, the payment in full for all the brittleness and frailty of flesh and breath.

And she is only a woman, like any woman, and the Lord knows I know what women are. And I know Margaret for what she is—mere woman; and yet I know, in the lover's soul of me, that she is somehow different. Her ways are not as the ways of other women, and all her ways are delightful to me. In the end, I suppose, I shall become a nest-builder, for of a surety nest-building is one of her pretty ways. And who shall say which is the worthier—the writing of a whole library or the building of a nest?

The monotonous days, bleak and gray and soggy cold, drag by. It is now a month since we began the passage of the Horn, and here we are, not so well forward as a month ago, because we are something like a hundred miles south of the Straits of Le Maire. Even this position is conjectural, being arrived at by dead reckoning, based on the leeway of a ship hove-to, now on the one tack, now on the other, with always the Great West Wind Drift making against us. It is four days since our last instrument-sight of the sun.

This storm-vexed ocean has become populous. No ships are getting round, and each day adds to our number. Never a brief day passes without our sighting from two or three to a dozen hove-to on port tack or starboard tack. Captain West estimates there must be at least two hundred sail of us. A ship hove-to with preventer tackles on the rudder-head is unmanageable. Each night we take our chance of unavoidable and disastrous collision. And at times, glimpsed through the snow-squalls, we see and curse the ships, east-bound, that drive past us with the West Wind and the West Wind Drift at their backs. And so wild is the mind of man that Mr. Pike and Mr. Mellaire still aver that on occasion they have known gales to blow ships from east to west around the Horn. It surely has been a year since we of the *Elsinore* emerged from under the lee of Tierra Del Fuego into the snorting south-west gales. A century, at least, has elapsed since we sailed from Baltimore.

* * * * *

And I don't give a snap of my fingers for all the wrath and fury of this dim-gray sea at the tip of the earth. I have told Margaret that I love her. The tale was told in the shelter of the weather cloth, where we clung together in the second dog-watch last evening. And it was told again, and by both of us, in the bright-lighted chart-room after the watches had been changed at eight bells. Yes, and her face was storm-bright, and all of her was very proud, save that her eyes were warm and soft and fluttered with lids that just would flutter maidenly and womanly. It was a great hour—our great hour.

A poor devil of a man is most lucky when, loving, he is loved. Grievous indeed must be the fate of the lover who is unloved. And I, for one, and for still other reasons, congratulate myself upon the vastitude of my good fortune. For see, were Margaret any other sort of a woman, were she . . . well, just the lovely and lovable and adorably snuggly sort who seem made just precisely for love and loving and nestling into the strong arms of a man—why, there wouldn't be anything remarkable or wonderful about her loving me. But Margaret is Margaret, strong, self-possessed, serene, controlled, a very mistress of herself. And there's the miracle—that such a woman should have been awakened to love by me. It is almost unbelievable. I go out of my way to get another peep into those long, cool, gray eyes of hers and see them grow melting soft as she looks at me. She is no Juliet, thank the Lord; and thank the Lord I am no Romeo. And yet I go up alone on the freezing poop, and under my breath chant defiantly at the snorting gale, and at the graybeards thundering down on us, that I am a lover. And I send messages to the lonely albatrosses veering through the murk that I am a lover. And I look at the wretched sailors crawling along the spray-swept bridge and know that never in ten thousand wretched lives could they experience the love I experience, and I wonder why God ever made them.

* * * * *

"And the one thing I had firmly resolved from the start," Margaret confessed to me this morning in the cabin, when I released her from my arms, "was that I would not permit you to make love to me."

"True daughter of Herodias," I gaily gibed, "so such was the drift of your thoughts even as early as the very start. Already you were looking upon me with a considerative female eye."

She laughed proudly, and did not reply.

"What possibly could have led you to expect that I would make love to you?" I insisted.

"Because it is the way of young male passengers on long voyages," she replied.

"Then others have . . . . ?"

"They always do," she assured me gravely.

And at that instant I knew the first ridiculous pang of jealousy; but I laughed it away and retorted:

"It was an ancient Chinese philosopher who is first recorded as having said, what doubtlessly the cave men before him gibbered, namely, that a woman pursues a man by fluttering away in advance of him."

"Wretch!" she cried. "I never fluttered. When did I ever flutter!"

"It is a delicate subject . . . " I began with assumed hesitancy.

"When did I ever flutter?" she demanded.

I availed myself of one of Schopenhauer's ruses by making a shift.

"From the first you observed nothing that a female could afford to miss observing," I charged. "I'll wager you knew as quickly as I the very instant when I first loved you."

"I knew the first time you hated me," she evaded.

"Yes, I know, the first time I saw you and learned that you were coming on the voyage," I said. "But now I repeat my challenge. You knew as quickly as I the first instant I loved you."

Oh, her eyes were beautiful, and the repose and certitude of her were tremendous, as she rested her hand on my arm for a moment and in a low, quiet voice said:

"Yes, I . . . I think I know. It was the morning of that pampero off the Plate, when you were thrown through the door into my father's stateroom. I saw it in your eyes. I knew it. I think it was the first time, the very instant."

I could only nod my head and draw her close to me. And she looked up at me and added:

"You were very ridiculous. There you sat, on the bed, holding on with one hand and nursing the other hand under your arm, staring at me, irritated, startled, utterly foolish, and then . . . how, I don't know . . . I knew that you had just come to know . . . "

"And the very next instant you froze up," I charged ungallantly.

"And that was why," she admitted shamelessly, then leaned away from me, her hands resting on my shoulders, while she gurgled and her lips parted from over her beautiful white teeth.

One thing I, John Pathurst, know: that gurgling laughter of hers is the most adorable laughter that was ever heard.

CHAPTER XXXVIII

I wonder. I wonder. Did the Samurai make a mistake? Or was it the darkness of oncoming death that chilled and clouded that star-cool brain of his, and made a mock of all his wisdom? Or was it the blunder that brought death upon him beforehand? I do not know, I shall never know; for it is a matter no one of us dreams of hinting at, much less discussing.

I shall begin at the beginning—yesterday afternoon. For it was yesterday afternoon, five weeks to a day since we emerged from the Straits of Le Maire into this gray storm-ocean, that once again we found ourselves hove to directly off the Horn. At the changing of the watches at four o'clock, Captain West gave the command to Mr. Pike to wear ship. We were on the starboard tack at the time, making leeway off shore. This manoeuvre placed us on the port tack, and the consequent leeway, to me, seemed on shore, though at an acute angle, to be sure.

In the chart-room, glancing curiously at the chart, I measured the distance with my eye and decided that we were in the neighbourhood of fifteen miles off Cape Horn.

"With our drift we'll be close up under the land by morning, won't we?" I ventured tentatively.

"Yes," Captain West nodded; "and if it weren't for the West Wind Drift, and if the land did not trend to the north-east, we'd be ashore by morning. As it is, we'll be well under it at daylight, ready to steal around if there is a change, ready to wear ship if there is no change."

It did not enter my head to question his judgment. What he said had to be. Was he not the Samurai?

And yet, a few minutes later, when he had gone below, I noticed Mr. Pike enter the chart-house. After several paces up and down, and a brief pause to watch Nancy and several men shift the weather cloth from lee to weather, I strolled aft to the chart-house. Prompted by I know not what, I peeped through one of the glass ports.

There stood Mr. Pike, his sou'wester doffed, his oilskins streaming rivulets to the floor, while he, dividers and parallel rulers in hand, bent over the chart. It was the expression of his face that startled me. The habitual sourness had vanished. All that I could see was anxiety and apprehension . . . yes, and age. I had never seen him look so old; for there, at that moment, I beheld the wastage and weariness of all his sixty-nine years of sea-battling and sea-staring.

I slipped away from the port and went along the deck to the break of the poop, where I held on and stood staring through the gray and spray in the conjectural direction of our drift. Somewhere, there, in the north-east and north, I knew was a broken, iron coast of rocks upon which the graybeards thundered. And there, in the chart-room, a redoubtable sailorman bent anxiously over a chart as he measured and calculated, and measured and calculated again, our position and our drift.

And I knew it could not be. It was not the Samurai but the henchman who was weak and wrong. Age was beginning to tell upon him at last, which could not be otherwise than expected when one considered that no man in ten thousand had weathered age so successfully as he.

I laughed at my moment's qualm of foolishness and went below, well content to meet my loved one and to rest secure in her father's wisdom. Of course he was right. He had proved himself right too often already on the long voyage from Baltimore.

At dinner Mr. Pike was quite distrait. He took no part whatever in the conversation, and seemed always to be listening to something from without— to the vexing clang of taut ropes that came down the hollow jiggermast, to the muffled roar of the gale in the rigging, to the smash and crash of the seas along our decks and against our iron walls.

Again I found myself sharing his apprehension, although I was too discreet to question him then, or afterwards alone, about his trouble. At eight he went on deck again to take the watch till midnight, and as I went to bed I dismissed all forebodings and speculated as to how many more voyages he could last after this sudden onslaught of old age.

I fell asleep quickly, and awoke at midnight, my lamp still burning, Conrad's *Mirror of the Sea* on my breast where it had dropped from my hands. I heard the watches change, and was wide awake and reading when Mr. Pike came below by the booby-hatch and passed down my hail by my open door, on his way to his room.

In the pause I had long since learned so well I knew he was rolling a cigarette. Then I heard him cough, as he always did, when the cigarette was lighted and the first inhalation of smoke flushed his lungs.

At twelve-fifteen, in the midst of Conrad's delightful chapter, "The Weight of the Burden," I heard Mr. Pike come along the hall.

Stealing a glance over the top of my book, I saw him go by, sea-booted, oilskinned, sou'westered. It was his watch below, and his sleep was meagre in this perpetual bad weather, yet he was going on deck.

I read and waited for an hour, but he did not return; and I knew that somewhere up above he was staring into the driving dark. I dressed fully, in all my heavy storm-gear, from sea-boots and sou'-wester to sheepskin under my oilskin coat. At the foot of the stairs I noted along the hall that Margaret's light was burning. I peeped in—she keeps her door open for ventilation—and found her reading.

"Merely not sleepy," she assured me.

Nor in the heart of me do I believe she had any apprehension. She does not know even now, I am confident, the Samurai's blunder—if blunder it was. As she said, she was merely not sleepy, although there is no telling in what occult ways she may have received though not recognized Mr. Pike's anxiety.

At the head of the stairs, passing along the tiny hall to go out the lee door of the chart-house, I glanced into the chart-room. On the couch, lying on his back, his head uncomfortably high, I thought, slept Captain West. The room was warm from the ascending heat of the cabin, so that he lay unblanketed, fully dressed save for oilskins and boots. He breathed easily and steadily, and the lean, ascetic lines of his face seemed softened by the light of the low-turned lamp. And that one glance restored to me all my surety and faith in his wisdom, so that I laughed at myself for having left my warm bed for a freezing trip on deck.

Under the weather cloth at the break of the poop I found Mr. Mellaire. He was wide awake, but under no strain. Evidently it had not entered his mind to consider, much less question, the manoeuvre of wearing ship the previous afternoon.

"The gale is breaking," he told me, waving his mittened hand at a starry segment of sky momentarily exposed by the thinning clouds.

But where was Mr. Pike? Did the second mate know he was on deck? I proceeded to feel Mr. Mellaire out as we worked our way aft, along the mad poop toward the wheel. I talked about the difficulty of sleeping in stormy weather, stated the restlessness and semi-insomnia that the violent motion of the ship caused in me, and raised the query of how bad weather affected the officers.

"I noticed Captain West, in the chart-room, as I came up, sleeping like a baby," I concluded.

We leaned in the lee of the chart-house and went no farther.

"Trust us to sleep just the same way, Mr. Pathurst," the second mate laughed. "The harder the weather the harder the demand on us, and the harder we sleep. I'm dead the moment my head touches the pillow. It takes Mr. Pike longer, because he always finishes his cigarette after he turns in. But he smokes while he's undressing, so that he doesn't require more than a minute to go deado. I'll wager he hasn't moved, right now, since ten minutes after twelve."

So the second mate did not dream the first was even on deck. I went below to make sure. A small sea-lamp was burning in Mr. Pike's room, and I saw his bunk unoccupied. I went in by the big stove in the dining-room and warmed up, then again came on deck. I did not go near the weather cloth, where I was certain Mr. Mellaire was; but, keeping along the lee of the poop, I gained the bridge and started for'ard.

I was in no hurry, so I paused often in that cold, wet journey. The gale was breaking, for again and again the stars glimmered through the thinning storm-clouds. On the 'midship-house was no Mr. Pike. I crossed it, stung by the freezing, flying spray, and carefully reconnoitred the top of the for'ard-house, where, in such bad weather, I knew the lookout was stationed. I was within twenty feet of them, when a wider clearance of starry sky showed me the figures of the lookout, whoever he was, and of Mr. Pike, side by side.

Long I watched them, not making my presence known, and I knew that the old mate's eyes were boring like gimlets into the windy darkness that separated the *Elsinore* from the thunder-surfed iron coast he sought to find.

Coming back to the poop I was caught by the surprised Mr. Mellaire.

"Thought you were asleep, sir," he chided.

"I'm too restless," I explained. "I've read until my eyes are tired, and now I'm trying to get chilled so that I can fall asleep while warming up in my blankets."

"I envy you, sir," he answered. "Think of it! So much of all night in that you cannot sleep. Some day, if ever I make a lucky strike, I shall make a voyage like this as a passenger, and have all watches below. Think of it! All blessed watches below! And I shall, like you, sir, bring a Jap servant along, and I'll make him call me at every changing of the watches, so that, wide awake, I can appreciate my good fortune in the several minutes before I roll over and go to sleep again."

We laughed good night to each other. Another peep into the chart-room showed me Captain West sleeping as before. He had not moved in general, though all his body moved with every roll and fling of the ship. Below, Margaret's light still burned, but a peep showed her asleep, her book fallen from her hands just as was the so frequent case with my books.

And I wondered. Half the souls of us on the *Elsinore* slept. The Samurai slept. Yet the old first mate, who should have slept, kept a bitter watch on the for'ard-house. Was his anxiety right? Could it be right? Or was it the crankiness of ultimate age? Were we drifting and leewaying to destruction? Or was it merely an old man being struck down by senility in the midst of his life-task?

Too wide awake to think of sleeping, I ensconced myself with *The Mirror of the Sea* at the dining-table. Nor did I remove aught of my storm-gear save the soggy mittens, which I wrung out and hung to dry by the stove. Four bells struck, and six bells, and Mr. Pike had not returned below. At

369

eight bells, with the changing of the watches, it came upon me what a night of hardship the old mate was enduring. Eight to twelve had been his own watch on deck. He had now completed the four hours of the second mate's watch and was beginning his own watch, which would last till eight in the morning—twelve consecutive hours in a Cape Horn gale with the mercury at freezing.

Next—for I had dozed—I heard loud cries above my head that were repeated along the poop. I did not know till afterwards that it was Mr. Pike's command to hard-up the helm, passed along from for'ard by the men he had stationed at intervals on the bridge.

All that I knew at this shock of waking was that something was happening above. As I pulled on my steaming mittens and hurried my best up the reeling stairs, I could hear the stamp of men's feet that for once were not lagging. In the chart-house hall I heard Mr. Pike, who had already covered the length of the bridge from the for'ard-house, shouting:

"Mizzen-braces! Slack, damn you! Slack on the run! But hold a turn! Aft, here, all of you! Jump! Lively, if you don't want to swim! Come in, port-braces! Don't let 'm get away! Lee-braces!—if you lose that turn I'll split your skull! Lively! Lively!—Is that helm hard over! Why in hell don't you answer?"

All this I heard as I dashed for the lee door and as I wondered why I did not hear the Samurai's voice.

Then, as I passed the chart-room door, I saw him.

He was sitting on the couch, white-faced, one sea-boot in his hands, and I could have sworn his hands were shaking. That much I saw, and the next moment was out on deck.

At first, just emerged from the light, I could see nothing, although I could hear men at the pin-rails and the mate snarling and shouting commands. But I knew the manoeuvre. With a weak crew, in the big, tail-end sea of a broken gale, breakers and destruction under her lee, the *Elsinore* was being worn around. We had been under lower-topsails and a reefed foresail all night. Mr. Pike's first action, after putting the wheel up, had been to square the mizzen-yards. With the wind-pressure thus eased aft, the stern could more easily swing against the wind while the wind-pressure on the for'ard-sails paid the bow off.

But it takes time to wear a ship, under short canvas, in a big sea. Slowly, very slowly, I could feel the direction of the wind altering against my cheek. The moon, dim at first, showed brighter and brighter as the last shreds of a *flying cloud* drove away from before it. In vain I looked for any land.

"Main-braces!—all of you!—jump!" Mr. Pike shouted, himself leading the rush along the poop. And the men really rushed. Not in all the months I had observed them had I seen such swiftness of energy.

I made my way to the wheel, where Tom Spink stood. He did not notice me. With one hand holding the idle wheel, he was leaning out to one side, his eyes fixed in a fascinated stare. I followed its direction, on between the chart-house and the port-jigger shrouds, and on across a mountain sea that was very vague in the moonlight. And then I saw it! The *Elsinore*'s stern was flung skyward, and across that cold ocean I saw land—black rocks and snow-covered slopes and crags. And toward this land the *Elsinore*, now almost before the wind, was driving.

From the 'midship-house came the snarls of the mate and the cries of the sailors. They were pulling and hauling for very life. Then came Mr. Pike, across the poop, leaping with incredible swiftness, sending his snarl before him.

"Ease that wheel there! What the hell you gawkin' at? Steady her as I tell you. That's all you got to do!"

From for'ard came a cry, and I knew Mr. Mellaire was on top of the for'ard-house and managing the fore-yards.

"Now!"—from Mr. Pike. "More spokes! Steady! Steady! And be ready to check her!"

He bounded away along the poop again, shouting for men for the mizzen-braces. And the men appeared, some of his watch, others of the second mate's watch, routed from sleep—men coatless, and hatless, and bootless; men ghastly-faced with fear but eager for once to spring to the orders of the man who knew and could save their miserable lives from miserable death. Yes—and I noted the delicate-handed cook, and Yatsuda, the sail-maker, pulling with his one unparalysed hand. It was all hands to save ship, and all hands knew it. Even Sundry Buyers, who had drifted aft in his stupidity instead of being for'ard with his own officer, forebore to stare about and to press his abdomen. For the nonce he pulled like a youngling of twenty.

The moon covered again, and it was in darkness that the *Elsinore* rounded up on the wind on the starboard tack. This, in her case, under lower-topsails only, meant that she lay eight points from the wind, or, in land terms, at right angles to the wind.

Mr. Pike was splendid, marvellous. Even as the *Elsinore* was rounding to on the wind, while the head-yards were still being braced, and even as he was watching the ship's behaviour and the wheel, in between his commands to Tom Spink of "A spoke! A spoke or two! Another! Steady! Hold her! Ease her!" he was ordering the men aloft to loose sail. I had thought, the manoeuvre of wearing achieved, that we were saved, but this setting of all three upper-topsails unconvinced me.

The moon remained hidden, and to leeward nothing could be seen. As each sail was set, the *Elsinore* was pressed farther and farther over, and I realized that there was plenty of wind left, despite the fact that the gale had broken or was breaking. Also, under this additional canvas, I could feel the *Elsinore* moving through the water. Pike now sent the Maltese Cockney to help Tom Spink at the wheel. As for himself, he took his stand beside the booby-hatch, where he could gauge the *Elsinore*, gaze to leeward, and keep his eye on the helmsmen.

"Full and by," was his reiterated command. "Keep her a good full—a rap-full; but don't let her fall away. Hold her to it, and drive her."

He took no notice whatever of me, although I, on my way to the lee of the chart-house, stood at his shoulder a full minute, offering him a chance to speak. He knew I was there, for his big shoulder brushed my arm as he swayed and turned to warn the helmsmen in the one breath to hold her up to it but to keep her full. He had neither time nor courtesy for a passenger in such a moment.

Sheltering by the chart-house, I saw the moon appear. It grew brighter and brighter, and I saw the land, dead to leeward of us, not three hundred yards away. It was a cruel sight—black rock and bitter snow, with cliffs so perpendicular that the *Elsinore* could have laid alongside of them in deep water, with great gashes and fissures, and with great surges thundering and spouting along all the length of it.

Our predicament was now clear to me. We had to weather the bight of land and islands into which we had drifted, and sea and wind worked directly on shore. The only way out was to drive through the water, to drive fast and hard, and this was borne in upon me by Mr. Pike bounding past to the break of the poop, where I heard him shout to Mr. Mellaire to set the mainsail.

Evidently the second mate was dubious, for the next cry of Mr. Pike's was:

"Damn the reef! You'd be in hell first! Full mainsail! All hands to it!"

The difference was appreciable at once when that huge spread of canvas opposed the wind. The *Elsinore* fairly leaped and quivered as she sprang to it, and I could feel her eat to windward as she at the same time drove faster ahead. Also, in the rolls and gusts, she was forced down till her lee-rail buried and the sea foamed level across to her hatches. Mr. Pike watched her like a hawk, and like certain death he watched the Maltese Cockney and Tom Spink at the wheel.

"Land on the lee bow!" came a cry from for'ard, that was carried on from mouth to mouth along the bridge to the poop.

I saw Mr. Pike nod his head grimly and sarcastically. He had already seen it from the lee-poop, and what he had not seen he had guessed. A score of times I saw him test the weight of the gusts on his cheek and with all the brain of him study the *Elsinore's* behaviour. And I knew what was in his mind. Could she carry what she had? Could she carry more?

Small wonder, in this tense passage of time, that I had forgotten the Samurai. Nor did I remember him until the chart-house door swung open and I caught him by the arm. He steadied and swayed beside me, while he watched that cruel picture of rock and snow and spouting surf.

"A good full!" Mr. Pike snarled. "Or I'll eat your heart out. God damn you for the farmer's hound you are, Tom Spink! Ease her! Ease her! Ease her into the big ones, damn you! Don't let her head fall off! Steady! Where in hell did you learn to steer? What cow-farm was you raised on?"

Here he bounded for'ard past us with those incredible leaps of his.

"It would be good to set the mizzen-topgallant," I heard Captain West mutter in a weak, quavery voice. "Mr. Pathurst, will you please tell Mr. Pike to set the mizzen-topgallant?"

And at that very instant Mr. Pike's voice rang out from the break of the poop:

"Mr. Mellaire!—the mizzen-topgallant!"

Captain West's head drooped until his chin rested on his breast, and so low did he mutter that I leaned to hear.

"A very good officer," he said. "An excellent officer. Mr. Pathurst, if you will kindly favour me, I should like to go in. I . . . I haven't got on my boots."

The muscular feat was to open the heavy iron door and hold it open in the rolls and plunges. This I accomplished; but when I had helped Captain West across the high threshold he thanked me and waived further services. And I did not know even then he was dying.

Never was a Blackwood ship driven as was the *Elsinore* during the next half-hour. The full-jib was also set, and, as it departed in shreds, the fore-topmast staysail was being hoisted. For'ard of the 'midship-house it was made unlivable by the bursting seas. Mr. Mellaire, with half the crew, clung on somehow on top the 'midship-house, while the rest of the crew was with us in the comparative safety of the poop. Even Charles Davis, drenched and shivering, hung on beside me to the brass ring-handle of the chart-house door.

Such sailing! It was a madness of speed and motion, for the *Elsinore* drove over and through and under those huge graybeards that thundered shore-ward. There were times, when rolls and gusts worked against her at the same moment, when I could have sworn the ends of her lower-yardarms swept the sea.

It was one chance in ten that we could claw off. All knew it, and all knew there was nothing more to do but await the issue. And we waited in silence. The only voice was that of the mate, intermittently cursing, threatening, and ordering Tom Spink and the Maltese Cockney at the wheel. Between whiles, and all the while, he gauged the gusts, and ever his eyes lifted to the main-topgallant-yard. He wanted to set that one more sail. A dozen times I saw him half-open his mouth to give the order he dared not give. And as I watched him, so all watched him. Hard-bitten, bitter-natured, sour-featured and snarling-mouthed, he was the one man, the henchman of the race, the master of the moment. "And where," was my thought, "O where was the Samurai?"

One chance in ten? It was one in a hundred as we fought to weather the last bold tooth of rock that gashed into sea and tempest between us and open ocean. So close were we that I looked to see our far-reeling skysail-yards strike the face of the rock. So close were we, no more than a biscuit toss from its iron buttress, that as we sank down into the last great trough between two seas I can swear every one of us held breath and waited for the *Elsinore* to strike.

Instead we drove free. And as if in very rage at our escape, the storm took that moment to deal us the mightiest buffet of all. The mate felt that monster sea coming, for he sprang to the wheel ere the blow fell. I looked for'ard, and I saw all for'ard blotted out by the mountain of water that fell aboard. The *Elsinore* righted from the shock and reappeared to the eye, full of water from rail to rail. Then a gust caught her sails and heeled her over, spilling half the enormous burden outboard again.

Along the bridge came the relayed cry of "Man overboard!"

I glanced at the mate, who had just released the wheel to the helmsmen. He shook his head, as if irritated by so trivial a happening, walked to the corner of the half-wheelhouse, and stared at the coast he had escaped, white and black and cold in the moonlight.

Mr. Mellaire came aft, and they met beside me in the lee of the chart-house.

"All hands, Mr. Mellaire," the mate said, "and get the mainsail off of her. After that, the mizzen-topgallant."

"Yes, sir," said the second.

"Who was it?" the mate asked, as Mr. Mellaire was turning away.

"Boney—he was no good, anyway," came the answer.

That was all. Boney the Splinter was gone, and all hands were answering the command of Mr. Mellaire to take in the mainsail. But they never took it in; for at that moment it started to blow away out of the bolt-ropes, and in but few moments all that was left of it was a few short, slatting ribbons.

"Mizzen-topgallant-sail!" Mr. Pike ordered. Then, and for the first time, he recognized my existence.

"Well rid of it," he growled. "It never did set properly. I was always aching to get my hands on the sail-maker that made it."

On my way below a glance into the chart-room gave me the cue to the Samurai's blunder—if blunder it can be called, for no one will ever know.

He lay on the floor in a loose heap, rolling willy-nilly with every roll of the *Elsinore*.

CHAPTER XXXIX

There is so much to write about all at once. In the first place, Captain West. Not entirely unexpected was his death. Margaret tells me that she was apprehensive from the start of the voyage—and even before. It was because of her apprehension that she so abruptly changed her plans and accompanied her father.

What really happened we do not know, but the agreed surmise is that it was some stroke of the heart. And yet, after the stroke, did he not come out on deck? Or could the first stroke have been followed by another and fatal one after I had helped him inside through the door? And even so, I have never heard of a heart-stroke being preceded hours before by a weakening of the mind. Captain West's mind seemed quite clear, and must have been quite clear, that last afternoon when he wore the *Elsinore* and started the lee-shore drift. In which case it was a blunder. The Samurai blundered, and his heart destroyed him when he became aware of the blunder.

At any rate the thought of blunder never enters Margaret's head. She accepts, as a matter of course, that it was all a part of the oncoming termination of his sickness. And no one will ever undeceive her. Neither Mr. Pike, Mr. Mellaire, nor I, among ourselves, mention a whisper of what so narrowly missed causing disaster. In fact, Mr. Pike does not talk about the matter at all.—And then, again, might it not have been something different from heart disease? Or heart disease complicated with something else that obscured his mind that afternoon before his death? Well, no one knows, and I, for one, shall not sit, even in secret judgment, on the event.

* * * * *

At midday of the day we clawed off Tierra Del Fuego the *Elsinore* was rolling in a dead calm, and all afternoon she rolled, not a score of miles off the land. Captain West was buried at four o'clock, and at eight bells that evening

Mr. Pike assumed command and made a few remarks to both watches. They were straight-from-the-shoulder remarks, or, as he called them, they were "brass tacks."

Among other things he told the sailors that they had another boss, and that they would toe the mark as they never had before. Up to this time they had been loafing in an hotel, but from this time on they were going to work.

"On this hooker, from now on," he perorated, "it's going to be like old times, when a man jumped the last day of the voyage as well as the first. And God help the man that don't jump. That's all. Relieve the wheel and lookout."

* * * * *

And yet the men are in terribly wretched condition. I don't see how they can jump. Another week of westerly gales, alternating with brief periods of calm, has elapsed, making a total of six weeks off the Horn. So weak are the men that they have no spirit left in them—not even the gangsters. And so afraid are they of the mate that they really do their best to jump when he drives them, and he drives them all the time. Mr. Mellaire shakes his head.

"Wait till they get around and up into better weather," he astonished me by telling me the other afternoon. "Wait till they get dried out, and rested up, with more sleep, and their sores healed, and more flesh on their bones, and more spunk in their blood—then they won't stand for this driving. Mr. Pike can't realize that times have changed, sir, and laws have changed, and men have changed. He's an old man, and I know what I am talking about."

"You mean you've been listening to the talk of the men?" I challenged rashly, all my gorge rising at the unofficerlike conduct of this ship's officer.

The shot went home, for, in a flash, that suave and gentle film of light vanished from the surface of the eyes, and the watching, fearful thing that lurked behind inside the skull seemed almost to leap out at me, while the cruel gash of mouth drew thinner and crueller. And at the same time, on my inner sight, was grotesquely limned a picture of a brain pulsing savagely against the veneer of skin that covered that cleft of skull beneath the dripping sou'-wester. Then he controlled himself, the mouth-gash relaxed, and the suave and gentle film drew again across the eyes.

"I mean, sir," he said softly, "that I am speaking out of a long sea experience. Times have changed. The old driving days are gone. And I trust, Mr. Pathurst, that you will not misunderstand me in the matter, nor misinterpret what I have said."

Although the conversation drifted on to other and calmer topics, I could not ignore the fact that he had not denied listening to the talk of the men. And yet, even as Mr. Pike grudgingly admits, he is a good sailorman and second mate save for his unholy intimacy with the men for'ard—an intimacy which even the Chinese cook and the Chinese steward deplore as unseamanlike and perilous.

Even though men like the gangsters are so worn down by hardship that they have no heart of rebellion, there remain three of the frailest for'ard who will not die, and who are as spunky as ever. They are Andy Fay, Mulligan Jacobs, and Charles Davis. What strange, abysmal vitality informs them is beyond all speculation. Of course, Charles Davis should have been overside with a sack of coal at his feet long ago. And Andy Fay and Mulligan Jacobs are only, and have always been, wrecked and emaciated wisps of men. Yet far stronger men than they have gone over the side, and far stronger men than they are laid up right now in absolute physical helplessness in the soggy forecastle bunks. And these two bitter flames of shreds of things stand all their watches and answer all calls for both watches.

Yes; and the chickens have something of this same spunk of life in them. Featherless, semi-frozen despite the oil-stove, sprayed dripping on occasion by the frigid seas that pound by sheer weight through canvas tarpaulins, nevertheless not a chicken has died. Is it a matter of selection? Are these the iron-vigoured ones that survived the hardships from Baltimore to the Horn, and are fitted to survive anything? Then for a De Vries to take them, save them, and out of them found the hardiest breed of chickens on the planet! And after this I shall always query that phrase, most ancient in our language—"chicken-hearted." Measured by the *Elsinore's* chickens, it is a misnomer.

Nor are our three Horn Gypsies, the storm-visitors with the dreaming, topaz eyes, spunkless. Held in superstitious abhorrence by the rest of the crew, aliens by lack of any word of common speech, nevertheless they are good sailors and are always first to spring into any enterprise of work or peril. They have gone into Mr. Mellaire's watch, and they are quite apart from the rest of the sailors. And when there is a delay, or wait, with nothing to do for long minutes, they shoulder together, and stand and sway to the heave of deck, and dream far dreams in those pale, topaz eyes, of a country, I am sure, where mothers, with pale, topaz eyes and sandy hair, birth sons and daughters that breed true in terms of topaz eyes and sandy hair.

But the rest of the crew! Take the Maltese Cockney. He is too keenly intelligent, too sharply sensitive, successfully to endure. He is a shadow of his former self. His cheeks have fallen in. Dark circles of suffering are under his eyes, while his eyes, Latin and English intermingled, are cavernously sunken and as bright-burning as if aflame with fever.

Tom Spink, hard-fibred Anglo-Saxon, good seaman that he is, long tried and always proved, is quite wrecked in spirit. He is whining and fearful. So broken is he, though he still does his work, that he is prideless and shameless.

"I'll never ship around the Horn again, sir," he began on me the other day when I greeted him good morning at the wheel. "I've sworn it before, but this time I mean it. Never again, sir. Never again."

"Why did you swear it before?" I queried.

"It was on the *Nahoma*, sir, four years ago. Two hundred and thirty days from Liverpool to 'Frisco. Think of it, sir. Two hundred and thirty days! And we was loaded with cement and creosote, and the creosote got loose. We buried the captain right here off the Horn. The grub gave out. Most of us nearly died of scurvy. Every man Jack of us was carted to hospital in 'Frisco. It was plain hell, sir, that's what it was, an' two hundred and thirty days of it."

"Yet here you are," I laughed; "signed on another Horn voyage."

And this morning Tom Spink confided the following tome:

"If only we'd lost the carpenter, sir, instead of Boney."

I did not catch his drift for the moment; then I remembered. The carpenter was the Finn, the Jonah, the warlock who played tricks with the winds and despitefully used poor sailormen.

* * * * *

Yes, and I make free to confess that I have grown well weary of this eternal buffeting by the Great West Wind. Nor are we alone in our travail on this desolate ocean. Never a day does the gray thin, or the snow-squalls cease that we do not sight ships, west-bound like ourselves, hove-to and trying to hold on to the meagre westing they possess. And occasionally, when the gray clears and lifts, we see a lucky ship, bound east, running before it and reeling off the miles. I saw Mr. Pike, yesterday, shaking his fist in a fury of hatred at one such craft that flew insolently past us not a quarter of a mile away.

And the men are jumping. Mr. Pike is driving with those block-square fists of his, as many a man's face attests. So weak are they, and so terrible is he, that I swear he could whip either watch single-handed. I cannot help but note that Mr. Mellaire refuses to take part in this driving. Yet I know that he is a trained driver, and that he was not averse to driving at the outset of the voyage. But now he seems bent on keeping on good terms with the crew. I should like to know what Mr. Pike thinks of it, for he cannot possibly be blind to what is going on; but I am too well aware of what would happen if I raised the question. He would insult me, snap my head off, and indulge in a three-days' sea-grouch. Things are sad and monotonous enough for Margaret and me in the cabin and at table, without invoking the blight of the mate's displeasure.

CHAPTER XL

Another brutal sea-superstition vindicated. From now on and for always these imbeciles of ours will believe that Finns are Jonahs. We are west of the Diego de Ramirez Rocks, and we are running west at a twelve-knot clip with an easterly gale at our backs. And the carpenter is gone. His passing, and the coming of the easterly wind, were coincidental.

It was yesterday morning, as he helped me to dress, that I was struck by the solemnity of Wada's face. He shook his head lugubriously as he broke the news. The carpenter was missing. The ship had been searched for him high and low. There just was no carpenter.

"What does the steward think?" I asked. "What does Louis think?—and Yatsuda?"

"The sailors, they kill 'm carpenter sure," was the answer. "Very bad ship this. Very bad hearts. Just the same pig, just the same dog. All the time kill. All the time kill. Bime-by everybody kill. You see."

The old steward, at work in his pantry, grinned at me when I mentioned the matter.

"They make fool with me, I fix 'em," he said vindictively. "Mebbe they kill me, all right; but I kill some, too."

He threw back his coat, and I saw, strapped to the left side of his body, in a canvas sheath, so that the handle was ready to hand, a meat knife of the heavy sort that butchers hack with. He drew it forth—it was fully two feet long—and, to demonstrate its razor-edge, sliced a sheet of newspaper into many ribbons.

"Huh!" he laughed sardonically. "I am Chink, monkey, damn fool, eh?—no good, eh? all rotten damn to hell. I fix 'em, they make fool with me."

And yet there is not the slightest evidence of foul play. Nobody knows what happened to the carpenter. There are no clues, no traces. The night was calm and snowy. No seas broke on board. Without doubt the clumsy, big-footed, over-grown giant of a boy is overside and dead. The question is: did he go over of his own accord, or was he put over?

At eight o'clock Mr. Pike proceeded to interrogate the watches. He stood at the break of the poop, in the high place, leaning on the rail and gazing down at the crew assembled on the main deck beneath him.

Man after man he questioned, and from each man came the one story. They knew no more about it than did we—or so they averred.

"I suppose you'll be chargin' next that I hove that big lummux overboard with me own hands," Mulligan Jacobs snarled, when he was questioned. "An' mebbe I did, bein' that husky an' rampagin' bull-like."

The mate's face grew more forbidding and sour, but without comment he passed on to John Hackey, the San Francisco hoodlum.

It was an unforgettable scene—the mate in the high place, the men, sullen and irresponsive, grouped beneath. A gentle snow drifted straight down through the windless air, while the *Elsinore*, with hollow thunder from her sails, rolled down on the quiet swells so that the ocean lapped the mouths of her scuppers with long-drawn, shuddering sucks and sobs. And all the men swayed in unison to rolls, their hands in mittens, their feet in sack-wrapped sea-boots, their faces worn and sick. And the three dreamers with the topaz eyes stood and swayed and dreamed together, incurious of setting and situation.

And then it came—the hint of easterly air. The mate noted it first. I saw him start and turn his cheek to the almost imperceptible draught. Then I felt it. A minute longer he waited, until assured, when, the dead carpenter forgotten, he burst out with orders to the wheel and the crew. And the men jumped, though in their weakness the climb aloft was slow and toilsome; and when the gaskets were off the topgallant-sails and the men on deck were hoisting yards and sheeting home, those aloft were loosing the royals.

While this work went on, and while the yards were being braced around, the *Elsinore*, her bow pointing to the west, began moving through the water before the first fair wind in a month and a half.

Slowly that light air fanned to a gentle breeze while all the time the snow fell steadily. The barometer, down to 28.80, continued to fall, and the breeze continued to grow upon itself. Tom Spink, passing by me on the poop to lend a hand at the final finicky trimming of the mizzen-yards, gave me a triumphant look. Superstition was vindicated. Events had proved him right.

Fair wind had come with the going of the carpenter, which said warlock had incontestably taken with him overside his bag of wind-tricks.

Mr. Pike strode up and down the poop, rubbing his hands, which he was too disdainfully happy to mitten, chuckling and grinning to himself, glancing at the draw of every sail, stealing adoring looks astern into the gray of snow out of which blew the favouring wind. He even paused beside me to gossip for a moment about the French restaurants of San Francisco and how, therein, the delectable California fashion of cooking wild duck obtained.

"Throw 'em through the fire," he chanted. "That's the way—throw 'em through the fire—a hot oven, sixteen minutes—I take mine fourteen, to the second—an' squeeze the carcasses."

By midday the snow had ceased and we were bowling along before a stiff breeze. At three in the afternoon we were running before a growing gale. It was across a mad ocean we tore, for the mounting sea that made from eastward bucked into the West End Drift and battled and battered down the huge south-westerly swell. And the big grinning dolt of a Finnish carpenter, already food for fish and bird, was astern there somewhere in the freezing rack and drive.

Make westing! We ripped it off across these narrowing degrees of longitude at the southern tip of the planet where one mile counts for two. And Mr. Pike, staring at his bending topgallant-yards, swore that they could carry away for all he cared ere he eased an inch of canvas. More he did. He set the huge crojack, biggest of all sails, and challenged God or Satan to start a seam of it or all its seams.

He simply could not go below. In such auspicious occasions all watches were his, and he strode the poop perpetually with all age-lag banished from his legs. Margaret and I were with him in the chart-room when he hurrahed the barometer, down to 28.55 and falling. And we were near him, on the poop, when he drove by an east-bound lime-juicer, hove-to under upper-topsails. We were a biscuit-toss away, and he sprang upon the rail at the jigger-shrouds and danced a war-dance and waved his free arm, and yelled his scorn and joy at their discomfiture to the several oilskinned figures on the stranger vessel's poop.

Through the pitch-black night we continued to drive. The crew was sadly frightened, and I sought in vain, in the two dog-watches, for Tom Spink, to ask him if he thought the carpenter, astern, had opened wide the bag-mouth and loosed all his tricks. For the first time I saw the steward apprehensive.

"Too much," he told me, with ominous rolling head. "Too much sail, rotten bad damn all to hell. Bime-by, pretty quick, all finish. You see."

"They talk about running the easting down," Mr. Pike chortled to me, as we clung to the poop-rail to keep from fetching away and breaking ribs and necks. "Well, this is running your westing down if anybody should ride up in a go-devil and ask you."

It was a wretched, glorious night. Sleep was impossible—for me, at any rate. Nor was there even the comfort of warmth. Something had gone wrong with the big cabin stove, due to our wild running, I fancy, and the steward was compelled to let the fire go out. So we are getting a taste of the hardship of the forecastle, though in our case everything is dry instead of soggy or afloat. The kerosene stoves burned in our state room, but so smelly was mine that I preferred the cold.

To sail on one's nerve in an over-canvassed harbour cat-boat is all the excitement any glutton can desire. But to sail, in the same fashion, in a big ship off the Horn, is incredible and terrible. The Great West Wind Drift, setting squarely into the teeth of the easterly gale, kicked up a tideway sea that was monstrous. Two men toiled at the wheel, relieving in pairs every half-hour, and in the face of the cold they streamed with sweat long ere their half-hour shift was up.

Mr. Pike is of the elder race of men. His endurance is prodigious. Watch and watch, and all watches, he held the poop.

"I never dreamed of it," he told me, at midnight, as the great gusts tore by and as we listened for our lighter spars to smash aloft and crash upon the deck. "I thought my last whirling sailing was past. And here we are! Here we are!

"Lord! Lord! I sailed third mate in the little *Vampire* before you were born. Fifty-six men before the mast, and the last Jack of 'em an able seaman. And there were eight boys, an' bosuns that was bosuns, an' sail-makers an' carpenters an' stewards an' passengers to jam the decks. An' three driving mates of us, an' Captain Brown, the Little Wonder. He didn't weigh a hundredweight, an' he drove *us*—he drove us, three drivin' mates that learned from him what drivin' was.

"It was knock down and drag out from the start. The first hour of puttin' the men to fair perished our knuckles. I've got the smashed joints yet to show. Every sea-chest broke open, every sea-bag turned out, and whiskey bottles, knuckle-dusters, sling-shots, bowie-knives, an' guns chucked overside by the armful. An' when we chose the watches, each man of fifty-six of 'em laid his knife on the main-hatch an' the carpenter broke the point square off.—Yes, an' the little *Vampire* only eight hundred tons. The *Elsinore* could carry her on her deck. But she was ship, all ship, an' them was men's days."

Margaret, save for inability to sleep, did not mind the driving, although Mr. Mellaire, on the other hand, admitted apprehension.

"He's got my goat," he confided to me. "It isn't right to drive a cargo-carrier this way. This isn't a ballasted yacht. It's a coal-hulk. I know what driving was, but it was in ships made to drive. Our iron-work aloft won't stand it. Mr. Pathurst, I tell you frankly that it is criminal, it is sheer murder, to run the *Elsinore* with that crojack on her. You can see yourself, sir. It's an after-sail. All its tendency is to throw her stern off and her bow up to it. And if it ever happens, sir, if she ever gets away from the wheel for two seconds and broaches to . . . "

"Then what?" I asked, or, rather, shouted; for all conversation had to be shouted close to ear in that blast of gale.

He shrugged his shoulders, and all of him was eloquent with the unuttered, unmistakable word—"finish."

At eight this morning Margaret and I struggled up to the poop. And there was that indomitable, iron old man. He had never left the deck all night. His eyes were bright, and he appeared in the pink of well-being. He rubbed his hands and chuckled greeting to us, and took up his reminiscences.

"In '51, on this same stretch, Miss West, the *Flying Cloud*, in twenty-four hours, logged three hundred and seventy-four miles under her topgallant-sails. That was sailing. She broke the record, that day, for sail an' steam."

"And what are we averaging, Mr. Pike?" Margaret queried, while her eyes were fixed on the main deck, where continually one rail and then the other dipped under the ocean and filled across from rail to rail, only to spill out and take in on the next roll.

"Thirteen for a fair average since five o'clock yesterday afternoon," he exulted. "In the squalls she makes all of sixteen, which is going some, for the *Elsinore*."

"I'd take the crojack off if I had charge," Margaret criticised.

"So would I, so would I, Miss West," he replied; "if we hadn't been six weeks already off the Horn."

She ran her eyes aloft, spar by spar, past the spars of hollow steel to the wooden royals, which bent in the gusts like bows in some invisible archer's hands.

"They're remarkably good sticks of timber," was her comment.

"Well may you say it, Miss West," he agreed. "I'd never a-believed they'd a-stood it myself. But just look at 'm! Just look at 'm!"

There was no breakfast for the men. Three times the galley had been washed out, and the men, in the forecastle awash, contented themselves with hard tack and cold salt horse. Aft, with us, the steward scalded himself twice ere he succeeded in making coffee over a kerosene-burner.

At noon we picked up a ship ahead, a lime-juicer, travelling in the same direction, under lower-topsails and one upper-topsail. The only one of her courses set was the foresail.

"The way that skipper's carryin' on is shocking," Mr. Pike sneered. "He should be more cautious, and remember God, the owners, the underwriters, and the Board of Trade."

Such was our speed that in almost no time we were up with the stranger vessel and passing her. Mr. Pike was like a boy just loosed from school. He altered our course so that we passed her a hundred yards away. She was a gallant sight, but, such was our speed, she appeared standing still. Mr. Pike jumped upon the rail and insulted those on her poop by extending a rope's end in invitation to take a tow.

Margaret shook her head privily to me as she gazed at our bending royal-yards, but was caught in the act by Mr. Pike, who cried out:

"What kites she won't carry she can drag!"

An hour later I caught Tom Spink, just relieved from his shift at the wheel and weak from exhaustion.

"What do you think now of the carpenter and his bag of tricks?" I queried.

"Lord lumme, it should a-ben the mate, sir," was his reply.

By five in the afternoon we had logged 314 miles since five the previous day, which was two over an average of thirteen knots for twenty-four consecutive hours.

"Now take Captain Brown of the little Vampire," Mr. Pike grinned to me, for our sailing made him good-natured. "He never would take in until the kites an' stu'n'sails was about his ears. An' when she was blown' her worst an' we was half-fairly shortened down, he'd turn in for a snooze, an' say to us, 'Call me if she moderates.' Yes, and I'll never forget the night when I called him an' told him that everything on top the houses had gone adrift, an' that two of the boats had been swept aft and was kindling-wood against the break of the cabin. 'Very well, Mr. Pike,' he says, battin' his eyes and turnin' over to go to sleep again. 'Very well, Mr. Pike,' says he. 'Watch her. An' Mr. Pike . . .' 'Yes, sir,' says I. 'Give me a call, Mr. Pike, when the windlass shows signs of comin' aft.' That's what he said, his very words, an' the next moment, damme, he was snorin'."

* * * * *

It is now midnight, and, cunningly wedged into my bunk, unable to sleep, I am writing these lines with flying dabs of pencil at my pad. And no more shall I write, I swear, until this gale is blown out, or we are blown to Kingdom Come.

CHAPTER XLI

The days have passed and I have broken my resolve; for here I am again writing while the *Elsinore* surges along across a magnificent, smoky, dusty sea. But I have two reasons for breaking my word. First, and minor, we had a real dawn this morning. The gray of the sea showed a streaky blue, and the cloud-masses were actually pink-tipped by a really and truly sun.

Second, and major, *we are around the Horn*! We are north of 50 in the Pacific, in Longitude 80.49, with Cape Pillar and the Straits of Magellan already south of east from us, and we are heading north-north-west. *We are around the Horn*! The profound significance of this can be appreciated only by one who has wind-jammed around from east to west. Blow high, blow low, nothing can happen to thwart us. No ship north of 50 was ever blown back. From now on it is plain sailing, and Seattle suddenly seems quite near.

All the ship's company, with the exception of Margaret, is better spirited. She is quiet, and a little down, though she is anything but prone to the wastage of grief. In her robust, vital philosophy God's always in heaven. I may describe her as being merely subdued, and gentle, and tender. And she is very wistful to receive gentle consideration and tenderness from me. She is, after all, the genuine woman. She wants the strength that man has to give, and I flatter myself that I am ten times a stronger man than I was when the voyage began, because I am a thousand times a more human man since I told the books to go hang and began to revel in the human maleness of the man that loves a woman and is loved.

Returning to the ship's company. The rounding of the Horn, the better weather that is continually growing better, the easement of hardship and toil and danger, with the promise of the tropics and of the balmy south-east trades before them—all these factors contribute to pick up our men again. The temperature has already so moderated that the men are beginning to shed their surplusage of clothing, and they no longer wrap sacking about their sea-boots. Last evening, in the second dog-watch, I heard a man actually singing.

The steward has discarded the huge, hacking knife and relaxed to the extent of engaging in an occasional sober romp with Possum. Wada's face is no longer solemnly long, and Louis' Oxford accent is more mellifluous than ever. Mulligan Jacobs and Andy Fay are the same venomous scorpions they have always been. The three gangsters, with the clique they lead, have again asserted their tyrany and thrashed all the weaklings and feeblings in the forecastle. Charles Davis resolutely refuses to die, though how he survived that wet and freezing room of iron through all the weeks off the Horn has elicited wonder even from Mr. Pike, who has a most accurate knowledge of what men can stand and what they cannot stand.

How Nietzsche, with his eternal slogan of "Be hard! Be hard!" would have delighted in Mr. Pike!

And—oh!—Larry has had a tooth removed. For some days distressed with a jumping toothache, he came aft to the mate for relief. Mr. Pike refused to "monkey" with the "fangled" forceps in the medicine-chest. He used a tenpenny nail and a hammer in the good old way to which he was brought up. I vouch for this. I saw it done. One blow of the hammer and the tooth was out, while Larry was jumping around holding his jaw. It is a wonder it wasn't fractured. But Mr. Pike avers he has removed hundreds of teeth by this method and never known a fractured jaw. Also, he avers he once sailed with a skipper who shaved every Sunday morning and never touched a razor, nor any cutting-edge, to his face. What he used, according to Mr. Pike, was a lighted candle and a damp towel. Another candidate for Nietzsche's immortals who are hard!

As for Mr. Pike himself, he is the highest-spirited, best-conditioned man on board. The driving to which he subjected the *Elsinore* was meat and drink. He still rubs his hands and chuckles over the memory of it.

"Huh!" he said to me, in reference to the crew; "I gave 'em a taste of real old-fashioned sailing. They'll never forget this hooker—at least them that don't take a sack of coal overside before we reach port."

"You mean you think we'll have more sea-burials?" I inquired.

He turned squarely upon me, and squarely looked me in the eyes for the matter of five long seconds.

"Huh!" he replied, as he turned on his heel. "Hell ain't begun to pop on this hooker."

He still stands his mate's watch, alternating with Mr. Mellaire, for he is firm in his conviction that there is no man for'ard fit to stand a second mate's watch. Also, he has kept his old quarters. Perhaps it is out of delicacy for Margaret; for I have learned that it is the invariable custom for the mate to occupy the captain's quarters when the latter dies. So Mr. Mellaire still eats by himself in the big after-room, as he has done since the loss of the carpenter, and bunks as before in the 'midship-house with Nancy.

CHAPTER XLII

Mr. Mellaire was right. The men would not accept the driving when the *Elsinore* won to easier latitudes. Mr. Pike was right. Hell had not begun to pop. But it has popped now, and men are overboard without even the kindliness of a sack of coal at their feet. And yet the men, though ripe for it, did not precipitate the trouble. It was Mr. Mellaire. Or, rather, it was Ditman Olansen, the crank-eyed Norwegian. Perhaps it was Possum. At any rate, it was an accident, in which the several-named, including Possum, played their respective parts.

To begin at the beginning. Two weeks have elapsed since we crossed 50, and we are now in 37—the same latitude as San Francisco, or, to be correct, we are as far south of the equator as San Francisco is north of it. The trouble was precipitated yesterday morning shortly after nine o'clock, and Possum started the chain of events that culminated in downright mutiny. It was Mr. Mellaire's watch, and he was standing on the bridge, directly under the mizzen-top, giving orders to Sundry Buyers, who, with Arthur Deacon and the Maltese Cockney, was doing rigging work aloft.

Get the picture and the situation in all its ridiculousness. Mr. Pike, thermometer in hand, was coming back along the bridge from taking the temperature of the coal in the for'ard hold. Ditman Olansen was just swinging into the mizzen-top as he went up with several turns of rope over one shoulder. Also, in some way, to the end of this rope was fastened a sizable block that might have weighed ten pounds. Possum, running free, was fooling around the chicken-coop on top the 'midship-house. And the chickens, featherless but indomitable, were enjoying the milder weather as they pecked at the grain and grits which the steward had just placed in their feeding-trough. The tarpaulin that covered their pen had been off for several days.

Now observe. I am at the break of the poop, leaning on the rail and watching Ditman Olansen swing into the top with his cumbersome burden. Mr. Pike, proceeding aft, has just passed Mr. Mellaire. Possum, who, on account of the Horn weather and the tarpaulin, has not seen the chickens for many weeks, is getting reacquainted, and is investigating them with that keen nose of his. And a hen's beak, equally though differently keen, impacts on Possum's nose, which is as sensitive as it is keen.

I may well say, now that I think it over, that it was this particular hen that started the mutiny. The men, well-driven by Mr. Pike, were ripe for an explosion, and Possum and the hen laid the train.

Possum fell away backwards from the coop and loosed a wild cry of pain and indignation. This attracted Ditman Olansen's attention. He paused and craned his neck out in order to see, and, in this moment of carelessness, the block he was carrying fetched away from him along with the several turns of rope around his shoulder. Both the mates sprang away to get out from under. The rope, fast to the block and following it, lashed about like a blacksnake, and, though the block fell clear of Mr. Mellaire, the bight of the rope snatched off his cap.

Mr. Pike had already started an oath aloft when his eyes caught sight of the terrible cleft in Mr. Mellaire's head. There it was, for all the world to read, and Mr. Pike's and mine were the only eyes that could read it. The sparse hair upon the second mate's crown served not at all to hide the cleft. It began out of sight in the thicker hair above the ears, and was exposed nakedly across the whole dome of head.

The stream of abuse for Ditman Olansen was choked in Mr. Pike's throat. All he was capable of for the moment was to stare, petrified, at that enormous fissure flanked at either end with a thatch of grizzled hair. He was in a dream, a trance, his great hands knotting and clenching unconsciously as he stared at the mark unmistakable by which he had said that he would some day identify the murderer of Captain Somers. And in that moment I remembered having heard him declare that some day he would stick his fingers in that mark.

Still as in a dream, moving slowly, right hand outstretched like a talon, with the fingers drawn downward, he advanced on the second mate with the evident intention of thrusting his fingers into that cleft and of clawing and tearing at the brain-life beneath that pulsed under the thin film of skin.

The second mate backed away along the bridge, and Mr. Pike seemed partially to come to himself. His outstretched arm dropped to his side, and he paused.

"I know you," he said, in a strange, shaky voice, blended of age and passion. "Eighteen years ago you were dismasted off the Plate in the *Cyrus*

Thompson. She foundered, after you were on your beam ends and lost your sticks. You were in the only boat that was saved. Eleven years ago, on the *Jason Harrison*, in San Francisco, Captain Somers was beaten to death by his second mate. This second mate was a survivor of the *Cyrus Thompson.* This second mate'd had his skull split by a crazy sea-cook. Your skull is split. This second mate's name was Sidney Waltham. And if you ain't Sidney Waltham . . . "

At this point Mr. Mellaire, or, rather, Sidney Waltham, despite his fifty years, did what only a sailor could do. He went over the bridge-rail side-wise, caught the running gear up-and-down the mizzen-mast, and landed lightly on his feet on top of Number Three hatch. Nor did he stop there. He ran across the hatch and dived through the doorway of his room in the 'midship-house.

Such must have been Mr. Pike's profundity of passion, that he paused like a somnambulist, actually rubbed his eyes with the back of his hand, and seemed to awaken.

But the second mate had not run to his room for refuge. The next moment he emerged, a thirty-two Smith and Wesson in his hand, and the instant he emerged he began shooting.

Mr. Pike was wholly himself again, and I saw him perceptibly pause and decide between the two impulses that tore at him. One was to leap over the bridge-rail and down at the man who shot at him; the other was to retreat. He retreated. And as he bounded aft along the narrow bridge the mutiny began. Arthur Deacon, from the mizzen-top, leaned out and hurled a steel marlin-spike at the fleeing mate. The thing flashed in the sunlight as it hurtled down. It missed Mr. Pike by twenty feet and nearly impaled Possum, who, afraid of firearms, was wildly rushing and ki-yi-ing aft. It so happened that the sharp point of the marlin-spike struck the wooden floor of the bridge, and it penetrated the planking with such force that after it had fetched to a standstill it vibrated violently for long seconds.

I confess that I failed to observe a tithe of what occurred during the next several minutes. Piece together as I will, after the event, I know that I missed much of what took place. I know that the men aloft in the mizzen descended to the deck, but I never saw them descend. I know that the second mate emptied the chambers of his revolver, but I did not hear all the shots. I know that Lars Johnson left the wheel, and on his broken leg, rebroken and not yet really mended, limped and scuttled across the poop, down the ladder, and gained for'ard. I know he must have limped and scuttled on that bad leg of his; I know that I must have seen him; and yet I swear that I have no impression of seeing him.

I do know that I heard the rush of feet of men from for'ard along the main deck. And I do know that I saw Mr. Pike take shelter behind the steel jiggermast. Also, as the second mate manoeuvred to port on top of Number Three hatch for his last shot, I know that I saw Mr. Pike duck around the corner of the chart-house to starboard and get away aft and below by way of the booby-hatch. And I did hear that last futile shot, and the bullet also as it ricochetted from the corner of the steel-walled chart-house.

As for myself, I did not move. I was too interested in seeing. It may have been due to lack of presence of mind, or to lack of habituation to an active part in scenes of quick action; but at any rate I merely retained my position at the break of the poop and looked on. I was the only person on the poop when the mutineers, led by the second mate and the gangsters, rushed it. I saw them swarm up the ladder, and it never entered my head to attempt to oppose them. Which was just as well, for I would have been killed for my pains, and I could never have stopped them.

I was alone on the poop, and the men were quite perplexed to find no enemy in sight. As Bert Rhine went past, he half fetched up in his stride, as if to knife me with the sheath knife, sharp-pointed, which he carried in his right hand; then, and I know I correctly measured the drift of his judgment, he unflatteringly dismissed me as unimportant and ran on.

Right here I was impressed by the lack of clear-thinking on any of their parts. So spontaneously had the ship's company exploded into mutiny that it was dazed and confused even while it acted. For instance, in the months since we left Baltimore there had never been a moment, day or night, even when preventer tackles were rigged, that a man had not stood at the wheel. So habituated were they to this, that they were shocked into consternation at sight of the deserted wheel. They paused for an instant to stare at it. Then Bert Rhine, with a quick word and gesture, sent the Italian, Guido Bombini, around the rear of the half-wheelhouse. The fact that he completed the circuit was proof that nobody was there.

Again, in the swift rush of events, I must confess that I saw but little. I was aware that more of the men were climbing up the ladder and gaining the poop, but I had no eyes for them. I was watching that sanguinary group aft near the wheel and noting the most important thing, namely, that it was Bert Rhine, the gangster, and not the second mate, who gave orders and was obeyed.

He motioned to the Jew, Isaac Chantz, who had been wounded earlier in the voyage by O'Sullivan, and Chantz led the way to the starboard chart-house door. While this was going on, all in flashing fractions of seconds, Bert Rhine was cautiously inspecting the lazarette through the open booby-hatch.

Isaac Chantz jerked open the chart-house door, which swung outward. Things did happen so swiftly! As he jerked the iron door open a two-foot hacking butcher knife, at the end of a withered, yellow hand, flashed out and down on him. It missed head and neck, but caught him on top of the left shoulder.

All hands recoiled before this, and the Jew reeled across to the rail, his right hand clutching at his wound, and between the fingers I could see the blood welling darkly. Bert Rhine abandoned his inspection of the booby-hatch, and, with the second mate, the latter still carrying his empty Smith & Wesson, sprang into the press about the chart-house door.

O wise, clever, cautious, old Chinese steward! He made no emergence. The door swung emptily back and forth to the rolling of the *Elsinore*, and no man knew but what, just inside, with that heavy, hacking knife upraised, lurked the steward. And while they hesitated and stared at the aperture that alternately closed and opened with the swinging of the door, the booby-hatch, situated between chart-house and wheel, erupted. It was Mr. Pike, with his .44 automatic Colt.

There were shots fired, other than by him. I know I heard them, like "red-heads" at an old-time Fourth of July; but I do not know who discharged them. All was mess and confusion. Many shots were being fired, and through the uproar I heard the reiterant, monotonous explosions from the Colt's .44

I saw the Italian, Mike Cipriani, clutch savagely at his abdomen and sink slowly to the deck. Shorty, the Japanese half-caste, clown that he was, dancing and grinning on the outskirts of the struggle, with a final grimace and hysterical giggle led the retreat across the poop and down the poop-ladder. Never had I seen a finer exemplification of mob psychology. Shorty, the most unstable-minded of the individuals who composed this mob, by his own instability precipitated the retreat in which the mob joined. When he broke before the steady discharge of the automatic in the hand of the mate, on the instant the rest broke with him. Least-balanced, his balance was the balance of all of them.

Chantz, bleeding prodigiously, was one of the first on Shorty's heels. I saw Nosey Murphy pause long enough to throw his knife at the mate. The missile went wide, with a metallic clang struck the brass tip of one of the spokes of the *Elsinore*'s wheel, and clattered on the deck. The second mate, with his empty revolver, and Bert Rhine with his sheath-knife, fled past me side by side.

Mr. Pike emerged from the booby-hatch and with an unaimed shot brought down Bill Quigley, one of the "bricklayers," who fell at my feet. The last man off the poop was the Maltese Cockney, and at the top of the ladder he paused to look back at Mr. Pike, who, holding the automatic in both hands, was taking careful aim. The Maltese Cockney, disdaining the ladder, leaped through the air to the main deck. But the Colt merely clicked. It was the last bullet in it that had fetched down Bill Quigley.

And the poop was ours.

Events still crowded so closely that I missed much. I saw the steward, belligerent and cautious, his long knife poised for a slash, emerge from the chart-house. Margaret followed him, and behind her came Wada, who carried my .22 Winchester automatic rifle. As he told me afterwards, he had brought it up under instructions from her.

Mr. Pike was glancing with cool haste at his Colt to see whether it was jammed or empty, when Margaret asked him the course.

"By the wind," he shouted to her, as he bounded for'ard. "Put your helm hard up or we'll be all aback."

Ah!—yeoman and henchman of the race, he could not fail in his fidelity to the ship under his command. The iron of all his years of iron training was there manifest. While mutiny spread red, and death was on the wing, he could not forget his charge, the ship, the *Elsinore*, the insensate fabric compounded of steel and hemp and woven cotton that was to him glorious with personality.

Margaret waved Wada in my direction as she ran to the wheel. As Mr. Pike passed the corner of the chart-house, simultaneously there was a report from amidships and the ping of a bullet against the steel wall. I saw the man who fired the shot. It was the cowboy, Steve Roberts.

As for the mate, he ducked in behind the sheltering jiggermast, and even as he ducked his left hand dipped into his side coat-pocket, so that when he had gained shelter it was coming out with a fresh clip of cartridges. The empty clip fell to the deck, the loader clip slipped up the hollow butt, and he was good for eight more shots.

Wada turned the little automatic rifle over to me, where I still stood under the weather cloth at the break of the poop.

"All ready," he said. "You take off safety."

"Get Roberts," Mr. Pike called to me. "He's the best shot for'ard. If you can't get 'm, jolt the fear of God into him anyway."

It was the first time I had a human target, and let me say, here and now, that I am convinced I am immune to buck fever. There he was before me, less than a hundred feet distant, in the gangway between the door to Davis' room and the starboard-rail, manoeuvring for another shot at Mr. Pike.

I must have missed Steve Roberts that first time, but I came so near him that he jumped. The next instant he had located me and turned his revolver on me. But he had no chance. My little automatic was discharging as fast as I could tickle the trigger with my fore-finger. The cowboy's first shot went wild of me, because my bullet arrived ere he got his swift aim. He swayed and stumbled backward, but the bullets—ten of them—poured from the muzzle of my Winchester like water from a garden hose. It was a stream of lead I played upon him. I shall never know how many times I hit him, but I am confident that after he had begun his long staggering fall at least three additional bullets entered him ere he impacted on the deck. And even as he was falling, aimlessly and mechanically, stricken then with death, he managed twice again to discharge his weapon.

And after he struck the deck he never moved. I do believe he died in the air.

As I held up my gun and gazed at the abruptly-deserted main-deck I was aware of Wada's touch on my arm. I looked. In his hand were a dozen little .22 long, soft-nosed, smokeless cartridges. He wanted me to reload. I threw on the safety, opened the magazine, and tilted the rifle so that he could let the fresh cartridges of themselves slide into place.

"Get some more," I told him.

Scarcely had he departed on the errand when Bill Quigley, who lay at my feet, created a diversion. I jumped—yes, and I freely confess that I yelled—with startle and surprise, when I felt his paws clutch my ankles and his teeth shut down on the calf of my leg.

It was Mr. Pike to the rescue. I understand now the Western hyperbole of "hitting the high places." The mate did not seem in contact with the deck. My impression was that he soared through the air to me, landing beside me, and, in the instant of landing, kicking out with one of those big feet of his. Bill Quigley was kicked clear away from me, and the next moment he was flying overboard. It was a clean throw. He never touched the rail.

Whether Mike Cipriani, who, till then, had lain in a welter, began crawling aft in quest of safety, or whether he intended harm to Margaret at the wheel, we shall never know; for there was no opportunity given him to show his purpose. As swiftly as Mr. Pike could cross the deck with those giant bounds, just that swiftly was the Italian in the air and following Bill Quigley overside.

The mate missed nothing with those eagle eyes of his as he returned along the poop. Nobody was to be seen on the main deck. Even the lookout had deserted the forecastle-head, and the *Elsinore*, steered by Margaret, slipped a lazy two knots through the quiet sea. Mr. Pike was apprehensive of a shot from ambush, and it was not until after a scrutiny of several minutes that he put his pistol into his side coat-pocket and snarled for'ard:

"Come out, you rats! Show your ugly faces! I want to talk with you!"

Guido Bombini, gesticulating peaceable intentions and evidently thrust out by Bert Rhine, was the first to appear. When it was observed that Mr. Pike did not fire, the rest began to dribble into view. This continued till all were there save the cook, the two sail-makers, and the second mate. The last to come out were Tom Spink, the boy Buckwheat, and Herman Lunkenheimer, the good-natured but simple-minded German; and these three came out only after repeated threats from Bert Rhine, who, with Nosey Murphy and Kid Twist, was patently in charge. Also, like a faithful dog, Guido Bombini fawned close to him.

"That will do—stop where you are," Mr. Pike commanded, when the crew was scattered abreast, to starboard and to port, of Number Three hatch.

It was a striking scene. *Mutiny on the high seas*! That phrase, learned in boyhood from my Marryatt and Cooper, recrudesced in my brain. This was it—mutiny on the high seas in the year nineteen thirteen—and I was part of it, a perishing blond whose lot was cast with the perishing but lordly blonds, and I had already killed a man.

Mr. Pike, in the high place, aged and indomitable; leaned his arm on the rail at the break of the poop and gazed down at the mutineers, the like of which I'll wager had never been assembled in mutiny before. There were the three gangsters and ex-jailbirds, anything but seamen, yet in control of this affair that was peculiarly an affair of the sea. With them was the Italian hound, Bombini, and beside them were such strangely assorted men as Anton Sorensen, Lars Jacobsen, Frank Fitzgibbon, and Richard Giller—also Arthur Deacon the white slaver, John Hackey the San Francisco hoodlum, the Maltese Cockney, and Tony the suicidal Greek.

I noticed the three strange ones, shouldering together and standing apart from the others as they swayed to the lazy roll and dreamed with their pale, topaz eyes. And there was the Faun, stone deaf but observant, straining to understand what was taking place. Yes, and Mulligan Jacobs and Andy Fay were bitterly and eagerly side by side, and Ditman Olansen, crank-eyed, as if drawn by some affinity of bitterness, stood behind them, his head appearing between their heads. Farthest advanced of all was Charles Davis, the man who by all rights should long since be dead, his face with its wax-like pallor startlingly in contrast to the weathered faces of the rest.

I glanced back at Margaret, who was coolly steering, and she smiled to me, and love was in her eyes—she, too, of the perishing and lordly race of blonds, her place the high place, her heritage government and command and mastery over the stupid lowly of her kind and over the ruck and spawn of the dark-pigmented breeds.

"Where's Sidney Waltham?" the mate snarled. "I want him. Bring him out. After that, the rest of you filth get back to work, or God have mercy on you."

The men moved about restlessly, shuffling their feet on the deck.

"Sidney Waltham, I want you—come out!" Mr. Pike called, addressing himself beyond them to the murderer of the captain under whom once he had sailed.

The prodigious old hero! It never entered his head that he was not the master of the rabble there below him. He had but one idea, an idea of passion, and that was his desire for vengeance on the murderer of his old skipper.

"You old stiff!" Mulligan Jacobs snarled back.

"Shut up, Mulligan!" was Bert Rhine's command, in receipt of which he received a venomous stare from the cripple.

"Oh, ho, my hearty," Mr. Pike sneered at the gangster. "I'll take care of your case, never fear. In the meantime, and right now, fetch out that dog."

Whereupon he ignored the leader of the mutineers and began calling, "Waltham, you dog, come out! Come out, you sneaking cur! Come out!"

Another lunatic, was the thought that flashed through my mind; another lunatic, the slave of a single idea. He forgets the mutiny, his fidelity to the ship, in his personal thirst for vengeance.

But did he? Even as he forgot and called his heart's desire, which was the life of the second mate, even then, without intention, mechanically, his sailor's considerative eye lifted to note the draw of the sails and roved from sail to sail. Thereupon, so reminded, he returned to his fidelity.

"Well?" he snarled at Bert Rhine. "Go on and get for'ard before I spit on you, you scum and slum. I'll give you and the rest of the rats two minutes to return to duty."

And the leader, with his two fellow-gangsters, laughed their weird, silent laughter.

"I guess you'll listen to our talk, first, old horse," Bert Rhine retorted. "—Davis, get up now and show what kind of a spieler you are. Don't get cold feet. Spit it out to Foxy Grandpa an' tell 'm what's doin'."

"You damned sea-lawyer!" Mr. Pike snarled as Davis opened his mouth to speak.

Bert Rhine shrugged his shoulders, and half turned on his heel as if to depart, as he said quietly:

"Oh, well, if you don't want to talk . . . "

Mr. Pike conceded a point.

"Go on!" he snarled. "Spit the dirt out of your system, Davis; but remember one thing: you'll pay for this, and you'll pay through the nose. Go on!"

The sea-lawyer cleared his throat in preparation.

"First of all, I ain't got no part in this," he began.

"I'm a sick man, an' I oughta be in my bunk right now. I ain't fit to be on my feet. But they've asked me to advise 'em on the law, an' I have advised 'em—"

"And the law—what is it?" Mr. Pike broke in.

But Davis was uncowed.

"The law is that when the officers is inefficient, the crew can take charge peaceably an' bring the ship into port. It's all law an' in the records. There was the *Abyssinia*, in eighteen ninety-two, when the master'd died of fever and the mates took to drinkin'—"

"Go on!" Mr. Pike shut him off. "I don't want your citations. What d'ye want? Spit it out."

"Well—and I'm talkin' as an outsider, as a sick man off duty that's been asked to talk—well, the point is our skipper was a good one, but he's gone. Our mate is violent, seekin' the life of the second mate. We don't care about that. What we want is to get into port with our lives. An' our lives is in danger. We ain't hurt nobody. You've done all the bloodshed. You've shot an' killed an' thrown two men overboard, as witnesses'll testify to in court. An' there's Roberts, there, dead, too, an' headin' for the sharks—an' what for? For defendin' himself from murderous an' deadly attack, as every man can

403

testify an' tell the truth, the whole truth, an' nothin' but the truth, so help 'm, God—ain't that right, men?"

A confused murmur of assent arose from many of them.

"You want my job, eh?" Mr. Pike grinned. "An' what are you goin' to do with me?"

"You'll be taken care of until we get in an' turn you over to the lawful authorities," Davis answered promptly. "Most likely you can plead insanity an' get off easy."

At this moment I felt a stir at my shoulder. It was Margaret, armed with the long knife of the steward, whom she had put at the wheel.

"You've got another guess comin', Davis," Mr. Pike said. "I've got no more talk with you. I'm goin' to talk to the bunch. I'll give you fellows just two minutes to choose, and I'll tell you your choices. You've only got two choices. You'll turn the second mate over to me an' go back to duty and take what's comin' to you, or you'll go to jail with the stripes on you for long sentences. You've got two minutes. The fellows that want jail can stand right where they are. The fellows that don't want jail and are willin' to work faithful, can walk right back to me here on the poop. Two minutes, an' you can keep your jaws stopped while you think over what it's goin' to be."

He turned his head to me and said in an undertone, "Be ready with that pop-gun for trouble. An' don't hesitate. Slap it into 'em—the swine that think they can put as raw a deal as this over on us."

It was Buckwheat who made the first move; but so tentative was it that it got no farther than a tensing of the legs and a sway forward of the shoulders. Nevertheless it was sufficient to start Herman Lunkenheimer, who thrust out his foot and began confidently to walk aft. Kid Twist gained him in a single spring, and Kid Twist, his wrist under the German's throat from behind; his knee pressed into the German's back, bent the man backward and held him. Even as the rifle came to my shoulder, the hound Bombini drew his knife directly beneath Kid Twist's wrist across the up-stretched throat of the man.

It was at this instant that I heard Mr. Pike's "Plug him!" and pulled the trigger; and of all ungodly things the bullet missed and caught the Faun, who staggered back, sat down on the hatch, and began to cough. And even as he coughed he still strained with pain-eloquent eyes to try to understand.

No other man moved. Herman Lunkenheimer, released by Kid Twist, sank down on the deck. Nor did I shoot again. Kid Twist stood again by the side of Bert Rhine and Guido Bombini fawned near.

Bert Rhine actually visibly smiled.

"Any more of you guys want to promenade aft?" he queried in velvet tones.

"Two minutes up," Mr. Pike declared.

"An' what are you goin' to do about it, Grandpa?" Bert Rhine sneered.

In a flash the big automatic was out of the mate's pocket and he was shooting as fast as he could pull trigger, while all hands fled to shelter. But, as he had long since told me, he was no shot and could effectively use the weapon only at close range—muzzle to stomach preferably.

As we stared at the main deck, deserted save for the dead cowboy on his back and for the Faun who still sat on the hatch and coughed, an eruption of men occurred over the for'ard edge of the 'midship-house.

"Shoot!" Margaret cried at my back.

"Don't!" Mr. Pike roared at me.

The rifle was at my shoulder when I desisted. Louis, the cook, led the rush aft to us across the top of the house and along the bridge. Behind him, in single file and not wasting any time, came the Japanese sail-makers, Henry the training-ship boy, and the other boy Buckwheat. Tom Spink brought up the rear. As he came up the ladder of the 'midship-house somebody from beneath must have caught him by a leg in an effort to drag him back. We saw half of him in sight and knew that he was struggling and kicking. He fetched clear abruptly, gained the top of the house in a surge, and raced aft along the bridge until he overtook and collided with Buckwheat, who yelled out in fear that a mutineer had caught him.

CHAPTER XLIII

We who are aft, besieged in the high place, are stronger in numbers than I dreamed until now, when I have just finished taking the ship's census. Of course Margaret, Mr. Pike, and myself are apart. We alone represent the ruling class. With us are servants and serfs, faithful to their salt, who look to us for guidance and life.

I use my words advisedly. Tom Spink and Buckwheat are serfs and nothing else. Henry, the training-ship boy, occupies an anomalous classification. He is of our kind, but he can scarcely be called even a cadet of our kind. He will some day win to us and become a mate or a captain, but in the meantime, of course, his past is against him. He is a candidate, rising from the serf class to our class. Also, he is only a youth, the iron of his heredity not yet tested and proven.

Wada, Louis, and the steward are servants of Asiatic breed. So are the two Japanese sail-makers—scarcely servants, not to be called slaves, but something in between.

So, all told, there are eleven of us aft in the citadel. But our followers are too servant-like and serf-like to be offensive fighters. They will help us defend the high place against all attack; but they are incapable of joining with us in an attack on the other end of the ship. They will fight like cornered rats to preserve their lives; but they will not advance like tigers upon the enemy. Tom Spink is faithful but spirit-broken. Buckwheat is hopelessly of the stupid lowly. Henry has not yet won his spurs. On our side remain Margaret, Mr. Pike, and myself. The rest will hold the wall of the poop and fight thereon to the death, but they are not to be depended upon in a sortie.

At the other end of the ship—and I may as well give the roster, are: the second mate, either to be called Mellaire or Waltham, a strong man of our own breed but a renegade; the three gangsters, killers and jackals, Bert Rhine, Nosey Murphy, and Kid Twist; the Maltese Cockney and Tony the crazy Greek; Frank Fitzgibbon and Richard Giller, the survivors of the trio of "bricklayers"; Anton Sorensen and Lars Jacobsen, stupid Scandinavian sailor-men; Ditman Olansen, the crank-eyed Berserk; John Hackey and Arthur Deacon, respectively hoodlum and white slaver; Shorty, the mixed-breed clown; Guido Bombini, the Italian hound; Andy Pay and Mulligan Jacobs, the bitter ones; the three topaz-eyed dreamers, who are unclassifiable; Isaac Chantz, the wounded Jew; Bob, the overgrown dolt; the feeble-minded Faun, lung-wounded; Nancy and Sundry Buyers, the two hopeless, helpless bosuns; and, finally, the sea-lawyer, Charles Davis.

This makes twenty-seven of them against the eleven of us. But there are men, strong in viciousness, among them. They, too, have their serfs and bravos. Guido Bombini and Isaac Chantz are certainly bravos. And weaklings like Sorensen, and Jacobsen, and Bob, cannot be anything else than slaves to the men who compose the gangster clique.

I failed to tell what happened yesterday, after Mr. Pike emptied his automatic and cleared the deck. The poop was indubitably ours, and there was no possibility of the mutineers making a charge on us in broad daylight. Margaret had gone below, accompanied by Wada, to see to the security of the port and starboard doors that open from the cabin directly on the main deck. These are still caulked and tight and fastened on the inside, as they have been since the passage of Cape Horn began.

Mr. Pike put one of the sail-makers at the wheel, and the steward, relieved and starting below, was attracted to the port quarter, where the patent log that towed astern was made fast. Margaret had returned his knife to him, and he was carrying it in his hand when his attention was attracted astern to our wake. Mike Cipriani and Bill Quigley had managed to catch the lazily moving log-line and were clinging to it. The *Elsinore* was moving just fast enough to keep them on the surface instead of dragging them under. Above them and about them circled curious and hungry albatrosses, Cape hens, and mollyhawks. Even as I glimpsed the situation one of the big birds, a ten-footer at least, with a ten-inch beak to the fore, dropped down on the Italian. Releasing his hold with one hand, he struck with his knife at the bird. Feathers flew, and the albatross, deflected by the blow, fell clumsily into the water.

Quite methodically, just as part of the day's work, the steward chopped down with his knife, catching the log-line between the steel edge and the rail. At once, no longer buoyed up by the *Elsinore's* two-knot drag ahead, the wounded men began to swim and flounder. The circling hosts of huge sea-birds descended upon them, with carnivorous beaks striking at their heads and shoulders and arms. A great screeching and squawking arose from the winged things of prey as they strove for the living meat. And yet, somehow, I was not very profoundly shocked. These were the men whom I had seen eviscerate the shark and toss it overboard, and shout with joy as they watched it devoured alive by its brethren. They had played a violent, cruel game with the things of life, and the things of life now played upon them the same violent, cruel game. As they that rise by the sword perish by the sword, just so did these two men who had lived cruelly die cruelly.

"Oh, well," was Mr. Pike's comment, "we've saved two sacks of mighty good coal."

* * * * *

Certainly our situation might be worse. We are cooking on the coal-stove and on the oil-burners. We have servants to cook and serve for us. And, most important of all, we are in possession of all the food on the *Elsinore*.

Mr. Pike makes no mistake. Realizing that with our crowd we cannot rush the crowd at the other end of the ship, he accepts the siege, which, as he says, consists of the besieged holding all food supplies while the besiegers are on the imminent edge of famine.

"Starve the dogs," he growls. "Starve 'm until they crawl aft and lick our shoes. Maybe you think the custom of carrying the stores aft just happened. Only it didn't. Before you and I were born it was long-established and it was established on brass tacks. They knew what they were about, the old cusses, when they put the grub in the lazarette."

Louis says there is not more than three days' regular whack in the galley; that the barrel of hard-tack in the forecastle will quickly go; and that our chickens, which they stole last night from the top of the 'midship-house, are equivalent to no more than an additional day's supply. In short, at the outside limit, we are convinced the men will be keen to talk surrender within the week.

We are no longer sailing. In last night's darkness we helplessly listened to the men loosing headsail-halyards and letting yards go down on the run. Under orders of Mr. Pike I shot blindly and many times into the dark, but without result, save that we heard the bullets of answering shots strike against the chart-house. So to-day we have not even a man at the wheel. The *Elsinore* drifts idly on an idle sea, and we stand regular watches in the shelter of chart-house and jiggermast. Mr. Pike says it is the laziest time he has had on the whole voyage.

I alternate watches with him, although when on duty there is little to be done, save, in the daytime, to stand rifle in hand behind the jiggermast, and, in the night, to lurk along the break of the poop. Behind the chart-house, ready to repel assault, are my watch of four men: Tom Spink, Wada, Buckwheat, and Louis. Henry, the two Japanese sail-makers, and the old steward compose Mr. Pike's watch.

It is his orders that no one for'ard is to be allowed to show himself, so, to-day, when the second mate appeared at the corner of the 'midship-house, I made him take a quick leap back with the thud of my bullet against the iron wall a foot from his head. Charles David tried the same game and was similarly stimulated.

Also, this evening, after dark, Mr. Pike put block-and-tackle on the first section of the bridge, heaved it out of place, and lowered it upon the poop. Likewise he hoisted in the ladder at the break of the poop that leads down to the main deck. The men will have to do some climbing if they ever elect to rush us.

I am writing this in my watch below. I came off duty at eight o'clock, and at midnight I go on deck to stay till four to-morrow morning. Wada shakes his head and says that the Blackwood Company should rebate us on the first-class passage paid in advance. We are working our passage, he contends.

Margaret takes the adventure joyously. It is the first time she has experienced mutiny, but she is such a thorough sea-woman that she appears like an old hand at the game. She leaves the deck to the mate and me; but, still acknowledging his leadership, she has taken charge below and entirely manages the commissary, the cooking, and the sleeping arrangements. We still keep our old quarters, and she has bedded the new-comers in the big after-room with blankets issued from the slop-chest.

In a way, from the standpoint of her personal welfare, the mutiny is the best thing that could have happened to her. It has taken her mind off her father and filled her waking hours with work to do. This afternoon, standing above the open booby-hatch, I heard her laugh ring out as in the old days coming down the Atlantic. Yes, and she hums snatches of songs under her breath as she works. In the second dog-watch this evening, after Mr. Pike had finished dinner and joined us on the poop, she told him that if he did not soon re-rig his phonograph she was going to start in on the piano. The reason she advanced was the psychological effect such sounds of revelry would have on the starving mutineers.

* * * * *

The days pass, and nothing of moment happens. We get nowhere. The *Elsinore*, without the steadying of her canvas, rolls emptily and drifts a lunatic course. Sometimes she is bow on to the wind, and at other times she is directly before it; but at all times she is circling vaguely and hesitantly to get somewhere else than where she is. As an illustration, at daylight this morning she came up into the wind as if endeavouring to go about. In the course of half an hour she worked off till the wind was directly abeam. In another half hour she was back into the wind. Not until evening did she manage to get the wind on her port bow; but when she did, she immediately paid off, accomplished the complete circle in an hour, and recommenced her morning tactics of trying to get into the wind.

And there is nothing for us to do save hold the poop against the attack that is never made. Mr. Pike, more from force of habit than anything else, takes his regular observations and works up the *Elsinore*'s position. This noon she was eight miles east of yesterday's position, yet to-day's position, in longitude, was within a mile of where she was four days ago. On the other hand she invariably makes nothing at the rate of seven or eight miles a day.

Aloft, the *Elsinore* is a sad spectacle. All is confusion and disorder. The sails, unfurled, are a slovenly mess along the yards, and many loose ends sway dismally to every roll. The only yard that is loose is the main-yard. It is fortunate that wind and wave are mild, else would the iron-work carry away and the mutineers find the huge thing of steel about their ears.

There is one thing we cannot understand. A week has passed, and the men show no signs of being starved into submission. Repeatedly and in vain has Mr. Pike interrogated the hands aft with us. One and all, from the cook to Buckwheat, they swear they have no knowledge of any food for'ard, save the small supply in the galley and the barrel of hardtack in the forecastle. Yet it is very evident that those for'ard are not starving. We see the smoke from the galley-stove and can only conclude that they have food to cook.

Twice has Bert Rhine attempted a truce, but both times his white flag, as soon as it showed above the edge of the 'midship-house, was fired upon by Mr. Pike. The last occurrence was two days ago. It is Mr. Pike's intention thoroughly to starve them into submission, but now he is beginning to worry about their mysterious food supply.

Mr. Pike is not quite himself. He is obsessed, I know beyond any doubt, with the idea of vengeance on the second mate. On divers occasions, now, I have come unexpectedly upon him and found him muttering to himself with grim set face, or clenching and unclenching his big square fists and grinding his teeth. His conversation continually runs upon the feasibility of our making a night attack for'ard, and he is perpetually questioning Tom

Spink and Louis on their ideas of where the various men may be sleeping—the point of which always is: *Where is the second mate likely to be sleeping?*

No later than yesterday afternoon did he give me most positive proof of his obsession. It was four o'clock, the beginning of the first dog-watch, and he had just relieved me. So careless have we grown, that we now stand in broad daylight at the exposed break of the poop. Nobody shoots at us, and, occasionally, over the top of the for'ard-house, Shorty sticks up his head and grins or makes clownish faces at us. At such times Mr. Pike studies Shorty's features through the telescope in an effort to find signs of starvation. Yet he admits dolefully that Shorty is looking fleshed-up.

But to return. Mr. Pike had just relieved me yesterday afternoon, when the second mate climbed the forecastle-head and sauntered to the very eyes of the *Elsinore*, where he stood gazing overside.

"Take a crack at 'm," Mr. Pike said.

It was a long shot, and I was taking slow and careful aim, when he touched my arm.

"No; don't," he said.

I lowered the little rifle and looked at him inquiringly.

"You might hit him," he explained. "And I want him for myself."

* * * * *

Life is never what we expect it to be. All our voyage from Baltimore south to the Horn and around the Horn has been marked by violence and death. And now that it has culminated in open mutiny there is no more violence, much less death. We keep to ourselves aft, and the mutineers keep to themselves for'ard. There is no more harshness, no more snarling and bellowing of commands; and in this fine weather a general festival obtains.

Aft, Mr. Pike and Margaret alternate with phonograph and piano; and for'ard, although we cannot see them, a full-fledged "foo-foo" band makes most of the day and night hideous. A squealing accordion that Tom Spink says was the property of Mike Cipriani is played by Guido Bombini, who sets the pace and seems the leader of the foo-foo. There are two broken-reeded harmonicas. Someone plays a jew's-harp. Then there are home-made fifes and whistles and drums, combs covered with paper, extemporized triangles, and bones made from ribs of salt horse such as negro minstrels use.

The whole crew seems to compose the band, and, like a lot of monkey-folk rejoicing in rude rhythm, emphasizes the beat by hammering kerosene cans, frying-pans, and all sorts of things metallic or reverberant. Some genius has rigged a line to the clapper of the ship's bell on the forecastle-head and clangs it horribly in the big foo-foo crises, though Bombini can be heard censuring him severely on occasion. And to cap it all, the fog-horn machine pumps in at the oddest moments in imitation of a big bass viol.

And this is mutiny on the high seas! Almost every hour of my deck-watches I listen to this infernal din, and am maddened into desire to join with Mr. Pike in a night attack and put these rebellious and inharmonious slaves to work.

Yet they are not entirely inharmonious. Guido Bombini has a respectable though untrained tenor voice, and has surprised me by a variety of selections, not only from Verdi, but from Wagner and Massenet. Bert Rhine and his crowd are full of rag-time junk, and one phrase that has caught the fancy of all hands, and which they roar out at all times, is: "*It's a bear*! *It's a bear*! *It's a bear*!" This morning Nancy, evidently very strongly urged, gave a doleful rendering of *Flying Cloud*. Yes, and in the second dog-watch last evening our three topaz-eyed dreamers sang some folk-song strangely sweet and sad.

And this is mutiny! As I write I can scarcely believe it. Yet I know Mr. Pike keeps the watch over my head. I hear the shrill laughter of the steward and Louis over some ancient Chinese joke. Wada and the sail-makers, in the pantry, are, I know, talking Japanese politics. And from across the cabin, along the narrow halls, I can hear Margaret softly humming as she goes to bed.

But all doubts vanish at the stroke of eight bells, when I go on deck to relieve Mr. Pike, who lingers a moment for a "gain," as he calls it.

413

"Say," he said confidentially, "you and I can clean out the whole gang. All we got to do is sneak for'ard and turn loose. As soon as we begin to shoot up, half of 'em'll bolt aft—lobsters like Nancy, an' Sundry Buyers, an' Jacobsen, an' Bob, an' Shorty, an' them three castaways, for instance. An' while they're doin' that, an' our bunch on the poop is takin' 'em in, you an' me can make a pretty big hole in them that's left. What d'ye say?"

I hesitated, thinking of Margaret.

"Why, say," he urged, "once I jumped into that fo'c's'le, at close range, I'd start right in, blim-blam-blim, fast as you could wink, nailing them gangsters, an' Bombini, an' the Sheeny, an' Deacon, an' the Cockney, an' Mulligan Jacobs, an' . . . an' . . . Waltham."

"That would be mine," I smiled. "You've only eight shots in your Colt."

Mr. Pike considered a moment, and revised his list. "All right," he agreed, "I guess I'll have to let Jacobs go. What d'ye say? Are you game?"

Still I hesitated, but before I could speak he anticipated me and returned to his fidelity.

"No, you can't do it, Mr. Pathurst. If by any luck they got the both of us . . . No; we'll just stay aft and sit tight until they're starved to it . . . But where they get their tucker gets me. For'ard she's as bare as a bone, as any decent ship ought to be, and yet look at 'em, rolling hog fat. And by rights they ought to a-quit eatin' a week ago."

CHAPTER XLIV

Yes, it is certainly mutiny. Collecting water from the leaders of the chart-house in a shower of rain this morning, Buckwheat exposed himself, and a long, lucky revolver-shot from for'ard caught him in the shoulder. The bullet was small-calibre and spent ere it reached him, so that he received no more than a flesh-wound, though he carried on as if he were dying until Mr. Pike hushed his noise by cuffing his ears.

I should not like to have Mr. Pike for my surgeon. He probed for the bullet with his little finger, which was far too big for the aperture; and with his little finger, while with his other hand he threatened another ear-clout, he gouged out the leaden pellet. Then he sent the boy below, where Margaret took him in charge with antiseptics and dressings.

I see her so rarely that a half-hour alone with her these days is an adventure. She is busy morning to night in keeping her house in order. As I write this, through my open door I can hear her laying the law down to the men in the after-room. She has issued underclothes all around from the slop-chest, and is ordering them to take a bath in the rain-water just caught. And to make sure of their thoroughness in the matter, she has told off Louis and the steward to supervise the operation. Also, she has forbidden them smoking their pipes in the after-room. And, to cap everything, they are to scrub walls, ceiling, everything, and then start to-morrow morning at painting. All of which serves to convince me almost that mutiny does not obtain and that I have imagined it.

But no. I hear Buckwheat blubbering and demanding how he can take a bath in his wounded condition. I wait and listen for Margaret's judgment. Nor am I disappointed. Tom Spink and Henry are told off to the task, and the thorough scrubbing of Buckwheat is assured.

* * * * *

The mutineers are not starving. To-day they have been fishing for albatrosses. A few minutes after they caught the first one its carcase was flung overboard. Mr. Pike studied it through his sea-glasses, and I heard him grit his teeth when he made certain that it was not the mere feathers and skin but the entire carcase. They had taken only its wing-bones to make into pipe-stems. The inference was obvious: *starving men would not throw meat away in such fashion.*

But where do they get their food? It is a sea-mystery in itself, although I might not so deem it were it not for Mr. Pike.

"I think, and think, till my brain is all frazzled out," he tells me; "and yet I can't get a line on it. I know every inch of space on the *Elsinore*, and know there isn't an ounce of grub anywhere for'ard, and yet they eat! I've overhauled the lazarette. As near as I can make it out, nothing is missing. Then where do they get it? That's what I want to know. Where do they get it?"

I know that this morning he spent hours in the lazarette with the steward and the cook, overhauling and checking off from the lists of the Baltimore agents. And I know that they came up out of the lazarette, the three of them, dripping with perspiration and baffled. The steward has raised the hypothesis that, first of all, there were extra stores left over from the previous voyage, or from previous voyages, and, next, that the stealing of these stores must have taken place during the night-watches when it was Mr. Pike's turn below.

At any rate, the mate takes the food mystery almost as much to heart as he takes the persistent and propinquitous existence of Sidney Waltham.

I am coming to realize the meaning of watch-and-watch. To begin with, I spend on deck twelve hours, and a fraction more, of each twenty-four. A fair portion of the remaining twelve is spent in eating, in dressing, and in undressing, and with Margaret. As a result, I feel the need for more sleep than I am getting. I scarcely read at all, now. The moment my head touches the pillow I am asleep. Oh, I sleep like a baby, eat like a navvy, and in years have not enjoyed such physical well-being. I tried to read George Moore last night, and was dreadfully bored. He may be a realist, but I solemnly aver he does not know reality on that tight, little, sheltered-life archipelago of his. If he could wind-jam around the Horn just one voyage he would be twice the writer.

And Mr. Pike, for practically all of his sixty-nine years, has stood his watch-and-watch, with many a spill-over of watches into watches. And yet he is iron. In a struggle with him I am confident that he would break me like so much straw. He is truly a prodigy of a man, and, so far as to-day is concerned, an anachronism.

The Faun is not dead, despite my unlucky bullet. Henry insisted that he caught a glimpse of him yesterday. To-day I saw him myself. He came to the corner of the 'midship-house and gazed wistfully aft at the poop, straining and eager to understand. In the same way I have often seen Possum gaze at me.

It has just struck me that of our eight followers five are Asiatic and only three are our own breed. Somehow it reminds me of India and of Clive and Hastings.

And the fine weather continues, and we wonder how long a time must elapse ere our mutineers eat up their mysterious food and are starved back to work.

We are almost due west of Valparaiso and quite a bit less than a thousand miles off the west coast of South America. The light northerly breezes, varying from north-east to west, would, according to Mr. Pike, work us in nicely for Valparaiso if only we had sail on the *Elsinore*. As it is, sailless, she drifts around and about and makes nowhere save for the slight northerly drift each day.

* * * * *

Mr. Pike is beside himself. In the past two days he has displayed increasing possession of himself by the one idea of vengeance on the second mate. It is not the mutiny, irksome as it is and helpless as it makes him; it is the presence of the murderer of his old-time and admired skipper, Captain Somers.

The mate grins at the mutiny, calls it a snap, speaks gleefully of how his wages are running up, and regrets that he is not ashore, where he would be able to take a hand in gambling on the reinsurance. But the sight of Sidney Waltham, calmly gazing at sea and sky from the forecastle-head, or astride the far end of the bowsprit and fishing for sharks, saddens him. Yesterday, coming to relieve me, he borrowed my rifle and turned loose the stream of tiny pellets on the second mate, who coolly made his line secure ere he scrambled inboard. Of course, it was only one chance in a hundred that Mr. Pike might have hit him, but Sidney Waltham did not care to encourage the chance.

417

And yet it is not like mutiny—not like the conventional mutiny I absorbed as a boy, and which has become classic in the literature of the sea. There is no hand-to-hand fighting, no crash of cannon and flash of cutlass, no sailors drinking grog, no lighted matches held over open powder-magazines. Heavens!—there isn't a single cutlass nor a powder-magazine on board. And as for grog, not a man has had a drink since Baltimore.

* * * * *

Well, it is mutiny after all. I shall never doubt it again. It may be nineteen-thirteen mutiny on a coal-carrier, with feeblings and imbeciles and criminals for mutineers; but at any rate mutiny it is, and at least in the number of deaths it is reminiscent of the old days. For things have happened since last I had opportunity to write up this log. For that matter, I am now the keeper of the *Elsinore's* official log as well, in which work Margaret helps me.

And I might have known it would happen. At four yesterday morning I relieved Mr. Pike. When in the darkness I came up to him at the break of the poop, I had to speak to him twice to make him aware of my presence. And then he merely grunted acknowledgment in an absent sort of way.

The next moment he brightened up, and was himself save that he was too bright. He was making an effort. I felt this, but was quite unprepared for what followed.

"I'll be back in a minute," he said, as he put his leg over the rail and lightly and swiftly lowered himself down into the darkness.

There was nothing I could do. To cry out or to attempt to reason with him would only have drawn the mutineers' attention. I heard his feet strike the deck beneath as he let go. Immediately he started for'ard. Little enough precaution he took. I swear that clear to the 'midship-house I heard the dragging age-lag of his feet. Then that ceased, and that was all.

I repeat. That was all. Never a sound came from for'ard. I held my watch till daylight. I held it till Margaret came on deck with her cheery "What ho of the night, brave mariner?" I held the next watch (which should have been the mate's) till midday, eating both breakfast and lunch behind

418

the sheltering jiggermast. And I held all afternoon, and through both dog-watches, my dinner served likewise on the deck.

And that was all. Nothing happened. The galley-stove smoked three times, advertising the cooking of three meals. Shorty made faces at me as usual across the rim of the for'ard-house. The Maltese Cockney caught an albatross. There was some excitement when Tony the Greek hooked a shark off the jib-boom, so big that half a dozen tailed on to the line and failed to land it. But I caught no glimpse of Mr. Pike nor of the renegade Sidney Waltham.

In short, it was a lazy, quiet day of sunshine and gentle breeze. There was no inkling to what had happened to the mate. Was he a prisoner? Was he already overside? Why were there no shots? He had his big automatic. It is inconceivable that he did not use it at least once. Margaret and I discussed the affair till we were well a-weary, but reached no conclusion.

She is a true daughter of the race. At the end of the second dog-watch, armed with her father's revolver, she insisted on standing the first watch of the night. I compromised with the inevitable by having Wada make up my bed on the deck in the shelter of the cabin skylight just for'ard of the jiggermast. Henry, the two sail-makers and the steward, variously equipped with knives and clubs, were stationed along the break of the poop.

And right here I wish to pass my first criticism on modern mutiny. On ships like the *Elsinore* there are not enough weapons to go around. The only firearms now aft are Captain West's .38 Colt revolver, and my .22 automatic Winchester. The old steward, with a penchant for hacking and chopping, has his long knife and a butcher's cleaver. Henry, in addition to his sheath-knife, has a short bar of iron. Louis, despite a most sanguinary array of butcher-knives and a big poker, pins his cook's faith on hot water and sees to it that two kettles are always piping on top the cabin stove. Buckwheat, who on account of his wound is getting all night in for a couple of nights, cherishes a hatchet.

419

The rest of our retainers have knives and clubs, although Yatsuda, the first sail-maker, carries a hand-axe, and Uchino, the second sail-maker, sleeping or waking, never parts from a claw-hammer. Tom Spink has a harpoon. Wada, however, is the genius. By means of the cabin stove he has made a sharp pike-point of iron and fitted it to a pole. To-morrow be intends to make more for the other men.

It is rather shuddery, however, to speculate on the terrible assortment of cutting, gouging, jabbing and slashing weapons with which the mutineers are able to equip themselves from the carpenter's shop. If it ever comes to an assault on the poop there will be a weird mess of wounds for the survivors to dress. For that matter, master as I am of my little rifle, no man could gain the poop in the day-time. Of course, if rush they will, they will rush us in the night, when my rifle will be worthless. Then it will be blow for blow, hand-to-hand, and the strongest pates and arms will win.

But no. I have just bethought me. We shall be ready for any night-rush. I'll take a leaf out of modern warfare, and show them not only that we are top-dog (a favourite phrase of the mate), but *why* we are top-dog. It is simple—night illumination. As I write I work opt the idea—gasoline, balls of oakum, caps and gunpowder from a few cartridges, Roman candles, and flares blue, red, and green, shallow metal receptacles to carry the explosive and inflammable stuff; and a trigger-like arrangement by which, pulling on a string, the caps are exploded in the gunpowder and fire set to the gasoline-soaked oakum and to the flares and candles. It will be brain as well as brawn against mere brawn.

* * * * *

I have worked like a Trojan all day, and the idea is realized. Margaret helped me out with suggestions, and Tom Spink did the sailorizing. Over our head, from the jiggermast, the steel stays that carry the three jigger-trysails descend high above the break of the poop and across the main deck to the mizzenmast. A light line has been thrown over each stay, and been thrown repeatedly around so as to form an unslipping knot. Tom Spink waited till dark, when he went aloft and attached loose rings of stiff wire around the stays

420

below the knots. Also he bent on hoisting-gear and connected permanent fastenings with the sliding rings. And further, between rings and fastenings, is a slack of fifty feet of light line.

This is the idea: after dark each night we shall hoist our three metal wash-basins, loaded with inflammables, up to the stays. The arrangement is such that at the first alarm of a rush, by pulling a cord the trigger is pulled that ignites the powder, and the very same pull operates a trip-device that lets the rings slide down the steel stays. Of course, suspended from the rings, are the illuminators, and when they have run down the stays fifty feet the lines will automatically bring them to rest. Then all the main deck between the poop and the mizzen-mast will be flooded with light, while we shall be in comparative darkness.

Of course each morning before daylight we shall lower all this apparatus to the deck, so that the men for'ard will not guess what we have up our sleeve, or, rather, what we have up on the trysail-stays. Even to-day the little of our gear that has to be left standing aroused their curiosity. Head after head showed over the edge of the for'ard-house as they peeped and peered and tried to make out what we were up to. Why, I find myself almost looking forward to an attack in order to see the device work.

CHAPTER XLV

And what has happened to Mr. Pike remains a mystery. For that matter, what has happened to the second mate? In the past three days we have by our eyes taken the census of the mutineers. Every man has been seen by us with the sole exception of Mr. Mellaire, or Sidney Waltham, as I assume I must correctly name him. He has not appeared—does not appear; and we can only speculate and conjecture.

In the past three days various interesting things have taken place. Margaret stands watch and watch with me, day and night, the clock around; for there is no one of our retainers to whom we can entrust the responsibility of a watch. Though mutiny obtains and we are besieged in the high place, the weather is so mild and there is so little call on our men that they have grown careless and sleep aft of the chart-house when it is their watch on deck. Nothing ever happens, and, like true sailors, they wax fat and lazy. Even have I found Louis, the steward, and Wada guilty of cat-napping. In fact, the training-ship boy, Henry, is the only one who has never lapsed.

Oh, yes, and I gave Tom Spink a thrashing yesterday. Since the disappearance of the mate he had had little faith in me, and had been showing vague signs of insolence and insubordination. Both Margaret and I had noted it independently. Day before yesterday we talked it over.

"He is a good sailor, but weak," she said. "If we let him go on, he will infect the rest."

"Very well, I'll take him in hand," I announced valorously.

"You will have to," she encouraged. "Be hard. Be hard. You must be hard."

Those who sit in the high places must be hard, yet have I discovered that it is hard to be hard. For instance, easy enough was it to drop Steve Roberts as he was in the act of shooting at me. Yet it is most difficult to be hard with a chuckle-headed retainer like Tom Spink—especially when he continually fails by a shade to give sufficient provocation. For twenty-four hours after my talk with Margaret I was on pins and needles to have it out with him, yet rather than have had it out with him I should have preferred to see the poop rushed by the gang from the other side.

Not in a day can the tyro learn to employ the snarling immediacy of mastery of Mr. Pike, nor the reposeful, voiceless mastery of a Captain West. Truly, the situation was embarrassing. I was not trained in the handling of men, and Tom Spink knew it in his chuckle-headed way. Also, in his chuckle-headed way, he was dispirited by the loss of the mate. Fearing the mate, nevertheless he had depended on the mate to fetch him through with a whole skin, or at least alive. On me he has no dependence. What chance had the gentleman passenger and the captain's daughter against the gang for'ard? So he must have reasoned, and, so reasoning, become despairing and desperate.

After Margaret had told me to be hard I watched Tom Spink with an eagle eye, and he must have sensed my attitude, for he carefully forebore from overstepping, while all the time he palpitated just on the edge of overstepping. Yes, and it was clear that Buckwheat was watching to learn the outcome of this veiled refractoriness. For that matter, the situation was not being missed by our keen-eyed Asiatics, and I know that I caught Louis several times verging on the offence of offering me advice. But he knew his place and managed to keep his tongue between his teeth.

At last, yesterday, while I held the watch, Tom Spink was guilty of spitting tobacco juice on the deck.

Now it must be understood that such an act is as grave an offence of the sea as blasphemy is of the Church.

It was Margaret who came to where I was stationed by the jiggermast and told me what had occurred; and it was she who took my rifle and relieved me so that I could go aft.

There was the offensive spot, and there was Tom Spink, his cheek bulging with a quid.

"Here, you, get a swab and mop that up," I commanded in my harshest manner.

Tom Spink merely rolled his quid with his tongue and regarded me with sneering thoughtfulness. I am sure he was no more surprised than was I by the immediateness of what followed. My fist went out like an arrow from a released bow, and Tom Spink staggered back, tripped against the corner of the tarpaulin-covered sounding-machine, and sprawled on the deck. He tried to make a fight of it, but I followed him up, giving him no chance to set himself or recover from the surprise of my first onslaught.

Now it so happens that not since I was a boy have I struck a person with my naked fist, and I candidly admit that I enjoyed the trouncing I administered to poor Tom Spink. Yes, and in the rapid play about the deck I caught a glimpse of Margaret. She had stepped out of the shelter of the mast and was looking on from the corner of the chart-house. Yes, and more; she was looking on with a cool, measuring eye.

Oh, it was all very grotesque, to be sure. But then, mutiny on the high seas in the year nineteen-thirteen is also grotesque. No lists here between mailed knights for a lady's favour, but merely the trouncing of a chuckle-head for spitting on the deck of a coal-carrier. Nevertheless, the fact that my lady looked on added zest to my enterprise, and, doubtlessly, speed and weight to my blows, and at least half a dozen additional clouts to the unlucky sailor.

Yes, man is strangely and wonderfully made. Now that I coolly consider the matter, I realize that it was essentially the same spirit with which I enjoyed beating up Tom Spink, that I have in the past enjoyed contests of the mind in which I have out-epigrammed clever opponents. In the one case, one proves himself top-dog of the mind; in the other, top-dog of the muscle. Whistler and Wilde were just as much intellectual bullies as I was a physical bully yesterday morning when I punched Tom Spink into lying down and staying down.

And my knuckles are sore and swollen. I cease writing for a moment to look at them and to hope that they will not stay permanently enlarged.

At any rate, Tom Spink took his disciplining and promised to come in and be good.

"Sir!" I thundered at him, quite in Mr. Pike's most bloodthirsty manner.

"Sir," he mumbled with bleeding lips. "Yes, sir, I'll mop it up, sir. Yes, sir."

I could scarcely keep from laughing in his face, the whole thing was so ludicrous; but I managed to look my haughtiest, and sternest, and fiercest, while I superintended the deck-cleansing. The funniest thing about the affair was that I must have knocked Tom Spink's quid down his throat, for he was gagging and hiccoughing all the time he mopped and scrubbed.

The atmosphere aft has been wonderfully clear ever since. Tom Spink obeys all orders on the jump, and Buckwheat jumps with equal celerity. As for the five Asiatics, I feel that they are stouter behind me now that I have shown masterfulness. By punching a man's face I verily believe I have doubled our united strength. And there is no need to punch any of the rest. The Asiatics are keen and willing. Henry is a true cadet of the breed, Buckwheat will follow Tom Spink's lead, and Tom Spink, a proper Anglo-Saxon peasant, will lead Buckwheat all the better by virtue of the punching.

* * * * *

Two days have passed, and two noteworthy things have happened. The men seem to be nearing the end of their mysterious food supply, and we have had our first truce.

I have noted, through the glasses, that no more carcasses of the mollyhawks they are now catching are thrown overboard. This means that they have begun to eat the tough and unsavoury creatures, although it does not mean, of course, that they have entirely exhausted their other stores.

It was Margaret, her sailor's eye on the falling barometer and on the "making" stuff adrift in the sky, who called my attention to a coming blow.

"As soon as the sea rises," she said, "we'll have that loose main-yard and all the rest of the top-hamper tumbling down on deck."

So it was that I raised the white flag for a parley. Bert Rhine and Charles Davis came abaft the 'midship-house, and, while we talked, many faces peered over the for'ard edge of the house and many forms slouched into view on the deck on each side of the house.

"Well, getting tired?" was Bert Rhine's insolent greeting. "Anything we can do for you?"

"Yes, there is," I answered sharply. "You can save your heads so that when you return to work there will be enough of you left to do the work."

"If you are making threats—" Charles Davis began, but was silenced by a glare from the gangster.

"Well, what is it?" Bert Rhine demanded. "Cough it off your chest."

"It's for your own good," was my reply. "It is coming on to blow, and all that unfurled canvas aloft will bring the yards down on your heads. We're safe here, aft. You are the ones who will run risks, and it is up to you to hustle your crowd aloft and make things fast and ship-shape."

"And if we don't?" the gangster sneered.

"Why, you'll take your chances, that is all," I answered carelessly. "I just want to call your attention to the fact that one of those steel yards, end-on, will go through the roof of your forecastle as if it were so much eggshell."

Bert Rhine looked to Charles Davis for verification, and the latter nodded.

"We'll talk it over first," the gangster announced.

"And I'll give you ten minutes," I returned. "If at the end of ten minutes you've not started taking in, it will be too late. I shall put a bullet into any man who shows himself."

"All right, we'll talk it over."

As they started to go back, I called:

"One moment."

They stopped and turned about.

"What have you done to Mr. Pike?" I asked.

Even the impassive Bert Rhine could not quite conceal his surprise.

"An' what have you done with Mr. Mellaire!" he retorted. "You tell us, an' we'll tell you."

I am confident of the genuineness of his surprise. Evidently the mutineers have been believing us guilty of the disappearance of the second mate, just as we have been believing them guilty of the disappearance of the first mate. The more I dwell upon it the more it seems the proposition of the Kilkenny cats, a case of mutual destruction on the part of the two mates.

"Another thing," I said quickly. "Where do you get your food?"

Bert Rhine laughed one of his silent laughs; Charles Davis assumed an expression of mysteriousness and superiority; and Shorty, leaping into view from the corner of the house, danced a jig of triumph.

I drew out my watch.

"Remember," I said, "you've ten minutes in which to make a start."

They turned and went for'ard, and, before the ten minutes were up, all hands were aloft and stowing canvas. All this time the wind, out of the north-west, was breezing up. The old familiar harp-chords of a rising gale were strumming along the rigging, and the men, I verily believe from lack of practice, were particularly slow at their work.

"It would be better if the upper-and-lower top-sails are set so that we can heave to," Margaret suggested. "They will steady her and make it more comfortable for us."

I seized the idea and improved upon it.

"Better set the upper and lower topsails so that we can handle the ship," I called to the gangster, who was ordering the men about, quite like a mate, from the top of the 'midship-house.

He considered the idea, and then gave the proper orders, although it was the Maltese Cockney, with Nancy and Sundry Buyers under him, who carried the orders out.

I ordered Tom Spink to the long-idle wheel, and gave him the course, which was due east by the steering compass. This put the wind on our port quarter, so that the *Elsinore* began to move through the water before a fair breeze. And due east, less than a thousand miles away, lay the coast of South America and the port of Valparaiso.

Strange to say, none of our mutineers objected to this, and after dark, as we tore along before a full-sized gale, I sent my own men up on top the chart-house to take the gaskets off the spanker. This was the only sail we could

427

set and trim and in every way control. It is true the mizzen-braces were still rigged aft to the poop, according to Horn practice. But, while we could thus trim the mizzen-yards, the sails themselves, in setting or furling, were in the hands of the for'ard crowd.

Margaret, beside me in the darkness at the break of the poop, put her hand in mine with a warm pressure, as both our tiny watches swayed up the spanker and as both of us held our breaths in an effort to feel the added draw in the *Elsinore*'s speed.

"I never wanted to marry a sailor," she said. "And I thought I was safe in the hands of a landsman like you. And yet here you are, with all the stuff of the sea in you, running down your easting for port. Next thing, I suppose, I'll see you out with a sextant, shooting the sun or making star-observations."

CHAPTER XLVI

Four more days have passed; the gale has blown itself out; we are not more than three hundred and fifty miles off Valparaiso; and the *Elsinore*, this time due to me and my own stubbornness, is rolling in the wind and heading nowhere in a light breeze at the rate of nothing but driftage per hour.

In the height of the gusts, in the three days and nights of the gale, we logged as much as eight, and even nine, knots. What bothered me was the acquiescence of the mutineers in my programme. They were sensible enough in the simple matter of geography to know what I was doing. They had control of the sails, and yet they permitted me to run for the South American coast.

More than that, as the gale eased on the morning of the third day, they actually went aloft, set top-gallant-sails, royals, and skysails, and trimmed the yards to the quartering breeze. This was too much for the Saxon streak in me, whereupon I wore the *Elsinore* about before the wind, fetched her up upon it, and lashed the wheel. Margaret and I are agreed in the hypothesis that their plan is to get inshore until land is sighted, at which time they will desert in the boats.

"But we don't want them to desert," she proclaims with flashing eyes. "We are bound for Seattle. They must return to duty. They've got to, soon, for they are beginning to starve."

"There isn't a navigator aft," I oppose.

Promptly she withers me with her scorn.

"You, a master of books, by all the sea-blood in your body should be able to pick up the theoretics of navigation while I snap my fingers. Furthermore, remember that I can supply the seamanship. Why, any squarehead peasant, in a six months' cramming course at any seaport navigation school, can pass the examiners for his navigator's papers. That means six hours for you. And less. If you can't, after an hour's reading and an hour's practice with the sextant, take a latitude observation and work it out, I'll do it for you."

"You mean you know?"

She shook her head.

"I mean, from the little I know, that I know I can learn to know a meridian sight and the working out of it. I mean that I can learn to know inside of two hours."

Strange to say, the gale, after easing to a mild breeze, recrudesced in a sort of after-clap. With sails untrimmed and flapping, the consequent smashing, crashing, and rending of our gear can be imagined. It brought out in alarm every man for'ard.

"Trim the yards!" I yelled at Bert Rhine, who, backed for counsel by Charles Davis and the Maltese Cockney, actually came directly beneath me on the main deck in order to hear above the commotion aloft.

"Keep a-runnin', an' you won't have to trim," the gangster shouted up to me.

"Want to make land, eh?" I girded down at him. "Getting hungry, eh? Well, you won't make land or anything else in a thousand years once you get all your top-hamper piled down on deck."

I have forgotten to state that this occurred at midday yesterday.

"What are you goin' to do if we trim?" Charles Davis broke in.

"Run off shore," I replied, "and get your gang out in deep sea where it will be starved back to duty."

"We'll furl, an' let you heave to," the gangster proposed.

I shook my head and held up my rifle. "You'll have to go aloft to do it, and the first man that gets into the shrouds will get this."

"Then she can go to hell for all we care," he said, with emphatic conclusiveness.

And just then the fore-topgallant-yard carried away—luckily as the bow was down-pitched into a trough of sea-and when the slow, confused, and tangled descent was accomplished the big stick lay across the wreck of both bulwarks and of that portion of the bridge between the foremast and the forecastle head.

Bert Rhine heard, but could not see, the damage wrought. He looked up at me challengingly, and sneered:

"Want some more to come down?"

It could not have happened more apropos. The port-brace, and immediately afterwards the starboard-brace, of the crojack-yard—carried away. This was the big, lowest spar on the mizzen, and as the huge thing of steel swung wildly back and forth the gangster and his followers turned and crouched as they looked up to see. Next, the gooseneck of the truss, on which it pivoted, smashed away. Immediately the lifts and lower-topsail sheets parted, and with a fore-and-aft pitch of the ship the spar up-ended and crashed to the deck upon Number Three hatch, destroying that section of the bridge in its fall.

All this was new to the gangster—as it was to me—but Charles Davis and the Maltese Cockney thoroughly apprehended the situation.

"Stand out from under!" I yelled sardonically; and the three of them cowered and shrank away as their eyes sought aloft for what new spar was thundering down upon them.

The lower-topsail, its sheets parted by the fall of the crojack-yard, was tearing out of the bolt-ropes and ribboning away to leeward and making such an uproar that they might well expect its yard to carry away. Since this wreckage of our beautiful gear was all new to me, I was quite prepared to see the thing happen.

The gangster-leader, no sailor, but, after months at sea, intelligent enough and nervously strong enough to appreciate the danger, turned his head and looked up at me. And I will do him the credit to say that he took his time while all our world of gear aloft seemed smashing to destruction.

"I guess we'll trim yards," he capitulated.

"Better get the skysails and royals off," Margaret said in my ear.

"While you're about it, get in the skysails and royals!" I shouted down. "And make a decent job of the gasketing!"

Both Charles Davis and the Maltese Cockney advertised their relief in their faces as they heard my words, and, at a nod from the gangster, they started for'ard on the run to put the orders into effect.

Never, in the whole voyage, did our crew spring to it in more lively fashion. And lively fashion was needed to save our gear. As it was, they cut away the remnants of the mizzen-lower-topsail with their sheath-knives, and they loosed the main-skysail out of its bolt-ropes.

The first infraction of our agreement was on the main-lower-topsail. This they attempted to furl. The carrying away of the crojack and the blowing away of the mizzen-lower-topsail gave me freedom to see and aim, and when the tiny messengers from my rifle began to spat through the canvas and to spat against the steel of the yard, the men strung along it desisted from passing the gaskets. I waved my will to Bert Rhine, who acknowledged me and ordered the sail set again and the yard trimmed.

"What is the use of running off-shore?" I said to Margaret, when the kites were snugged down and all yards trimmed on the wind. "Three hundred and fifty miles off the land is as good as thirty-five hundred so far as starvation is concerned."

So, instead of making speed through the water toward deep sea, I hove the *Elsinore* to on the starboard tack with no more than leeway driftage to the west and south.

But our gallant mutineers had their will of us that very night. In the darkness we could hear the work aloft going on as yards were run down, sheets let go, and sails dewed up and gasketed. I did try a few random shots, and all my reward was to hear the whine and creak of ropes through sheaves and to receive an equally random fire of revolver-shots.

It is a most curious situation. We of the high place are masters of the steering of the *Elsinore*, while those for'ard are masters of the motor power. The only sail that is wholly ours is the spanker. They control absolutely—sheets, halyards, clewlines, buntlines, braces, and down-hauls—every sail on the fore and main. We control the braces on the mizzen, although they control the canvas on the mizzen. For that matter, Margaret and I fail to comprehend why they do not go aloft any dark night and sever the mizzen-braces at the yard-ends. All that prevents this, we are decided, is laziness. For if they did sever the braces that lead aft into our hands, they would be compelled to rig new braces for'ard in some fashion, else, in the rolling, would the mizzenmast be stripped of every spar.

And still the mutiny we are enduring is ridiculous and grotesque. There was never a mutiny like it. It violates all standards and precedents. In the old classic mutinies, long ere this, attacking like tigers, the seamen should have swarmed over the poop and killed most of us or been most of them killed.

Wherefore I sneer at our gallant mutineers, and recommend trained nurses for them, quite in the manner of Mr. Pike. But Margaret shakes her head and insists that human nature is human nature, and that under similar circumstances human nature will express itself similarly. In short, she points to the number of deaths that have already occurred, and declares that on some dark night, sooner or later, whenever the pinch of hunger sufficiently sharpens, we shall see our rascals storming aft.

And in the meantime, except for the tenseness of it, and for the incessant watchfulness which Margaret and I alone maintain, it is more like a mild adventure, more like a page out of some book of romance which ends happily.

It is surely romance, watch and watch for a man and a woman who love, to relieve each other's watches. Each such relief is a love passage and unforgettable. Never was there wooing like it—the muttered surmises of wind and weather, the whispered councils, the kissed commands in palms of hands, the dared contacts of the dark.

Oh, truly, I have often, since this voyage began, told the books to go hang. And yet the books are at the back of the race-life of me. I am what I am out of ten thousand generations of my kind. Of that there is no discussion. And yet my midnight philosophy stands the test of my breed. I must have selected my books out of the ten thousand generations that compose me. I have killed a man—Steve Roberts. As a perishing blond without an alphabet I should have done this unwaveringly. As a perishing blond with an alphabet, plus the contents in my brain of the philosophizing of all philosophers, I have killed this same man with the same unwaveringness. Culture has not emasculated me. I am quite unaffected. It was in the day's work, and my kind have always been day-workers, doing the day's work, whatever it might be, in high adventure or dull ploddingness, and always doing it.

Never would I ask to set back the dial of time or event. I would kill Steve Roberts again, under the same circumstances, as a matter of course. When I say I am unaffected by this happening I do not quite mean it. I am affected. I am aware that the spirit of me is informed with a sober elation of efficiency. I have done something that had to be done, as any man will do what has to be done in the course of the day's work.

Yes, I am a perishing blond, and a man, and I sit in the high place and bend the stupid ones to my will; and I am a lover, loving a royal woman of my own perishing breed, and together we occupy, and shall occupy, the high place of government and command until our kind perish from the earth.

CHAPTER XLVII

Margaret was right. The mutiny is not violating standards and precedents. We have had our hands full for days and nights. Ditman Olansen, the crank-eyed Berserker, has been killed by Wada, and the training-ship boy, the one lone cadet of our breed, has gone overside with the regulation sack of coal at his feet. The poop has been rushed. My illuminating invention has proved a success. The men are getting hungry, and we still sit in command in the high place.

First of all the attack on the poop, two nights ago, in Margaret's watch. No; first, I have made another invention. Assisted by the old steward, who knows, as a Chinese ought, a deal about fireworks, and getting my materials from our signal rockets and Roman candles, I manufactured half a dozen bombs. I don't really think they are very deadly, and I know our extemporized fuses are slower than our voyage is at the present time; but nevertheless the bombs have served the purpose, as you shall see.

And now to the attempt to rush the poop. It was in Margaret's watch, from midnight till four in the morning, when the attack was made. Sleeping on the deck by the cabin skylight, I was very close to her when her revolver went off, and continued to go off.

My first spring was to the tripping-lines on my illuminators. The igniting and releasing devices worked cleverly. I pulled two of the tripping-lines, and two of the contraptions exploded into light and noise and at the same time ran automatically down the jigger-trysail-stays, and automatically fetched up at the ends of their lines. The illumination was instantaneous and gorgeous. Henry, the two sail-makers, and the steward—at least three of them awakened from sound sleep, I am sure—ran to join us along the break of the poop. All the advantage lay with us, for we were in the dark, while our foes were outlined against the light behind them.

But such light! The powder crackled, fizzed, and spluttered and spilled out the excess of gasolene from the flaming oakum balls so that streams of fire dripped down on the main deck beneath. And the stuff of the signal-flares dripped red light and blue and green.

There was not much of a fight, for the mutineers were shocked by our fireworks. Margaret fired her revolver haphazardly, while I held my rifle for any that gained the poop. But the attack faded away as quickly as it had come. I did see Margaret overshoot some man, scaling the poop from the port-rail, and the next moment I saw Wada, charging like a buffalo, jab him in the chest with the spear he had made and thrust the boarder back and down.

That was all. The rest retreated for'ard on the dead run, while the three trysails, furled at the foot of the stays next to the mizzen and set on fire by the dripping gasolene, went up in flame and burned entirely away and out without setting the rest of the ship on fire. That is one of the virtues of a ship steel-masted and steel-stayed.

And on the deck beneath us, crumpled, twisted, face hidden so that we could not identify him, lay the man whom Wada had speared.

And now I come to a phase of adventure that is new to me. I have never found it in the books. In short, it is carelessness coupled with laziness, or vice versa. I had used two of my illuminators. Only one remained. An hour later, convinced of the movement aft of men along the deck, I let go the third and last and with its brightness sent them scurrying for'ard. Whether they were attacking the poop tentatively to learn whether or not I had exhausted my illuminators, or whether or not they were trying to rescue Ditman Olansen, we shall never know. The point is: they did come aft; they were compelled to retreat by my illuminator; and it was my last illuminator. And yet I did not start in, there and then, to manufacture fresh ones. This was carelessness. It was laziness. And I hazarded our lives, perhaps, if you please, on a psychological guess that I had convinced our mutineers that we had an inexhaustible stock of illuminators in reserve.

The rest of Margaret's watch, which I shared with her, was undisturbed. At four I insisted that she go below and turn in, but she compromised by taking my own bed behind the skylight.

At break of day I was able to make out the body, still lying as last I had seen it. At seven o'clock, before breakfast, and while Margaret still slept, I sent the two boys, Henry and Buckwheat, down to the body. I stood above them, at the rail, rifle in hand and ready. But from for'ard came no signs of life; and the lads, between them, rolled the crank-eyed Norwegian over so that we could recognize him, carried him to the rail, and shoved him stiffly across and into the sea. Wada's spear-thrust had gone clear through him.

But before twenty-four hours were up the mutineers evened the score handsomely. They more than evened it, for we are so few that we cannot so well afford the loss of one as they can. To begin with—and a thing I had anticipated and for which I had prepared my bombs—while Margaret and I ate a deck-breakfast in the shelter of the jiggermast a number of the men sneaked aft and got under the overhang of the poop. Buckwheat saw them coming and yelled the alarm, but it was too late. There was no direct way to get them out. The moment I put my head over the rail to fire at them, I knew they would fire up at me with all the advantage in their favour. They were hidden. I had to expose myself.

Two steel doors, tight-fastened and caulked against the Cape Horn seas, opened under the overhang of the poop from the cabin on to the main deck. These doors the men proceeded to attack with sledge-hammers, while the rest of the gang, sheltered by the 'midship-house, showed that it stood ready for the rush when the doors were battered down.

Inside, the steward guarded one door with his hacking knife, while with his spear Wada guarded the other door. Nor, while I had dispatched them to this duty, was I idle. Behind the jiggermast I lighted the fuse of one of my extemporized bombs. When it was sputtering nicely I ran across the poop to the break and dropped the bomb to the main deck beneath, at the same time making an effort to toss it in under the overhang where the men battered at the port-door. But this effort was distracted and made futile by a popping of several revolver shots from the gangways amidships. One *is* jumpy when soft-nosed bullets putt-putt around him. As a result, the bomb rolled about on the open deck.

Nevertheless, the illuminators had earned the respect of the mutineers for my fireworks. The sputtering and fizzling of the fuse were too much for them, and from under the poop they ran for'ard like so many scuttling rabbits. I know I could have got a couple with my rifle had I not been occupied with lighting the fuse of a second bomb. Margaret managed three wild shots with her revolver, and the poop was immediately peppered by a scattering revolver fire from for'ard.

Being provident (and lazy, for I have learned that it takes time and labour to manufacture home-made bombs), I pinched off the live end of the fuse in my hand. But the fuse of the first bomb, rolling about on the main deck, merely fizzled on; and as I waited I resolved to shorten my remaining fuses. Any of the men who fled, had he had the courage, could have pinched off the fuse, or tossed the bomb overboard, or, better yet, he could have tossed it up amongst us on the poop.

It took fully five minutes for that blessed fuse to burn its slow length, and when the bomb did go off it was a sad disappointment. I swear it could have been sat upon with nothing more than a jar to one's nerves. And yet, in so far as the intimidation goes, it did its work. The men have not since ventured under the overhang of the poop.

That the mutineers were getting short of food was patent. The *Elsinore*, sailless, drifted about that morning, the sport of wind and wave; and the gang put many lines overboard for the catching of mollyhawks and albatrosses. Oh, I worried the hungry fishers with my rifle. No man could show himself for'ard without having a bullet whop against the iron-work perilously near him. And still they caught birds—not, however, without danger to themselves, and not without numerous losses of birds due to my rifle.

Their procedure was to toss their hooks and bait over the rail from shelter and slowly to pay the lines out as the slight windage of the *Elsinore's* hull, spars, and rigging drifted her through the water. When a bird was hooked they hauled in the line, still from shelter, till it was alongside. This was the ticklish moment. The hook, merely a hollow and acute-angled triangle of sheet-copper floating on a piece of board at the end of the line, held the bird by pinching its curved beak into the acute angle. The moment the line slacked the bird was released. So, when alongside, this was the problem: to lift the bird out of the water, straight up the side of the ship, without once jamming and easing and slacking. When they tried to do this from shelter invariably they lost the bird.

They worked out a method. When the bird was alongside the several men with revolvers turned loose on me, while one man, overhauling and keeping the line taut, leaped to the rail and quickly hove the bird up and over and inboard. I know this long-distance revolver fire seriously bothered me. One cannot help jumping when death, in the form of a piece of flying lead, hits the rail beside him, or the mast over his head, or whines away in a ricochet from the steel shrouds. Nevertheless, I managed with my rifle to bother the exposed men on the rail to the extent that they lost one hooked bird out of two. And twenty-six men require a quantity of albatrosses and mollyhawks every twenty-four hours, while they can fish only in the daylight.

As the day wore along I improved on my obstructive tactics. When the *Elsinore* was up in the eye of the wind, and making sternway, I found that by putting the wheel sharply over, one way or the other, I could swing her bow off. Then, when she had paid off till the wind was abeam, by reversing the wheel hard across to the opposite hard-over I could take advantage of her momentum away from the wind and work her off squarely before it. This made all the wood-floated triangles of bird-snares tow aft along her sides.

The first time I was ready for them. With hooks and sinkers on our own lines aft, we tossed out, grappled, captured, and broke off nine of their lines. But the next time, so slow is the movement of so large a ship, the mutineers hauled all their lines safely inboard ere they towed aft within striking distance of my grapnels.

Still I improved. As long as I kept the *Elsinore* before the wind they could not fish. I experimented. Once before it, by means of a winged-out spanker coupled with patient and careful steering, I could keep her before it. This I did, hour by hour one of my men relieving another at the wheel. As a result all fishing ceased.

Margaret was holding the first dog-watch, four to six. Henry was at the wheel steering. Wada and Louis were below cooking the evening meal over the big coal-stove and the oil-burners. I had just come up from below and was standing beside the sounding-machine, not half a dozen feet from Henry at the wheel. Some obscure sound from the ventilator must have attracted me, for I was gazing at it when the thing happened.

But first, the ventilator. This is a steel shaft that leads up from the coal-carrying bowels of the ship beneath the lazarette and that wins to the outside-world via the after-wall of the chart-house. In fact, it occupies the hollow inside of the double walls of the afterwall of the chart-house. Its opening, at the height of a man's head, is screened with iron bars so closely set that no mature-bodied rat can squeeze between. Also, this opening commands the wheel, which is a scant fifteen feet away and directly across the booby-hatch. Some mutineer, crawling along the space between the coal and the deck of the lower hold, had climbed the ventilator shaft and was able to take aim through the slits between the bars.

Practically simultaneously, I saw the out-rush of smoke and heard the report. I heard a grunt from Henry, and, turning my head, saw him cling to the spokes and turn the wheel half a revolution as he sank to the deck. It must have been a lucky shot. The boy was perforated through the heart or very near to the heart—we have no time for post-mortems on the *Elsinore*.

Tom Spink and the second sail-maker, Uchino, sprang to Henry's side. The revolver continued to go off through the ventilator slits, and the bullets thudded into the front of the half wheel-house all about them. Fortunately they were not hit, and they immediately scrambled out of range. The boy quivered for the space of a few seconds, and ceased to move; and one more cadet of the perishing breed perished as he did his day's work at the wheel of the *Elsinore* off the west coast of South America, bound from Baltimore to Seattle with a cargo of coal.

CHAPTER XLVIII

The situation is hopelessly grotesque. We in the high place command the food of the *Elsinore*, but the mutineers have captured her steering-gear. That is to say, they have captured it without coming into possession of it. They cannot steer, neither can we. The poop, which is the high place, is ours. The wheel is on the poop, yet we cannot touch the wheel. From that slitted opening in the ventilator-shaft they are able to shoot down any man who approaches the wheel. And with that steel wall of the chart-house as a shield they laugh at us as from a conning tower.

I have a plan, but it is not worth while putting into execution unless its need becomes imperative. In the darkness of night it would be an easy trick to disconnect the steering-gear from the short tiller on the rudder-head, and then, by re-rigging the preventer tackles, steer from both sides of the poop well enough for'ard to be out of the range of the ventilator.

In the meantime, in this fine weather, the *Elsinore* drifts as she lists, or as the windage of her lists and the sea-movement of waves lists. And she can well drift. Let the mutineers starve. They can best be brought to their senses through their stomachs.

* * * * *

And what are wits for, if not for use? I am breaking the men's hungry hearts. It is great fun in its way. The mollyhawks and albatrosses, after their fashion, have followed the *Elsinore* up out of their own latitudes. This means that there are only so many of them and that their numbers are not recruited. Syllogism: major premise, a definite and limited amount of bird-meat; minor premise, the only food the mutineers now have is bird-meat; conclusion, destroy the available food and the mutineers will be compelled to come back to duty.

I have acted on this bit of logic. I began experimentally by tossing small chunks of fat pork and crusts of stale bread overside. When the birds descended for the feast I shot them. Every carcass thus left floating on the surface of the sea was so much less meat for the mutineers.

But I bettered the method. Yesterday I overhauled the medicine-chest, and I dosed my chunks of fat pork and bread with the contents of every bottle that bore a label of skull and cross-bones. I even added rough-on-rats to the deadliness of the mixture—this on the suggestion of the steward.

And to-day, behold, there is no bird left in the sky. True, while I played my game yesterday, the mutineers hooked a few of the birds; but now the rest are gone, and that is bound to be the last food for the men for'ard until they resume duty.

Yes; it is grotesque. It is a boy's game. It reads like Midshipman Easy, like Frank Mildmay, like Frank Reade, Jr.; and yet, i' faith, life and death's in the issue. I have just gone over the toll of our dead since the voyage began.

First, was Christian Jespersen, killed by O'Sullivan when that maniac aspired to throw overboard Andy Fay's sea-boots; then O'Sullivan, because he interfered with Charles Davis' sleep, brained by that worthy with a steel marlin-spike; next Petro Marinkovich, just ere we began the passage of the Horn, murdered undoubtedly by the gangster clique, his life cut out of him with knives, his carcass left lying on deck to be found by us and be buried by us; and the Samurai, Captain West, a sudden though not a violent death, albeit occurring in the midst of all elemental violence as Mr. Pike clawed the *Elsinore* off the lee-shore of the Horn; and Boney the Splinter, following, washed overboard to drown as we cleared the sea-gashing rock-tooth where the southern tip of the continent bit into the storm-wrath of the Antarctic; and the big-footed, clumsy youth of a Finnish carpenter, hove overside as a Jonah by his fellows who believed that Finns control the winds; and Mike Cipriani and Bill Quigley, Rome and Ireland, shot down on the poop and flung overboard alive by Mr. Pike, still alive and clinging to the log-line, cut adrift by the steward to be eaten alive by great-beaked albatrosses, mollyhawks, and sooty-plumaged Cape hens; Steve Roberts, one-time cowboy, shot by me as he tried to shoot me; Herman Lunkenheimer, his throat cut before all of us by the hound Bombini as Kid Twist stretched the throat taut from behind; the two mates, Mr. Pike and Mr. Mellaire, mutually destroying each other in what must have been an unwitnessed epic combat; Ditman Olansen, speared by Wada as he charged Berserk at the head of the mutineers in the attempt to rush the poop; and last, Henry, the cadet of the perishing house, shot at the wheel, from the ventilator-shaft, in the course of his day's work.

No; as I contemplate this roll-call of the dead which I have just made I see that we are not playing a boy's game. Why, we have lost a third of us, and the bloodiest battles of history have rarely achieved such a percentage of mortality. Fourteen of us have gone overside, and who can tell the end?

Nevertheless, here we are, masters of matter, adventurers in the micro-organic, planet-weighers, sun-analysers, star-rovers, god-dreamers, equipped with the human wisdom of all the ages, and yet, quoting Mr. Pike, to come down to brass tacks, we are a lot of primitive beasts, fighting bestially, slaying bestially, pursuing bestially food and water, air for our lungs, a dry space above the deep, and carcasses skin-covered and intact. And over this menagerie of beasts Margaret and I, with our Asiatics under us, rule top-dog. We are all dogs—there is no getting away from it. And we, the fair-pigmented ones, by the seed of our ancestry rulers in the high place, shall remain top-dog over the rest of the dogs. Oh, there is material in plenty for the cogitation of any philosopher on a windjammer in mutiny in this Year of our Lord 1913.

* * * * *

Henry was the fourteenth of us to go overside into the dark and salty disintegration of the sea. And in one day he has been well avenged; for two of the mutineers have followed him. The steward called my attention to what was taking place. He touched my arm half beyond his servant's self, as he gloated for'ard at the men heaving two corpses overside. Weighted with coal, they sank immediately, so that we could not identify them.

"They have been fighting," I said. "It is good that they should fight among themselves."

But the old Chinese merely grinned and shook his head.

"You don't think they have been fighting?" I queried.

"No fight. They eat'm mollyhawk and albatross; mollyhawk and albatross eat'm fat pork; two men he die, plenty men much sick, you bet, damn to hell me very much glad. I savve."

And I think he was right. While I was busy baiting the sea-birds the mutineers were catching them, and of a surety they must have caught some that had eaten of my various poisons.

The two poisoned ones went over the side yesterday. Since then we have taken the census. Two men only have not appeared, and they are Bob, the fat and overgrown feebling youth, and, of all creatures, the Faun. It seems my fate that I had to destroy the Faun—the poor, tortured Faun, always willing and eager, ever desirous to please. There is a madness of ill luck in all this. Why couldn't the two dead men have been Charles Davis and Tony the Greek? Or Bert Rhine and Kid Twist? or Bombini and Andy Fay? Yes, and in my heart I know I should have felt better had it been Isaac Chantz and Arthur Deacon, or Nancy and Sundry Buyers, or Shorty and Larry.

* * * * *

The steward has just tendered me a respectful bit of advice.

"Next time we chuck'm overboard like Henry, much better we use old iron."

"Getting short of coal?" I asked.

He nodded affirmation. We use a great deal of coal in our cooking, and when the present supply gives out we shall have to cut through a bulkhead to get at the cargo.

CHAPTER XLIX

443

The situation grows tense. There are no more sea-birds, and the mutineers are starving. Yesterday I talked with Bert Rhine. To-day I talked with him again, and he will never forget, I am certain, the little talk we had this morning.

To begin with, last evening, at five o'clock, I heard his voice issuing from between the slits of the ventilator in the after-wall of the chart-house. Standing at the corner of the house, quite out of range, I answered him.

"Getting hungry?" I jeered. "Let me tell you what we are going to have for dinner. I have just been down and seen the preparations. Now, listen: first, caviare on toast; then, clam bouillon; and creamed lobster; and tinned lamb chops with French peas—you know, the peas that melt in one's mouth; and California asparagus with mayonnaise; and—oh, I forgot to mention fried potatoes and cold pork and beans; and peach pie; and coffee, real coffee. Doesn't it make you hungry for your East Side? And, say, think of the free lunch going to waste right now in a thousand saloons in good old New York."

I had told him the truth. The dinner I described (principally coming out of tins and bottles, to be sure) was the dinner we were to eat.

"Cut that," he snarled. "I want to talk business *with you.*"

"Right down to brass tacks," I gibed. "Very well, when are you and the rest of your rats going to turn to?"

"Cut that," he reiterated. "I've got you where I want you now. Take it from me, I'm givin' it straight. I'm not tellin' you how, but I've got you under my thumb. When I come down on you, you'll crack."

"Hell is full of cocksure rats like you," I retorted; although I never dreamed how soon he would be writhing in the particular hell preparing for him.

"Forget it," he sneered back. "I've got you where I want you. I'm just tellin' you, that's all."

"Pardon me," I replied, "when I tell you that I'm from Missouri. You'll have to show *me.*"

And as I thus talked the thought went through my mind of how I naturally sought out the phrases of his own vocabulary in order to make myself intelligible to him. The situation was bestial, with sixteen of our complement already gone into the dark; and the terms I employed, perforce, were terms of bestiality. And I thought, also, of I who was thus compelled to dismiss the dreams of the utopians, the visions of the poets, the king-thoughts of the king-thinkers, in a discussion with this ripened product of the New York City inferno. To him I must talk in the elemental terms of life and death, of food and water, of brutality and cruelty.

"I give you your choice," he went on. "Give in now, an' you won't be hurt, none of you."

"And if we don't?" I dared airily.

"You'll be sorry you was ever born. You ain't a mush-head, you've got a girl there that's stuck on you. It's about time you think of her. You ain't altogether a mutt. You get my drive?"

Ay, I did get it; and somehow, across my brain flashed a vision of all I had ever read and heard of the siege of the Legations at Peking, and of the plans of the white men for their womenkind in the event of the yellow hordes breaking through the last lines of defence. Ay, and the old steward got it; for I saw his black eyes glint murderously in their narrow, tilted slits. He knew the drift of the gangster's meaning.

"You get my drive?" the gangster repeated.

And I knew anger. Not ordinary anger, but cold anger. And I caught a vision of the high place in which we had sat and ruled down the ages in all lands, on all seas. I saw my kind, our women with us, in forlorn hopes and lost endeavours, pent in hill fortresses, rotted in jungle fastnesses, cut down to the last one on the decks of rocking ships. And always, our women with us, had we ruled the beasts. We might die, our women with us; but, living, we had ruled. It was a royal vision I glimpsed. Ay, and in the purple of it I grasped the ethic, which was the stuff of the fabric of which it was builded. It was the sacred trust of the seed, the bequest of duty handed down from all ancestors.

And I flamed more coldly. It was not red-brute anger. It was intellectual. It was based on concept and history; it was the philosophy of action of the strong and the pride of the strong in their own strength. Now at last I knew Nietzsche. I knew the rightness of the books, the relation of high thinking to high-conduct, the transmutation of midnight thought into action in the high place on the poop of a coal-carrier in the year nineteen-thirteen, my woman beside me, my ancestors behind me, my slant-eyed servitors under me, the beasts beneath me and beneath the heel of me. God! I felt kingly. I knew at last the meaning of kingship.

My anger was white and cold. This subterranean rat of a miserable human, crawling through the bowels of the ship to threaten me and mine! A rat in the shelter of a knot-hole making a noise as beast-like as any rat ever made! And it was in this spirit that I answered the gangster.

"When you crawl on your belly, along the open deck, in the broad light of day, like a yellow cur that has been licked to obedience, and when you show by your every action that you like it and are glad to do it, then, and not until then, will I talk with you."

Thereafter, for the next ten minutes, he shouted all the Billingsgate of his kind at me through the slits in the ventilator. But I made no reply. I listened, and I listened coldly, and as I listened I knew why the English had blown their mutinous Sepoys from the mouths of cannon in India long years ago.

* * * * *

And when, this morning, I saw the steward struggling with a five-gallon carboy of sulphuric acid, I never dreamed the use he intended for it.

In the meantime I was devising another way to overcome that deadly ventilator shaft. The scheme was so simple that I was shamed in that it had not occurred to me at the very beginning. The slitted opening was small. Two sacks of flour, in a wooden frame, suspended by ropes from the edge of the chart-house roof directly above, would effectually cover the opening and block all revolver fire.

No sooner thought than done. Tom Spink and Louis were on top the chart-house with me and preparing to lower the flour, when we heard a voice issuing from the shaft.

"Who's in there now?" I demanded. "Speak up."

"I'm givin' you a last chance," Bert Rhine answered.

And just then, around the corner of the house, stepped the steward. In his hand he carried a large galvanized pail, and my casual thought was that he had come to get rain-water from the barrels. Even as I thought it, he made a sweeping half-circle with the pail and sloshed its contents into the ventilator-opening. And even as the liquid flew through the air I knew it for what it was—undiluted sulphuric acid, two gallons of it from the carboy.

The gangster must have received the liquid fire in the face and eyes. And, in the shock of pain, he must have released all holds and fallen upon the coal at the bottom of the shaft. His cries and shrieks of anguish were terrible, and I was reminded of the starving rats which had squealed up that same shaft during the first months of the voyage. The thing was sickening. I prefer that men be killed cleanly and easily.

The agony of the wretch I did not fully realize until the steward, his bare fore-arms sprayed by the splash from the ventilator slats, suddenly felt the bite of the acid through his tight, whole skin and made a mad rush for the water-barrel at the corner of the house. And Bert Rhine, the silent man of soundless laughter, screaming below there on the coal, was enduring the bite of the acid in his eyes!

We covered the ventilator opening with our flour-device; the screams from below ceased as the victim was evidently dragged for'ard across the coal by his mates; and yet I confess to a miserable forenoon. As Carlyle has said: "Death is easy; all men must die"; but to receive two gallons of full-strength sulphuric acid full in the face is a vastly different and vastly more horrible thing than merely to die. Fortunately, Margaret was below at the time, and, after a few minutes, in which I recovered my balance, I bullied and swore all our hands into keeping the happening from her.

* * * * *

Oh, well, and we have got ours in retaliation. Off and on, through all of yesterday, after the ventilator tragedy, there were noises beneath the cabin floor or deck. We heard them under the dining-table, under the steward's pantry, under Margaret's stateroom.

This deck is overlaid with wood, but under the wood is iron, or steel rather, such as of which the whole *Elsinore* is builded.

Margaret and I, followed by Louis, Wada, and the steward, walked about from place to place, wherever the sounds arose of tappings and of cold-chisels against iron. The tappings seemed to come from everywhere; but we concluded that the concentration necessary on any spot to make an opening large enough for a man's body would inevitably draw our attention to that spot. And, as Margaret said:

"If they do manage to cut through, they must come up head-first, and, in such emergence, what chance would they have against us?"

So I relieved Buckwheat from deck duty, placed him on watch over the cabin floor, to be relieved by the steward in Margaret's watches.

In the late afternoon, after prodigious hammerings and clangings in a score of places, all noises ceased. Neither in the first and second dog-watches, nor in the first watch of the night, were the noises resumed. When I took charge of the poop at midnight Buckwheat relieved the steward in the vigil over the cabin floor; and as I leaned on the rail at the break of the poop, while my four hours dragged slowly by, least of all did I apprehend danger from the cabin—especially when I considered the two-gallon pail of raw sulphuric acid ready to hand for the first head that might arise through an opening in the floor not yet made. Our rascals for'ard might scale the poop; or cross aloft from mizzenmast to jigger and descend upon our heads; but how they could invade us through the floor was beyond me.

But they did invade. A modern ship is a complex affair. How was I to guess the manner of the invasion?

It was two in the morning, and for an hour I had been puzzling my head with watching the smoke arise from the after-division of the for'ard-house and with wondering why the mutineers should have up steam in the donkey-engine at such an ungodly hour. Not on the whole voyage had the donkey-engine been used. Four bells had just struck, and I was leaning on the rail at the break of the poop when I heard a prodigious coughing and choking from aft. Next, Wada ran across the deck to me.

"Big trouble with Buckwheat," he blurted at me. "You go quick."

I shoved him my rifle and left him on guard while I raced around the chart-house. A lighted match, in the hands of Tom Spink, directed me. Between the booby-hatch and the wheel, sitting up and rocking back and forth with wringings of hands and wavings of arms, tears of agony bursting from his eyes, was Buckwheat. My first thought was that in some stupid way he had got the acid into his own eyes. But the terrible fashion in which he coughed and strangled would quickly have undeceived me, had not Louis, bending over the booby-companion, uttered a startled exclamation.

I joined him, and one whiff of the air that came up from below made me catch my breath and gasp. I had inhaled sulphur. On the instant I forgot the *Elsinore*, the mutineers for'ard, everything save one thing.

The next I know, I was down the booby-ladder and reeling dizzily about the big after-room as the sulphur fumes bit my lungs and strangled me. By the dim light of a sea-lantern I saw the old steward, on hands and knees, coughing and gasping, the while he shook awake Yatsuda, the first sail-maker. Uchino, the second sail-maker, still strangled in his sleep.

It struck me that the air might be better nearer the floor, and I proved it when I dropped on my hands and knees. I rolled Uchino out of his blankets with a quick jerk, wrapped the blankets about my head, face, and mouth, arose to my feet, and dashed for'ard into the hall. After a couple of collisions with the wood-work I again dropped to the floor and rearranged the blankets so that, while my mouth remained covered, I could draw or withdraw, a thickness across my eyes.

The pain of the fumes was bad enough, but the real hardship was the dizziness I suffered. I blundered into the steward's pantry, and out of it, missed the cross-hall, stumbled through the next starboard opening in the long hall, and found myself bent double by violent collision with the dining-room table.

But I had my bearings. Feeling my way around the table and bumping most of the poisoned breath out of me against the rotund-bellied stove, I emerged in the cross-hall and made my way to starboard. Here, at the base of the chart-room stairway, I gained the hall that led aft. By this time my own situation seemed so serious that, careless of any collision, I went aft in long leaps.

Margaret's door was open. I plunged into her room. The moment I drew the blanket-thickness from my eyes I knew blindness and a modicum of what Bert Rhine must have suffered. Oh, the intolerable bite of the sulphur in my lungs, nostrils, eyes, and brain! No light burned in the room. I could only strangle and stumble for'ard to Margaret's bed, upon which I collapsed.

She was not there. I felt about, and I felt only the warm hollow her body had left in the under-sheet. Even in my agony and helplessness the intimacy of that warmth her body had left was very dear to me. Between the lack of oxygen in my lungs (due to the blankets), the pain of the sulphur, and the mortal dizziness in my brain, I felt that I might well cease there where the linen warmed my hand.

Perhaps I should have ceased, had I not heard a terrible coughing from along the hall. It was new life to me. I fell from bed to floor and managed to get upright until I gained the hall, where again I fell. Thereafter I crawled on hands and knees to the foot of the stairway. By means of the newel-post I drew myself upright and listened. Near me something moved and strangled. I fell upon it and found in my arms all the softness of Margaret.

How describe that battle up the stairway? It was a crucifixion of struggle, an age-long nightmare of agony. Time after time, as my consciousness blurred, the temptation was upon me to cease all effort and let myself blur down into the ultimate dark. I fought my way step by step. Margaret was now quite unconscious, and I lifted her body step by step, or dragged it several steps at a time, and fell with it, and back with it, and lost much that had been so hardly gained. And yet out of it all this I remember: that warm soft body of hers was the dearest thing in the world—vastly more dear than the pleasant land I remotely remembered, than all the books and all the humans I had ever known, than the deck above, with its sweet pure air softly blowing under the cool starry sky.

As I look back upon it I am aware of one thing: the thought of leaving her there and saving myself never crossed my mind. The one place for me was where she was.

Truly, this which I write seems absurd and purple; yet it was not absurd during those long minutes on the chart-room stairway. One must taste death for a few centuries of such agony ere he can receive sanction for purple passages.

And as I fought my screaming flesh, my reeling brain, and climbed that upward way, I prayed one prayer: that the chart-house doors out upon the poop might not be shut. Life and death lay right there in that one point of the issue. Was there any creature of my creatures aft with common sense and anticipation sufficient to make him think to open those doors? How I yearned for one man, for one proved henchman, such as Mr. Pike, to be on the poop! As it was, with the sole exception of Tom Spink and Buckwheat, my men were Asiatics.

I gained the top of the stairway, but was too far gone to rise to my feet. Nor could I rise upright on my knees. I crawled like any four-legged animal—nay, I wormed my way like a snake, prone to the deck. It was a matter of several feet to the doorway. I died a score of times in those several feet; but ever I endured the agony of resurrection and dragged Margaret with me. Sometimes the full strength I could exert did not move her, and I lay with her and coughed and strangled my way through to another resurrection.

And the door was open. The doors to starboard and to port were both open; and as the *Elsinore* rolled a draught through the chart-house hall my lungs filled with pure, cool air. As I drew myself across the high threshold and pulled Margaret after me, from very far away I heard the cries of men and the reports of rifle and revolver. And, ere I fainted into the blackness, on my side, staring, my pain gone so beyond endurance that it had achieved its own anæsthesia, I glimpsed, dream-like and distant, the sharply silhouetted poop-rail, dark forms that cut and thrust and smote, and, beyond, the mizzen-mast brightly lighted by our illuminators.

*　*　*　*　*

Well, the mutineers failed to take the poop. My five Asiatics and two white men had held the citadel while Margaret and I lay unconscious side by side.

The whole affair was very simple. Modern maritime quarantine demands that ships shall not carry vermin that are themselves plague-carriers. In the donkey-engine section of the for'ard house is a complete fumigating apparatus. The mutineers had merely to lay and fasten the pipes aft across the coal, to chisel a hole through the double-deck of steel and wood under the cabin, and to connect up and begin to pump. Buckwheat had fallen asleep and been awakened by the strangling sulphur fumes. We in the high place had been smoked out by our rascals like so many rats.

It was Wada who had opened one of the doors. The old steward had opened the other. Together they had attempted the descent of the stairway and been driven back by the fumes. Then they had engaged in the struggle to repel the rush from for'ard.

Margaret and I are agreed that sulphur, excessively inhaled, leaves the lungs sore. Only now, after a lapse of a dozen hours, can we draw breath in anything that resembles comfort. But still my lungs were not so sore as to prevent my telling her what I had learned she meant to me. And yet she is only a woman—I tell her so; I tell her that there are at least seven hundred and fifty millions of two-legged, long-haired, gentle-voiced, soft-bodied, female humans like her on the planet, and that she is really swamped by the immensity of numbers of her sex and kind. But I tell her something more. I tell her that of all of them she is the only one. And, better yet, to myself and for myself, I believe it. I know it. The last least part of me and all of me proclaims it.

Love *is* wonderful. It is the everlasting and miraculous amazement. Oh, trust me, I know the old, hard scientific method of weighing and calculating and classifying love. It is a profound foolishness, a cosmic trick and quip, to the contemplative eye of the philosopher—yes, and of the futurist. But when one forsakes such intellectual flesh-pots and becomes mere human and male human, in short, a lover, then all he may do, and which is what he cannot help doing, is to yield to the compulsions of being and throw both his arms around love and hold it closer to him than is his own heart close to him. This is the summit of his life, and of man's life. Higher than this no man may rise. The philosophers toil and struggle on mole-hill peaks far below. He who has not loved has not tasted the ultimate sweet of living. I know. I love Margaret, a woman. She is desirable.

CHAPTER L

In the past twenty-four hours many things have happened. To begin with, we nearly lost the steward in the second dog-watch last evening. Through the slits in the ventilator some man thrust a knife into the sacks of flour and cut them wide open from top to bottom. In the dark the flour poured to the deck unobserved.

Of course, the man behind could not see through the screen of empty sacks, but he took a blind pot-shot at point-blank range when the steward went by, slip-sloppily dragging the heels of his slippers. Fortunately it was a miss, but so close a miss was it that his cheek and neck were burned with powder grains.

At six bells in the first watch came another surprise. Tom Spink came to me where I stood guard at the for'ard end of the poop. His voice shook as he spoke.

"For the love of God, sir, they've come," he said.

"Who?" I asked sharply.

"Them," he chattered. "The ones that come aboard off the Horn, sir, the three drownded sailors. They're there, aft, sir, the three of 'em, standin' in a row by the wheel."

"How did they get there?"

"Bein' warlocks, they flew, sir. You didn't see 'm go by you, did you, sir?"

"No," I admitted. "They never went by me."

Poor Tom Spink groaned.

"But there are lines aloft there on which they could cross over from mizzen to jigger," I added. "Send Wada to me."

When the latter relieved me I went aft. And there in a row were our three pale-haired storm-waifs with the topaz eyes. In the light of a bull's-eye, held on them by Louis, their eyes never seemed more like the eyes of great cats. And, heavens, they purred! At least, the inarticulate noises they made sounded more like purring than anything else. That these sounds meant friendliness was very evident. Also, they held out their hands, palms upward, in unmistakable sign of peace. Each in turn doffed his cap and placed my hand for a moment on his head. Without doubt this meant their offer of fealty, their acceptance of me as master.

I nodded my head. There was nothing to be said to men who purred like cats, while sign-language in the light of the bull's-eye was rather difficult. Tom Spink groaned protest when I told Louis to take them below and give them blankets.

I made the sleep-sign to them, and they nodded gratefully, hesitated, then pointed to their mouths and rubbed their stomachs.

"Drowned men do not eat," I laughed to Tom Spink. "Go down and watch them. Feed them up, Louis, all they want. It's a good sign of short rations for'ard."

At the end of half an hour Tom Spink was back.

"Well, did they eat?" I challenged him.

But he was unconvinced. The very quantity they had eaten was a suspicious thing, and, further, he had heard of a kind of ghost that devoured dead bodies in graveyards. Therefore, he concluded, mere non-eating was no test for a ghost.

The third event of moment occurred this morning at seven o'clock. The mutineers called for a truce; and when Nosey Murphy, the Maltese Cockney, and the inevitable Charles Davis stood beneath me on the main deck, their faces showed lean and drawn. Famine had been my great ally. And in truth, with Margaret beside me in that high place of the break of the poop, as I looked down on the hungry wretches I felt very strong. Never had the inequality of numbers fore and aft been less than now. The three deserters, added to our own nine, made twelve of us, while the mutineers, after subtracting Ditman Olansen, Bob and the Faun, totalled only an even score. And of these Bert Rhine must certainly be in a bad way, while there were many weaklings, such as Sundry Buyers, Nancy, Larry, and Lars Jacobsen.

"Well, what do you want?" I demanded. "I haven't much time to waste. Breakfast is ready and waiting."

Charles Davis started to speak, but I shut him off.

"I'll have nothing out of you, Davis. At least not now. Later on, when I'm in that court of law you've bothered me with for half the voyage, you'll get your turn at talking. And when that time comes don't forget that I shall have a few words to say."

Again he began, but this time was stopped by Nosey Murphy.

"Aw, shut your trap, Davis," the gangster snarled, "or I'll shut it for you." He glanced up to me. "We want to go back to work, that's what we want."

"Which is not the way to ask for it," I answered.

"Sir," he added hastily.

"That's better," I commented.

"Oh, my God, sir, don't let 'm come aft." Tom Spink muttered hurriedly in my ear. "That'd be the end of all of us. And even if they didn't get you an' the rest, they'd heave me over some dark night. They ain't never goin' to forgive me, sir, for joinin' in with the afterguard."

I ignored the interruption and addressed the gangster.

"There's nothing like going to work when you want to as badly as you seem to. Suppose all hands get sail on her just to show good intention."

"We'd like to eat first, sir," he objected.

"I'd like to see you setting sail, first," was my reply. "And you may as well get it from me straight that what I like goes, aboard this ship."—I almost said "hooker."

Nosey Murphy hesitated and looked to the Maltese Cockney for counsel. The latter debated, as if gauging the measure of his weakness while he stared aloft at the work involved. Finally he nodded.

"All right, sir," the gangster spoke up. "We'll do it . . . but can't something be cookin' in the galley while we're doin' it?"

I shook my head.

"I didn't have that in mind, and I don't care to change my mind now. When every sail is stretched and every yard braced, and all that mess of gear cleared up, food for a good meal will be served out. You needn't bother about the spanker nor the mizzen-braces. We'll make your work lighter by that much."

In truth, as they climbed aloft they showed how miserably weak they were. There were some too feeble to go aloft. Poor Sundry Buyers continually pressed his abdomen as he toiled around the deck-capstans; and never was Nancy's face quite so forlorn as when he obeyed the Maltese Cockney's command and went up to loose the mizzen-skysail.

In passing, I must note one delicious miracle that was worked before our eyes. They were hoisting the mizzen-upper-topsail-yard by means of one of the patent deck-capstans. Although they had reversed the gear so as to double the purchase, they were having a hard time of it. Lars Jacobsen was limping on his twice-broken leg, and with him were Sundry Buyers, Tony the Greek, Bombini, and Mulligan Jacobs. Nosey Murphy held the turn.

When they stopped from sheer exhaustion Murphy's glance chanced to fall on Charles Davis, the one man who had not worked since the outset of the voyage and who was not working now.

"Bear a hand, Davis," the gangster called.

Margaret gurgled low laughter in my ear as she caught the drift of the episode.

The sea-lawyer looked at the other in amazement ere he answered:

"I guess not."

After nodding Sundry Buyers over to him to take the turn Murphy straightened his back and walked close to Davis, then said very quietly:

"I guess yes."

That was all. For a space neither spoke. Davis seemed to be giving the matter judicial consideration. The men at the capstan panted, rested, and looked on—all save Bombini, who slunk across the deck until he stood at Murphy's shoulder.

Under such circumstances the decision Charles Davis gave was eminently the right one, although even then he offered a compromise.

"I'll hold the turn," he volunteered.

"You'll lump around one of them capstan-bars," Murphy said.

The sea-lawyer made no mistake. He knew in all absoluteness that he was choosing between life and death, and he limped over to the capstan and found his place. And as the work started, and as he toiled around and

457

around the narrow circle, Margaret and I shamelessly and loudly laughed our approval. And our own men stole for'ard along the poop to peer down at the spectacle of Charles Davis at work.

All of which must have pleased Nosey Murphy, for, as he continued to hold the turn and coil down, he kept a critical eye on Davis.

"More juice, Davis!" he commanded with abrupt sharpness.

And Davis, with a startle, visibly increased his efforts.

This was too much for our fellows, who, Asiatics and all, applauded with laughter and hand-clapping. And what could I do? It was a gala day, and our faithful ones deserved some little recompense of amusement. So I ignored the breach of discipline and of poop etiquette by strolling away aft with Margaret.

At the wheel was one of our storm-waifs. I set the course due east for Valparaiso, and sent the steward below to bring up sufficient food for one substantial meal for the mutineers.

"When do we get our next grub, sir?" Nosey Murphy asked, as the steward served the supplies down to him from the poop.

"At midday," I answered. "And as long as you and your gang are good, you'll get your grub three times each day. You can choose your own watches any way you please. But the ship's work must be done, and done properly. If it isn't, then the grub stops. That will do. Now go for'ard."

"One thing more, sir," he said quickly. "Bert Rhine is awful bad. He can't see, sir. It looks like he's going to lose his face. He can't sleep. He groans all the time."

* * * * *

It was a busy day. I made a selection of things from the medicine-chest for the acid-burned gangster; and, finding that Murphy knew how to manipulate a hypodermic syringe, entrusted him with one.

Then, too, I practised with the sextant and think I fairly caught the sun at noon and correctly worked up the observation. But this is latitude, and is comparatively easy. Longitude is more difficult. But I am reading up on it.

All afternoon a gentle northerly fan of air snored the *Elsinore* through the water at a five-knot clip, and our course lay east for land, for the habitations of men, for the law and order that men institute whenever they organize into groups. Once in Valparaiso, with police flag flying, our mutineers will be taken care of by the shore authorities.

Another thing I did was to rearrange our watches aft so as to split up the three storm-visitors. Margaret took one in her watch, along with the two sail-makers, Tom Spink, and Louis. Louis is half white, and all trustworthy, so that, at all times, on deck or below, he is told off to the task of never letting the topaz-eyed one out of his sight.

In my watch are the steward, Buckwheat, Wada, and the other two topaz-eyed ones. And to one of them Wada is told off; and to the other is assigned the steward. We are not taking any chances. Always, night and day, on duty or off, these storm-strangers will have one of our proved men watching them.

* * * * *

Yes; and I tried the stranger men out last evening. It was after a council with Margaret. She was sure, and I agreed with her, that the men for'ard are not blindly yielding to our bringing them in to be prisoners in Valparaiso. As we tried to forecast it, their plan is to desert the *Elsinore* in the boats as soon as we fetch up with the land. Also, considering some of the bitter lunatic spirits for'ard, there would be a large chance of their drilling the *Elsinore*'s steel sides and scuttling her ere they took to the boats. For scuttling a ship is surely as ancient a practice as mutiny on the high seas.

So it was, at one in the morning, that I tried out our strangers. Two of them I took for'ard with me in the raid on the small boats. One I left beside Margaret, who kept charge of the poop. On the other side of him stood the steward with his big hacking knife. By signs I had made it clear to him, and to his two comrades who were to accompany me for'ard, that at the first sign of treachery he would be killed. And not only did the old steward, with signs emphatic and unmistakable, pledge himself to perform the execution, but we were all convinced that he was eager for the task.

With Margaret I also left Buckwheat and Tom Spink. Wada, the two sail-makers, Louis, and the two topaz-eyed ones accompanied me. In addition to fighting weapons we were armed with axes. We crossed the main deck unobserved, gained the bridge by way of the 'midship-house, and by way of the bridge gained the top of the for'ard-house. Here were the first boats we began work on; but, first of all, I called in the lookout from the forecastle-head.

He was Mulligan Jacobs; and he picked his way back across the wreck of the bridge where the fore-topgallant-yard still lay, and came up to me unafraid, as implacable and bitter as ever.

"Jacobs," I whispered, "you are to stay here beside me until we finish the job of smashing the boats. Do you get that?"

"As though it could fright me," he growled all too loudly. "Go ahead for all I care. I know your game. And I know the game of the hell's maggots under our feet this minute. 'Tis they that'd desert in the boats. 'Tis you that'll smash the boats an' jail 'm kit an' crew."

"S-s-s-h," I vainly interpolated.

"What of it?" he went on as loudly as ever. "They're sleepin' with full bellies. The only night watch we keep is the lookout. Even Rhine's asleep. A few jolts of the needle has put a clapper to his eternal moanin'. Go on with your work. Smash the boats. 'Tis nothin' I care. 'Tis well I know my own crooked back is worth more to me than the necks of the scum of the world below there."

"If you felt that way, why didn't you join us?" I queried.

"Because I like you no better than them an' not half so well. They are what you an' your fathers have made 'em. An' who in hell are you an' your fathers? Robbers of the toil of men. I like them little. I like you and your fathers not at all. Only I like myself and me crooked back that's a livin' proof there ain't no God and makes Browning a liar."

"Join us now," I urged, meeting him in his mood. "It will be easier for your back."

"To hell with you," was his answer. "Go ahead an' smash the boats. You can hang some of them. But you can't touch me with the law. 'Tis me that's a crippled creature of circumstance, too weak to raise a hand against any man—a feather blown about by the windy contention of men strong in their back an' brainless in their heads."

"As you please," I said.

"As I can't help pleasin'," he retorted, "bein' what I am an' so made for the little flash between the darknesses which men call life. Now why couldn't I a-ben a butterfly, or a fat pig in a full trough, or a mere mortal man with a straight back an' women to love me? Go on an' smash the boats. Play hell to the top of your bent. Like me, you'll end in the darkness. And your darkness'll be—as dark as mine."

"A full belly puts the spunk back into you," I sneered.

"'Tis on an empty belly that the juice of my dislike turns to acid. Go on an' smash the boats."

"Whose idea was the sulphur?" I asked.

"I'm not tellin' you the man, but I envied him until it showed failure. An' whose idea was it—to douse the sulphuric into Rhine's face? He'll lose that same face, from the way it's shedding."

"Nor will I tell you," I said. "Though I will tell you that I am glad the idea was not mine."

"Oh, well," he muttered cryptically, "different customs on different ships, as the cook said when he went for'ard to cast off the spanker sheet."

461

Not until the job was done and I was back on the poop did I have time to work out the drift of that last figure in its terms of the sea. Mulligan Jacobs might have been an artist, a philosophic poet, had he not been born crooked with a crooked back.

And we smashed the boats. With axes and sledges it was an easier task than I had imagined. On top of both houses we left the boats masses of splintered wreckage, the topaz-eyed ones working most energetically; and we regained the poop without a shot being fired. The forecastle turned out, of course, at our noise, but made no attempt to interfere with us.

And right here I register another complaint against the sea-novelists. A score of men for'ard, desperate all, with desperate deeds behind them, and jail and the gallows facing them not many days away, should have only begun to fight. And yet this score of men did nothing while we destroyed their last chance for escape.

"But where did they get the grub?" the steward asked me afterwards.

This question he has asked me every day since the first day Mr. Pike began cudgelling his brains over it. I wonder, had I asked Mulligan Jacobs the question, if he would have told me? At any rate, in court at Valparaiso that question will be answered. In the meantime I suppose I shall submit to having the steward ask me it daily.

"It is murder and mutiny on the high seas," I told them this morning, when they came aft in a body to complain about the destruction of the boats and to demand my intentions.

And as I looked down upon the poor wretches from the break of the poop, standing there in the high place, the vision of my kind down all its mad, violent, and masterful past was strong upon me. Already, since our departure from Baltimore, three other men, masters, had occupied this high place and gone their way—the Samurai, Mr. Pike, and Mr. Mellaire. I stood here, fourth, no seaman, merely a master by the blood of my ancestors; and the work of the *Elsinore* in the world went on.

Bert Rhine, his head and face swathed in bandages, stood there beneath me, and I felt for him a tingle of respect. He, too, in a subterranean, ghetto way was master over his rats. Nosey Murphy and Kid Twist stood shoulder to shoulder with their stricken gangster leader. It was his will, because of his terrible injury, to get in to land and doctors as quickly as possible. He preferred taking his chance in court against the chance of losing his life, or, perhaps, his eyesight.

The crew was divided against itself; and Isaac Chantz, the Jew, his wounded shoulder with a hunch to it, seemed to lead the revolt against the gangsters. His wound was enough to convict him in any court, and well he knew it. Beside him, and at his shoulders, clustered the Maltese Cockney, Andy Fay, Arthur Deacon, Frank Fitzgibbon, Richard Giller, and John Hackey.

In another group, still allegiant to the gangsters, were men such as Shorty, Sorensen, Lars Jacobsen, and Larry. Charles Davis was prominently in the gangster group. A fourth group was composed of Sundry Buyers, Nancy, and Tony the Greek. This group was distinctly neutral. And, finally, unaffiliated, quite by himself, stood Mulligan Jacobs—listening, I fancy, to far echoes of ancient wrongs, and feeling, I doubt not, the bite of the iron-hot hooks in his brain.

"What are you going to do with us, sir?" Isaac Chantz demanded of me, in defiance to the gangsters, who were expected to do the talking.

Bert Rhine lurched angrily toward the sound of the Jew's voice. Chantz's partisans drew closer to him.

"Jail you," I answered from above. "And it shall go as hard with all of you as I can make it hard."

"Maybe you will an' maybe you won't," the Jew retorted.

"Shut up, Chantz!" Bert Rhine commanded.

"And you'll get yours, you wop," Chantz snarled, "if I have to do it myself."

I am afraid that I am not so successfully the man of action that I have been priding myself on being; for, so curious and interested was I in observing the moving drama beneath me that for the moment I failed to glimpse the tragedy into which it was culminating.

"Bombini!" Bert Rhine said.

His voice was imperative. It was the order of a master to the dog at heel. Bombini responded. He drew his knife and started to advance upon the Jew. But a deep rumbling, animal-like in its *sound* and menace, arose in the throats of those about the Jew.

Bombini hesitated and glanced back across his shoulder at the leader, whose face he could not see for bandages and who he knew could not see.

"'Tis a good deed—do it, Bombini," Charles Davis encouraged.

"Shut your face, Davis!" came out from Bert Rhine's bandages.

Kid Twist drew a revolver, shoved the muzzle of it first into Bombini's side, then covered the men about the Jew.

Really, I felt a momentary twinge of pity for the Italian. He was caught between the mill-stones, "Bombini, stick that Jew," Bert Rhine commanded.

The Italian advanced a step, and, shoulder to shoulder, on either side, Kid Twist and Nosey Murphy advanced with him.

"I cannot see him," Bert Rhine went on; "but by God I will see him!"

And so speaking, with one single, virile movement he tore away the bandages. The toll of pain he must have paid is beyond measurement. I saw the horror of his face, but the description of it is beyond the limits of any English I possess. I was aware that Margaret, at my shoulder, gasped and shuddered.

"Bombini!—stick him," the gangster repeated. "And stick any man that raises a yap. Murphy! See that Bombini does his work."

Murphy's knife was out and at the bravo's back. Kid Twist covered the Jew's group with his revolver. And the three advanced.

It was at this moment that I suddenly recollected myself and passed from dream to action.

"Bombini!" I said sharply.

He paused and looked up.

"Stand where you are," I ordered, "till I do some talking.—Chantz! Make no mistake. Rhine is boss for'ard. You take his orders . . . until we get into Valparaiso; then you'll take your chances along with him in jail. In the meantime, what Rhine says goes. Get that, and get it straight. I am behind Rhine until the police come on board.—Bombini! do whatever Rhine tells you. I'll shoot the man who tries to stop you.—Deacon! Stand away from Chantz. Go over to the fife-rail."

All hands knew the stream of lead my automatic rifle could throw, and Arthur Deacon knew it. He hesitated barely a moment, then obeyed.

"Fitzgibbon!—Giller!—Hackey!" I called in turn, and was obeyed. "Fay!" I called twice, ere the response came.

Isaac Chantz stood alone, and Bombini now showed eagerness.

"Chantz!" I said; "don't you think it would be healthier to go over to the fife-rail and be good?"

He debated the matter not many seconds, resheathed his knife, and complied.

The tang of power! I was minded to let literature get the better of me and read the rascals a lecture; but thank heaven I had sufficient proportion and balance to refrain.

"Rhine!" I said.

He turned his corroded face up to me and blinked in an effort to see.

"As long as Chantz takes your orders, leave him alone. We'll need every hand to work the ship in. As for yourself, send Murphy aft in half an hour and I'll give him the best the medicine-chest affords. That is all. Go for'ard."

And they shambled away, beaten and dispirited.

"But that man—his face—what happened to him?" Margaret asked of me.

Sad it is to end love with lies. Sadder still is it to begin love with lies. I had tried to hide this one happening from Margaret, and I had failed. It could no longer be hidden save by lying; and so I told her the truth, told her how and why the gangster had had his face dashed with sulphuric acid by the old steward who knew white men and their ways.

* * * * *

There is little more to write. The mutiny of the *Elsinore* is over. The divided crew is ruled by the gangsters, who are as intent on getting their leader into port as I am intent on getting all of them into jail. The first lap of the voyage of the *Elsinore* draws to a close. Two days, at most, with our present sailing, will bring us into Valparaiso. And then, as beginning a new voyage, the *Elsinore* will depart for Seattle.

* * * * *

One thing more remains for me to write, and then this strange log of a strange cruise will be complete. It happened only last night. I am yet fresh from it, and athrill with it and with the promise of it.

Margaret and I spent the last hour of the second dog-watch together at the break of the poop. It was good again to feel the *Elsinore* yielding to the wind-pressure on her canvas, to feel her again slipping and sliding through the water in an easy sea.

Hidden by the darkness, clasped in each other's arms, we talked love and love plans. Nor am I shamed to confess that I was all for immediacy. Once in Valparaiso, I contended, we would fit out the *Elsinore* with fresh crew and officers and send her on her way. As for us, steamers and rapid travelling would fetch us quickly home. Furthermore, Valparaiso being a place where such things as licences and ministers obtained, we would be married ere we caught the fast steamers for home.

466

But Margaret was obdurate. The Wests had always stood by their ships, she urged; had always brought their ships in to the ports intended or had gone down with their ships in the effort. The *Elsinore* had cleared from Baltimore for Seattle with the Wests in the high place. The *Elsinore* would re-equip with officers and men in Valparaiso, and the *Elsinore* would arrive in Seattle with a West still on board.

"But think, dear heart," I objected. "The voyage will require months. Remember what Henley has said: 'Every kiss we take or give leaves us less of life to live.'"

She pressed her lips to mine.

"We kiss," she said.

But I was stupid.

* * * * *

"Oh, the weary, weary months," I complained. "You dear silly," she gurgled. "Don't you understand?"

"I understand only that it is many a thousand miles from Valparaiso to Seattle," I answered.

"You won't understand," she challenged.

"I am a fool," I admitted. "I am aware of only one thing: I want you. I want you."

"You are a dear, but you are very, very stupid," she said, and as she spoke she caught my hand and pressed the palm of it against her cheek. "What do you feel?" she asked.

"Hot cheeks—cheeks most hot."

"I am blushing for what your stupidity compels me to say," she explained. "You have already said that such things as licences and ministers obtain in Valparaiso . . . and . . . and, well . . . "

"You mean . . . ?" I stammered.

467

"Just that," she confirmed.

"The honeymoon shall be on the *Elsinore* from Valparaiso all the way to Seattle?" I rattled on.

"The many thousands of miles, the weary, weary months," she teased in my own intonations, until I stifled her teasing with my lips.

About Author

John Griffith London (born **John Griffith Chaney**; January 12, 1876 – November 22, 1916) was an American novelist, journalist, and social activist. A pioneer in the world of commercial magazine fiction, he was one of the first writers to become a worldwide celebrity and earn a large fortune from writing. He was also an innovator in the genre that would later become known as science fiction.

His most famous works include The Call of the Wild and White Fang, both set in the Klondike Gold Rush, as well as the short stories "To Build a Fire", "An Odyssey of the North", and "Love of Life". He also wrote about the South Pacific in stories such as "The Pearls of Parlay", and "The Heathen".

London was part of the radical literary group "The Crowd" in San Francisco and a passionate advocate of unionization, workers' rights, socialism, and eugenics. He wrote several works dealing with these topics, such as his dystopian novel The Iron Heel, his non-fiction exposé The People of the Abyss, The War of the Classes, and Before Adam.

Family

Jack London's mother, Flora Wellman, was the fifth and youngest child of Pennsylvania Canal builder Marshall Wellman and his first wife, Eleanor Garrett Jones. Marshall Wellman was descended from Thomas Wellman, an early Puritan settler in the Massachusetts Bay Colony. Flora left Ohio and moved to the Pacific coast when her father remarried after her mother died. In San Francisco, Flora worked as a music teacher and spiritualist, claiming to channel the spirit of a Sauk chief, Black Hawk.

Biographer Clarice Stasz and others believe London's father was astrologer William Chaney. Flora Wellman was living with Chaney in San Francisco when she became pregnant. Whether Wellman and Chaney were legally married is unknown. Stasz notes that in his memoirs, Chaney refers to London's mother Flora Wellman as having been his "wife"; he also cites an advertisement in which Flora called herself "Florence Wellman Chaney".

According to Flora Wellman's account, as recorded in the San Francisco Chronicle of June 4, 1875, Chaney demanded that she have an abortion. When she refused, he disclaimed responsibility for the child. In desperation, she shot herself. She was not seriously wounded, but she was temporarily deranged. After giving birth, Flora turned the baby over for care to Virginia Prentiss, an African-American woman and former slave. She was a major maternal figure throughout London's life. Late in 1876, Flora Wellman married John London, a partially disabled Civil War veteran, and brought her baby John, later known as Jack, to live with the newly married couple. The family moved around the San Francisco Bay Area before settling in Oakland, where London completed public grade school.

In 1897, when he was 21 and a student at the University of California, Berkeley, London searched for and read the newspaper accounts of his mother's suicide attempt and the name of his biological father. He wrote to William Chaney, then living in Chicago. Chaney responded that he could not be London's father because he was impotent; he casually asserted that London's mother had relations with other men and averred that she had slandered him when she said he insisted on an abortion. Chaney concluded by saying that he was more to be pitied than London. London was devastated by his father's letter; in the months following, he quit school at Berkeley and went to the Klondike during the gold rush boom.

Early life

London was born near Third and Brannan Streets in San Francisco. The house burned down in the fire after the 1906 San Francisco earthquake; the California Historical Society placed a plaque at the site in 1953. Although the family was working class, it was not as impoverished as London's later accounts claimed. London was largely self-educated.

In 1885, London found and read Ouida's long Victorian novel Signa. He credited this as the seed of his literary success. In 1886, he went to the Oakland Public Library and found a sympathetic librarian, Ina Coolbrith, who encouraged his learning. (She later became California's first poet laureate and an important figure in the San Francisco literary community).

472

In 1889, London began working 12 to 18 hours a day at Hickmott's Cannery. Seeking a way out, he borrowed money from his foster mother Virginia Prentiss, bought the sloop Razzle-Dazzle from an oyster pirate named French Frank, and became an oyster pirate himself. In his memoir, John Barleycorn, he claims also to have stolen French Frank's mistress Mamie. After a few months, his sloop became damaged beyond repair. London hired on as a member of the California Fish Patrol.

In 1893, he signed on to the sealing schooner Sophie Sutherland, bound for the coast of Japan. When he returned, the country was in the grip of the panic of '93 and Oakland was swept by labor unrest. After grueling jobs in a jute mill and a street-railway power plant, London joined Coxey's Army and began his career as a tramp. In 1894, he spent 30 days for vagrancy in the Erie County Penitentiary at Buffalo, New York. In The Road, he wrote:

> Man-handling was merely one of the very minor unprintable horrors of the Erie County Pen. I say 'unprintable'; and in justice I must also say undescribable. They were unthinkable to me until I saw them, and I was no spring chicken in the ways of the world and the awful abysses of human degradation. It would take a deep plummet to reach bottom in the Erie County Pen, and I do but skim lightly and facetiously the surface of things as I there saw them.

—Jack London, The Road

After many experiences as a hobo and a sailor, he returned to Oakland and attended Oakland High School. He contributed a number of articles to the high school's magazine, The Aegis. His first published work was "Typhoon off the Coast of Japan", an account of his sailing experiences.

As a schoolboy, London often studied at Heinold's First and Last Chance Saloon, a port-side bar in Oakland. At 17, he confessed to the bar's owner, John Heinold, his desire to attend university and pursue a career as a writer. Heinold lent London tuition money to attend college.

London desperately wanted to attend the University of California, located in Berkeley. In 1896, after a summer of intense studying to pass certification exams, he was admitted. Financial circumstances forced him to leave in 1897 and he never graduated. No evidence has surfaced that he ever wrote for student publications while studying at Berkeley.

While at Berkeley, London continued to study and spend time at Heinold's saloon, where he was introduced to the sailors and adventurers who would influence his writing. In his autobiographical novel, John Barleycorn, London mentioned the pub's likeness seventeen times. Heinold's was the place where London met Alexander McLean, a captain known for his cruelty at sea. London based his protagonist Wolf Larsen, in the novel The Sea-Wolf, on McLean.

Heinold's First and Last Chance Saloon is now unofficially named Jack London's Rendezvous in his honor.

Gold rush and first success

On July 12, 1897, London (age 21) and his sister's husband Captain Shepard sailed to join the Klondike Gold Rush. This was the setting for some of his first successful stories. London's time in the harsh Klondike, however, was detrimental to his health. Like so many other men who were malnourished in the goldfields, London developed scurvy. His gums became swollen, leading to the loss of his four front teeth. A constant gnawing pain affected his hip and leg muscles, and his face was stricken with marks that always reminded him of the struggles he faced in the Klondike. Father William Judge, "The Saint of Dawson", had a facility in Dawson that provided shelter, food and any available medicine to London and others. His struggles there inspired London's short story, "To Build a Fire" (1902, revised in 1908), which many critics assess as his best.

His landlords in Dawson were mining engineers Marshall Latham Bond and Louis Whitford Bond, educated at Yale and Stanford, respectively. The brothers' father, Judge Hiram Bond, was a wealthy mining investor. The Bonds, especially Hiram, were active Republicans. Marshall Bond's diary mentions friendly sparring with London on political issues as a camp pastime.

London left Oakland with a social conscience and socialist leanings; he returned to become an activist for socialism. He concluded that his only hope of escaping the work "trap" was to get an education and "sell his brains". He saw his writing as a business, his ticket out of poverty, and, he hoped, a means of beating the wealthy at their own game. On returning to California in 1898, London began working to get published, a struggle described in his novel, Martin Eden (serialized in 1908, published in 1909). His first published story since high school was "To the Man On Trail", which has frequently been collected in anthologies. When The Overland Monthly offered him only five dollars for it—and was slow paying—London came close to abandoning his writing career. In his words, "literally and literarily I was saved" when The Black Cat accepted his story "A Thousand Deaths", and paid him $40—the "first money I ever received for a story".

London began his writing career just as new printing technologies enabled lower-cost production of magazines. This resulted in a boom in popular magazines aimed at a wide public audience and a strong market for short fiction. In 1900, he made $2,500 in writing, about $77,000 in today's currency. Among the works he sold to magazines was a short story known as either "Diable" (1902) or "Bâtard" (1904), two editions of the same basic story; London received $141.25 for this story on May 27, 1902. In the text, a cruel French Canadian brutalizes his dog, and the dog retaliates and kills the man. London told some of his critics that man's actions are the main cause of the behavior of their animals, and he would show this in another story, The Call of the Wild.

In early 1903, London sold The Call of the Wild to The Saturday Evening Post for $750, and the book rights to Macmillan for $2,000. Macmillan's promotional campaign propelled it to swift success.

While living at his rented villa on Lake Merritt in Oakland, California, London met poet George Sterling; in time they became best friends. In 1902, Sterling helped London find a home closer to his own in nearby Piedmont. In his letters London addressed Sterling as "Greek", owing to Sterling's aquiline nose and classical profile, and he signed them as "Wolf". London was later to depict Sterling as Russ Brissenden in his autobiographical novel Martin Eden (1910) and as Mark Hall in The Valley of the Moon (1913).

In later life London indulged his wide-ranging interests by accumulating a personal library of 15,000 volumes. He referred to his books as "the tools of my trade".

First marriage (1900–04)

London married Elizabeth "Bessie" Maddern on April 7, 1900, the same day The Son of the Wolf was published. Bess had been part of his circle of friends for a number of years. She was related to stage actresses Minnie Maddern Fiske and Emily Stevens. Stasz says, "Both acknowledged publicly that they were not marrying out of love, but from friendship and a belief that they would produce sturdy children." Kingman says, "they were comfortable together... Jack had made it clear to Bessie that he did not love her, but that he liked her enough to make a successful marriage."

London met Bessie through his friend at Oakland High School, Fred Jacobs; she was Fred's fiancée. Bessie, who tutored at Anderson's University Academy in Alameda California, tutored Jack in preparation for his entrance exams for the University of California at Berkeley in 1896. Jacobs was killed aboard the USAT Scandia in 1897, but Jack and Bessie continued their friendship, which included taking photos and developing the film together. This was the beginning of Jack's passion for photography.

During the marriage, London continued his friendship with Anna Strunsky, co-authoring The Kempton-Wace Letters, an epistolary novel contrasting two philosophies of love. Anna, writing "Dane Kempton's" letters, arguing for a romantic view of marriage, while London, writing "Herbert Wace's" letters, argued for a scientific view, based on Darwinism and eugenics. In the novel, his fictional character contrasted two women he had known.

London's pet name for Bess was "Mother-Girl" and Bess's for London was "Daddy-Boy". Their first child, Joan, was born on January 15, 1901, and their second, Bessie (later called Becky), on October 20, 1902. Both children were born in Piedmont, California. Here London wrote one of his most celebrated works, The Call of the Wild.

While London had pride in his children, the marriage was strained. Kingman says that by 1903 the couple were close to separation as they were "extremely incompatible". "Jack was still so kind and gentle with Bessie that when Cloudsley Johns was a house guest in February 1903 he didn't suspect a breakup of their marriage."

London reportedly complained to friends Joseph Noel and George Sterling:

> [Bessie] is devoted to purity. When I tell her morality is only evidence of low blood pressure, she hates me. She'd sell me and the children out for her damned purity. It's terrible. Every time I come back after being away from home for a night she won't let me be in the same room with her if she can help it.

Stasz writes that these were "code words for fear that was consorting with prostitutes and might bring home venereal disease."

On July 24, 1903, London told Bessie he was leaving and moved out. During 1904, London and Bess negotiated the terms of a divorce, and the decree was granted on November 11, 1904.

War correspondent (1904)

London accepted an assignment of the San Francisco Examiner to cover the Russo-Japanese War in early 1904, arriving in Yokohama on January 25, 1904. He was arrested by Japanese authorities in Shimonoseki, but released through the intervention of American ambassador Lloyd Griscom. After travelling to Korea, he was again arrested by Japanese authorities for straying too close to the border with Manchuria without official permission, and was sent back to Seoul. Released again, London was permitted to travel with the Imperial Japanese Army to the border, and to observe the Battle of the Yalu.

London asked William Randolph Hearst, the owner of the San Francisco Examiner, to be allowed to transfer to the Imperial Russian Army, where he felt that restrictions on his reporting and his movements would be less severe. However, before this could be arranged, he was arrested for a third time in four months, this time for assaulting his Japanese assistants, whom he accused of stealing the fodder for his horse. Released through the personal intervention of President Theodore Roosevelt, London departed the front in June 1904.

Bohemian Club

On August 18, 1904, London went with his close friend, the poet George Sterling, to "Summer High Jinks" at the Bohemian Grove. London was elected to honorary membership in the Bohemian Club and took part in many activities. Other noted members of the Bohemian Club during this time included Ambrose Bierce, Gelett Burgess, Allan Dunn, John Muir, Frank Norris, and Herman George Scheffauer.

Beginning in December 1914, London worked on The Acorn Planter, A California Forest Play, to be performed as one of the annual Grove Plays, but it was never selected. It was described as too difficult to set to music. London published The Acorn Planter in 1916.

Second marriage

After divorcing Maddern, London married Charmian Kittredge in 1905. London had been introduced to Kittredge in 1900 by her aunt Netta Eames, who was an editor at Overland Monthly magazine in San Francisco. The two met prior to his first marriage but became lovers years later after Jack and Bessie London visited Wake Robin, Netta Eames' Sonoma County resort, in 1903. London was injured when he fell from a buggy, and Netta arranged for Charmian to care for him. The two developed a friendship, as Charmian, Netta, her husband Roscoe, and London were politically aligned with socialist causes. At some point the relationship became romantic, and Jack divorced his wife to marry Charmian, who was five years his senior.

Biographer Russ Kingman called Charmian "Jack's soul-mate, always at his side, and a perfect match." Their time together included numerous trips, including a 1907 cruise on the yacht Snark to Hawaii and Australia. Many of London's stories are based on his visits to Hawaii, the last one for 10 months beginning in December 1915.

The couple also visited Goldfield, Nevada, in 1907, where they were guests of the Bond brothers, London's Dawson City landlords. The Bond brothers were working in Nevada as mining engineers.

London had contrasted the concepts of the "Mother Girl" and the "Mate Woman" in The Kempton-Wace Letters. His pet name for Bess had been "Mother-Girl;" his pet name for Charmian was "Mate-Woman."Charmian's aunt and foster mother, a disciple of Victoria Woodhull, had raised her without prudishness.Every biographer alludes to Charmian's uninhibited sexuality.

Joseph Noel calls the events from 1903 to 1905 "a domestic drama that would have intrigued the pen of an Ibsen.... London's had comedy relief in it and a sort of easy-going romance." In broad outline, London was restless in his first marriage, sought extramarital sexual affairs, and found, in Charmian Kittredge, not only a sexually active and adventurous partner, but his future life-companion. They attempted to have children; one child died at birth, and another pregnancy ended in a miscarriage.

In 1906, London published in Collier's magazine his eye-witness report of the San Francisco earthquake.

Beauty Ranch (1905–16)

In 1905, London purchased a 1,000 acres (4.0 km2) ranch in Glen Ellen, Sonoma County, California, on the eastern slope of Sonoma Mountain.He wrote: "Next to my wife, the ranch is the dearest thing in the world to me." He desperately wanted the ranch to become a successful business enterprise. Writing, always a commercial enterprise with London, now became even more a means to an end: "I write for no other purpose than to add to the beauty that now belongs to me. I write a book for no other reason than to add three or four hundred acres to my magnificent estate."

Stasz writes that London "had taken fully to heart the vision, expressed in his agrarian fiction, of the land as the closest earthly version of Eden ... he educated himself through the study of agricultural manuals and scientific tomes. He conceived of a system of ranching that today would be praised for its ecological wisdom." He was proud to own the first concrete silo in California, a circular piggery that he designed. He hoped to adapt the wisdom of Asian sustainable agriculture to the United States. He hired both Italian and Chinese stonemasons, whose distinctly different styles are obvious.

The ranch was an economic failure. Sympathetic observers such as Stasz treat his projects as potentially feasible, and ascribe their failure to bad luck or to being ahead of their time. Unsympathetic historians such as Kevin Starr suggest that he was a bad manager, distracted by other concerns and impaired by his alcoholism. Starr notes that London was absent from his ranch about six months a year between 1910 and 1916 and says, "He liked the show of managerial power, but not grinding attention to detail .... London's workers laughed at his efforts to play big-time rancher the operation a rich man's hobby."

London spent $80,000 ($2,280,000 in current value) to build a 15,000-square-foot (1,400 m2) stone mansion called Wolf House on the property. Just as the mansion was nearing completion, two weeks before the Londons planned to move in, it was destroyed by fire.

London's last visit to Hawaii, beginning in December 1915, lasted eight months. He met with Duke Kahanamoku, Prince Jonah Kūhiō Kalaniana'ole, Queen Lili'uokalani and many others, before returning to his ranch in July 1916. He was suffering from kidney failure, but he continued to work.

The ranch (abutting stone remnants of Wolf House) is now a National Historic Landmark and is protected in Jack London State Historic Park.

Animal activism

London witnessed animal cruelty in the training of circus animals, and his subsequent novels Jerry of the Islands and Michael, Brother of Jerry included a foreword entreating the public to become more informed about this practice. In 1918, the Massachusetts Society for the Prevention of Cruelty to Animals and the American Humane Education Society teamed up to create the Jack London Club, which sought to inform the public about cruelty to circus animals and encourage them to protest this establishment. Support from Club members led to a temporary cessation of trained animal acts at Ringling-Barnum and Bailey in 1925.

Death

London died November 22, 1916, in a sleeping porch in a cottage on his ranch. London had been a robust man but had suffered several serious illnesses, including scurvy in the Klondike. Additionally, during travels on the Snark, he and Charmian picked up unspecified tropical infections, and diseases, including yaws. At the time of his death, he suffered from dysentery, late-stage alcoholism, and uremia; he was in extreme pain and taking morphine.

London's ashes were buried on his property not far from the Wolf House. London's funeral took place on November 26, 1916, attended only by close friends, relatives, and workers of the property. In accordance with his wishes, he was cremated and buried next to some pioneer children, under a rock that belonged to the Wolf House. After Charmian's death in 1955, she was also cremated and then buried with her husband in the same spot that her husband chose. The grave is marked by a mossy boulder. The buildings and property were later preserved as Jack London State Historic Park, in Glen Ellen, California.

Suicide debate

Because he was using morphine, many older sources describe London's death as a suicide, and some still do. This conjecture appears to be a rumor, or speculation based on incidents in his fiction writings. His death certificate gives the cause as uremia, following acute renal colic.

The biographer Stasz writes, "Following London's death, for a number of reasons, a biographical myth developed in which he has been portrayed as an alcoholic womanizer who committed suicide. Recent scholarship based upon firsthand documents challenges this caricature." Most biographers, including Russ Kingman, now agree he died of uremia aggravated by an accidental morphine overdose.

London's fiction featured several suicides. In his autobiographical memoir John Barleycorn, he claims, as a youth, to have drunkenly stumbled overboard into the San Francisco Bay, "some maundering fancy of going out with the tide suddenly obsessed me". He said he drifted and nearly succeeded in drowning before sobering up and being rescued by fishermen. In the dénouement of The Little Lady of the Big House, the heroine, confronted by the pain of a mortal gunshot wound, undergoes a physician-assisted suicide by morphine. Also, in Martin Eden, the principal protagonist, who shares certain characteristics with London, drowns himself.

Plagiarism accusations

London was vulnerable to accusations of plagiarism, both because he was such a conspicuous, prolific, and successful writer and because of his methods of working. He wrote in a letter to Elwyn Hoffman, "expression, you see—with me—is far easier than invention." He purchased plots and novels from the young Sinclair Lewis and used incidents from newspaper clippings as writing material.

In July 1901, two pieces of fiction appeared within the same month: London's "Moon-Face", in the San Francisco Argonaut, and Frank Norris' "The Passing of Cock-eye Blacklock", in Century Magazine. Newspapers showed the similarities between the stories, which London said were "quite different in manner of treatment, patently the same in foundation and motive." London explained both writers based their stories on the same newspaper account. A year later, it was discovered that Charles Forrest McLean had published a fictional story also based on the same incident.

Egerton Ryerson Young claimed The Call of the Wild (1903) was taken from Young's book My Dogs in the Northland (1902). London acknowledged using it as a source and claimed to have written a letter to Young thanking him.

In 1906, the New York World published "deadly parallel" columns showing eighteen passages from London's short story "Love of Life" side by side with similar passages from a nonfiction article by Augustus Biddle and J. K. Macdonald, titled "Lost in the Land of the Midnight Sun". London noted the World did not accuse him of "plagiarism", but only of "identity of time and situation", to which he defiantly "pled guilty".

The most serious charge of plagiarism was based on London's "The Bishop's Vision", Chapter 7 of his novel The Iron Heel (1908). The chapter is nearly identical to an ironic essay that Frank Harris published in 1901, titled "The Bishop of London and Public Morality". Harris was incensed and suggested he should receive 1/60th of the royalties from The Iron Heel, the disputed material constituting about that fraction of the whole novel. London insisted he had clipped a reprint of the article, which had appeared in an American newspaper, and believed it to be a genuine speech delivered by the Bishop of London.

Views

Atheism

London was an atheist. He is quoted as saying, "I believe that when I am dead, I am dead. I believe that with my death I am just as much obliterated as the last mosquito you and I squashed."

Socialism

London wrote from a socialist viewpoint, which is evident in his novel The Iron Heel. Neither a theorist nor an intellectual socialist, London's socialism grew out of his life experience. As London explained in his essay, "How I Became a Socialist", his views were influenced by his experience with people at the bottom of the social pit. His optimism and individualism faded, and he vowed never to do more hard physical work than necessary. He wrote that his individualism was hammered out of him, and he was politically reborn. He often closed his letters "Yours for the Revolution."

London joined the Socialist Labor Party in April 1896. In the same year, the San Francisco Chronicle published a story about the twenty-year-old London's giving nightly speeches in Oakland's City Hall Park, an activity he was arrested for a year later. In 1901, he left the Socialist Labor Party and joined the new Socialist Party of America. He ran unsuccessfully as the high-profile Socialist candidate for mayor of Oakland in 1901 (receiving 245 votes) and 1905 (improving to 981 votes), toured the country lecturing on socialism in 1906, and published two collections of essays about socialism: The War of the Classes (1905) and Revolution, and other Essays (1906).

Stasz notes that "London regarded the Wobblies as a welcome addition to the Socialist cause, although he never joined them in going so far as to recommend sabotage." Stasz mentions a personal meeting between London and Big Bill Haywood in 1912.

In his late (1913) book The Cruise of the Snark, London writes about appeals to him for membership of the Snark's crew from office workers and other "toilers" who longed for escape from the cities, and of being cheated by workmen.

In his Glen Ellen ranch years, London felt some ambivalence toward socialism and complained about the "inefficient Italian labourers" in his employ. In 1916, he resigned from the Glen Ellen chapter of the Socialist Party, but stated emphatically he did so "because of its lack of fire and fight, and its loss of emphasis on the class struggle." In an unflattering portrait of London's ranch days, California cultural historian Kevin Starr refers to this period as "post-socialist" and says "... by 1911 ... London was more bored by the class struggle than he cared to admit."

Race

London shared common concerns among many European Americans in California about Asian immigration, described as "the yellow peril"; he used the latter term as the title of a 1904 essay. This theme was also the subject of a story he wrote in 1910 called "The Unparalleled Invasion". Presented as an historical essay set in the future, the story narrates events between 1976 and 1987, in which China, with an ever-increasing population, is taking over and colonizing its neighbors with the intention of taking over the entire Earth. The western nations respond with biological warfare and bombard China with dozens of the most infectious diseases. On his fears about China, he admits, "it must be taken into consideration that the above postulate is itself a product of Western race-egotism, urged by our belief in our own righteousness and fostered by a faith in ourselves which may be as erroneous as are most fond race fancies."

By contrast, many of London's short stories are notable for their empathetic portrayal of Mexican ("The Mexican"), Asian ("The Chinago"), and Hawaiian ("Koolau the Leper") characters. London's war correspondence from the Russo-Japanese War, as well as his unfinished novel Cherry, show he admired much about Japanese customs and capabilities. London's writings have been popular among the Japanese, who believe he portrayed them positively.

In "Koolau the Leper", London describes Koolau, who is a Hawaiian leper—and thus a very different sort of "superman" than Martin Eden—and who fights off an entire cavalry troop to elude capture, as "indomitable spiritually—a ... magnificent rebel". This character is based on Hawaiian leper Kaluaikoolau, who in 1893 revolted and resisted capture from forces of the Provisional Government of Hawaii in the Kalalau Valley.

An amateur boxer and avid boxing fan, London reported on the 1910 Johnson–Jeffries fight, in which the black boxer Jack Johnson vanquished Jim Jeffries, known as the "Great White Hope". In 1908, London had reported on an earlier fight of Johnson's, contrasting the black boxer's coolness and intellectual style, with the apelike appearance and fighting style of his Canadian opponent, Tommy Burns:

> [What won] on Saturday was bigness, coolness, quickness, cleverness, and vast physical superiority ... Because a white man wishes a white man to win, this should not prevent him from giving absolute credit to the best man, even when that best man was black. All hail to Johnson. ... superb. He was impregnable ... as inaccessible as Mont Blanc.

Those who defend London against charges of racism cite the letter he wrote to the Japanese-American Commercial Weekly in 1913:

> In reply to yours of August 16, 1913. First of all, I should say by stopping the stupid newspaper from always fomenting race prejudice. This of course, being impossible, I would say, next, by educating the people of Japan so that they will be too intelligently tolerant to respond to any call to race prejudice. And, finally, by realizing, in industry and

485

government, of socialism—which last word is merely a word that stands for the actual application of in the affairs of men of the theory of the Brotherhood of Man.

In the meantime the nations and races are only unruly boys who have not yet grown to the stature of men. So we must expect them to do unruly and boisterous things at times. And, just as boys grow up, so the races of mankind will grow up and laugh when they look back upon their childish quarrels.

In 1996, after the City of Whitehorse, Yukon, renamed a street in honor of London's alleged racism forced the city to change the name of "Jack London Boulevard"[failed verification] back to "Two-mile Hill".

Eugenics

London supported eugenics, including forced sterilization of criminals or those deemed feeble minded. His novel Before Adam(1906–07) has been described as having pro-eugenic themes.

London wrote to Frederick H. Robinson of the periodical Medical Review of Reviews, stating, "I believe the future belongs to eugenics, and will be determined by the practice of eugenics."

Works

Short stories

Western writer and historian Dale L. Walker writes:

London's true métier was the short story ... London's true genius lay in the short form, 7,500 words and under, where the flood of images in his teeming brain and the innate power of his narrative gift were at once constrained and freed. His stories that run longer than the magic 7,500 generally—but certainly not always—could have benefited from self-editing.

London's "strength of utterance" is at its height in his stories, and they are painstakingly well-constructed. "To Build a Fire" is the best known of all his stories. Set in the harsh Klondike, it recounts the haphazard trek of a new arrival who has ignored an old-timer's warning about the risks of traveling alone. Falling through the ice into a creek in seventy-five-below weather, the unnamed man is keenly aware that survival depends on his untested skills at quickly building a fire to dry his clothes and warm his extremities. After publishing a tame version of this story—with a sunny outcome—in The Youth's Companion in 1902, London offered a second, more severe take on the man's predicament in The Century Magazine in 1908. Reading both provides an illustration of London's growth and maturation as a writer. As Labor (1994) observes: "To compare the two versions is itself an instructive lesson in what distinguished a great work of literary art from a good children's story."

Other stories from the Klondike period include: "All Gold Canyon", about a battle between a gold prospector and a claim jumper; "The Law of Life", about an aging American Indian man abandoned by his tribe and left to die; "Love of Life", about a trek by a prospector across the Canadian tundra; "To the Man on Trail," which tells the story of a prospector fleeing the Mounted Police in a sled race, and raises the question of the contrast between written law and morality; and "An Odyssey of the North," which raises questions of conditional morality, and paints a sympathetic portrait of a man of mixed White and Aleut ancestry.

London was a boxing fan and an avid amateur boxer. "A Piece of Steak" is a tale about a match between older and younger boxers. It contrasts the differing experiences of youth and age but also raises the social question of the treatment of aging workers. "The Mexican" combines boxing with a social theme, as a young Mexican endures an unfair fight and ethnic prejudice to earn money with which to aid the revolution.

Several of London's stories would today be classified as science fiction. "The Unparalleled Invasion" describes germ warfare against China; "Goliath" is about an irresistible energy weapon; "The Shadow and the Flash" is a tale about two brothers who take different routes to achieving invisibility; "A

Relic of the Pliocene" is a tall tale about an encounter of a modern-day man with a mammoth. "The Red One" is a late story from a period when London was intrigued by the theories of the psychiatrist and writer Jung. It tells of an island tribe held in thrall by an extraterrestrial object.

Some nineteen original collections of short stories were published during London's brief life or shortly after his death. There have been several posthumous anthologies drawn from this pool of stories. Many of these stories were located in the Klondike and the Pacific. A collection of Jack London's San Francisco Stories was published in October 2010 by Sydney Samizdat Press.

Novels

London's most famous novels are The Call of the Wild, White Fang, The Sea-Wolf, The Iron Heel, and Martin Eden.

In a letter dated December 27, 1901, London's Macmillan publisher George Platt Brett, Sr., said "he believed Jack's fiction represented 'the very best kind of work' done in America."

Critic Maxwell Geismar called The Call of the Wild "a beautiful prose poem"; editor Franklin Walker said that it "belongs on a shelf with Walden and Huckleberry Finn"; and novelist E.L. Doctorow called it "a mordant parable ... his masterpiece."

The historian Dale L. Walker commented:

> Jack London was an uncomfortable novelist, that form too long for his natural impatience and the quickness of his mind. His novels, even the best of them, are hugely flawed.

Some critics have said that his novels are episodic and resemble linked short stories. Dale L. Walker writes:

> The Star Rover, that magnificent experiment, is actually a series of short stories connected by a unifying device ... Smoke Bellew is a series of stories bound together in a novel-like form by their reappearing

protagonist, Kit Bellew; and John Barleycorn ... is a synoptic series of short episodes.

Ambrose Bierce said of The Sea-Wolf that "the great thing—and it is among the greatest of things—is that tremendous creation, Wolf Larsen ... the hewing out and setting up of such a figure is enough for a man to do in one lifetime. "However, he noted, "The love element, with its absurd suppressions, and impossible proprieties, is awful."

The Iron Heel is an example of a dystopian novel that anticipates and influenced George Orwell's Nineteen Eighty-Four. London's socialist politics are explicitly on display here. The Iron Heel meets the contemporary definition of soft science fiction. The Star Rover (1915) is also science fiction.

Apocrypha

Jack London Credo

London's literary executor, Irving Shepard, quoted a Jack London Credo in an introduction to a 1956 collection of London stories:

> I would rather be ashes than dust!
>
> I would rather that my spark should burn out in a brilliant blaze than it should be stifled by dry-rot.
>
> I would rather be a superb meteor, every atom of me in magnificent glow, than a sleepy and permanent planet.
>
> The function of man is to live, not to exist.
>
> I shall not waste my days in trying to prolong them.
>
> I shall use my time.

The biographer Stasz notes that the passage "has many marks of London's style" but the only line that could be safely attributed to London was the first. The words Shepard quoted were from a story in the San Francisco Bulletin, December 2, 1916, by journalist Ernest J. Hopkins, who visited the ranch just weeks before London's death. Stasz notes, "Even more so than today journalists' quotes were unreliable or even sheer inventions," and says no direct source in London's writings has been found. However, at least one line, according to Stasz, is authentic, being referenced by London and written in his own hand in the autograph book of Australian suffragette Vida Goldstein:

> Dear Miss Goldstein:–
>
> Seven years ago I wrote you that I'd rather be ashes than dust. I still subscribe to that sentiment.
>
> Sincerely yours,
>
> Jack London
>
> Jan. 13, 1909

In his short story "By The Turtles of Tasman", a character, defending her "ne'er-do-well grasshopperish father" to her "antlike uncle", says: "... my father has been a king. He has lived .... Have you lived merely to live? Are you afraid to die? I'd rather sing one wild song and burst my heart with it, than live a thousand years watching my digestion and being afraid of the wet. When you are dust, my father will be ashes."

"The Scab"

A short diatribe on "The Scab" is often quoted within the U.S. labor movement and frequently attributed to London. It opens:

> After God had finished the rattlesnake, the toad, and the vampire, he had some awful substance left with which he made a scab. A scab is a two-legged animal with a corkscrew soul, a water brain, a combination backbone of jelly and glue. Where others have hearts, he carries a tumor of rotten principles. When a scab comes down the street, men turn their backs and Angels weep in Heaven, and the Devil shuts the gates of hell to keep him out....

In 1913 and 1914, a number of newspapers printed the first three sentences with varying terms used instead of "scab", such as "knocker","stool pigeon"or "scandal monger"

This passage as given above was the subject of a 1974 Supreme Court case, Letter Carriers v. Austin, in which Justice Thurgood Marshall referred to it as "a well-known piece of trade union literature, generally attributed to author Jack London". A union newsletter had published a "list of scabs," which was granted to be factual and therefore not libelous, but then went on to quote the passage as the "definition of a scab". The case turned on the question of whether the "definition" was defamatory. The court ruled that "Jack London's... 'definition of a scab' is merely rhetorical hyperbole, a lusty and imaginative expression of the contempt felt by union members towards those who refuse to join", and as such was not libelous and was protected under the First Amendment.

Despite being frequently attributed to London, the passage does not appear at all in the extensive collection of his writings at Sonoma State University's website. However, in his book The War of the Classes he published a 1903 speech entitled "The Scab", which gave a much more balanced view of the topic:

> The laborer who gives more time or strength or skill for the same wage than another, or equal time or strength or skill for a less wage, is a scab. The generousness on his part is hurtful to his fellow-laborers, for it compels them to an equal generousness which is not to their liking, and which gives them less of food and shelter. But a word may be said for the scab. Just as his act makes his rivals compulsorily generous, so do they, by fortune of birth and training, make compulsory his act of generousness.
>
> [...]
>
> Nobody desires to scab, to give most for least. The ambition of every individual is quite the opposite, to give least for most; and, as a result, living in a tooth-and-nail society, battle royal is waged by the ambitious individuals. But in its most salient aspect, that of the struggle over the division of the joint product, it is no longer a battle between individuals, but between groups of individuals. Capital and labor apply

themselves to raw material, make something useful out of it, add to its value, and then proceed to quarrel over the division of the added value. Neither cares to give most for least. Each is intent on giving less than the other and on receiving more.

Legacy and honors

Mount London, also known as Boundary Peak 100, on the Alaska-British Columbia boundary, in the Boundary Ranges of the Coast Mountains of British Columbia, is named for him.

Jack London Square on the waterfront of Oakland, California was named for him.

He was honored by the United States Postal Service with a 25¢ Great Americans series postage stamp released on January 11, 1986.

Jack London Lake (Russian), a mountain lake located in the upper reaches of the Kolyma River in Yagodninsky district of Magadan Oblast.

Fictional portrayals of London include Michael O'Shea in the 1943 film Jack London, Jeff East in the 1980 film Klondike Fever, Aaron Ashmore in the Murdoch Mysteries episode "Murdoch of the Klondike" from 2012, and Johnny Simmons in the 2014 miniseries Klondike. (Source: Wikipedia)

NOTABLE WORKS

NOVELS

The Cruise of the Dazzler (1902)

A Daughter of the Snows (1902)

The Call of the Wild (1903)

The Kempton-Wace Letters (1903) (published anonymously, co-authored with Anna Strunsky)

The Sea-Wolf (1904)

The Game (1905)

White Fang (1906)

Before Adam (1907)

The Iron Heel (1908)

Martin Eden (1909)

Burning Daylight (1910)

Adventure (1911)

The Scarlet Plague (1912)

A Son of the Sun (1912)

The Abysmal Brute (1913)

The Valley of the Moon (1913)

The Mutiny of the Elsinore (1914)

The Star Rover (1915) (published in England as The Jacket)

The Little Lady of the Big House (1916)

Jerry of the Islands (1917)

Michael, Brother of Jerry (1917)

Hearts of Three (1920) (novelization of a script by Charles Goddard)

The Assassination Bureau, Ltd (1963) (left half-finished, completed by Robert L. Fish)

SHORT STORIES

"An Old Soldier's Story" (1894)

"Who Believes in Ghosts!" (1895)

"And 'FRISCO Kid Came Back" (1895)

"Night's Swim In Yeddo Bay" (1895)

"One More Unfortunate" (1895)

"Sakaicho, Hona Asi And Hakadaki" (1895)

"A Klondike Christmas" (1897)

"Mahatma's Little Joke" (1897)

"O Haru" (1897)

"Plague Ship" (1897)

"The Strange Experience Of A Misogynist" (1897)

"Two Gold Bricks" (1897)

"The Devil's Dice Box" (1898)

"A Dream Image" (1898)

"The Test: A Clondyke Wooing" (1898)

"To the Man on Trail" (1898)

"In a Far Country" (1899)

"The King of Mazy May" (1899)

"The End Of The Chapter" (1899)

"The Grilling Of Loren Ellery" (1899)

"The Handsome Cabin Boy" (1899)

"In The Time Of Prince Charley" (1899)

"Old Baldy" (1899)

"The Men of Forty Mile" (1899)

"Pluck and Pertinacity" (1899)

"The Rejuvenation of Major Rathbone" (1899)

"The White Silence" (1899)

"A Thousand Deaths" (1899)

"Wisdom of the Trail" (1899)

"An Odyssey of the North" (1900)

"The Son of the Wolf" (1900)

"Even unto Death" (1900)

"The Man with the Gash" (1900)

"A Lesson in Heraldry" (1900)

"A Northland Miracle" (1900)

"Proper "GIRLIE"" (1900)

"Thanksgiving on Slav Creek" (1900)

"Their Alcove" (1900)

"Housekeeping in the Klondike" (1900)

"Dutch Courage" (1900)

"Where the Trail Forks" (1900)

"Hyperborean Brew" (1901)

"A Relic of the Pliocene" (1901)

"The Lost Poacher" (1901)

"The God of His Fathers" (1901)

""FRISCO Kid's" Story" (1901)

"The Law of Life" (1901)

"The Minions of Midas" (1901)

"In the Forests of the North" (1902)

"The "Fuzziness" of Hoockla-Heen" (1902)

"The Story of Keesh" (1902)

"Keesh, Son of Keesh" (1902)

"Nam-Bok, the Unveracious" (1902)

"Li Wan the Fair" (1902)

"Lost Face"

"Master of Mystery" (1902)

"The Sunlanders" (1902)

"The Death of Ligoun" (1902)

"Moon-Face" (1902)

"Diable—A Dog" (1902), renamed Bâtard in 1904

"To Build a Fire" (1902, revised 1908)

"The League of the Old Men" (1902)

"The Dominant Primordial Beast" (1903)

"The One Thousand Dozen" (1903)

"The Marriage of Lit-lit" (1903)

"The Shadow and the Flash" (1903)

"The Leopard Man's Story" (1903)

"Negore the Coward" (1904)

"All Gold Cañon" (1905)

"Love of Life" (1905)

"The Sun-Dog Trail" (1905)

"The Apostate" (1906)

"Up the Slide" (1906)

"Planchette" (1906)

"Brown Wolf" (1906)

"Make Westing" (1907)

"Chased by the Trail" (1907)

"Trust" (1908)

"A Curious Fragment" (1908)

"Aloha Oe" (1908)

"That Spot" (1908)

"The Enemy of All the World" (1908)

"The House of Mapuhi" (1909)

"Good-by, Jack" (1909)

"Samuel" (1909)

"South of the Slot" (1909)

"The Chinago" (1909)

"The Dream of Debs" (1909)

"The Madness of John Harned" (1909)

"The Seed of McCoy" (1909)

"A Piece of Steak" (1909)

"Mauki" (1909)

"The Whale Tooth" (1909)

"Goliath" (1910)

"The Unparalleled Invasion" (1910)

"Told in the Drooling Ward" (1910)

"When the World was Young" (1910)

"The Terrible Solomons" (1910)

"The Inevitable White Man" (1910)

"The Heathen" (1910)

"Yah! Yah! Yah!" (1910)

"By the Turtles of Tasman" (1911)

"The Mexican" (1911)

"War" (1911)

"The Unmasking of the Cad" (1911)

"The Scarlet Plague" (1912)

"The Captain of the Susan Drew" (1912)

"The Sea-Farmer" (1912)

"The Feathers of the Sun" (1912)

"The Prodigal Father" (1912)

"Samuel" (1913)

"The Sea-Gangsters" (1913)

"The Strength of the Strong" (1914)

"Told in the Drooling Ward" (1914)

"The Hussy" (1916)

"Like Argus of the Ancient Times" (1917)

"Jerry of the Islands" (1917)

"The Red One" (1918)

"Shin-Bones" (1918)

"The Bones of Kahekili" (1919)

SHORT STORY COLLECTIONS

Son of the Wolf (1900)

Chris Farrington, Able Seaman (1901)

The God of His Fathers & Other Stories (1901)

Children of the Frost (1902)

The Faith of Men and Other Stories (1904)

Tales of the Fish Patrol (1906)

Moon-Face and Other Stories (1906)

Love of Life and Other Stories (1907)

Lost Face (1910)

South Sea Tales (1911)

When God Laughs and Other Stories (1911)

The House of Pride & Other Tales of Hawaii (1912)

Smoke Bellew (1912)

A Son of the Sun (1912)

The Night Born (1913)

The Strength of the Strong (1914)

The Turtles of Tasman (1916)

The Human Drift (1917)

The Red One (1918)

On the Makaloa Mat (1919)

Dutch Courage and Other Stories (1922)

AUTOBIOGRAPHICAL MEMOIRS

The Road (1907)

The Cruise of the Snark (1911)

John Barleycorn (1913)

NON-FICTION AND ESSAYS

Through the Rapids on the Way to the Klondike (1899)

From Dawson to the Sea (1899)

What Communities Lose by the Competitive System (1900)

The Impossibility of War (1900)

Phenomena of Literary Evolution (1900)

A Letter to Houghton Mifflin Co. (1900)

Husky, Wolf Dog of the North (1900)

Editorial Crimes — A Protest (1901)

Again the Literary Aspirant (1902)

The People of the Abyss (1903)

How I Became a Socialist (1903)

The War of the Classes (1905)

The Story of an Eyewitness (1906)

A Letter to Woman's Home Companion (1906)

Revolution, and other Essays (1910)

Mexico's Army and Ours (1914)

Lawgivers (1914)

Our Adventures in Tampico (1914)

Stalking the Pestilence (1914)

The Red Game of War (1914)

The Trouble Makers of Mexico (1914)

With Funston's Men (1914)

POETRY

A Heart (1899)

Abalone Song (1913)

And Some Night (1914)

Ballade of the False Lover (1914)

Cupid's Deal (1913)

Daybreak (1901)

Effusion (1901)

George Sterling (1913)

Gold (1915)

He Chortled with Glee (1899)

He Never Tried Again (1912)

His Trip to Hades (1913)

Homeland (1914)

Hors de Saison (1913)

If I Were God (1899)

In a Year (1901)

In and Out (1911)

Je Vis en Espoir (1897)

Memory (1913)

Moods (1913)

My Confession (1912)

My Little Palmist (1914)

Of Man of the Future (1915)

Oh You Everybody's Girl (19)

On the Face of the Earth You are the One (1915)

Rainbows End (1914)

Republican Rallying Song (1916)

Sonnet (1901)

The Gift of God (1905)

The Klondyker's Dream (1914)

The Lover's Liturgy (1913)

The Mammon Worshippers (1911)

The Republican Battle-Hymn (1905)

The Return of Ulysses (1915)

The Sea Sprite and the Shooting Star (1916)

The Socialist's Dream (1912)

The Song of the Flames (1903)

The Way of War (1906)

The Worker and the Tramp (1911)

Tick! Tick! Tick! (1915)

Too Late (1912)

Weasel Thieves (1913)

When All the World Shouted my Name (1905)

Where the Rainbow Fell (1902)

Your Kiss (1914)

PLAYS

Theft (1910)

Daughters of the Rich: A One Act Play (1915)

The Acorn Planter: A California Forest Play (1916)